Emotion in
Social Relations

D0219729

Emotion in Social Relations

CULTURAL, GROUP, AND INTERPERSONAL PROCESSES

BRIAN PARKINSON

AGNETA H. FISCHER

ANTONY S.R. MANSTEAD

Psychology Press
New York • Hove

Published in 2005 by
Psychology Press
270 Madison Avenue
New York, NY 10016
www.psypress.com

Published in Great Britain by
Psychology Press
27 Church Road
Hove, East Sussex
BN3 2FA
www.psypress.co.uk

Psychology Press is an imprint of the Taylor & Francis Group.
Printed in the United States of America on acid-free paper.

10 9 8 7 6 5 4 3 2 1

Library of Congress Cataloging-in-Publication Data

Parkinson, Brian, 1958–
   Emotion in social relations : cultural, group, and interpersonal processes /
Brian Parkinson, Agneta H. Fischer, Antony S.R. Manstead.
      p. cm.
   Includes bibliographical references and indexes.
   ISBN 1-84169-045-7 (hardcover : alk. paper)—ISBN 1-84169-046-5 (pbk. : alk.
paper) 1. Emotions—Sociological aspects. 2. Emotions—Social aspects.
3. Emotions—Cross-cultural studies. 4. Social interaction. 5. Social psychology.
6. Interpersonal communication. I. Fischer, Agneta, 1958– II. Manstead, A. S. R.
III. Title.

HM1033.P37 2004
152.4--dc22   2004009848

CONTENTS

ABOUT THE AUTHORS

Brian Parkinson first studied Psychology at Manchester University, where he received his PhD in 1983. He is currently employed as Lecturer in Experimental Psychology at Oxford University. His research has concerned the social psychology of emotion and mood, and he has published in a range of international academic journals. He is the author of *Ideas and Realities of Emotion* (Routledge, 1995) and coauthor of *Changing Moods* (Longman, 1996). He is currently chief editor of the *British Journal of Social Psychology*.

Agneta H. Fischer studied Psychology at Leiden University (the Netherlands), where she received her PhD in 1991. She is currently chair of the department of Social Psychology and professor in Social Psychology, with special emphasis on emotion theory and research. She currently is president of ISRE (International Society for Research on Emotion). She is the editor of *Gender and Emotion: Social Psychological Perspectives* (Cambridge, 2000) and has published articles and book chapters in the area of the social and cultural context of emotion and emotion expression.

Antony S. R. Manstead studied Psychology and Sociology at the University of Bristol and gained his PhD in Social Psychology from the University of Sussex. Prior to his present position at Cardiff University, he has held positions at the Universities of Sussex, Manchester, California at Berkeley, Amsterdam, and Cambridge. He has been chief editor of the *British Journal of Social Psychology* and associate editor of *Personality and Social Psychology Bulletin* and of *Cognition and Emotion*. In 2004 he was the recipient of the British Psychological Society's Presidents' Award for distinguished contributions to psychological knowledge.

PREFACE

If you knew any of us from another time or place, in a different context, you may well not fully recognize the positions we take here. This collective project has changed us for now or for good, for better or worse, in all kinds of ways. Even our voices sound different. By some strange ventriloquism, we opened our mouths and heard one of the others speaking (or at least ran our fingers across the keyboard and read someone else's phrasing on the screen).

Of course, none of this happened instantly. Although consensus was intended from the start, it sometimes required a few back-and-forth exchanges to arrive. And even then it didn't always seem stable. Like emotions, opinions, judgments, and explanations adjust, and adjust to, the unfolding social relations that surround them.

To start at the beginning (or at least one version of it), Agneta and Tony convened a symposium on social aspects of emotion at the 1999 conference of the European Association of Experimental Social Psychology in Oxford. We all met for lunch afterward. This was where the structure of this book first took shape—over chips, chops, pies, and burgers at *Browns* on Woodstock Road. Instead of taking individual experiences as the primary phenomenon, the idea was that we would start from the most inclusive social processes relating to society and culture and zoom in on emotion, taking in group and interpersonal factors on the way. That structure is one of the few things that remain from that original discussion.

A lot of things have happened in the mean time. All of us have new jobs or work roles. Tony moved from Amsterdam to Cambridge, Brian moved from Brunel to Oxford, Agneta was made Head of Department. Two of us had babies. The transitions we made set back our schedules but also gave us time and space to refine and reformulate ideas. We met up at conferences and during vacations in Winchester, San Sebastian, Cuenca, and Amsterdam. Imagine us sitting inside or outside, in a restaurant or bar, arguing the toss or in fervent agreement over coffee or beer. Tony's gentle corrections, Agneta's direct criticism or endorsement,

Brian's reluctance to reconsider. Mediation and moderation of all kinds from all of us. We worked through endless drafts and picked over theories, methods, and typographies. On many occasions, we felt like the thing was nearly finished. Somehow, eventually, we got to the end of it.

So this is a book that sees emotion from a social perspective, as something that reflects and affects relations between individuals and groups within a broader society. We are certainly not the first to adopt such an approach, but we feel that the growing literature on the social psychology of emotion has not, until now, been thoroughly reviewed and integrated. In particular, group-level processes are often ignored, and connections between different levels of analysis are rarely considered. In fact, we have been surprised at the lack of available literature on the question of how cultural, group, and interpersonal factors influence each other in the production of emotion. If nothing else, this book raises the profile of this issue.

Each of us took responsibility for two or more of the chapters, but none of them should be seen as single-authored. We tried to adopt a common style but inevitable variations in modes of presentation appear, depending on topic as well as writer. Although two of the authors are close to bilingual, none of us found a way of perfectly translating the Manstead style into Fischerish or Parkinsonese (or vice versa). In many ways this is reassuring as much as frustrating. We always wrote with one another in mind, but something specific about the nature of our individual presentation toward this and other imagined audiences still remains. It is left to the reader to identify who might have said what to whom and in what context.

As for acknowledgements, our ideas were inspired by Jim Averill, Alan Fogel, Nico Frijda, Erving Goffman, Henri Tajfel, Colwyn Trevarthen, Lev Vygotsky, Geoffrey White, and Jamie Walker Symon, and by discussions with many of our colleagues in the International Society for Research on Emotions (ISRE). We have also received invaluable advice and encouragement along the way from José-Miguel Fernández-Dols, Keith Oatley, Jerry Parrott, Patricia Rodriguez Mosquera, Jim Russell, Stephanie Shields, Heather Smith, Russell Spears, Lara Tiedens, Colin Wayne Leach, as well as one another.

You may not agree with all that we say, but we hope that any disagreements may be productive.

Brian Parkinson

Agneta Fischer

Tony Manstead

Emotion's Place in the Social World

Think of the last time you experienced an emotion. Love, hate, fear, anger, embarrassment; it doesn't matter which. Where were you and what were you doing? What was it that excited, pleased, or upset you? Chances are there was at least one other person around (even if only in your otherwise private thoughts), and that something that they did or didn't do (or something that was done or not done to them) was part of what made you emotional. Now think about what happened next. Perhaps someone else reacted to your emotion, tried to calm you down, or responded with antagonism. Later still, maybe you discussed your feelings with someone close to you. Maybe, in some ways, the experience affected other people almost as much as it affected you.

What is it about people's behavior that causes emotional effects? Why should some things they do matter to us whereas others do not? How do we tell what is emotionally important? This book proposes that one answer is that we make reference to others' reactions to whatever is happening, especially when we share relationships or affiliations with those others. We know we should care about something at an emotional level if people close to us also seem to care. Further, to the extent that we are members of a common society, we have also learned to perceive, interpret, and act toward things in broadly similar ways, to recognize their conventional significance, and this too partly determines their emotional power. Those raised in different cultural contexts might not always share our emotional perspective on events.

Although emotions are often seen as intensely personal experiences, it also seems clear that most of them have an intimate relationship to other people's thoughts, words, and deeds and bring direct consequences for how social life proceeds. Further, our position within groups, subcultures, and the broader society helps to determine our emotional outlook on the world. This chapter considers the range of ways in which emotions relate to social life, and explores how their personal and social aspects might be reconciled. The aim is to set the stage for the book's more extensive consideration of how emotions are shaped by their social context.

☐ Levels of Social Analysis

Social life involves a vast variety of processes that operate at a number of different levels (see also Doise, 1986; Keltner & Haidt, 1999). Three of these levels are of particular relevance to the present discussion. The first and most obvious level is the interpersonal level, which focuses on direct relations and interactions with other people, and on how their conduct influences and is influenced by our own. One person says something and another replies, a glance is acknowledged or ignored, and so on. Working at this level, we can start to understand what role emotions play in the course of unfolding encounters between people, and in the development of more articulated relationships.

Scaling up the analysis to a second level permits consideration of how individuals' conduct is shaped by the fact that they belong to groups. Here, our focus will be on how collections of three or more people are implicated in emotional life. For example, what difference does it make if another person is "one of us" rather than "one of them"—a member of an in-group as opposed to an out-group? How does our sharing (or not) of a common social identity influence our emotional interactions? It seems that our membership of sports teams, work committees, fan clubs, gender categories, and so on can help to set the range of emotional options that are open to us. Groups segment the social world into the good and bad, the praiseworthy and blameworthy, the desirable and undesirable, with obvious consequences for our emotions.

As groups get larger over the course of history, they tend to subdivide and stratify. They develop traditions and rules, both formal and informal. Large-scale and relatively permanent groups with internal structures and established norms, values, and practices may be treated at a separate, cultural level. Because shared culture provides a constant backdrop for our emotional activities, its impact is often less obvious to us than that of our changing group and interpersonal allegiances. We become aware of cultural assumptions, rules, or practices only when brought into contact with direct alternatives. For example, for some English people, North Americans can seem effusive, upbeat, and relentlessly confident. Prolonged interaction with them can lead to the recognition of a contrasting implicit norm about understatement. We all grow up with emotional habits, some of which remain invisible to us until we are forced to acknowledge their cultural specificity.

Distinctions between interpersonal, group, and cultural factors often seem fuzzy. For example, when do three people who are talking stop engaging in interpersonal interaction and start operating as a group? When should groups be treated as cultures and when shouldn't they? Indeed, what is a society, apart from a very large group? One of the reasons for maintaining these contestable distinctions is that research into social aspects of emotion has tended to treat them separately, however artificial this separation might sometimes seem. It therefore makes sense to review the evidence in these accepted categories. For most of this book, then, we will continue to divide social life into its interpersonal, group-level, and cultural aspects, but our ultimate aim will be to provide an integrative analysis of their interactive operation.

☐ Pieces of the Emotional Jigsaw

Setting out what we mean by an emotion turns out to be even more problematic than demarcating social life. Although we all have an intuitive sense of what the word means, a surprising degree of disagreement exists about its precise definition (e.g., Fehr & Russell, 1984; Kleinginna & Kleinginna, 1981). Unfortunately, it is not possible to evade this issue entirely because definitions have important consequences for the interpretation of theory and research. For example, if we see emotion as a private experience, its relationship to the social world cannot be direct, but if we see emotion as communicative then it has a more obvious place in the social world (see following discussion). Because of the difficulty of the definitional issue and the significance of its implications, we will postpone detailed consideration of emotion's meaning until we have identified some key landmarks in the relevant conceptual terrain. For now, it should suffice to say that the occurrence of an emotion is usually associated with a range of events and subcomponents that we can specify more easily than emotion itself. By setting out these different aspects of emotional processes, we get a better handle on the phenomenon in question.

The first thing to note is that emotions are related to events that happen in the world (objects and causes). We are therefore led to consider what it is about these events that make them emotional events. Second, emotion implies taking a particular perspective toward events, by liking or disliking what is happening, for example, or treating it as a cause for congratulation or condemnation (appraisal). Third, when we are emotional, our bodies usually react in some way: We break into a cold sweat or feel a warm glow, our pulse quickens or our heart stops, and so on (physiological change). Fourth, in addition to our sensations of bodily turmoil, we often feel strong impulses to act in certain ways when emotional (action tendencies). We may experience a desire to hurt or hug someone, for instance, or to run away, hide, or just stay very still. Fifth, particular emotions often seem to be associated with distinctive muscular movements that can express what we are feeling to others (expression or display). We smile or frown, lean forward or turn away, or clench our fists or open our arms, for example. Finally, we often try to do something about one or more of these different aspects of emotional episodes (regulation). We may seek to influence the course of events, change our perspective toward these events, work on our bodily reactions, or modify our gestures and expressions. For instance, imagine someone is being insulting in front of people whose opinions matter to you. You may try to silence her criticisms, wonder whether she really intends offense, take a deep breath to maintain your relaxation, or keep a tight lip to hide how upset you are.

Although we cannot yet say exactly what emotions are, then, we can at least agree that when we get emotional, some subset of the previously mentioned processes is probably also operating. Indeed, according to many definitions, emotion is constituted from the overall combination of these subprocesses. Alternatively, one or more component may be seen as more central to what emotion really is. In either case, separate consideration of these six different aspects of emotional function may bring us closer to understanding the nature of emotion and how it relates to social life.

☐ Appraisal and Feedback Theories

Although the identification of component processes takes us a step closer to understanding what emotion is, we also need to say something about how those processes fit together. Indeed, the whole may be greater than the sum of its proverbial parts. Our ultimate aim, therefore, will be to reconstruct the bigger picture from the different pieces of the jigsaw. In the present section, we start to address this aim by considering which stages of the emotion process come first and how each stage influences what follows.

In William James's (1884) classic paper "What is an emotion?" he contrasted a commonsense view of emotion causation with his own alternative, which has come to be known as "feedback theory":

> Our natural way of thinking is that the mental perception of some fact excites the mental affection called the emotion, and that this latter state of mind gives rise to the bodily expression. My thesis, on the contrary, is that *the bodily changes follow directly the perception of the exciting fact, and that our feeling of the same changes as they occur* IS *the emotion* . Common sense says, we lose our fortune, are sorry and weep; we meet a bear, are frightened and run; we are insulted by a rival, are angry and strike. The hypothesis here to be defended says that this order of sequence is incorrect … and that the more rational statement is that we feel sorry because we cry, angry because we strike, afraid because we tremble, and not that we cry, strike, or tremble because we are sorry, angry, or fearful, as the case may be. (pp. 189–190, emphasis in original)

According to feedback theory, then, the physiological changes, expressions, and actions come first, followed by the experience of the emotion, which is directly based on their perception (see Figure 1.1). Indeed, according to James, if these changes did not occur, the emotional quality would disappear from our experience:

> Without the bodily states following on the perception, the latter would be purely cognitive in form: pale, colorless, destitute of emotional warmth. We might then see the bear, and judge it best to run,

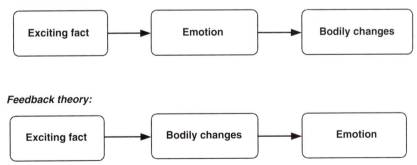

FIGURE 1.1. James's reversal of common sense

receive the insult, and deem it right to strike, but we could not actually feel afraid or angry. (p. 190)

In other words, "A purely disembodied emotion is a non-entity" (p. 194).

For James, not only is bodily feedback what makes emotion emotional, it also defines what is different about different emotions. We know what we are feeling because the particular pattern of felt changes is thought to be distinctive in fear, anger, happiness, sadness, guilt, and so on:

> The various permutations and combinations of which these organic activities are susceptible make it abstractly possible that no shade of emotion, however slight, should be without a bodily reverberation as unique, when taken in its totality, as is the mental mood itself. (p. 172)

The most popular alternative to feedback theory is *appraisal theory* (e.g., Arnold, 1960; Ellsworth, 1991; Lazarus, 1991a; Roseman, 1984; Scherer, 2001; Smith & Lazarus, 1993, *inter alia*), which in many ways is closer to what James claimed was "our natural way of thinking" about emotions. In this view, what makes emotion emotional is not the feeling of the various bodily responses, but rather what makes facts exciting in the first place—the realization that they matter to us personally:

> Both perception and emotion have an object; but in emotion the object is known in a particular way. To perceive or apprehend something means that I know what it is like as a thing, apart from any effect on me. To like it or dislike it means that I know it not only objectively, as it is apart from me, but also that I estimate its relation to me, that I appraise it as desirable or undesirable, valuable or harmful for me, so that I am drawn to it or repelled by it. (Arnold, 1960, p. 171)

The basic idea, then, is that our emotional reactions depend not on the specific characteristics of stimulus events, but rather on the way that we interpret and evaluate what is happening to us (appraisal). Furthermore, the particular character of our appraisal of events is what underlies the differences between different emotions. At the crudest level, this means that: "when we appraise something as good for us, we like it. When we appraise something as bad for us, we dislike it" (Arnold, 1960, p. 194).

Some of the more specific relationships between appraisals and emotions according to Smith and Lazarus's (1993) more recent version of appraisal theory are set out in Figure 1.2. The *sine qua non* for emotion according to this model is an appraisal of *motivational relevance*, meaning that unless what is happening has an impact on the goals or projects that

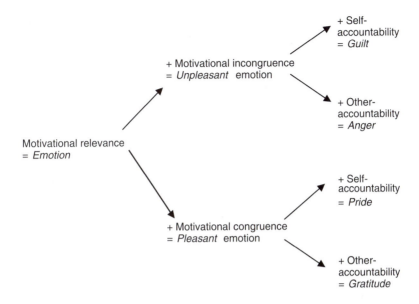

FIGURE 1.2. Appraisal components associated with selected emotions

the person is currently pursuing, there will be no emotion. In other words, we don't care about things that don't affect our lives (or those of other people we care about) in some way. Whether the resulting emotion is pleasant or unpleasant depends on appraisal of *motivational congruence*, which determines whether current developments help or hinder pursuit of our goals. The specific nature of the pleasant or unpleasant emotion in turn depends on further so-called "secondary" appraisals, which assess how the motivationally relevant event is to be explained (*accountability*) and what options are available for dealing with it (*coping potential*). For example, if someone insults us, this is usually a motivationally relevant and incongruent event and therefore leads to an unpleasant emotion. However, the kind of unpleasant emotion we experience depends on more specific appraisals relating to who is responsible (or accountable) for the insult. In particular, we will experience anger if we perceive the person doing the insulting as to blame for what they are doing, but guilt if we blame ourselves for doing something that led to the insult in the first place. In short, whether emotion occurs, and what form it takes, depends on our specific understanding of what is going on.

Although the connections between appraisals and emotions specified by appraisal models of this kind mainly seem logical and rational, most of us would resist the idea that we are always *aware* of explicitly interpreting events in terms of these appraisals in advance of the occurrence of emotion itself. We can all think of times, for example, when anger, fear, or guilt, came over us without any apparent warning. Appraisal theorists deal readily with such experiences by proposing that appraisal can proceed unconsciously as well as consciously. The empirical challenge, then, is to demonstrate the occurrence of unconscious appraisal prior to the experience of emotion. As yet, few usable criteria have been proposed for establishing the presence of such processes.

Another possible misconception that should be dispelled at this stage is that appraisals necessarily occur in a fixed order working from primary through secondary to produce an increasingly differentiated emotion. Instead, according to Smith and Lazarus (1993), the overall relational meaning of a situation may be grasped holistically all at once. Scherer's (1984, 2001) model, by contrast, does argue that the appraisal process unfolds as a series of logically sequenced stimulus evaluation checks, starting from more basic judgments relating to novelty and pleasantness and ending with more complex appraisals concerning the compatibility of events with norms and values.

Other versions of appraisal theory also differ in their interpretations of some of the specific dimensions or components of meaning involved in producing particular emotions, but most still overlap with Smith and Lazarus's account in many ways (see Roseman & Smith, 2001). Further, all of them agree that relational meaning usually initiates the emotion process and shapes its course. In other words, appraisals of emotional events lead to the specific bodily changes, expressions, and action tendencies that constitute the emotional reaction. Appraisal thus becomes a central organizing principle explaining how the different aspects of emotion fit together, and how the overall syndrome fits into the social world.

The function of appraisal, according to most theorists, is to allow detection of adaptively consequential situations. Appraisal provides a signal that something that is happening requires action and selects the form that action should take. The emotional response prepares the individual for dealing with the current concern by setting mind and body in an appropriate state of readiness (Lazarus, 1991a; Smith, 1989). For example, appraisals of uncertain coping potential lead to fear, which involves release of metabolic energy to muscles that might help with any flight reaction, enhanced alertness, and a pattern of facial movement that informs others about the threatening situation (potentially enlisting their help). Thus, appraisals precede internal physiological reactions, action tendencies, and expressive movements as the emotion unfolds. At a less automatic level, appraisals also determine what modes of coping might be directed at the emotional situation (problem-focused coping) and at the feelings engendered by that situation (emotion-focused coping). Coping, as well as the behaviors precipitated more directly by action

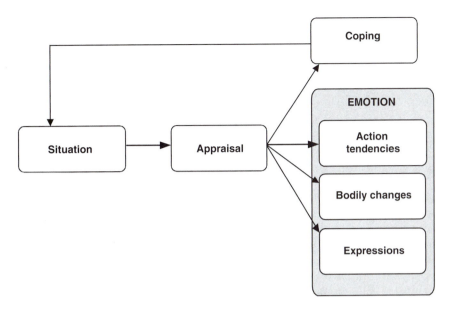

FIGURE 1.3. Appraisal theory

tendencies, in turn influence the emotional situation, which is then reappraised in accordance with any resultant changes (see Figure 1.3).

As we have seen, feedback theory argues, by contrast, that the heart, guts, and face react before any emotion is experienced. Indeed, feedback theorists believe that emotional experience derives precisely from the body reactions triggered by emotional stimuli. A sudden movement may make us jump, for example, and only then do the associated sensations start to produce feelings of shock. Of course, if the body responds selectively to the emotional meaning of situations (rather than their objective characteristics), it would be hard to discount the role of appraisal in discerning this meaning. Indeed, how does the body know how to react unless the emotional implications of what is happening have already been registered at some level?

This is not the place to get embroiled in debates about the correct sequence of events characterizing emotion episodes. For present purposes, it will suffice to acknowledge that emotions often do unfold as a function of appraisals of events, and that any bodily changes and facial movements that occur are often tightly dependent on these appraisals. However, as will become apparent later in the book, we do not believe that relations between appraisals and emotions are always as simple or clear-cut as appraisal theorists often seem to imply.

☐ Social Influences on Emotion Components

We are now in a position to discuss how the three kinds of social influence deriving from interpersonal encounters and relationships, group allegiances and conflicts, and cultural values and practices impact the various stages and aspects of unfolding emotions identified earlier. Our preliminary assumption, derived from appraisal theory, is that emotions develop as reactions to events that are appraised as good or bad by individuals, and that they involve some forms of expression and reaction that in turn may be subject to regulation of various kinds. Something happens, this something is recognized as emotionally relevant, and we consequently get emotional. The emotion manifests itself in bodily changes, action impulses, and facial expressions that we may or may not attempt to control. We see the bear, realize that it may be dangerous, become physiologically aroused, and want to escape. Our eyes widen and our jaw drops, but we try not to panic so much that we run into a tree instead of toward a likely hiding place. In this narrative, emotion may seem like an entirely personal affair, but as we shall see, interpersonal, group, and cultural factors are implicated in all aspects of the story, as well as how the story gets represented.

☐ Causes and Objects

Philosophers often classify emotions as intentional states (e.g., Gordon, 1974), meaning that they are always about something. We don't just feel angry, for example, we feel angry with someone else, about something that they have done. It turns out that most of the things we get emotional about are social in one way or another. Someone's unfeeling comment upsets us, we fall in love with somebody, or fall out with them, we are anxious about meeting a person for the first time, and so on. Questionnaire-based surveys support this observation that other people's actions or experiences comprise one of the largest classes of emotion-inducing events (e.g., Scherer, Wallbott, & Summerfield, 1986).

But the emotional effects of what people do also depend on who these people are. In particular, we need to be in some kind of relationship with others before their lives impact our own. This relationship need not be one of friendship or affiliation. In fact, people we despise, envy, or resent can make as much of a difference to our feelings as loved ones. Similarly, we can get excited or upset about what happens both to heroes and villains in action movies (though obviously in different ways). What seems to be necessary is some level of involvement or association: the fact that we share common or conflicting goals, or that the other's conduct can directly influence goal attainment. We work together or against one another on various formal and informal projects. These connections between people are what make us care about their conduct.

Furthermore, the specific nature of our interpersonal connections determines the particular meaning of the emotional object. For example, the same compliment has very different affective implications when it comes from our boss, our employee, or from someone with whom we are romantically involved. Both intimacy and relative status can make a big difference in how people react to interpersonal events.

Involvement, affiliation, and status differentials do not simply operate between pairs of people (e.g., "I am friends with John but an enemy of Jack who gets on with Jane but not Julie," and so on). Instead, more inclusive social arrangements also influence the way allegiances, antipathies, and power structures are formed. In particular, we are all members of certain kinds of groups or collectivities, ranging from families, sports teams, and clubs to broader social categories relating to class, gender, social status, and so on. As a general rule, what happens to members of our own groups also affects us personally. Further, because groups often define themselves in distinction to other groups (e.g., Catholics versus Protestants, Mac users versus PC users, suits or casuals, social or cognitive psychologists), what happens to members of specific out-groups also has corresponding emotional effects. For example, a Manchester United supporter might be happy when United win and when Arsenal lose (depending also on how rarely or commonly those particular contingencies might arise).

Groups also operate in the broader social context of societies. Manchester United can only produce emotionally relevant outcomes, for instance, because of the various institutions constituting the UK premier league, and their conduct only has meaning when set in the framework of the accepted rules of the game. If we could somehow transpose the act of kicking a ball into the net into some remote tribal setting in which its spectators had no previous knowledge of games like soccer, its emotional impact would certainly be different.

In sum, what people get emotional about can be social in three ways. At the interpersonal level, things that other people do or experience depress or elate us in different ways depending on our relationship with them. At the group level, outcomes experienced by in-groups and out-groups are of emotional concern. And finally, at the cultural level, pre-existing conventions, norms, values, and rules define what is emotionally significant and provide guidelines about appropriate or proper response.

Although people often account for their emotions in everyday conversation by reference to their objects ("I got angry about what she said"), we need additionally to specify their *causes* to explain them fully (e.g., Kenny, 1963; Ryle, 1949). The distinction may seem a subtle one: The object is the focus of the emotion, the thing that it is directed at, but the cause is what actually gets and keeps the emotion process going. Sometimes the cause of emotion is pretty much the same as its object, but at other times it is not. Most frequently, the emotion's object is just one aspect of one of its many causes. For example, I am angry that you failed to acknowledge that I had arrived at your party. However, what caused my anger is not only what you did or didn't do on that particular occasion, but also the history of our relationship, the presence of other people who noticed you ignoring me and their apparent reactions, the fact that someone else had just been rude to me too, the irritable mood I was already in, and so on. Clearly, social factors of various kinds may enter into the complex of emotion causes in many ways that are not purely restricted to their impact on the specific definition of emotional objects.

☐ Appraisal

As noted previously, emotions are often related to the ways in which people interpret and evaluate events and objects. Getting angry with people, for example, typically involves disapproval of their conduct, whereas feeling proud of our group's performance implies that we think they have done well. In addition to the nature of the object itself, then, part of what distinguishes one emotion from another (anger from guilt, love from hate) seems to involve the particular stance taken toward this object. Whether or not appraisal is the central and exclusive determinant of emotion, it seems incontrovertible that processes relating to appraisal represent an important aspect of emotional functioning. Whatever their precise causal status, social factors make an important difference to the appraisals associated with emotions. These social factors again can be seen as impacting at the interpersonal, group, and cultural levels.

We have already described how our emotions often take someone else's experiences as their object. It also seems that we take into account their evaluations and interpretations when making our own appraisals of other emotional objects. For example, we may enjoy a comedy film less when our companions are evidently offended by its content, or become more anxious partly because those sharing our fate seem to find the situation worrying (cf. Schachter, 1959). In effect, we calibrate perceptions of emotional meaning against the apparent perspective of key others. Because these processes of social appraisal (Manstead & Fischer, 2001) work in both directions, others are also affected by our own apparent evaluations. Indeed, sometimes we may only arrive at emotional conclusions as a consequence of discussion with each other, or by otherwise registering mutual reactions (in smiles, frowns, or diverted gazes). In either of these cases, the appraisals shaping emotions are influenced by a fundamentally interpersonal process (see Parkinson, 1995; 2001b).

At the group level, emotional appraisals may be normatively determined. Things matter to us to the extent that they affect group goals, projects, and identities (e.g., Smith, 1993). For example, derogatory comments about other United supporters, Tarantino aficionados, Radiohead fans, Volkswagen drivers, or social psychologists may upset you not because you know the insulted individuals personally but because you align yourself with them at a more general level. Indeed, group members may coordinate their appraisals with one another during the formation of common norms.

At the cultural level, socialized interpretations change the way we make sense of emotional events, and societal values provide criteria for their appraisal as good or bad. For example, Americans are brought up to value personal achievement, whereas certain other societies place more emphasis on shared family or group goals. Therefore, becoming top of one's class at school may be appraised rather differently within these contrasting cultural frames. In the same vein, Anglo-American culture tends to see the causation of behavior in primarily individual terms, whereas some Eastern societies foster more fatalistic views (e.g., Miller, 1984). These differing perspectives on causality have obvious implications for appraisals of accountability associated with emotions such as anger and pride (e.g., Roseman, 2001). More generally, a cultural emphasis on self versus others, or on personal uniqueness as opposed to social position, has clear consequences for the evaluation and interpretation of a wide variety of interpersonal events (e.g., Markus & Kitayama, 1991).

☐ Bodily Changes

Although it is obviously important to think about emotional objects and their appraisals when explaining emotions, most people would still say that the core of emotion itself is something separate, namely an inner feeling. James's (1884) feedback theory provides one possible explanation for this perceived personal essence. As noted previously, his view is that the experience of emotion results entirely from perception of bodily changes, which differentiate emotion from nonemotion, and different emotions from each other. However, one of the main problems facing

James's account is that subsequent research has failed to discern dramatically different patterns of bodily activity even when widely contrasting emotions are compared (e.g., Ax, 1953; Cannon, 1927; Ekman, Levenson, & Friesen, 1983). Not wishing to abandon the intuitively plausible idea that emotions depend on internal sensations, Schachter (1964) proposed that an undifferentiated state of metabolic activation (autonomic arousal) provides the heat behind emotional reactions (distinguishing emotion from nonemotion), but that their specific quality depends on appraisal of the prevailing situation. For example, if I sense my heart beating after someone has insulted me, I may interpret my reaction as anger, but if the same symptom occurs when someone is raising their fist to strike me, the sensation may be perceived as a symptom of fear.

In situations where we experience the internal symptoms of emotion but do not immediately know their origins, Schachter argued that we may engage in a process of social comparison to make sense of what we are feeling. For example, if arousal symptoms occur when you are with someone who seems euphoric, you may conclude that you too are experiencing joy, but if the same symptoms arise in the company of an evidently irritated individual, you may infer that you are angry instead (Schachter & Singer, 1962, but see Reisenzein, 1983 for a critical review of this evidence). Thus, according to this view, the emotional meaning of bodily changes may be disambiguated partly as a function of interpersonal processes.

Evidence also exists that when we are engaged in interactions with close others, our physiological states may converge at a more basic level. For example, Levenson and Gottmann (1983) demonstrated "autonomic linkages" between members of married couples engaged in dialogue with one another. Further, the extent of the interconnections between the respective internal processes of the two parties to the conversation proved a useful index of the quality of their relationship. Similar social attunement of bodily changes may also occur at a group level. The famous phenomenon of synchronized menstruation among women who are living together is one example of this. Related to this, the rhythms of group emotion may permeate into individual group members' internal states.

The fact that we seem to feel emotions inside our bodies tends to reinforce the common perception that emotions are essentially individual, even private states. It is my heart alone that I feel pounding when anxious, even if what I am anxious about directly concerns other people, and even when other people's hearts are pounding too. Although no one would want to deny the role of bodily activity in emotion, it is possible that its centrality has been overestimated. For example, patients continue to experience and express emotion even after spinal injuries that remove any sensations from the neck down (e.g., Bermond, Nieuwenhuyse, Fasotti, & Schuerman, 1991; Chwalisz, Diener, & Gallagher, 1988). Although there may be changes in some of the symptoms associated with emotion in such cases (e.g., Hohmann, 1966), in no cases do the participants report a complete absence of emotion.

Questions have also been raised about the accuracy of our perceptions of bodily change during emotion (e.g., Pennebaker, 1982, and see Cornelius, 1996). What we experience may not simply be an objective reflection of internal reality, but rather a culturally framed interpretation. Indeed, different cultures have very different views about where emotions are located and how they influence the body. In this regard, Averill (1974) contends that the association of emotions with gut reactions reflects culturally specific ideological prejudices about their primitive nature. Similarly, Rimé, Phillipot, and Cisamolo (1990) demonstrate that reports of bodily change experiences during specific remembered emotional incidents correspond closely with reports of bodily changes for typical emotional incidents, and conclude that stereotypical representations underlie both kinds of report.

However, it would be surprising if our ideas about how our bodies react during emotion had no basis in reality whatsoever. A compromise position suggested by Cacioppo and colleagues (2000) is that when internal signals are ambiguous, we may apply ready-made interpretations to make sense of them (as Schachter's theory implies), whereas strong emotions tend to produce more distinctive patterns of change. Further, these ready-made interpretations may derive, at least partly, from our veridical perceptions of the bodily changes felt during these extreme cases of emotion.

Some emotion theories see bodily changes as simple reactions to emotional stimuli or appraisals of these stimuli. However, it is also true that our internal physiology adjusts as we change our mode of action with respect to the environment. The autonomic processes implicated in emotion do not simply provide signals about emotional significance; rather, they reflect our developing engagement with emotional concerns. When we become involved in an argument, for instance, the blood that rushes to our face is part of the stance we are adopting with respect to our antagonist (cf. Sarbin, 1986). This need not imply that we work ourselves up into a state of physiological excitement deliberately, however. Instead, our role in the encounter develops a cognitive, behavioral, and physiological momentum of its own as the other person's own engagement similarly escalates. Each party to the exchange continually shapes the other's responses without any explicit attempt at manipulation.

In sum, physiological changes are usually neither the first stage of an emotional process nor the core components of emotional experience. It is therefore misleading to claim that emotions depend directly on signals from the body. More accurately, emotions are embodied actions and reactions in the first place. Our perceptions of physiological symptoms merely reflect the fact that emotion is associated with high levels of involvement, which in turn tend to be associated with more pronounced internal adjustments. Thus, to the extent that levels of involvement are determined by interpersonal, group, and cultural factors (as suggested previously), even literally internal aspects of emotion are also indirectly subject to social influence.

☐ Action Tendencies

One of the functions of the bodily changes experienced during emotion is to prepare muscles to move in ways that help to deal with the emotional event. For example, Cannon (1927) saw emotions as reactions to emergency situations requiring vigorous response. The body therefore releases metabolic energy to support any action that might be required. According to appraisal theories, the body is prepared more specifically for the particular kind of action required by the current situation as appraised. For example, appraisal of danger may lead to energy being released to the leg muscles to facilitate running away.

The mind too seems to ready itself for potentially necessary emotional responses. Emotion directs our attention to current events requiring action of some kind and makes us want to do something about them. For example, objects appraised as good generally encourage approach, whereas objects appraised as bad invoke withdrawal tendencies (Arnold, 1960). At a more specific level, an overheard derogatory remark may intrude into our consciousness even if we are occupied with something else, and we may immediately experience an urge to dispute it, or to strike or shout at the person making it.

Action tendencies are intended to change the relation between the emotional person and the current environment. As the earlier examples imply, they often specifically change the relation between the individual and other individuals as part of the social environment. We want to move away from people who are doing repellent things, and to move toward those who are behaving in more attractive ways. In addition to this interpersonal aspect, action tendencies may also be directed at changing the relation of a group member to other members of the group, or of the group to other groups. For example, when our team performs well, we are willing to bask in reflected glory, whereas we usually feel like distancing ourselves from its failures (e.g., Cialdini et al., 1976).

At a cultural level, the particular form our action impulses take depends on cultural conventions. For example, even in states of intense fury, members of Anglo-American society rarely feel the urge to literally "run amok," but may instead have a strong inclination to drive their cars very fast, or to play music at high volume. Thus, culture not only provides norms about what we are allowed to do, and opportunities for doing those things, but it also sets the agenda for our emotional desires and impulses in the first place.

☐ Expression

The ways in which people present and display their emotional appraisals of objects and events is intrinsically a social affair. What we show on our faces, for example, depends largely on who is there to read them. The common experience of attempting to disguise a socially unacceptable expression is often explained by reference to the psychological concept of "display rules" (e.g., Ekman, 1973). The idea is that people follow culturally learned conventions about what it is (and is not) appropriate to express in any given situation by explicitly regulating their facial movements. The resulting facial positions thus reflect a combination of automatic and controlled processes. Similar principles may also underlie gestural and vocal expressions.

The operation of display rules is clearly influenced by the interpersonal context, because there is little need to modify our expressions if no one else can see them. Further, different display rules probably apply when the other people who are present are in-group or out-group members. In a competitive situation, for example, a Manchester United fan might normally play up displays of triumph in front of fans of the losing team, but tone down her exuberance if she is in love with any of them.

Because display rules were originally invoked to explain cultural differences in emotional expression (Ekman, 1973), many examples of their societal specificity are available. One obvious cross-cultural contrast concerns reactions to formal ceremonies and rites of passage. For instance, Iranian funerals involve intensive outpourings of exuberant grief from some mourners, whereas in the United Kingdom, the norm is for somber restraint throughout (with the occasional surfacing of anguish for those particularly close to the deceased). Because it seems unlikely that British people are initially any less upset than others by the death of loved ones, these differences probably relate to the conventional presentation of emotion rather than its underlying quality or quantity. Presumably, people pick up these manners of emotional expression over the course of cultural socialization.

The display rules idea implies that an emotional impulse to expression is subsequently controlled. Alternatively, it has been argued that our emotional displays are attuned to others' reactions in the first place. According to this view, the only reason we frown when someone does something to offend us is to convey to them or others that we are prepared to retaliate (see Fridlund, 1994, and Chapter 6, this volume). Facial movements, then, would signal interpersonal motives rather than express individual emotions. If this is true, movements that are taken to be expressive of emotion are always fundamentally socially oriented.

☐ Regulation

It is not only the more obvious external manifestations of emotion that may be controlled in response to social considerations. We also make more direct attempts to adjust the way we feel about things. For example, when something uncontrollable upsets us, we often tell ourselves that it cannot be helped. Instead of giving ourselves this kind of advice, others might also encourage the use of specific affect-regulation strategies. Our friends also tell us that "what's done is done," remind us "how terrible" the tragedy was, or advise us to let our feelings out.

Emotion regulation may also be dictated by group membership, as in the case of service professionals who sometimes need to work up their level of caring for, or empathy with, clients (e.g., Hochschild, 1983). Finally, the culture provides a tool-kit of strategies for our use, as well as guidelines concerning when it is appropriate to deploy them. For example, when a child misbehaves in a supermarket, a Japanese mother might say: "It is not Mommy alone who is shopping. Other people are also here to shop, and the store owners have neatly lined things up so that the customers will buy them. Therefore it will be annoying to them if you behave this way" (Conroy, Hess, Azuma, & Kashigawa, 1980, p. 168). United States mothers, on the other hand, are more likely to tell their children off more directly or hold them tightly close by to prevent them going astray in the first place.

Interpersonal recommendations of this kind clearly relate to cultural norms and values about proper conduct, some of which are explicitly embodied in religious or philosophical teachings. For example, Christians may recite the Serenity Prayer: "Lord grant me the serenity to accept the things I cannot change, the courage to change the things I can, and the wisdom to know the difference." The Buddha also offered advice concerning emotion regulation, including the following: "Holding on to anger is like grasping a hot coal with the intent of throwing it at someone else; you are the one who gets burned." More generally, the collective knowledge of every society includes tried and tested strategies for coping with unpleasant events that are common in that particular cultural setting.

☐ Emotion Itself

So far, we have discussed how social factors affect various aspects of emotional functioning, ranging from causes and objects to means of control. But what about emotion itself? It seems obvious to many people that the essence of emotion is something wholly individual and private, an internal experience that we cannot easily put into words, let alone share directly with others. Think, for example, of the Vulcan mind meld as featured in the first television series of *Star Trek*, when Mr. Spock puts his hand to another's head to get properly in touch with their feelings. Ordinary interpersonal interaction somehow doesn't seem to be sufficient to get through to others completely. Everyone would agree that subjective aspects are involved in getting emotional. We see things from a particular perspective that no one else can entirely appreciate. However, having considered how emotion is hemmed in on all sides by aspects that are (at least partly) socially determined, the question of what exactly it is that is left untouched by these forces inevitably arises (see also Parkinson, 1996).

One view, corresponding more or less to the commonsense ideas just outlined, is that a core essence exists to emotion insulated from all the contingent influences of social life. Ekman (1971), for example, argues that culture and learning determine what people get emotional about, and whether they modulate their expression of emotion, but not emotion itself.

However, whether emotions really do have a detachable essence of this sort, independent of the various processes surrounding it, is debatable. Averill and Nunley (1992), for example, call this the "myth of the emotional artichoke:" the idea that if you peel away all the external layers you will get to the heart of emotion. They suggest that emotion may be more like an onion; you can keep peeling away, but all there is to it are the layers themselves. Another relevant metaphor here is Ryle's (1949) notion of a "category mistake." He imagines a foreign tourist being shown around the city of Oxford who has seen the various colleges, libraries, and departments yet is still expectantly waiting for his first sight of the university itself. Similarly, someone following an essentialist approach might say, "You've presented me with the appraisals, expressions, and regulation processes, but where is the *emotion*?" Ryle's answer would be that no localized phenomenon exists corresponding to the word in question and that it instead denotes a superordinate concept whose meaning is constituted from these various aspects, just as "Oxford University" is distributed around the various buildings and institutions that underlie its operations. By the final chapter of this book, readers should be in a better position to decide between these alternative accounts.

☐ Individual and Social Conceptions of Emotion

We shall be considering various theoretical approaches to emotion in subsequent chapters of this book, but it makes sense to set out some of the basic alternative positions that have been taken at this early stage. Although it is commonplace to emphasize individualistic aspects of emotions—how they are based on our idiosyncratic reactions, and how they affect us at a personal level—it should be clear that our focus here is on how relational, group, and cultural factors impinge on this process. In short, this book tries to understand emotion from the "outside," by examining the everyday social settings in which it operates. By taking this perspective, we do not mean to deny that intrapsychic or biological aspects to the emotional process exist. Rather, we want to draw attention to how emotions are always produced in particular contexts that give them their meaning and shape the ways in which they unfold.

The extent to which social factors are prioritized in understanding emotions depends in part on whether emotion is seen as a core essence apart from its various manifestations, components, and aspects as considered previously. Obviously, if emotion is a distinctive feeling (or "qualia") separate from appraisals, bodily changes, facial movements, and so on, it makes more sense to see it as located internally. Where else could the heart of this kind of experience be? On the other hand, if emotion is seen as a syndrome constituted from various interlocking processes that unfold as part of ongoing transactions with the world, it becomes much easier to see their direct relation with social life.

At one end of the spectrum, then, are several influential thinkers who define emotions in terms of feelings, experiences, or other internal events. For example, Oatley (1992) argued that

> Emotions can be described scientifically in a way that corresponds recognizably to emotions as referred to in ordinary language. We should continue to refer to emotions as mental states, just as we talk

about seeing and hearing even though more than a hundred years of research has taught us much more about them than is known to a layperson. (p. 18)

If Oatley is correct that emotions are intrinsically intrapsychic conditions, then their connection to the outside world must necessarily be indirect and mediated. The role of social factors in emotion thus boils down to one of external influence. Emotions may be caused or take as their object social events, and may influence the course of social life in their expression, but emotions themselves remain individual and internal (cf. Ekman, 1972, as discussed earlier). For example, according to Ortony, Clore, and Collins' (1988) definitions, anger is an affective mental state produced by "disapproving of someone else's blameworthy action" and "being displeased about ... [the related] undesirable event" (p. 147), and emotions more generally are "valenced reactions to events, agents, or objects, with their particular nature being determined by the way in which the eliciting condition is construed" (p. 13). Although, as Oatley points out, such a view is consistent with many of our commonsense ideas, it is also worth noting that not all humans (let alone psychologists) share this conception. As we shall see in the next chapter, many languages locate emotions more within the realm of social relations than the private world of the mind.

Schachter's (1964) theory acknowledges the internal component of emotion, but argues that it only gains specific emotional meaning when linked up to cognitions about the current situation, including its social aspects. In this view, emotion has a private as well as a public aspect, and the latter may be directly influenced by social considerations. Similarly, Russell and Feldman-Barrett (1999; see also Russell, 2003) contend that internal feelings of pleasantness and arousal constitute "core affect," but external and often culturally specific considerations determine the way the emotional episode is classified and regulated. According to both of these views, emotion is only partly internal and cannot be completely understood without reference to its context.

Averill (1980) attaches even greater emphasis to the social contexts that shape emotional life. He defines emotions not as private events but as "transitory social roles" supplied by the culture. For example, getting angry is seen as a way of upholding justice without any deliberate aggression (Averill, 1982). Because the anger response is seen as largely involuntary and controlled by spontaneous bodily changes, responsibility may be disowned for any acts carried out in the "heat of the moment" (Averill, 1974). Performance of the emotional role involves a variety of changes in appraisals, bodily involvement, facial expression, and so on, none of which can be seen as exhaustively defining the emotion itself.

Instead, it is the overall pattern of events that is important: "An emotional syndrome may include many diverse elements, some of them biological and some of social origin, but none of which is essential to the identification of the syndrome as a whole" (Averill, 1980).

Seeing emotions as syndromes of components does not necessarily imply that these syndromes are assembled by sociocultural forces, however. Plutchik (1980), for example, argues that the cognitive appraisals that lead to the subjective aspects of emotion are themselves biologically determined (see also Tooby & Cosmides, 2001). Similarly, Scherer (e.g., 2001) views emotions as self-organizing coordinations between different response systems that are shaped by an incremental series of stimulus evaluation checks whose existence depends on evolutionary selection.

Although apparently major disagreements exist between different theorists about the centrality of social factors, even the staunchest individualist would agree that emotions are related in some way to social life. Correspondingly, even the most extreme social constructionist would acknowledge that some of the processes that contribute to emotional syndromes can be profitably studied at an individual level (e.g., Averill, 1992). Arguments may be reduced to more specific issues about which emotion-relevant aspects and processes are influenced by social factors and to what extent. For example, is facial movement an expression of an internal feeling, or is it part of a communication addressed to other people? Are appraisals privately calculated or negotiated between people? Do individuals formulate regulation intentions to control their feelings, or is the process more accurately described in terms of interpersonal alignment with each party subject to continual mutual influence? Do other people directly catch our feelings as a function of contact with us? All of these questions will be addressed in subsequent chapters of this book.

As a final point, it is worth noting that disagreements about the role of social factors in emotion are often mistakenly seen as reflecting the well-worn nature-nurture controversy. To be clear, our claim that there are irreducibly social aspects to emotion exist does not imply that biology plays no role in the phenomenon. For one thing, social and biological are overlapping, not mutually exclusive, categories. Indeed, both our sensitivity to others' responses and our capacity for learning about emotional meanings derive from evolutionary origins. Although we believe that biological factors have often been over-emphasized in the explanation of emotion, they are clearly implicated at all levels. For example, many of the specific response components involved in emotional syndromes have biological aspects. In practice, all psychological functions reflect culture and biology, learning and instinct, ontogenesis and phylogenesis, and their respective interactions are so tight that it rarely makes sense to view either side of the equation in isolation (see also Ellsworth, 1994). However, important questions still remain about the relative emphasis of alternative accounts, and about the specific processes whereby the interlocking factors exert their influence. In particular, a live issue concerns whether it is only emotional components that are biologically determined (Ortony & Turner, 1990) or whether biology also provides an organizing principle that links these components together (e.g., Plutchik, 1980; Tooby & Cosmides, 2001). Clearly, the latter view leaves little space for social factors to work their influence. In this book, we hope to raise the conceptual profile of cultural, group, and interpersonal factors in the understanding of emotion and to counter any tendency to relegate social processes to a secondary role.

☐ Subsequent Chapters

In the following chapters, we focus in turn on cultural, group, and interpersonal processes and their effects on emotion. Chapter 2 is concerned with the ways in which emotion is represented and conceptualized in different societies, whereas chapter 3 concentrates on the processes whereby culture affects emotion itself. Moving to group processes, chapter 4 reviews research into the emotional impact of relations between groups (intergroup emotion), and chapter 5 is devoted to the effects of group membership on emotion (intragroup emotion). The first interpersonal chapter (chapter 6) considers how a specific aspect of emotional functioning, facial movement, affects and is affected by changing relationships between people, and chapter 7 provides a more general discussion of emotions as processes that operate interpersonally rather than at a purely intrapsychic level. In the final chapter (chapter 8), we shall revisit many of the themes raised in the present chapter, and attempt to develop an integrative theory drawing on the insights from cultural, group, and interpersonal theory and research reviewed in chapters 2 to 7.

In particular, chapter 8 will consider two directions of relationship between the three modes of social influence outlined earlier. First, we discuss how cultures influence groups, and groups influence interpersonal relations from above. Second, we suggest that a complementary process operates "bottom-up," through the establishment of group emotion via interpersonal processes, and cultural emotion via group processes. For example, interpersonal co-ordination may lead to a shared group affect contributing to the establishment of a common frame of reference for action. Intergroup alignment in turn has cultural effects resulting from negotiation, struggle, revolution, or the evolution of consensus. This analysis implies not only that there are both bottom-up and top-down relations between cultural, group, and relational processes, but also that the three levels are mutually interacting and determining. This leads us to a final reconceptualization of social and emotional life in which many of the traditional distinctions cease to apply.

Emotional Meaning Across Cultures

Opportunities for interacting with members of other cultures have grown immensely over the last decades. Not only have many societies become increasingly multicultural, but also processes of globalization have tended to increase intercultural contact more generally. It has never been so easy to travel to countries all over the world, and we can also interact with people from different societies via the internet without traveling at all. When we meet people, either directly or remotely, in addition to communicating thoughts and attitudes, we also transmit emotions. However artificial or short-lived interpersonal encounters and social relations may be, they typically involve some degree of affective commitment or involvement, prompting pangs or passions of envy, admiration, love, hate, hope, or disappointment. Social interaction thus implies both experience and expression of feelings.

However, abundant evidence exists that emotions do not provide a universal currency for direct exchange. They may be experienced or expressed in different ways, regulated and shared in different situations, or recognized and interpreted differently from one culture to the next. Smiles, for example, may be interpreted as signs of approval rather than courtesy. Saying that you are angry may imply childishness or honesty. Shame may be treated as an act of social repair and not an acknowledgement of one's stupidity, and so on. In other words, emotions may be understood and evaluated differently because they mean different things in different cultural contexts. When interacting with people from other countries, therefore, we are confronted not only with a language barrier, but also with an emotion barrier.

In this chapter and the next, we shall be concerned with cross-cultural differences in emotion. The present chapter focuses on what emotion words and concepts mean in different languages and societies, whereas chapter 3 is concerned with variations relating more directly to emotional experience and expression. Before addressing either topic, however, a few remarks should be made about the usage and meaning of the central concept of "culture" itself.

☐ Operationalizing "Culture"

Two approaches to culture are often distinguished in the social sciences. The first is the *emic* approach adopted by many cultural anthropologists. Here, a single culture is intensively analyzed from inside. The focus is on the meanings of concepts and customs within the society's own frames of reference, and, to fully appreciate their significance, emic researchers need to live among the populace and to suspend or unlearn any of their own culturally specific habits of interpretation. As a result of such participant observation, an ethnography (literally, a "writing of the culture") is derived, which details the many interlocking aspects of the society's way of life. For example, "emotion" is interpreted emically by reference to the functions it serves within broader social practices.

For emic researchers, culture is not an isolated independent variable that has a causal impact on other variables, but rather something that permeates everyday activities. By contrast, the *etic* approach adopted by many psychologists involves directly comparing different cultures with each other along supposedly common dimensions. Cultures are thus understood in relation to one another rather than on their own terms. For example, an etic researcher might look for similarities and differences in the experience, expression, and representation of emotion in two or more different countries.

Each of these approaches has corresponding limitations. The emic tradition makes it hard to disentangle emotion from the systems of meaning that surround it, whereas the etic tradition is always open to the criticism that its dimensions of comparison do not apply in precisely the same way within different cultural frameworks. In effect, emic researchers may seem trapped inside specific cultural representations, whereas etic researchers are left outside unable to find a point of entry. Emic researchers are accused of not seeing the forest for the trees, and etic researchers are condemned for missing vital subtleties.

In this book, therefore, we shall attempt to flesh out the etic framework by incorporating relevant emic insights. For example, a common problem with many comparative studies of emotion concerns their reliance on unquestioned common knowledge or stereotypes in operationalizing "culture" (see also Oyserman, Coon, & Kemmelmeier, 2002; Rodriguez et al., in press). It is assumed that geographical boundaries (e.g., Western vs. Eastern) directly map to loosely defined ideological divisions. Ethnographic findings enable us to make finer and more accurate distinctions.

Probably the most popular basis for distinguishing cultures according to the etic tradition is Hofstede's (1984) cultural dimension of individualism-collectivism. Individualistic cultures (found mostly in North-Western Europe and the English speaking countries) place a premium on personal agency and autonomy, whereas collectivistic cultures (mostly found in Asian and African countries) attach more value to group goals and interpersonal relations (Triandis, 1989; Kitayama & Markus, 1994; Markus & Kitayama, 1991). These contrasting meaning systems are thought to have particular implications for the forms of self-construals and modes of agency experienced by members of the societies in question (e.g., Markus & Kitayama, 1992), bringing consequent effects on emotion and its representation.

In our view, it is not enough to divide cultures into broad categories on the basis of highly abstract dimensions of this kind before making comparisons. Culture first needs to be "unpackaged"—that is, clearly defined and operationalized (see Bond & Tedesachi, 2001; Matsumoto, 2001; Rodriguez et al., in press) before its implications can be fully appreciated. One advantage of emic approaches may be their ability to distinguish cultural values and representations from emotions themselves, so that their mutual influences can be examined. On the other hand, a pitfall lies in their tendency to treat culture as an unproblematic independent variable exerting a top-down influence, instead of seeing relations between emotion and culture in more dialectical terms. However, we believe that it is possible to disentangle emotional processes and the surrounding culture, without assuming that connections between them are mechanistic. This possibility will be further elaborated in the final chapter.

☐ Emotional Meaning

The central topic of the present chapter, emotional meaning, refers to our everyday understanding of emotions: how we conceive of emotions, how they are represented in language, how we think they work, how positively or negatively they are viewed, and so on. It includes people's classifications of specific emotion terms on the basis of similarities and contrasts, as well as how the category of emotion is distinguished from nonemotion at a general level. In addition, emotional meaning incorporates more elaborate ethnotheories and prescriptive bodies of knowledge about emotion (making it similar to concepts such as emotionology, Stearns & Stearns, 1985, and emotional culture, Gordon, 1989). By focusing on these topics, we aim to emphasize that emotions convey culturally specific representations rather than carry a universal and biologically determined semantic content (see also White, 2000). In addition to determining how we label and communicate affect, emotional meaning systems also shape the ways in which we experience, express, organize, and modulate our emotions.

A range of views are possible concerning the relationship between emotional meaning and emotion itself. According to some authors (e.g., Harris, 1995), no necessary correspondence exists between our representations of emotion and the emotional phenomena that are represented. In this view, the way that emotion is understood by members of a society may reflect cultural prejudice or ideology as much as the structure of emotional reality. Thus, differences in emotional meaning across cultures may be reconciled with a putatively universal set of emotion processes. Emotion may be the same across the world but represented in different, more or less accurate, ways. Other theorists (e.g., Harré, 1986; Lutz, 1988), on the other hand, have claimed that emotional meaning is not merely an imperfect reflection of emotional reality, but it also helps to shape emotional experience in the first place. On this account, it is impossible to view emotion language, or the way in which emotions get their cultural meaning more generally, as wholly separate from emotion itself. According to Heelas (1986), for example, the social importance of any given emotion is reflected in the extent of its conceptual articulation, which in turn affects its identification, representation, and regulation.

Clearly, the relationship between emotion representation and emotional experience is not a direct one-way mapping, with words describing after the fact a discrete emotional state that is already fully articulated. Instead, a more complex dynamic operates, with representations of emotion influencing emotion itself as well as vice versa (see also Besnier, 1990; Parkinson, 1998; White, 2000). Neither emotion nor its representation should be seen as the simple prerequisite of the other. We can feel something without exactly knowing what we feel, and we may know about emotions we have never personally experienced. More commonly, however, experience and understanding are more tightly integrated than these examples imply. In particular, the meaning we attach to emotion may make us more aware of our feelings, intensify emotional experience, prompt attempts at regulation, and otherwise change the character of our emotional conduct. To quote Heelas (1986): "How raw experiences are constituted as emotions depends on how they are illuminated. Emotions experienced as organ talk are not the same as emotions experienced in the light of gods" (p. 257).

This chapter reviews studies directed at three aspects of emotional meaning. First, we consider investigations of the structure of emotion vocabularies. At issue here are questions concerning which phenomena are included in the general category of emotion and how much its content is subject to cultural variation. Second, we discuss research into the specific meanings of particular emotion words. For example, cross-cultural differences in the events and reactions associated with typical examples of emotions are elucidated, as well as variations in the ways emotion names are used in everyday discourse. Third, we identify ethnotheories of emotions (see also D'Andrade, 1984; Lutz, 1983; Lutz & White, 1986), which can be found in metaphors and broader common-sense views on the nature and workings of emotion.

At the end of this chapter, we return to the question of how emotional meaning may impact emotional phenomena. How does emotional meaning get integrated in emotional experience? How does it influence emotional responses, and which processes account for its effects?

□ Emotion Vocabularies Across Cultures

"Emotion" as a General Category

The study of emotion words is not new. Anthropologists (e.g., Geertz, 1973) and psychologists (e.g., Davitz, 1969) have been analyzing the semantic content of emotion concepts for several decades. What is more novel, however, is the systematic attempt to relate differences in emotional meanings to cross-cultural variation in emotion itself. Some basic questions arise from such a project. Are people talking about the same things when they talk about "emotions" in different cultures or at different times (e.g., Averill, 1980; Harré & Finlay-Jones, 1986; Russell, 1991a; Wierzbicka, 1991b)? What exactly counts as an emotion in one culture compared to another? Is there precisely the same variety and number of "emotions" in all cultures and languages? Is it self-evident that there must be phenomena corresponding to our own idea of what emotions are in all other cultures?

The answer to each of these questions is no. Just as other psychological categories such as "mental illness" (e.g., Rosenhan, 1973; Szasz, 1974), "self" (e.g., Gergen & Davis, 1984) and "personality trait" (e.g., Mischel, 1972) have proved slippery when subjected to sustained analysis, "emotion" turns out to be a more problematic concept than it might seem at first glance. Emotions are not straightforward, hard-wired essences that may simply be observed or revealed, but rather are complex, multicomponential phenomena needing interpretation to be identified as proper instances of the category in question (see also van Brakel, 1994). For example, screaming or sitting silently for hours with your eyes closed may be seen as signs of emotion in one culture, but not another.

What English speakers label as an emotion is usually a set of symptoms, or a syndrome (Averill, 1980). Other languages may selectively emphasize different aspects of this syndrome and exclude other aspects. Alternatively, their closest equivalent term may not denote a syndrome in the first place. Thus, cultural representations may differ greatly from culture to culture, and from one historical era to the next.

Defining emotion even within a single language or culture is often far from straightforward. Attempts to specify the related concept of "passion" can be traced as far back as Aristotle and Plato, and have been sources of disagreement among philosophers and psychologists ever since. Many of these disputes center on the common assumption that emotions can be defined precisely on the basis of a delimited set of necessary and sufficient features, so that a sharp dividing line separates instances of the category from nonemotions (the "classical view"). Several theorists have explicitly denied that all everyday concepts can be defined in this way (Rosch, 1973; Wittgenstein, 1953). For example, the definition of a square is that it is a geometric shape with four sides of equal length at right angles to one another. However, what would be the necessary and jointly sufficient features of an emotion? The occurrence of a feeling accompanied by physiological changes, perhaps? But would that specification always apply to all supposed emotions? What about guilt, pity, or serenity, for example? And wouldn't pain, dizziness, and thirst also count as emotions according to these criteria?

The most popular alternative to the classical approach to definition is Rosch's (1973) prototype theory. According to this view, many concepts can only be defined in terms of their prototypes—that is, the clearest examples around which the category in question is organized (Fehr & Russell, 1984). The line demarcating the category from other categories thus becomes blurred rather than sharply drawn, and decisions about category membership become probabilistic instead of definitive. The prototype approach has been productively applied to psychological concepts such as "intelligence" (Neisser, 1979), "disposition" (Buss & Craik, 1980), and "traits" (Cantor & Mischel, 1977), as well as to "emotion" (Fehr & Russell, 1984; Shaver, Schwartz, Kirson, & O'Connor, 1987).

"Emotion" is seen as a "fuzzy set" because it often seems impossible to demarcate a strict boundary between what belongs inside and what belongs outside the category, even within a single language. For example, professional emotion theorists as well as laypeople disagree about questions such as whether "surprise" is or is not an emotion (e.g., Ortony & Turner, 1990). Similar disputes surround the emotional status of states such as "boredom," "admiration," "pride," "frustration," and "tiredness." According to prototype theory, no simple and conclusive test exists that can be deployed to resolve such ambiguities. Instead, judgments can only be made on the basis of comparisons with whatever are seen as the clearest defining examples of emotion. Because these prototypical instances may differ from one language or society to another, the range of phenomena falling under the banner of "emotion" (or broadly equivalent terms) also shows cultural variability.

Most, but not all, languages seem to have words or expressions that denote the broad range of phenomena that English-speakers call emotions. In the Anglo-Saxon world, the emotion category is relatively inclusive, typically referring to combinations of thoughts, feelings, and bodily processes (Wierzbicka, 1999). Some languages, such as Samoan, Tahitian, or Papuan, do not appear to have such a general emotion term. However, words exist in these languages referring to "our insides" (Ifaluk), to feelings and sensations (Samoa), or to thoughts and feelings that originate in the liver (Chewong). Another variation of the emotion category can be found in the Japanese language, which contains two different general labels: *kanjo* and *jodo*. It is not clear whether these concepts refer to the same type of feelings and intensity of feelings as the English concept of emotion. *Jodo*, for example, covers concepts like considerate, motivating, lucky, and calculating (Russell, 1991a), which the English would call "personal attributes," in addition to apparently more emotional terms (corresponding loosely to "anger," "happiness," "shame," etc.).

There also seem to be differences in the number of words that fall into the "emotion" category in different languages. For example, according to some researchers, English contains about 2,000 emotion words, Dutch about 1,500, Taiwanese Chinese about 750, Malaysian about 230, and the language of the Chewong (a small aboriginal group in central Malaysia [Howell, 1981]) only seven (Heelas, 1986; Russell, 1991a). Such variations may reflect the inclusiveness of the category, how fine-grained its internal distinctions are, or how many synonyms are provided in the language

In sum, the general concept of "emotion" forms a category that does not have a similar meaning across cultures, and does not even seem to exist in all languages. The fact that not every language contains a term that refers to the same range of phenomena, or is characterized by the same features as the English-language "emotion," may lead us to question the universality of the phenomena that such a concept picks out (Russell, 1991a and b; Wierzbicka, 1999). Alternatively, it might be argued that emotions themselves are universal but that different languages encode them in very different ways and to very different degrees.

"Basic" or Prototypical Emotions

Another approach to investigating the universality of the emotion category is to ask people which terms can be counted as its members. The results of such studies provide insight into whether specific emotions are represented in the general category of emotion, which examples are most prototypical, and which emotional domains are highlighted, ignored, or repressed in a particular language.

In one of the first investigations of the lexical structure of the emotion domain, Fehr and Russell (1984) asked English speaking students to list as many emotion words as they could think of. Three hundred eighty-three different emotion words were generated in total. The 10 most frequently mentioned emotions were "happiness," "anger," "sadness," "love," "fear," "hate," "joy," "excitement," "anxiety," and "depression." Examples of less frequently mentioned emotion terms were "withdrawn," "weak," "uptight," "relaxed," and "malicious."

In a second study, respondents were asked to state the general category to which 20 target emotion words belonged. "Love," "sadness," "hate," "happiness," "joy," and "anger" were most often rated as belonging to the category "emotion." Moreover, these same emotion words were also rated as the most prototypical. Shaver and colleagues (1987) obtained similar results from U.S. participants using a different, card-sorting task, involving the categorization of 213 emotion words. A hierarchical cluster analysis of the results suggested that 25 low-level clusters were organized into five basic categories: "love," "joy," "anger," "sadness," and "fear."

These studies suggest that five commonly identified categories are the most prototypical in the English language domain of "emotion." These categories also correspond approximately to several lists of so-called "basic emotions" proposed by theorists such as Ekman (1992a) and Izard (1977). However, other supposedly basic emotions do not seem to be prototypical. In particular, surprise is considered by Ekman (1992a) to be a basic emotion, partly because it has a unique facial expression. However, Shaver and colleagues (1987) argued that surprise does not qualify as a basic category, because it is too small (including only three words), and because it is mentioned by very few persons in free-listing studies.

Can the same prototypical categories of emotion also be found in other languages? Van Goozen and Frijda (1993) collected free lists of emotion words from respondents in six different European countries (Belgium, England, France, Italy, Switzerland, and the Netherlands). Although there were large differences in the average number of total emotions mentioned (ranging from 137 in Switzerland to 429 in Italy), equivalents of "joy," "sadness," "fear," and "anger" were among the first 12 most frequently mentioned emotion words in all countries. "Love" and "happiness" also came in the top 12 for five out of the six countries. Further, correlations between the frequencies with which equivalent emotion words were mentioned across countries were all positive, indicating some level of similarity in their relative prominence in the different languages. Including Fehr and Russell's (1984) Canadian data in the sample revealed further evidence of similarity across national samples, but also suggested that shared language was a factor. In particular, the two English-speaking groups (Canada and England) produced similar patterns of data, both of which could be more easily distinguished from patterns obtained in non English-speaking countries. Of course, to the extent that shared language tends also to have implications concerning shared culture, these findings hardly provide unambiguous support for a primarily linguistic explanation.

Results of cross-cultural studies of non-Western languages also suggest that many parts of the emotion lexicon are universally shared (Church, Katigbak, Reyes, & Jensen, 1999; Fontaine, Poortinga, Setiadi, & Markam, 2002; Moore, Romney & Hsia, 2002; Shaver, Wu, & Schwartz, 1989). Hupka, Lenton, and Hutchison (1999), for example, showed that 47 of 65 sampled languages had emotion terms for at least 15 of the 25 low-level clusters identified by Shaver and colleagues (1987), such as "alarm," "amusement," "arousal," and "aggravation." Ethnographic studies (Heider, 1991; Lutz, 1988) also suggest that basic-level emotion concepts are similar across languages. In most languages across the world, the vocabulary seems to be organized around the categories of "love," "joy," "fear," "anger," and "sadness."

However, some studies also show that additional prototypical categories can be found in some non-Western languages. For example, Shaver, Wu, and Schwartz (1989) derived a distinctive "sad love" category from Chinese participants' sortings of emotion words, suggesting that a tendency to associate concepts such as "unrequited love" and "infatuation" with "longing," "nostalgia," and "sorrow." Moreover, "love" itself seemed to be part of the "joy" cluster rather than representing a category in its own right. A separate "shame" cluster was also apparent in the Chinese data, unlike the U.S. results that suggested that "shame," "guilt," and "remorse" were subcategories of "sadness." This final difference may reflect the Chinese emphasis on shame during the process of socialization. Indeed, Chinese children already appear to possess a clear understanding of the shame concept by the age of 2 and a half (e.g., Fung, 1999, and see chapter 3).

There are also languages that seem to lack any word for an emotion usually considered to be basic. In particular, Levy (1973) found that "sadness" is not part of the vocabulary of inhabitants of the village Piri, on the island of Huahine (one of the Society Islands). According to Levy (1973):

There are words for severe grief and for lamentation. There are, how-ever, no unambiguous terms that represent the concepts of sadness, longing, or loneliness. . . . People would name their condition, where I supposed that the body signs and the context called for "sadness" or "depression" as "feeling troubled." (p. 305)

Differences in basic emotion categories occur across historical eras as well as geographically defined cultures. For example, the Rasādhyāya (a Sanskrit text written by Hindu philosophers between the third and elev-enth centuries A.D.) delineates eight "basic emotions," roughly trans-lated as (a) sexual passion–love, (b) amusement–laughter–humor, (c) sorrow, (d) anger, (e) fear–terror, (f) perseverance–energy–heroism, (g) disgust–disillusion, and (h) amusement–wonder–astonishment. Accor-ding to Shweder and Haidt (2000), only three of these concepts (sorrow, anger, and fear) show a substantial correspondence with the basic emo-tions listed by Ekman (1992a).

To summarize, this review of emotion vocabularies indicates that pro-totypical concepts that seem close to English notions of "joy," "fear," "sadness," and "anger" feature in a wide range of languages. However, these categories are not unproblematically universal: Differences exist in their precise meaning and usage, two or more of them are sometimes fused together in broader categories, and some languages apparently fail to specify them all in the first place. Taken together, these data present a powerful case for cultural variability in the emotion lexicon (see van Brakel, 1994, for further examples). Culture-specific basic categories like "love," "shame," "surprise," "sad love," or "compassion" offer further testament to this verdict.

☐ Meanings of Specific Emotion Words

In the previous section, we tried to elaborate the meaning of the general category of emotion by reference to its specific exemplars. In the present section, we refocus our attention on the particular meaning of these exemplars across cultures. Research on this topic has consistently demon-strated that the internal meanings of supposedly equivalent emotion words may differ widely across cultures.

Culturally Specific Emotion Words

Abundant evidence now exists that some languages have emotion words without close equivalents in other languages. The apparent absence of a sadness term in Piri as noted by Levy (1973) and mentioned above is one example of this phenomenon. In this case, a word that is widely used in most cultures does not seem to feature in one specific culture. Conversely, many emotion concepts also seem to be distinctive to a single culture but are rarely represented elsewhere. The present section will focus on concepts of this latter variety.

The Japanese language contains several words that fall into this category. In particular, *itoshii* refers to longing for an absent loved one, *ijirashii* means seeing someone praiseworthy overcoming an obstacle (Russell, 1991a), *oime* describes the unpleasant sense of being indebted to another person (Triandis, 1990b), and *amae*, probably the best known example, refers to a kind of sweet dependence on people close to you (Doi, 1973; Morsbach & Tyler, 1986).

The Korean words *dapdaphada* (approximately translated as "helplessness") and *uulhada* (roughly speaking, "depression" or "loneliness") do not seem to map directly to European or North American emotion terms either. In a study of these concepts, Schmidt-Atzert and Hyun-Sook Park (1999) asked Korean and German participants to list emotions that they would feel in response to 10 prototypical situations that had been constructed to elicit dapdaphada, uulhada, fear, sadness, loneliness, anger, hate, love, joy, and happiness. Most of the Korean respondents used the words *dapdaphada* and *uulhada* to express how they felt in reaction to the corresponding scenarios, but much less frequently in response to other scenarios. None of the closest German words were used as frequently, confirming that these emotion concepts have no direct equivalents in the German language.

Examples also appear within Western society. The German word *Schadenfreude* (referring to pleasure arising from the misfortune of others [e.g., Ben-Ze'ev, 1992]), for instance, has equivalents in French and Dutch, but not in English. In addition, Crespo (1986) discusses a specific Spanish emotion, *verguenza ajena*, which is literally translated as "shame because of a stranger." This condition arises not because of one's own improper actions (as in most Western instances of "shame"), but as a result of the improper or inadequate conduct of another person. Verguenza ajena seems to reflect the importance of correct social conduct, especially of face-saving rules in Spanish society. The social function of the emotion may be to attach stigma to those who cause its occurrence.

As a final illustration, Milan Kundera writes about a specifically Czechoslovakian emotion in his novel *The book of laughter and forgetting* (1980):

> *Litost* is a Czech word with no exact translation into any other language. It designates a feeling as infinite as an open accordion, a feeling that is the synthesis of many others: grief, sympathy, remorse,

and an indefinable longing. The first syllable which is long and stressed sounds like the wail of an abandoned dog.

Under certain circumstances, however, it can have a very narrow meaning, a meaning as definite, precise, and sharp as a well-honed cutting edge. I have never found an equivalent in other languages for this sense of the word either, though I do not see how anyone can understand the human soul without it. (p. 121; see also Russell, 1991a)

Obviously, we could extend the above list of examples almost indefinitely. It should, however, be noted that the absence of a specific word does not necessarily imply that the emotion it refers to does not exist in the culture, or that it cannot be imagined or acted out. For example, most English people can readily grasp the meaning of *Schadenfreude* when it is explained to them. Similarly, people outside Japan do not usually find it difficult to imagine situations in which they would feel the uncomfortable sense of indebtedness captured by the word *oime*. Think, for example, of how you feel when someone gives you a present that is inappropriately expensive. In general, it seems that it is not the emotional reaction itself that seems unfamiliar in cases of untranslatable emotion words, but rather the particular form of the emotion that the word picks out (see also van Brakel, 1994, p. 197). These terms often relate specific feelings to particular situations or events, and make more precise distinctions than we are accustomed to making. One of the ways in which different languages differ, then, seems to relate to how coarsely or finely they depict the grain of emotional experience. Because the availability of a single term tends to make the represented construct more accessible, however, these cultural variations in emotional vocabulary may also have a corresponding impact on emotional awareness and regulation. In other words, even if culturally distinctive emotion words do not identify culturally different emotions in the first place, their use in interpreting and modulating experiences may lead to deeper changes in the phenomena underlying their original use.

☐ Evaluating Semantic Equivalence

In the previous section we considered indigenous emotion terms that present seemingly intractable problems for would-be translators. But how precise are the translations we make more routinely between supposedly equivalent words? How can we assess their degree of correspondence? For example, does the English word *angry* really mean the same as *boos* (in Dutch), *böse* (in German), *fâché* (in French), or *song* (in the Ifaluk language)? On what basis can this kind of comparison be made?

The Semantic Primitive Approach

Wierzbicka (1992, 1999) argues that this problem may be solved by breaking down the meanings of individual emotion words into their underlying components. According to this approach, translating local terms into a universal metalanguage of "semantic primitives" such as "feel," "like," "want," "know," or "body" permits an exact assessment of their equivalence. Working from such shared concepts, Wierzbicka (1992) is able to identify distinctive meanings for comparable culturally specific emotion concepts. For example, her analysis suggests that thoughts such as "I don't want this," and "I would want to do something bad to this person," are implied by the English word *anger*, whereas "This person should know this," and "Because of this, I should do something," are the corresponding component meanings for *song* on Ifaluk. In other words, unlike *anger*, *song* does not involve wishing to hurt the person that provoked the associated feelings. Wierzbicka (1994) concludes that:

> The fact that the Ifaluk language has no words corresponding to the English word anger and that the closest Ifaluk counterpart of this concept is much "softer" and closer to admonition, seems to constitute a lexical confirmation of this difference between the two cultures. (p. 138)

Although Wierzbicka's methods seem capable of producing informative results, they have clear limitations. First, some of the differences between the meanings of emotion terms may be too local, specific, or context-dependent to be captured in the abstract language of semantic primitives. For example, *rage* may represent a more intense form of *anger*, but no way exists of discerning this difference within the terms of the model because emotional intensity does not feature as a semantic universal. Similarly, the particular meanings of emotion words that specify distinctive antecedent events or behavioral consequences (see discussion below) often do not easily reduce to the abstract level required by the approach.

A second, deeper problem concerns the very notion of universal components of meaning. Can we really be sure that words exist that map to identical concepts of "feel," "think," and "know" in all languages? Even within the English language, the relevant words are used in a variety of senses depending on their context. How then can we pin down the common essence of their universal meaning? In addition, the relations and oppositions between so-called primitive terms may be culturally specific. For example, it has been suggested that some languages do not even clearly distinguish supposedly universal concepts such as feeling and thinking (e.g., in the case of the Ifaluk [Lutz, 1985]). The inclusion of words conveying evaluative and moral connotations in lists of semantic primitives seems to present still further problems. Calling something "good" or "bad" surely makes sense only after reference to prevailing cultural standards, which obviously vary from place to place and time to time.

Of course, a completely universal metalanguage is not necessary for specific comparisons between concepts across two or more cultures. All that is required is that corresponding semantic components can be identified across all languages that are currently being compared. Thus, a scaled down version of Wierzbicka's approach may well continue to be valuable in certain contexts.

A final concern with the semantic universal approach relates to its apparent claims to scientific objectivity. Conclusions are presented as deriving from a systematic, data-driven process whereby basic semantic elements are identified. In practice, however, no researcher has direct access to the lexicon or grammar of any language. Instead, meanings must always be inferred from observations of how words are used in context, and such inferences will always be subject to potential interpretational biases. In short, even if other linguistic researchers were in agreement about the structure and content of Wierzbicka's metalanguage, there is no reason to suppose that they would arrive at identical translations of the emotion words in question.

Ultimately, Wierzbicka's main contribution to the cultural psychology of emotion may lie not with her meticulous dissections of linguistic concepts, but rather with her unsettling of cruder notions of universality and difference. Too often, Anglo-American researchers have used English-language emotion terms as the frame of reference for cross-cultural comparisons. Thus, the existence of biologically "basic emotions" is inferred from the availability of foreign words that Westerners can easily understand. But as we have seen above, "anger," "fear," and "happiness" are not unproblematically neutral descriptions of preexisting emotions, but instead culturally specific representations carrying their own ideological implications. Languages don't differ only by virtue of being more or less accurate approximations of our own. Wierzbicka's alternative is to replace English with a conceptual version of Esperanto that supposedly carries no cultural baggage. However, in our view, there is no easy way to get outside local linguistic conventions. Although specific points of contact between different systems of cultural meaning may be identified, it does not seem possible to divide through across the board by any lowest common denominator.

☐ Comparing Emotion Scripts

As we have argued above, cross-language comparisons of emotion terms do not require an atomistic universal metalanguage. To the extent that broad commonality exists between the kinds of phenomena described, similarities and differences in meaning can still be specified at a more local level to some extent. For example, emotion words in many languages seem to imply a typical sequence of events that unfolds when specific emotions occur. At minimum, some antecedent event and some response to that event are specified. Commonly, the representation also includes the subsequent regulation of the response to the event or an evaluation of its appropriateness (see Kövecses, 1990; Lutz, 1987; Russell, 1991b; Shaver et al., 1987). Consideration of the extent to which these events and their sequencing correspond across cultures thus provides important information about the degree of semantic variability. This kind of evidence is frequently interpreted using a prototype approach (De Souza, 1987; Lutz, 1987; White, 2000). The meanings of particular emotion words, like the concept of emotion in general, are considered to have fuzzy boundaries so that distinctions are most apparent when considering their most central and defining instances.

In the following sections, we consider in turn cultural differences in emotion meanings relating to the typical antecedents of emotional response, the typical responses that occur, and the evaluative meanings attached to these responses.

Emotional Antecedents

According to some cultural anthropologists (e.g., Lutz, 1987; White, 1990), contexts, and specifically social contexts, are more central to the meaning of emotion in many non-Western cultures than in Western cultures (see discussion below). For example, the common Ifaluk word *metagu* covers emotions arising from situations when people have to visit strangers, when they are in the middle of a large group of people, or when they encounter malevolent ghosts. The term cannot easily be understood except by reference to the contexts for the occurrence of the associated emotion. In Western cultures, by contrast, emotions are often seen as primarily individual responses that are more detachable from their context.

However, even in Western languages, emotion words typically carry implications about the range of eliciting situations. Shaver and colleagues (1987), for example, showed that emotion knowledge of Western respondents may also be represented as a sequence starting with a specified set of possible antecedents. Indeed, White (2000) argues that event schemas are universally deployed in commonsense reasoning about emotion. Thus, cross-language differences in the meanings of emotion words may relate to the specific types of antecedent or emotional situation typically indicated, or the level of abstraction at which they are encoded, rather than to whether or not they are contextualized in the first place.

One of the primary reasons for these differences, of course, is that different environmental conditions are experienced by users of the different languages. Dangers on Ifaluk, for example, refer to open wells, lagoon waters, sloping trunks, or roots of trees (Lutz, 1983), whereas in Israel, interactions with strangers or use of public transport constitute the most typical fear antecedents (see also Scherer et al., 1988). Generally speaking, no language is likely to encode contexts that are outside the typical range of experience of its current and previous users.

Among the events experienced by members of any culture, however, are some that attain particular significance, because of their relevance to widely held values and "focal concerns" (Mesquita & Frijda, 1992). For example, the Cree language has 30 different words referring to different antecedents of anger, such as anger resulting from insults, mutual ill feeling, taking leave of an individual on a walk, or offensive visual sights (Hupka, Lenton, & Hutchison, 1999). These specified occasions for anger do not seem to lie outside the range of experiences of members of other cultures. Further, other domains of emotion are not linguistically overrepresented to a similar extent. Therefore, the most plausible explanation for the selective emphasis is the historical importance of distinguishing occasions for anger among Cree society.

These cross-cultural differences are most pronounced when antecedents are represented in concrete rather than abstract terms. For example, Galati and Sciaky (1995) found only 8.5% correspondence between low-level, concrete codings of reported antecedents across two samples from different part of Italy, but complete agreement when antecedents were coded at the most abstract level (e.g., in terms of loss, separation, wrongdoing, danger, or achievement). In short, specific differences in the content of scripts do not necessarily rule out a deeper equivalence in emotional meaning. However, a large-scale cross-cultural study by Scherer and colleagues (Scherer, Wallbott, Matsumoto, & Kudoh, 1988) showed that even when antecedents were coded in terms of general categories like "relationships," "body," "achievement," or "strangers," there were still striking differences in their reporting by respondents from European countries, Japan, and the United States. Cultural differences in represented emotion antecedents therefore seem to run deeper than superficial aspects of eliciting situations.

Responses

Emotion scripts from different cultures also seem to specify different kinds of emotional response. In many European languages, *anger* is associated with antagonism, assertiveness, open criticism, hostility, and sometimes even aggression. This emphasis on the overt interpersonal expression of anger also characterizes the language of the Kaluli (Fajans, 1983), and for the Pukhtun, anger is specifically associated with cold-blooded revenge (Lindholm, 1982). However, very different modes of response are implied by corresponding concepts in other languages. Ifalukian *song*, for example, is thought to involve less hostility than Anglo-American *anger*, because the urge to do something bad is not directed at another person (see discussion of Wierzbicka's account above). *Song*, therefore, seems to be a more indirect form of anger. Similarly, the Inuit word for getting angry, *qiquq*, implies silent withdrawal, and being clogged up (see van Brakel, 1994). Other languages contain anger words that imply a lack of any kind of expression (e.g., the Temiars, the Faeroe Islanders, the inhabitants of Santa Isabel, the Utku Inuit, the Tahitians, and the Samoans; see Briggs, 1973; Gerber, 1985; Roseman, 1988).

Different responses are also specified in scripts for emotions other than anger. For example, research comparing the prototypical contents of pride scenarios revealed that Spanish respondents typically associated pride with acting arrogantly, whereas Dutch respondents associated it with telling everybody good news (Fischer, Manstead, & Rodriguez, 1999). In a similar vein, Shweder and Haidt (2000) argue that medieval Hindu *amusement* was quite different from contemporary Western *happiness*, because it did not have celebratory features, but was instead more associated with contempt, indignation, and *Schadenfreude*, thus implying derogation of others. Jealousy scripts in different cultures also appear to specify a wide variety of expressions (Hupka, 1981, 2003), such as slaying one's wife and her lover, seizing the lover's property, and the lover's friends formally presenting the wife to her lover, accompanied with gifts, or simply getting divorced. A final example is "biting your tongue," an idiomatic expression used by women in Orissa (India) to indicate that they realize that they have failed to uphold social norms and are ashamed (Shweder & Haidt, 2000).

Evaluative and Moral Implications

The content of emotion scripts may also reflect implicit or explicit norms and values concerning the appropriateness and importance of an emotion. In particular, terms for corresponding emotions may have more positive connotations in some cultures than they do in others. *Uzüntu* in

Turkish, for example, is usually translated as "sadness," but has a less negative connotation than this English word or its Dutch equivalent. Similarly, the Chinese word for "pride," *jiaoao*, describes an emotion that is not very positive to experience.

Many of the cultural differences in evaluations of specific emotions may be understood by reference to the pervasive individualism-collectivism dimension first popularized by Hofstede (1980), and described above. Individualistic cultures emphasize personal choice as the source of action, whereas collectivist cultures define identities in terms of attachment to broader groups and institutions. Within these contrasting interpretative frames, the same emotion may accrue different value. For example, *shame* is seen as a "bad" emotion in many individualistic societies, because it is associated with weakness and personal failure or wrongdoing. In collectivistic cultures, however, *shame* has a more positive connotation, and is used to socialize children into being good citizens. Thus, according to Goddard (1997), the shame-related emotion *malu* in Malay is seen as a particularly moral value, reflecting sensitivity to what other people think about the person experiencing it.

A related but more specific set of cultural values that have implications for shame concerns *honor* (e.g., Cohen & Nisbett, 1994, 1997; Peristiany, 1965). In this context, *honor* refers to personal integrity as well as social reputation (Rodriguez, 1999). In Spain, for example, the individual's place in the social and moral order contributes directly to his or her sense of well-being and self-esteem. Within such a cultural setting, *shame* reflects an admirable sensitivity to honor-related concerns. Consistent with this conclusion, Fischer and colleagues (1999) found that Spanish respondents were more likely to mention positive beliefs concerning shame (*vergüenza*) than respondents from the Netherlands (a more individualistic, nonhonor culture).

According to Cohen and Nisbett (1994), honor cultures have developed particularly in societies with historically ineffective law enforcement, where citizens learned to protect themselves by showing that they were not the kind of people to be trifled with: "Allowing oneself to be pushed around, insulted, or affronted without retaliations amounts to announcing that one is an easy mark" (p. 552).

Retribution for public threats to honor is therefore a common and accepted social practice in honor cultures. For example, respondents from the southern United States find aggression more acceptable than their northern counterparts when it is motivated by self-defense or intended to protect family or possessions. When honor is at stake, aggression (including even the use of firearms) is not only considered legitimate, but essential.

In many other Western cultures too, anger is seen as a positive sign of assertiveness or deserved power, as long as the emotional reaction remains proportionate to the seriousness of the provoking offence. Similar representations are also found in some non-Western cultures. For example, among the Ifaluk, *song* is described as "justified anger," an emotion that it is good to feel and express when a wrong-doing has occurred (Lutz, 1986). In other cultures, however, anger has a much worse reputation. For the Utku Inuit in particular, it is seen as a bad emotion that is never justified and therefore has to be avoided or suppressed at all costs (Briggs, 1970; see also Gaffin, 1995; White, 1990).

The examples presented so far might be read as implying that the evaluative connotations of emotion words are fixed and consistent within any culture. In practice, however, how highly any emotion is valued partly depends on the context in which it occurs. *Mamaja* in the Cheke Holo language on Santa Isabel (similar to the English "be ashamed" [White, 2000]) provides a clear example of this point. Specifically, this emotion may be considered bad if it disturbs a relationship with another person, but good if it involves acknowledging the transgression of a norm in an interpersonal relation by not showing respect. It is likely that other emotions in other languages similarly attract different evaluations depending on when and where they occur and how they are expressed.

☐ Methodological Recommendations

To establish the extent of cross-cultural variation in emotion vocabularies, it seems necessary both to develop a close understanding of the specific systems of meaning operating in the languages in question (the emic approach), and to deploy some overarching frame of reference to allow their meaningful comparison (the etic approach). Each of these tasks brings its own problems. Some form of ethnographic observation seems to be required for the former project, because no purely linguistic analysis adequately taps into the pragmatic use of words in context. However, the results of anthropological investigations of this kind are crucially shaped by the researcher's particular perspective and theoretical commitments and need to be evaluated accordingly. The fact that compatible findings often emerge from different methods may, of course, increase our confidence in the validity of the conclusions. Imposition of standard tasks assists with the latter comparative task, but again each of these tasks has its associated limitations. For example, sorting procedures can provide information about associations between emotional meanings and about the relative centrality of category exemplars, but tell us very little about how words are actually used in less abstract contexts. Here, as in the semantic primitive approach, attention is exclusively directed toward the referential meaning of emotion words. However, emotional communication is not only about describing internal or external states of affairs, but it also serves to exert practical influence over the addressees to whom it is directed. Thus, to say that you are feeling *anger* or *song* is to frame the current situation for other people as well as yourself and calls for specific responses from those others. Emotion words are not only names for things but also tools that may serve different kinds of purposes in different societal contexts (see also chapter 8, this volume).

In principle, these pragmatic functions of emotion language may be identified from ethnographic analysis, and intensive, qualitative studies of this kind may help to supplement the more quantitative findings. However, with some notable exceptions (e.g., Besnier, 1995), anthropological investigations too have often tended to concentrate on semantic aspects of emotional meaning (e.g., Lutz, 1983). How to fill the resulting research gap is an issue we shall return to in a moment.

Most of the research into emotional language is also limited by the assumption that meanings show a simple and direct relation to words taken in isolation. *Anger* and *song* are assumed to mean roughly the same thing whenever and however they are used in practice. The prototype approach takes one step beyond this assumption by suggesting that each emotion word covers a variety of related instances rather than always indicating a single and definite meaning (e.g., Russell & Fehr, 1994). Just as the general category of emotion is considered to have fuzzy boundaries, so too *anger, love, amae, verguenza*, and so on only loosely specify their range of application.

But if words are tools rather than names, it is flexibility rather than fuzziness that is at issue (see Edwards, 1997; Parkinson, 1998). Each term may have multiple uses, depending on the linguistic and extralinguistic context in which it is deployed. For example, a variety of language games (Wittgenstein, 1953) with quite different rules surround the usage of the English emotion word *love*, each making a difference to the pragmatic effects it exerts. Saying "I love you" at a certain stage in the development of a romantic relationship is not just about labeling a feeling but also involves entering into a commitment of a kind (especially if reciprocation is forthcoming). However, it is also possible to "love" popcorn, sunny days, or having nothing to do, without similar interpersonal consequences (see also Solomon, 1981). Because the range of activities, joint projects, and rituals in which emotion talk is embedded varies from society to society as well as setting to setting, the words themselves may not be so easily or directly comparable as the naming account implies. Without an understanding of the forms of life that give them their purpose and function, there may be occasions when researchers miss the point of emotional language use in unfamiliar cultures.

One solution to this problem is to study the structure and flow of everyday conversations across cultures, instead of trying to extract and pin down a separable, decontextualized meaning for each term. The pragmatic implications of an emotion word may be elucidated by examining how it is used by speakers and how hearers respond to its intended effects (e.g., Edwards, 1997). The close attention to the workings of dialogue achieved by some forms of discourse or conversational analysis, coupled with the immersion in cultural practices required by ethnographic research, should help to enrich our depiction of relational processes of emotional meaning.

☐ Emotion Ethnotheories

Most of the research considered so far in this chapter has been directed at the semantic meaning of individual emotion words. However, investigations of the actual usage of emotion names suggest that they occur relatively infrequently in everyday discourse (see White, 2000). Thus, emotions may not always be labeled or expressed directly, but rather may be conveyed more implicitly using gestures, tone of voice, expressions, or metaphors (e.g., Besnier, 1995; Irvine, 1990; White, 2000).

To fully understand emotional meaning, it is therefore important to go beyond purely linguistic studies to get at underlying beliefs and norms. Material presented in the previous section concerning the differing cultural values attached to individual emotions as specified in script-based representations is clearly relevant to this enterprise. In the present section, we broaden our focus to include emotional ethnotheories. Ethnotheories (or "emotionologies" [Stearns & Stearns, 1985]) are implicated in the ways people understand and deal with their own and others' emotions, and further reveal culture-specific beliefs about the nature, importance, and value of emotions and emotional events.

Beliefs About the Nature of Emotion

Socialization into any culture involves acquiring knowledge about specific emotions and how to deal with them, for example, through the social sharing of emotions (e.g., Rimé, 1995; Rimé, Philippot, Boca, & Mesquita, 1992). In all societies, we find ideas telling us where emotions are located in the body, which emotions are good or bad, what they reveal about a person or that person's situation, and how we can deal with them. Some beliefs about emotions may be more or less universal, but a great number appear to be culture-specific, deriving their particular character from more general systems of meaning characterizing the society in question. In the following sections, we will provide examples of differing views on the nature and significance of emotions. The review is not intended to be exhaustive; our aim is simply to illustrate the general point that in addition to examining lexical representations of emotions, it is necessary to consider the more general cultural meaning system in which emotions are embedded.

Emotion in contrast to reason?

The prevalent view in Western societies is that emotionality and rationality are diametrically opposed (e.g., Lutz, 1990). According to this conception, emotions are antithetical to logical thinking and tend to be impulsive and intuitive. A related idea is that emotions are involuntary, implying that the emotional individual is coerced into doing things that he or she has not really chosen to do. However, unlike in some other cultures (see discussion below), this lack of control is seen as relative rather than absolute, leaving open some possibilities for regulation.

Uncontrollability and irrationality in turn are often explained by reference to the supposedly primitive nature of emotions: They are often treated as remnants of our bestial past, and as residing in the least evolved part of the brain (see Averill, 1974). Thus, emotional expressions of children, animals, and "uncivilized" beings represent the best illustrations of the phenomenon, because in them one can see emotion in its purest and most raw form.

It is also commonplace to think of emotions as coming from the heart rather than the head. This "psychophysiological symbolism" (Averill), which identifies emotion with visceral processes, with the blood, sweat, and tears of reactivity, has pervaded Western academic thinking as well as popular discourse for centuries. The same features are also nicely reflected in many metaphors found in English as well as other languages (see Kövecses, 1990). Anger, for example, is often depicted as hot fluid in a container, which may boil over when pressure becomes too intense (e.g., "anger was welling up inside her," "his blood was boiling," "she got all steamed up," "he nearly burst a blood vessel," etc.). Despite these common associations of emotion with body rather than brain, Westerners are not usually very specific about the precise location of emotions. The heart that is often alluded to, for example, is usually symbolic rather than the physical organ. By contrast, other ethnotheories seem to make perfectly literal claims about the internal seat of emotions, whether it is found in the intestines (Levy, 1973), the liver (Howell, 1981), or other parts of the body (Heelas, 1986).

The idea that emotions are irrational, hard-to-control, bodily reactions is not only an ancient idea reflected in metaphors, or found in the works of some great Western philosophers, but also characterizes laypeople's contemporary definitions (e.g., Fehr & Russell, 1984). For example, high correlations are found between ratings of the prototypicality of emotions and endorsement of statements such as, "We should be careful not to allow our emotion to control our actions completely," and "Sometimes emotion is hard to control" (p. 473). Similar findings were reported by Parrott (1995) and Shields (1987), who asked informants to describe the characteristics of an "emotional" person. In these studies, emotionality was not only associated with observable emotional expressions and behaviors, but also by the notion of irrationality and being out of control. This is precisely why emotionality is more closely associated with women than with men (cf. Fischer, 1993; Shields, 1987, 2002). We call people "emotional" not on the basis of objective criteria, but because we *believe* that they are overreacting, that their response is over the top, and that they lack a sense of perspective.

Partly because the primitive and irrational aspects of Western emotions are attributed to internal bodily processes, some residual control over the functions remains possible. People can try to relax or take drugs of various kinds to quell the turmoil within. By contrast, ethnotheories viewing emotions as external agencies that invade or take possession of people leave much less room for maneuver. For example, Maoris think of emotional experiences as coming from outside and thus beyond control (van Brakel, 1994).

How widespread is the view of emotions as antithetical to rational thought and behavior? Some non-Western cultures also appear to talk about emotions as primitive and uncontrollable forces. Levy (1973), for example, notes that the people of Piri and Roto on Tahiti distrust strong emotions because "strong passions force one out of control, make one do things one does not want to do" (p. 273). Similar ideas can be found among the Ifaluk where "the head and the heart, or rationality and passion, are dichotomized and hierarchically arranged" (Lutz, 1983, p. 251).

Counterexamples also exist, however. The Illongot, for instance, do not seem to make any direct contrast between reason and emotion. In Rosaldo's (1980, p. 47) words: "The energy that is liget can generate both chaos and concentration, distress and industry, a loss of sense and reason, and an experience of clarification and release." However, she also notes that "liget is associated most readily with a variety of words suggesting chaos, separation, and confusion, words that point to the disruptive qualities of 'anger' uncontrolled by 'knowledge.'"

The lack of solid cross-cultural research on emotional ethnotheories makes it difficult to reach a general conclusion about the universality or variability of the opposition between reason and emotion. Further, one of the basic implicit criteria for translating a folk concept in "emotional" terms may be precisely that it connotes unreasonable or involuntary response. To the extent that irrationality is a presupposed defining feature of emotion, all rational phenomena are excluded by fiat in the first place. At any rate, beliefs about how irrational or primitive emotions are considered to be, how concerned people are about their strength and uncontrollability, and which emotion-regulation strategies are believed to be most efficient all seem to vary across cultures, and to depend on more general values.

A final issue concerns whether emotions are irrational in reality or only according to certain ethnotheories. From the 1960s onwards, the former view has been attacked by several philosophers and psychologists (e.g., Averill, 1980, De Souza, 1987; Solomon, 1976). One of their central points is that emotions are shaped by people's beliefs about what is happening to them, and it may be these beliefs or the nature of what is happening that is irrational rather than emotion itself. Further, although "emotionality" as a general factor may be associated with irrational or involuntary behavior, the connection is less clear when considering specific emotions arising in specific circumstances. My anger makes sense by reference to the insult that provoked it, but my more pervasive emotional reactivity (whether arising from temperament or current mood) is harder to justify on the grounds of reason. In other words, "having an emotion" is seen as more unreasonable than "being emotional" (Parrott, 1995). Despite these observations, it still seems to be the case that Western culture imposes relatively strict norms about social conduct, and when these norms are transgressed, the reaction is often interpreted as "emotional," and hence as irrational.

Self or social relations?

Ethnotheories also differ according to whether they locate the primary site of emotional phenomena exclusively within or between people. For some cultures, emotion resides in the self; for others, it is distributed across social relations. These differences in turn are related to the broader cultural dimension of individualism-collectivism (e.g., Hofstede, 1980; Kim, Triandis, Kagitcibasi, Choi, & Yoon, 1994; Triandis, 1995, inter alia) described above. By emphasizing the needs and goals of a single individual and fostering independence, emotions are seen as an expression of the unique self in individualistic cultures. In contrast, collectivistic cultures view emotion as a response to a social context, underlining relations within groups, and the promotion of harmony and interdependence.

Markus and Kitayama (1991, 1994) argue that individualistic and collectivistic cultures encourage the development of different kinds of selves, which are linked to culture-specific emotion patterns. Individualistic cultures promote independent selves containing unique internal attributes that guide behavior. These selves are therefore fundamentally detached from their social context. By contrast, the interdependent selves arising from collectivistic societies are not separate from others, but instead are defined by their social roles and relationships.

Western, independent selves experience and conceive of emotions as inner feelings (e.g., van Brakel, 1994) that express a person's authentic individuality. Correspondingly, Western psychologists tend to study the physiological and neural mechanisms supposedly underlying emotional responses or the facial expressions that only imperfectly reveal these emotional responses to others. Emotions experienced by interdependent selves, on the other hand, are always already part of social relations and arrangements. Thus, the Japanese emotion domain is dominated by interpersonal emotions, such as *amae*, indulgent dependence on the other; *sugari*, a desire to lean toward another; and *tanomi*, a desire to rely on others. Further, "feeling good" is positively correlated with socially engaging emotions, and negatively correlated with socially disengaging emotions in Japan, whereas the reverse pattern of associations is found among U.S. respondents (Kitayama, Markus, & Kurokawa, 2000). In short, Japanese emotions are perceived as more relevant to social status and place in society than personal achievements or dispositions.

According to Lutz (1985, 1987), Ifaluk ethnotheory similarly views emotions as evoked in, and inseparable from, social activity. Here the central criterion for distinguishing emotions is the pleasantness or unpleasantness not of the associated feeling state, but of the consequences of the situation. Further, emotions are not thought to arise as part of an individual development, but rather because the child gradually becomes aware of the norms concerning appropriate emotions in various social situations. This suggests that emotions like shame (*metagu*) have explicit social functions for the Ifaluk. Similarly, among the Pacific islanders, there is no noun equivalent to "shame" that is used to describe a mental state, but the verb-form translated as "shaming" is used to emphasize the action or performance aspect of this emotion (White, 2000).

This last example suggests that specific grammatical features of emotion language may have deeper implications for associated ethnotheories. According to the linguistic category model (Semin & Fiedler, 1991), emotion state verbs (e.g., "to hate") draw attention to the relationship between the subject and object of the sentence (the person who does the hating and the person who is hated), rather than locating the described phenomenon purely within a single psyche. By contrast, emotional adjectives (e.g., "aggressive hatred") tend to imply a dispositional inference (describing a quality inherent to the emotional person), and thus can be considered self-markers rather than relationship-markers (Semin, Görts, Nandram, & Semin-Goossens, 2002). In a series of studies Semin and colleagues (2002) have demonstrated that members of more collectivistic cultures (i.e., Turks and Hindustani Surinamese) use emotion state verbs in greater proportions than respondents from individualistic cultures. They conclude that emotions and emotional events are represented in more interpersonal terms in collectivistic societies.

Are emotions really internal or external to the self? Which ethnotheory is more accurate? Most psychological researchers seem to subscribe to the independent-self idea, interpreting emotions as individual bodily or behavioral reactions to private appraisals about personal significance, whose manifestations in the social world are always indirect and often deliberately distorted. Taking seriously the collectivistic conception of emotions as social relations may therefore provide a valuable corrective to any bias and selectivity of such a single-mindedly individualist view (e.g., De Rivera, 1984; Parkinson, 1995, inter alia).

☐ Historical Changes in Ethnotheory

In the previous section, we have shown how beliefs about emotion often reflect more general cultural values and representations. However, we have said very little about the origins of these ideas. This latter issue is clarified by examining the historical development of ethnotheories within a single society. Stearns' (1994) analysis of U.S. emotional culture from the Victorian era to the present day provides an exemplary illustration of such an approach.

Victorian culture has often been characterized as repressive, especially with regard to emotional and sexual life. According to Stearns (see also Foucault, 1976), this picture is too simplistic. He shows that Victorian life not only involved intolerance of emotion, but also, by contrast, an insistence on emotional intensity. At the start of this era, for example, a burgeoning genre of family advice literature proclaimed the crucial importance of loving relationships between husbands, wives, sons, and daughters. Only negative, bestial emotions, such as fear, anger, and jealousy were explicitly discouraged because of their potential for disrupting the affectionate ties between family members.

However, because absence of emotion was also seen as a sign of indifference and insensibility, the idea of putting dangerous emotions to good use became a common theme in this literature from the 1840s onwards. For example, although anger was considered to be a bad emotion in the setting of the home, it was also viewed as vital to productive functioning in the worlds of work and politics, at least for men. In other words, the capacity for experiencing intense emotions ("to be passionate") was valued as an indication of "appropriate emotional vigor" (Stearns, 1994, p. 53). Thus, the theme of control was combined with a positive emphasis on passion: "emotional excess was obviously condemned, but so was emotional vapidity" (p. 42). However, these recommendations did not apply irrespective of gender, because it was men specifically who were required to be passionate, whereas the sweetness and calm demanded by the feminine domestic role meant that the burden of emotional control fell more heavily on women.

In twentieth-century advice literature, management of emotions became a more central theme. Parenting manuals, for example, were increasingly concerned with children's experiences of fear, anger, and jealousy, but any potentially valuable function of these "bad" emotions was rejected. The new cultural standards that began to emerge from the 1920s onwards were characterized by a strong negative evaluation of these three particular emotions, with an emphasis on their destructive potential. This focus on the problems caused by emotions persisted throughout the twentieth century, but progressively widened to encompass other negative emotions, such as grief, and even positive emotions, like love. The norm was one of emotional control: "to keep not only unpleasant experiences, but even agreeable emotions under careful wraps" (Stearns, 1994).

The recent growth in the popularity of the notion of emotional intelligence (Goleman, 1995; Salovey & Mayer, 1990) may have introduced a new shift in emotional standards in Western culture. Although the implied emphasis on emotional control might be seen as a continuation of the twentieth century style of "coolness," the additional focus on understanding one's own and others' emotions suggests the development of a new norm in which regulation is secondary to insight and empathy. In the present view, nothing is wrong with emotion per se, but it needs to be managed strategically to properly serve its personal and interpersonal purposes.

☐ Emotion and Meaning

In this chapter, we have argued that "emotions" do not constitute a natural category defined by a hard-wired biological essence, but instead depend on specific systems of cultural meaning. Indeed, the general category, or its nearest equivalent, includes different phenomena in different cultural contexts. These differences are apparent not only in studies of emotion vocabularies but also from ethnographic research and from the investigations of the contents of emotion scripts. But what difference do these differences make? Does it matter whether a language has 1 or 20 words for anger, or whether fear is elicited by gods rather than by fellow human beings? For some theorists, the answer is "not much." Their view is that emotional meanings are simply irrelevant to the study of emotions themselves, because the psychological processes in question operate at an entirely different and independent level.

Our view, by contrast, is that emotional meanings are important not only in their own right, but also because they may influence processes of actual, real-time emotional functioning in several ways. Emotions cannot be seen as separate from the cultural systems of meaning within which they are experienced, enacted, regulated, and represented. Emotion words, beliefs about the nature and workings of emotions, and emotional attitudes and rules pervade our emotional lives. Thus, the issue is not whether, but rather how (and how closely) emotions are related to the ways that they are represented and understood.

Linguistic Effects

If someone is reacting in an abrupt manner toward a friend who just won a prize in the lottery, does that mean that person is "emotional?" If so, which particular label is most appropriate? Is the person "envious," "frustrated," "disappointed," "irritated," or simply "tired?" Several different emotion words may apply, depending on which aspects of the situation or of the reaction to that situation are emphasized. Different emotion words imply different perspectives on events. Therefore, to the extent that different languages demarcate emotional reality in different ways, they also facilitate different ways of interpreting that reality. According to this reasoning, culture-specific emotion words contain culture-specific schematic knowledge about emotional reactions in particular emotional situations.

Further, languages that contain more emotion words than others within particular domains also permit a wider variety of representations to be applied to those domains. These differences probably reflect the relative salience of emotion themes. For example, the occurrence of many fine-grained emotion words for "shame" in the Chinese language confirms the cultural significance of this realm of experience.

Levy's (1973) analysis of hypercognized and hypocognized emotion domains explicitly endorses this kind of connection between the availability of emotion words and a culture's emotion knowledge. An emotion domain is hypocognized if hardly any explicit knowledge is available, and is hypercognized if it is the focus of considerable cultural attention. For example, the fact that 47 of the 301 emotion words in the missionary dictionary for Tahiti refer to angry feelings suggests that this emotion is hypercognized in this culture. Sadness, on the other hand, is a hypocognized emotion on Tahiti, because no specific word exists for this emotion.

The idea that knowledge and use of emotion language reflects a cultural focus on emotions is also supported by research on the relation between culture and alexithymia, a clinical disorder involving the inability to identify and label emotions (Huynh-Nhu, Berenbaum, & Raghavan, 2002). In these studies, Asian respondents showed higher levels of alexithymia than European Americans. Moreover, this difference depended on variations in the extent of parental socialization of emotions, suggesting that alexithymia occurs more often in social environments that do not foster the ability to verbally communicate emotions.

It seems, then, that societies develop words for the issues that are important and need to be communicated, but not for the issues that are unimportant, or irrelevant. Hyper- or hypocognition does not reflect the emotional richness or poverty of the speakers of any language, but rather the relevance of communicating specific emotions in the social interactions between individuals in that culture. Thus, emotion words may provide clues concerning which themes are important, which "emotions" are explicitly verbalized, and which are emphasized, valued, rejected, or suppressed in a society. A rich domain of emotion words suggests that the conditions they describe are relevant and important, and can be easily identified. However, this does not necessarily mean that these conditions are valued positively by the society. On the contrary, we may talk more about matters on which sanctions are explicitly imposed (e.g., Foucault, 1976).

Ethnotheoretical Effects

The cultural meaning of emotions extends beyond differences in vocabularies to the particular ways in which emotions are "theorized." We have considered various examples of such ethnotheories of emotion, illustrating how cultures may differ in their beliefs about the origins and workings of emotions. The normative or prescriptive content of ethnotheories is particularly relevant to the regulation and communication of emotion. Culture-specific feeling rules and display rules encourage individuals to bring their experience and expression of emotions into line with these norms, and to socialize children into regulating their emotions in culturally appropriate ways. Thus, we may selectively expose ourselves to situations that elicit only approved emotions, reappraise what is happening so that unwanted emotions are avoided, or try to distract ourselves from events that should not concern us. For example, several historical and anthropological studies have explored the implications of different norms about anger or fear for emotion regulation.

Cultural prescriptions about emotion not only influence individual regulation processes but also other people's direct reactions to our emotions (see chapter 8). For example, if anger is considered an illegitimate emotion within a certain society, then people will react negatively to its occurrence, and their reactions are likely to shape the course of its expression on line.

The influence of the descriptive (rather than prescriptive) aspects of ethnotheories is less obvious. How do representations of the causes and consequences of emotions influence their actual experience and expression? Little evidence is available on the specific impact of descriptive representations partly because they tend to covary so closely with normative prescriptions across cultures. Further, it is difficult to assess effects on emotional experience because this is typically conveyed within the terms available in the language of the culture. Thus, any apparent modification of experience may in fact simply reflect the associated linguistic differences.

Despite the lack of evidence, our view is that specific ethnotheories make people selectively aware of particular aspects of emotional syndromes, resulting in specific individual and interpersonal regulation strategies. For example, if people believe that emotions are uncontrollable, they are less likely to expend effort in attempts to suppress them (in themselves or in others). Similarly, if people believe that emotions arise from some external agency, worshipping the relevant gods becomes more likely than trying to change the practicalities of the current situation. Finally, if men believe that anger is a sign of power, and fear a sign of weakness and femininity, they will be more likely to show the former emotion but conceal the latter.

In conclusion, emotions have meanings and these meanings can be culture-specific in various ways. Our view is that these emotional meanings are relevant not only for cultural anthropologists, linguists, or ethnographers, but also for emotion researchers. Examining how people label, conceptualize, and theorize about emotions is not only an interesting enterprise in its own right, but also directly relevant to our understanding of the actual experience, expression, and communication of emotions. The next chapter pursues this latter theme.

3

Cultural Variation in Emotion

In individualistic societies, many adolescents go through a solipsistic phase, when they question whether other people really experience the world in the same way as they do. What often seems most in doubt during these musings is whether overt expressions genuinely correspond to deeper private feelings, or whether friends, family, and strangers in particular are simply going through the motions in a more calculated manner. This theme is frequently dramatized in popular books and films. For example, the extraterrestrial pod creatures in *Invasion of the Body Snatchers* are incapable of experiencing emotion but try to infiltrate North American society by becoming exact replicas of human beings in all other respects. They look like us, and even act like us in many ways, but something barely perceptible seems to be missing inside.

Attributing emotions to people from other cultures rather than aliens usually presents less severe problems. Once we get over our teenage egocentrism and ethnocentrism, we are usually quite ready to believe that a common core of affective experience is shared across humanity, despite dissimilarities in language and conventions of expression. Although we may be uncertain about how to read their emotions precisely, we are usually confident that people from very different societies can feel many of the same things that we do (even if they may sometimes lack our finer sentiments [see Leyens et al., 2000 and chapter 5, this volume]).

But is this confidence misplaced? Our conclusion in the previous chapter was that different cultures theorize and label emotions in quite different ways. Does this also imply that the emotions that they are theorizing and labeling must be different too? Not necessarily. According to many theorists, languages and ethnotheories simply pick out different aspects of the same underlying phenomenon, rather like the fabled blind men trying to grasp the totality of the unseen elephant, one feeling the shape of its tail, another its ears, and so on (cf. Russell & Feldman Barrett, 1999). However, even if cultural influence only went this far and no further, the relative emphasis of different cultural frames would still change the way in which people represented, reacted to, and regulated emotions (see chapter 2).

The question raised by the present chapter is how deeply cultural differences penetrate into emotion itself. Although people with different societal traditions have different ideas about emotions and try to control them in different ways, is the reality of what they are trying to control and represent different in the first place? Are emotions universal prior to the imposition of their cultural meanings? Yes and no is the rather unsatisfying answer. Most theorists would agree that some aspects of emotional functioning are mainly fixed by human biology, whereas others are primarily the consequence of cultural socialization. Further, these two kinds of force overlap and interact in complicated ways over the course of phylogenetic and ontogenetic development (as well as in the real-time control of behavior). The questions that remain unresolved, then, do not relate to whether emotions are biological or cultural, a product of nature or nurture, but rather to the precise nature and extent of each relative contribution, and to the processes underlying their reciprocal influence.

Regardless of the position taken on these issues, there is no question that the cultural differences in emotional meaning discussed in the previous chapter present serious difficulties for researchers interested in comparing actual emotions across cultures. One of these difficulties concerns translation. How do we identify which phenomena are to be compared in the first place? For example, how do we find an equivalent for the Anglo-American emotion called anger in other cultures with different languages? Dictionaries or interpreters don't entirely solve this problem because the available concepts fail to correspond in any precise way. We might end up comparing "anger" with something that is actually closer to what we would call "irritation" or "moral outrage," or, even more problematically, something for which we have no words at all (see chapter 2).

The translation problem means that participants' reports of emotion do not usually provide a sound basis for cross-cultural comparisons of emotion itself. When Ifaluk people say that they are experiencing *song*, for example, we cannot simply assume that this means exactly what English speakers mean by *anger*. But without a common language, how can we develop a set of independent criteria for establishing whether or not the same emotion has occurred? If emotions are complex syndromes that cannot be defined by any single component, then comparison of appraisals, bodily changes, facial movements, and so on is necessary before equivalence can be established with any confidence. But even the most ardent universalist would be unwilling to claim that all aspects of emotional functioning are identical across cultures. Such a position would fly in the face of accepted facts. Emotions really are different even if the differences are seen as superficial ones. The problem then is to identify a culture-independent core or essence of emotion that can be identified in ways that bypass cultural representations. Needless to say, theorists have disagreements about what this core might be, and whether it really exists in the first place (see chapter 1). In practice, at any rate, it is extremely difficult to escape from cultural meaning systems when examining emotions. Even if researchers found a way of getting around informants' own interpretations, they would still remain trapped within their own culturally derived preconceptions when formulating identification criteria.

In the sections that follow, we review research addressing the questions of which emotions and which emotional components are affected by cultural factors. We begin by considering the issue of whether a small set of biologically basic emotions can be identified across all human societies. This debate has centered on the evidence concerning cross-cultural similarities in facial expressions, which many claim provides the most important empirical support for the universality thesis. In later sections, we will discuss anthropological and psychological studies of cultural variations in the experience, expression, and regulation of specific emotions.

☐ Basic Emotions and Expressions

Are There Basic Emotions?

For several decades, a great deal of theory and research in the cultural psychology of emotion has focused on the seemingly straightforward issue of whether or not some emotions are universal. Several investigators (e.g., Ekman, 1972; Izard, 1977; Oatley & Johnson-Laird, 1989; Plutchik, 1980; Tomkins, 1962; Tooby & Cosmides, 2001) have argued that a circumscribed set of "basic emotions" are preprogrammed into our mental system by evolution. Other secondary or non-basic emotions develop during socialization as a function of cognitive articulation or blending of these basic emotions, and are therefore more subject to cultural influence. Some of the linguistic and ethnotheoretical evidence for and against basic emotions was reviewed in the previous chapter. Here, our attention shifts to cross-cultural studies that have examined the cultural meaning not of emotion as a concept but of one of the central components of the phenomenon itself: facial expression. If facial expressions turn out to have consistent emotional meanings across all cultures, then it seems likely that the emotions that they convey are universal too. Before examining the evidence on this issue, however, it is worth examining an influential theoretical critique of the notion of basic emotions (Ortony & Turner, 1990).

The first problem for proponents of basic emotions is that their agreement that some emotions are basic is undermined by their disagreement about which (Contempt? Interest? Pain?), and how many there are (Two? Seven plus or minus two? Eighteen?). In Ortony and Turner's (1990) words: "The divergence of opinion about the number of basic emotions is matched by the divergence of opinion about their identity" (p. 315). According to Ortony and Turner, it is even debatable whether some of the proposed basic emotions, such as surprise or interest, should really be categorized as emotions in the first place (because neither necessarily involves the experience of pleasant or unpleasant feelings). Part of this confusion derives from the lack of consensus about what it actually means for an emotion to be basic in the first place (or, indeed, for an emotion to be an emotion; see chapters 1 and 2). In this regard, Ortony and Turner distinguish three conceptually distinct interpretations: An emotion may be "basic" at the conceptual level (i.e., a basic category of emotion in a semantic hierarchy, see chapter 2), the biological level (i.e., an evolutionarily determined basic process or state), the psychological level (a basic building block out of which other nonbasic emotions are made), or at two or more of these levels. However, some emotions that seem to be basic at one of these levels are not basic at other levels, making it difficult for researchers using different definitions to agree about which emotions should be given "basic" status.

Ortony and Turner's (1990) appealing alternative to the basic emotion idea is to argue that it is not emotions themselves that are biologically basic, but rather some of their component processes. Similarly, Camras (1992) argues that "basic emotions" are emergent structures arising from the developing interdependencies between environmental, social, and individual processes. Again, it should be clear from this discussion of competing theoretical positions that the debate is not about whether emotions are biological or not, but rather about which aspects of their constitution are evolutionarily determined (e.g., Manstead & Fischer, 2002). The fact that some aspects of the response syndrome are universal does not necessarily mean that they are always part of the same emotion process. Although many of the strands that interweave in emotion production may have natural origins, the way that they are stitched together and the patterns that they yield might nevertheless be based on cultural traditions.

Are There Basic Emotion Expressions?

Much of the empirical debate concerning basic emotions has centered on evidence deriving from cross-cultural studies of one particular aspect of emotion, namely facial "expression." The guiding idea is that distinctive facial positions characterize each of the basic emotions, facilitating their communication (Darwin, 1872, and see chapter 6, this volume). If this is correct, then members of all cultures should recognize a smile as indicating happiness, a scowl as indicating anger, and so on (assuming that happiness and anger are "basic emotions"). In the 1960s, pioneering research by Ekman, Tomkins, and Izard systematically compared different cultures' interpretations of facial expressions to address this issue.

For example, Ekman and his collaborators (e.g., Ekman 1972, 1989, 1992a and b; Ekman & Friesen, 1971; Ekman, Friesen, et al., 1987; Ekman & Heider, 1988) showed a set of photographs of Western expressions (indicating happiness, sadness, anger, fear, disgust, and surprise; see Figure 3.1) to respondents from various countries around the world, and asked them to choose an appropriate emotion name for each (from a list supplied by the researchers).

Even in preliterate cultures, having minimal previous contact with Westerners, selection of the "correct" responses was significantly above chance levels. In other words, people seem to know something about the emotional meanings of certain facial positions regardless of their level of exposure to Western conventions. "Recognition accuracy" therefore does not wholly depend on learning what expressions are supposed to mean in Western culture.

The findings of later studies were also broadly concordant (e.g., Biehl et al., 1997; Boucher & Carlson, 1980; Ducci, Arcuri, Georgies, & Sineshaw, 1982; Keltner & Haidt, 1999; Kirouac & Dore, 1982 inter alia). This apparent consensus led Ekman (1998) to the following conclusion:

> Our evidence, and that of others, shows only that when people are experiencing strong emotions, are not making any attempt to mask their expressions, the expression will be the same regardless of age, race, culture, sex and education. That is a powerful finding. (p. 391)

However, such a strong conclusion may not be warranted by the evidence. Russell's (1994) thorough review of the literature on judgments of facial expression suggested that the level of cross-cultural consistency provides weaker and less direct support for basic emotions than is often

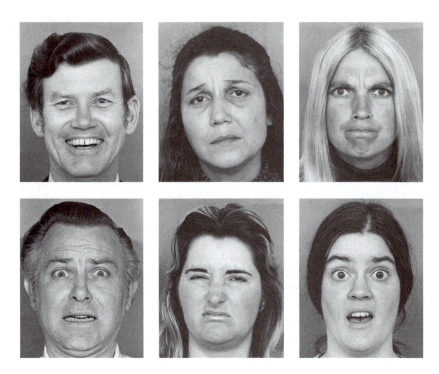

FIGURE 3.1. Photos of six posed facial expressions used in Ekman's cross-cultural studies. Copyright Paul Ekman.

implied. In particular, he argued that the use of a forced choice task (together with other procedural aspects) may have artificially boosted performance. In addition to this methodological critique, Russell identified several important limitations of the data even when taken at face value. His central argument was that judges do not need to know the specific emotion that a face is supposed to express to perform at above-chance levels on the "recognition" task.

For example, when presented with a supposedly "angry" face, the fixed gaze may indicate to participants that attention was being specifically directed toward someone, the tightened facial muscles may suggest tension, and the absence of a smile may tell them that the experience was not pleasant. Piecing together this information rules out some of the possible emotional interpretations, and makes others more likely. More generally, Russell (1994) argues that there may be a universal ability to pick up evidence about levels of pleasure and arousal from faces, but not about particular basic emotions. Alternatively, Fridlund (1994, and see chapter 6) argues that facial positions signal behavioral intentions or social motives (e.g., impulses to aggress, play, or run away) rather than emotions per se (e.g., anger, happiness, or fear). Either of these theories is capable of accounting for some level of cross-cultural consistency in judgments without assuming that faces directly express basic emotions. Indeed, when participants are not explicitly told to make emotional interpretations, faces are often explained in terms of current situations or motives rather than emotions (e.g., Frijda, 1953). A "fear" face, for example, may be described in terms of staring intently at something unpleasant yet strangely compelling (or in the words of one of Frijda's participants: "as if looking at something with fixed attention, a game or something tense, two cars which almost get into collision but nothing happens. . . . Gosh, who would do anything so stupid! [p. 314]").

If respondents from other cultures infer emotion indirectly from faces, it would not be surprising if their inferences were sometimes inconsistent. In fact, although performance on judgment tasks is significantly better than would be expected if people were just guessing at random, it is also rather less than perfect (Russell, 1994). Further, culture does make a difference to emotion judgments except in the case of smiles, which seem to be universally recognized as indicating happiness (although the fact that this was the only unambiguously pleasant emotion included on Ekman's list may have made its identification easier too). For all five of the other supposedly basic emotions, allocation of the "correct" label decreased in frequency the more remote their judges were from Anglo-American culture (Russell, 1994, and see Figure 3.2). Indeed, preliterate cultures attached the label "disgust" (or rather its nearest equivalent in their own language) to faces with flared nostrils on less than a third of trials.

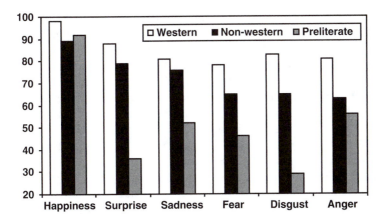

FIGURE 3.2. Cross-cultural differences in emotion-expression matching (adapted from Russell, 1994)

If basic emotions are directly expressed in distinctive facial expressions, why should cultures differ in the recognition of these expressions, and why should remote cultures perform at such low levels? Surely if everyone were so familiar with the emotion-expression connection, the meaning of the faces should be self-evident. Ekman (e.g., 1994) suggests three solutions to this problem.

First, he points out that there may have been translation problems with some of the different languages' words for basic emotions. For example, as noted in the previous chapter, some cultures have no terms that directly correspond to some of the emotions that Anglo-Americans consider basic. Thus, to the extent that the words supplied to participants did not precisely match what the face apparently showed, performance might be impaired. However, if participants knew exactly what emotion the facial expression conveyed, it is hard to imagine why they would fail to select the closest possible translation for it rather than one that was actually closer to another of the emotions with which they were supposedly equally familiar. Even if no word precisely meaning "disgust" had been presented to them, for example, surely they should still know that a word meaning something similar was a better description of the disgust expression than a word meaning something more similar to "fear," "anger," "sadness," "happiness," or "surprise." In short, inexactness (as opposed to serious error) in translation does not in itself explain why a majority of preliterate participants got the answer wrong for some of the faces. Further, we have the issue of why any language would fail to encode an emotion that is supposedly basic in the first place (Russell, 1994, and see chapter 2; hypocognition is one possible answer). Finally, Elfenbein and Ambady (2002) have recently presented evidence that it is shared culture rather than shared language that enhances performance on expression judgment tasks.

Ekman's second explanation for imperfect recognition accuracy is that members of preliterate cultures had problems with the experimental task itself. One of these problems was that the unavailability of any written language meant that the six alternative emotion words had to be presented orally, imposing demands on participants' memory. Although this may certainly have been a confounding factor, memory demands would nevertheless be substantially reduced if faces really did give such a clear indication of an associated basic emotion that participants immediately recognized the correct answer when it came along. Of course, if none of the options was perfect, because of the translation problems noted above, the memory issue might still resurface to some degree.

A further methodological complication noted by Ekman is that participants' unfamiliarity with experimental procedures meant that they did not properly understand what was being asked of them when presented with pictures of faces and emotion words. Indeed, it is certainly true that unless one has prior experience of the conventions of scientific assessment, many of the questions asked by experimenters may seem ambiguous, not to say odd. Thus, the cross-cultural communications of researchers and participants might have been at cross purposes, potentially explaining why tribespeople's supposed underlying knowledge was not fully tapped. As Russell (1994) points out, however, the near-perfect results obtained for smiles suggest that even participants from preliterate cultures understood the experimenter's questions well enough when they actually knew the right answer. The question then arises of why they recognized these facial expressions so much better than any of the other supposedly equally basic ones.

Ekman's final explanation for cultural differences in performance concerns display rules. Although his theory proposes that each basic emotion is linked to a distinctive facial expression, this expression can also be masked or modulated in conformance to societal norms about its appropriateness. Thus, a culture that disapproves of anger (e.g., Briggs, 1970) may encourage its members to cover up or suppress any expression of this emotion on the face. If such display rules are pervasive, then perhaps this leads to some confusion about the meaning of some facial expressions and their links to emotion. Does an angry face continue to mean "anger" when it is never actually shown in public, for example? This reasoning leads to further unresolved questions about how display rules are supposed to operate in practice. In particular, if people consciously adjust their expression to meet social demands, they must surely be aware at some level of the nature of the expression that they are trying to avoid showing (cf. Wegner, 1994). Ekman's account therefore seems to imply that display rules sometimes become so engrained that their operation goes unnoticed. But if this is true, how exactly are children taught to follow these rules? Surely, the society needs to know what the forbidden expression means at some level to maintain sanctions against its occurrence.

To summarize, it is clear that emotion-relevant faces are interpreted with some consistency across cultures, suggesting a universal link between facial position and at least some aspect or correlate of emotion. However, it is also apparent that variation exists both within and across societies in the extent of this consistency. This suggests at minimum that cultural expertise and socialization play some role in the attribution of emotional meaning to facial expressions.

☐ Decoding Rules

If the impact of display rules changes cultural perceptions of facial expressions as Ekman's account implies, then it becomes possible to argue that culture influences the interpretation as well as the presentation of basic emotions. Indeed, evidence suggests that culture-specific decoding rules alter people's responses to other people's faces (e.g., Biehl et al., 1997; Ekman et al., 1987; Matsumoto & Ekman, 1989; Mandal, Bryden, & Bulman-Fleming, 1996; Matsumoto, 1989, 1992; Schimmack, 1996). These decoding rules lead members of a culture to amplify, deamplify, neutralize, or qualify their perceptions and interpretations of others' emotional expressions to take into account the corresponding effects of display rules on the expressions themselves. Further, some decoding rules are thought to minimize perception of emotions that would otherwise be disruptive to the flow of social interaction in a particular culture. As well as compensating for display rules, then, decoding rules can also reinforce their effects.

Studies of differences between respondents from collectivistic and individualistic cultures illustrate the operation of the latter, reinforcing form of decoding rules. For example, it has been repeatedly demonstrated that Japanese tend to give lower ratings of the intensity of facial expressions (regardless of the culture of the poser) than do Western respondents (Ekman et al., 1987; Matsumoto, 1989; Matsumoto & Ekman, 1989). This difference has been explained in terms of the Japanese prescriptive norm to suppress emotions that damage social relations. Not only does this prescription discourage intense emotional expression, it also makes people reluctant to perceive intense emotion in others' faces.

If Japanese judges underestimate the intensity of negative emotions as a function of a reinforcing decoding rule, this seems to imply that their judgments of expressions produced by other Japanese people will be doubly inaccurate. First, the sender minimizes the expression of the emotion, and second the receiver minimizes its perception. However, in fact, the cross-cultural evidence tends to support an in-group advantage rather than disadvantage in emotion judgment (Elfenbein & Ambady, 2002). The paradox is partly resolved by invoking compensatory decoding rules that correct for display rules. But then why don't reinforcing and compensatory decoding rules simply cancel each other out? One answer is provided by research that distinguishes between the perceived intensity of an expression (how pronounced the facial movements are seen to be) and the perceived intensity of the underlying emotion (how strong the experience that the face conveys is thought to be). It seems that reinforcing decoding rules affect perceived expression intensity, whereas compensatory decoding rules modify perceived emotion intensity.

Results of an experiment by Matsumoto, Kasri, and Kooken (1999) are consistent with this reasoning. In this study, American and Japanese respondents were asked to make two different intensity ratings—one for experience and one for expression—for seven facial expressions. The results showed that the Americans rated emotional expressions as more intense than did the Japanese, but that the Japanese rated the emotional experience as more intense than did the Americans. Moreover, the Japanese rated the emotional expression and experience as equally intense, whereas the Americans rated the expression as more intense than the experience. This latter finding was explained as an attempt by U.S. participants to compensate for their culture's encouragement of exaggerated emotion expression (both positive and negative). Japanese participants' higher ratings of experience intensity were correspondingly explained as correcting for deamplifying display rules.

A subsequent study (Matsumoto, Consolacion, et al., 2002) directly addressed the relation between decoding rules and the cultural dimensions of individualism–collectivism and status differentiation. The first of these dimensions was introduced in the previous chapter. The second status differentiation dimension reflects the extent to which members of a culture adjust their social behavior in response to status differences that exist between them and the people with whom they are interacting. In particular, high status differentiation might lead to modulation of facial expression on the basis of the perceived status of the other. Matsumoto and colleagues found that almost all of the effects of country on decoding of expressions could be accounted for in terms of these two dimensions. In other words, judgments of emotional intensity depend crucially on basic cultural values. Because people high in collectivism or status orientation follow the cultural display rule to mask negative emotional expressions themselves, they tend to think that others' subjective experiences too are more intense than the facial expression implies.

What does the operation of decoding rules tell us about the universality of basic emotions? According to Ekman (1994) and Matsumoto (2002), they provide an explanation for cross-cultural differences in recognition rates that doesn't lapse into an extreme form of cultural relativism. Faces that are produced according to culturally specific display rules are likely to be better interpreted by members of the same culture because they are more familiar with the operation of these display rules and can therefore compensate for them. Thus, differences in recognition rates for facial expressions across cultures would only reflect differing degrees of familiarity with expressive conventions. However, as we have seen above, some (reinforcing) decoding rules seem to render culturally unwanted emotions less, instead of more, visible. Indeed, if members of a culture could easily compensate for display rules, there would be little point in conforming to them in the first place. Why bother to disguise something when others will immediately see through your disguise anyway?

On the basis of their recent meta-analysis, Elfenbein and Ambady (2002) concluded that emotion-recognition accuracy was particularly good when senders and receivers were members of the same national, ethnic, or regional group. They argue that this apparent "in-group advantage" arises not from shared display rules and encoding rules, but rather from common exposure to local "dialects" of emotion expression. Familiarity with the idiosyncrasies of these dialects enhances decoding of faces produced by other people who have been socialized in similar ways. Instead of seeing facial expressions as culturally distorted versions of biological signals, then, they argue that they are simply local variations on a universal theme. It is not that something is covered up then exposed during intracultural emotion recognition, but rather that something expressed in a distinctive way is interpreted competently. In support of their rejection of the decoding rule interpretation, Elfenbein and Ambady (2002) show that studies using facial stimuli supposedly devoid of display rules still lead to an in-group recognition advantage. If no display-rule-based distortions exist to correct for in the first place, why should familiarity with display rules improve performance?

As argued in chapter 2, different ethnotheories attach differential importance to different aspects of emotional presentation, selectively discounting some components of the syndrome and selectively emphasizing others. According to this view, it may even be the case that no common underlying basic emotion is more or less accurately perceived, but rather that different cultures deploy varying emotion representations to make sense of others' varying conduct. The metaphor of "decoding" implies that a true signal exists to be extracted from the surrounding noise (Parkinson, 1995). Instead, it seems that whatever emotional meaning is formulated from an emotional communication depends on the cultural frame of the receiver as well as the sender. When the respective systems of representation are congruent, we get something that looks like unproblematic transparent transmission of emotion. However, when senders and receivers are from different cultures, the resulting discrepancies between conventional interpretations may lead us to question whether either has a correct idea of the emotion in the first place.

□ Cultural Differences in Emotion

A vast and rapidly expanding literature has evolved around cultural differences in emotion over recent decades (e.g., Cohen & Nisbett, 1994, 1997; Cohen, Nisbett, Bowdle, & Schwartz, 1996; Kitayama & Markus,

1994; Kitayama, Markus, & Matsumoto, 1995; Markus & Kitayama, 1991; Matsumoto, 1989, 1990, 1999; Matsumoto, Consolacion, et al., 2002; Matsumoto, Kasri, & Kooken, 1999; Matsumoto & Kupperbusch, 2001; Mesquita, 2001; Scherer & Wallbott, 1994; Watson-Gegeo & White, 1990). In all of these studies, one or more components of the emotion process were compared across culture to discern similarities or differences. The following sections review some of this evidence and discuss its implications. We will focus in particular on a handful of specific emotions that have been the focus of most of the cross-cultural research: namely happiness, shame, anger, and sadness. For each of these emotions, we will first briefly describe its cultural meaning, and then focus on whether it is experienced more frequently or more intensely in some cultures than in others. In the previous chapter, we argued that emotions may be hyper- or hypocognized. In the present chapter, we will show that this selective emphasis on, and visibility of, certain emotions may have an impact on the actual frequency or intensity with which they are reported. Finally, we will review studies that assess one or more of the various components of each of these emotions, including appraisals, action tendencies, physiological symptoms, and expressions. Before addressing specific emotions, however, we shall consider cultural variations relating to emotion in general and to the broad categories of positive and negative emotions.

Emotion in Collectivistic and Individualistic Cultures

As argued in chapter 2, different cultures may interpret and deal with emotions in different ways. For example, because emotions are more important signifiers of social relations in collectivistic cultures (see also Markus & Kitayama, 1991; Matsumoto, 2001; Semin et al., 2002), social role and position are more likely to influence their expression or suppression. In individualistic cultures, on the other hand, emotions are important not as indicators of social position and relation but in their own right and for their own sake, because they are believed to reflect the true and inner self. Individualistic emotion norms and display rules may therefore develop to protect or enhance the individual self rather than to support social relations or reflect status.

A study by Suh, Diener, Oishi, and Triandis (1998) demonstrates the differing implications of experiencing emotion in the two contrasting types of culture. In this study, emotions were a stronger determinant of judgments about life satisfaction in individualistic cultures than in collectivistic cultures. Relevant social norms and emotions made equal contributions to the prediction of life satisfaction for the latter participants, whereas norms were much less influential for individualists (see also Lu, Gilmour, & Kao, 2001).

The internal focus of emotion-related judgments in individualistic societies is also illustrated by Levenson, Ekman, Heider, and Friesen's (1992) cross-cultural study of bodily changes as determinants of the subjective experience of emotion. These authors showed that North American and Indonesian respondents showed identical patterns of ANS (autonomic nervous system) changes after having displayed a specific emotional expression like frowning or smiling, but that their reported emotional experience differed. The American respondents reported feeling emotional after the expression manipulation (and its consequent effects on internal physiology), but the Indonesian respondents did not. Levenson and colleagues explained this difference by reference to the Indonesians' collectivistic interpretation of emotion as context-dependent, rather than internally determined.

Cultural differences in the perceived personal and interpersonal significance of emotion are also reflected in culture-specific patterns of expression, with members of collectivistic cultures more likely to play down their emotions than members of individualistic cultures (see, e.g., Tsai, Chentsova-Dutton, Freire-Bebeau, & Przymus, 2002). Indeed, Scherer and colleagues (Scherer, Wallbott, Matsumoto, & Kudoh, 1988) found that Japanese participants reported fewer emotion-associated bodily expressions, verbal reactions (except in the case of joy), and physiological symptoms than North Americans or Europeans.

All of these findings are consistent with the argument that contrasting cultural meaning systems lead to different types of self-construals, on the basis of independent (or idiocentric) or interdependent (or allocentric) views of the self (Markus & Kitayama, 1991, and see chapter 2). Independent self-construals highlight a person's uniqueness and independence from others, suggesting that his or her behavior arises from a unique set of internal attributes. Thus, an important cultural task in individualistic societies is to express oneself, to promote personal goals, and to be direct. Collectivistic cultures, by contrast, emphasize the "self in relation to others," as part of a social context. The resulting interdependent self is seen as flexible, and behavior is caused by the social context, rather than by internal will or desire. In this view, then, others are relatively salient, a continuous awareness exists of their presence, and the focus is on their needs, desires, and goals, at least when they are part of the in-group. These different forms of self-construal alter the experience and expression not only of emotion in general, but also of specific emotions.

Pleasant and Unpleasant Emotions

To the extent that differing ethnotheories also imply differing value systems, we would expect individualistic and collectivistic cultures to encourage the experience and expression of different emotions. For example, collectivistic norms of politeness toward strangers and social harmony with in-group members might lead to the masking of negative emotions and the enforcement of smiling and congeniality. Individualistic prescriptions, on the other hand, might underline the importance of expressing one's authentic emotions, regardless of their valence.

Culture-specific patterns of emotional expressiveness of this sort were apparently found in early demonstrations of the operation of display rules. For example, Ekman and Friesen (1971; see also chapter 6) found that Japanese and American students showed similar facial expressions when watching an unpleasant film alone, but Japanese students showed fewer negative and more positive expressions when viewing the same film while being interviewed by the researcher. One possible interpretation is that Japanese politeness norms led to the suppression of negative expressions during the interview phase (but see Fridlund, 1994 and chapter 6, this volume for alternative interpretations).

A more recent study by Matsumoto and Kupperbusch (2001; see also chapter 6) used a better controlled version of the same procedure to examine the correspondence between felt and displayed emotions in European American participants reporting collectivistic or individualistic orientations. The hypothesis was that display would be more concordant with experience for participants with individualistic values (e.g., "It is appropriate to express your feelings."). Collectivistic values, by contrast, should discourage them from showing emotions that are potentially disruptive to social relations ("Do not offend others with your emotions.").

Each participant first watched a variety of positive and negative film-clips and rated his or her subjective experience of seven emotions (anger, contempt, disgust, sadness, happiness, fear, and surprise). In the second phase, this procedure was either repeated (for participants in the control condition), or the films were shown again, but this time in the presence of the experimenter (for participants in the experimental condition). When the experimenter was present, participants with collectivistic values smiled more and showed less negative emotion in response to the unpleasant film clips, but smiled less and showed more negative emotion in response to the pleasant film clips. However, ratings of emotional experience were unaffected by the experimenter's presence. Participants with more individualistic values showed similar but weaker tendencies to attenuate their emotional expressions when observed. In other words, it seems that social pressures to conceal both positive and negative emotions apply more strongly to people holding collectivistic values.

Additional support for the operation of culture-specific display rules was obtained by Matsumoto, Takeuchi, Andayani, Kouznetsova, and Krupp (1998). In this study, respondents from four different countries

(United States, Japan, Korea, and Russia) reported on regulation strategies deployed in connection with seven different emotions (anger, contempt, disgust, fear, happiness, sadness, and surprise) experienced in various social contexts (with family, friends, colleagues, and strangers). Americans reported the lowest levels of downplaying or masking their emotions when with family, friends, and colleagues (although not all the effects were significant). However, a different pattern of results emerged for regulation in the presence of strangers. In this condition, Americans reported suppressing anger, contempt, and disgust more than Russians, but expressing happiness more than the other three groups.

Overall, participants with collectivistic values reported greater regulation of anger, contempt, and disgust (emotions threatening social harmony and connectedness) than of happiness, sadness, fear, and surprise, especially in relation to family members. These findings are consistent with the notion that collectivists show a general tendency to mask both positive and negative feelings, but that a more specific focus also exists on suppressing negative emotions within the in-group to preserve social harmony. Americans, on the other hand, exerted more control on emotional expressions toward strangers (except in the case of smiling).

Further support for these conclusions comes from a study by Tsai and colleagues (2002), who compared facial and physiological responses of European and Hmong Americans (Native Americans with a more collectivist culture) while they were reliving an emotional episode. The measures of skin conductance (considered to be an index of physiological arousal) showed no differences across the two groups suggesting similar levels of emotional reactivity to the task. However, codings of a particular form of smile thought to indicate deliberate control of expression (non-Duchenne smiles, see Figure 3.3) were significantly higher for European Americans. The authors conclude that European Americans attempt to convey a greater intensity of happiness by forcing a smile.

In summary, the evidence tends to suggest that collectivistic cultures are more likely to discourage expression of negative emotions than individualistic cultures, although the nature and size of this difference may depend on the specific social context in which the emotion is displayed. Some inconsistencies also appear between studies, and to date there has been little systematic investigation of when and how emotion expressions are regulated by different cultural groups. Indeed, it seems likely that different kinds of display rules apply in different settings. So far, however, studies have focused almost exclusively on the degree of emotion regulation, and not on the selective application of rules that underlie such regulation and the variety of effects that are produced.

The precise nature of the processes underlying the operation of display rules is also unclear. For example, socialization of expressive norms

FIGURE 3.3. Faces showing a Duchenne and a non-Duchenne smile. Copyright Paul Ekman.

among family members might seem to imply automatic or habitual regulation of emotional responses. On the other hand, the apparently strategic adjustment of expressive regulation to meet the perceived requirements of different social contexts suggests that senders are aware of the display rules that they are following. Further consideration of these processes is provided in the final chapter of this book.

Happiness

In addition to valence or pleasantness, a further dimension of emotional meaning relating to social orientation seems especially important in distinguishing individualistic and collectivistic cultures (Kitayama, Markus, & Matsumoto, 1995). This dimension contrasts emotions that promote interdependence of self and others (social engagement) with those that involve separation of self from the social world (social disengagement). Individualistic cultures emphasize pleasant feelings that highlight the successful attributes of the independent self (socially disengaging pleasant emotions). In these cultures, feeling good, or being happy, is strongly associated with personal achievement, success, and self-promotion. In American culture especially, maintenance of self-esteem is a key concern that is strongly associated with the norm to display happiness (Mesquita & Markus, 2004).

Similarly, Franks and Hefferman (1998) argue that the pursuit of happiness is a central characteristic of American culture. Americans create and maintain happiness in many different ways, including praising, complimenting, and offering encouragement to each other, to a far greater extent than Europeans, for whom this extravagant and effusive boosting of others' egos is often seen as exaggerated and insincere. In U.S. culture, happiness has become more than an emotion that is simply felt in pleasant situations; it has also become a goal in itself, the essence of what is sought in an authentic self.

By contrast, members of collectivistic cultures place more emphasis on pleasant feelings that highlight connectedness with other people (socially engaging pleasant emotions). For example, the respect for the feeling of others captured by the positive emotion of *simpatico* is considered particularly important among Hispanics (Triandis, Marin, Lysansky, & Betancourt, 1984). Similarly, Hindus consider interpersonal fusion as an ideal (Kakar, 1978), Ifaluks particularly value the compassionate emotion of *fago*, which serves to reinforce mutual caring responsibilities (Lutz, 1988), and the Japanese enjoy the dependence on others captured by *amae* (e.g., Doi, 1973).

The correspondence between socially engaged and disengaged emotions and cultural concerns relating to interdependence or independence was specifically addressed in a diary study conducted by Mesquita and Karasawa (2002). In this study, Japanese and American students answered questions about what emotions they had experienced and what concerns had led to these emotions at three hourly intervals every day for a week. The reported concerns were then classified either as independent (e.g., relating to sense of control, or being able to cope) or as interdependent (e.g., relating to closeness to others, or fit of behavior in relationship). The results revealed that interdependent concerns were more closely related to pleasant emotions for Japanese participants, but that independent and interdependent concerns were equally predictive of pleasant emotions for American participants.

Evidence also indicates that differences in cultural frameworks and concerns lead to differences in the frequency or intensity with which particular emotions are experienced. For example, Kitayama, Markus, and Kurokawa (2000) looked for differences between collectivists and individualists in the prevalence of pleasant emotions that either highlight the self or others. In this study, Japanese and American respondents reported the frequency with which they experienced six different categories of emotion: general pleasant feelings (calm, elated, relaxed), socially engaging pleasant emotions (friendly feelings, respect, closeness), socially disengaging pleasant emotions (proud, feeling superior), socially engaging unpleasant emotions (ashamed, guilty, concerned for another), socially disengaging unpleasant emotions (angry, frustrated, sulky), and *amae*-related emotions (feel like being babied, leaning on another). It was found that American, but not Japanese, participants reported more pleasant than unpleasant emotions. In addition, there were higher correlations between general pleasant feelings and socially engaging emotions in Japan, and between general pleasant feelings and socially disengaging emotions among American respondents. Overall, interpersonal orientation was more important in differentiating the emotions of Japanese participants, whereas pleasantness was more important in differentiating the emotions of American participants.

A range of other studies also support the idea that Americans are more concerned with self-esteem and with the encouragement of pleasant emotions. For example, Americans see the expression of happiness as more important than do respondents from other cultures (Matsumoto, 1990), European Americans report higher levels of life satisfaction than Asian Americans (Diener, Oishi, & Lucas, 2003), and Americans tend to report more intense joy and more physiological symptoms during joy than either Japanese or European participants (Scherer, Wallbott, Matsumoto, & Kudoh, 1988). Although none of the studies directly assessed the cultural significance of these emotions, their findings are all consistent with the notion that the importance Americans attach to pleasant emotions influences the frequency with which these emotions are experienced.

A culture's focus on particular emotions may also lead to a tendency to approach or avoid specific objects or events that alter the likelihood of experiencing these emotions. For example, Americans seem to gravitate more toward pleasant situations, and to appraise situations as more pleasant than East Asians, who are more concerned with avoiding unpleasant situations that may lead to shame (Kitayama, Markus, & Kurokawa, 2000; Mesquita & Karasawa, 2002). Similarly, in Scherer and colleagues' (1988) cross-national survey, achievement related situations were all reported more frequently by U.S. respondents than by Japanese respondents.

Cultural differences in the appraisal of positive and negative events have also been reported by Kitayama, Markus, Matsumoto, and Norasak-kurkit (1997). In their study, American and Japanese participants described situations in which their self-esteem was either impaired (failure) or enhanced (success). Participants' descriptions of these situations were then classified as indicating "self-appraisal" (self-esteem influenced by one's own actions), "other-appraisal" (self-esteem influenced by other people's actions), or "social comparison." For reported successes, both Japanese and American participants were found to use more self-appraisals than other-appraisals. However, in the failure condition, Japanese participants reported fewer self-appraisals than other-appraisals, whereas the reverse pattern was found among American participants. When a second group of participants rated their appraisals of these events after reading the descriptions, further interesting cultural differences emerged. Americans appraised the success situations more in terms of self-esteem enhancement, especially when the situations were ones originally provided by American participants. In addition, they reported that their self-esteem would increase more in success situations than it would decrease in failure situations. By contrast, Japanese readers reported that their self-esteem would decrease more in failure situations than it would increase in success situations, evidencing a more self-critical tendency.

Other studies confirming this culture-specific relation between appraisals and emotions were conducted by Roseman, Dhawan, Rettek, Naidu, and Thapa (1995), who found that cultural differences in appraisals predicted cultural differences in emotions. Moreover, Mauro, Sato, and Tucker (1992) found that Chinese respondents reported more pride as a consequence of events that they appraised as uncontrollable, whereas Americans reported more pride as a consequence of their own actions. Once more, this supports the general idea that personal control is emphasized to a greater extent in individualistic cultures. The belief that individuals can master and effectively modify their environment stands in sharp contrast to the emphasis on mutual obligations and collective goals found in more collectivist cultures. In a large-scale cross-national study, Sastry and Ross (1998) specifically examined the relation between the sense of personal control and well-being. Participants from Asian countries were found to have a lower sense of control, but this was not associated with higher depression or anxiety ratings. By contrast, the American data showed an inverse relationship between feelings of personal control and anxiety or depression. The authors explained these cultural differences in terms of the greater valuation of personal control in the United States.

In conclusion, abundant empirical evidence now exists that happiness is a hypercognized emotion in American culture. To meet cultural expectations arising from the promotion of happy experiences and expressions, people from the United States actively seek out happy events and appraise situations in more positive terms.

Shame

Unlike happiness, shame seems to be a socially engaging emotion in all cultures, because it fosters interdependence by motivating people to restore harmony in relationships. Because of this important social function, shame seems to be generally hypercognized in collectivistic cultures, and also in cultures with high power–distance or status differentiation. Indeed, shame is closely associated with feelings of indebtedness for interdependent selves (Markus, Kitayama, & Matsumoto, 1995). Chinese and Asian cultures that place a particular emphasis on shame in socialization and interpersonal life are sometimes even termed "shame cultures" (Doi, 1973).

Shame cultures have often been contrasted with guilt cultures (Benedict, 1946; Mead, 1934). In shame cultures, individuals worry about what others will think when they have done wrong, whereas in guilt cultures the concern is more about falling short of personal standards. Shame or the threat of shame represents an interpersonally based sanction for losing face as a consequence of wrongdoing in shame cultures. Guilt cultures, on the other hand, operate more on the private conscience of individuals.

Although it may be oversimplistic to draw a hard and fast distinction between shame and guilt cultures at a general level (Miyake & Yamazaki, 1995), it is nevertheless a fact that shame is a more important emotion in many collectivistic cultures. This difference is not only apparent from the number of shame-related words contained in the vocabularies of those cultures (Russell & Yik, 1996; see chapter 2, this volume), but also from studies of cultural differences in children's knowledge of shame and in socialization practices involving this emotion. For example, Japanese parents often use phrases like "if you do that, people will laugh at you" (Miyake & Yamazaki, 1995) as an indirect way of disciplining children without using direct reprimands. Shaming is thus a mechanism of social control, imposed on children who must learn to submit to the social hierarchy. In collectivistic cultures, then, the ability to experience shame signifies awareness of one's position in society.

The developmental function of shame in collectivist cultures is evident from various studies. Shaver, Wu, and Schwartz (1992), for example, showed that 95% of Chinese mothers claimed that their children understood the meaning of *xiu* ("shame") by the age of three. Fung (1999) also reports evidence that 43% of Taiwanese parents reported that children should be ashamed if they break social rules, whereas none of their American counterparts agreed with this statement. In a similar vein, Rodriguez and colleagues (2000) compared the knowledge of shame in an honor culture and an individualistic culture by asking Dutch and Spanish children of different age groups (7, 12, and 15) what emotions they would experience in response to specific events. The youngest group of Dutch children reported that they did not know what "shame" meant, whereas the youngest group of Spanish children knew what shame was, but were ignorant about the meaning of "pride."

Ethnographic investigations also document the use of shame by parents. Lutz (1983), for example, describes the importance of Ifalukian *metagu* ("shame") in establishing parental goals, mostly in relation to meeting strangers. Ifaluk infants are described as experiencing *metagu* before they are 1 year old. Parents specifically elicit this emotion when their offspring behave improperly by summoning a special type of ghost who is reputed to kidnap and eat children. Similarly, Myers (1979) observes that shame is a significant emotion in the life of the Pintupi Aborigines. For members of this culture, experiencing shame involves awareness of others, and signifies the separation between what is defined as public and private. According to Myers, shame reflects the desire to avoid self-focus: Individuals are denied their personal will and are required to submit themselves to the social hierarchy. This is illustrated by the fact that younger men in this community are not allowed to speak in public occasions, because this is seen as an example of pushing themselves too much.

Shame also comprises a central element of women's honor in honor cultures. To maintain their honor, they must behave modestly, and take care that the men in their family are not offended by their behavior. Only women who behave in the proper way are said to have shame (see also Rodriguez Mosquera, Manstead, & Fischer, 2000). In honor cultures, then, having shame refers not so much to an emotion, but rather to an attitude, a way in which one should behave in interactions with others. This idea of shame as a highly valued dispositional state is also characteristic of many collectivistic cultures (e.g., Menon & Shweder, 1994).

Taken together, these studies suggest that shame is a salient emotion in many kinds of collectivistic cultures. Children's sensitivity to situations that may lead to shame is higher in collectivist and honor cultures than in individualistic cultures and they learn shame's meaning together with its associated practices at a very early age (Cole, Bruschi, & Tamang, 2002; Oyserman et al., 2002; Singelis & Sharky, 1995; Singelis, Bond, Sharkey, & Lai, 1999).

In individualistic as well as collectivistic cultures, shame is one of a cluster of socially engaging unpleasant emotions (Markus, Kitayama, & Matsumoto, 1995). Here, however, shame seems to be associated with self-failure rather than trouble in ongoing social relationships. For example, Fischer and colleagues (1999) found that shame was more often elicited by the behavior of others in Spain than in the Netherlands. Further, the emotion was assumed to have more negative social implications for oneself in individualistic cultures than in honor cultures. In individualistic cultures, then, shame seems more an emotion to be avoided and suppressed, even to be ashamed of. This may explain why so few shame-related words are contained in the English language and in the languages of other relatively individualistic countries.

Do the contrasting cultural meanings attached to shame translate into differences in the actual experience of this emotion? Kitayama and colleagues (2000) showed that Japanese participants reported more negative socially engaging emotions, such as shame, than did American participants. Further, Spanish respondents in a study by Rodriguez and colleagues (2000, 2002a and b) reported more intense shame in connection with various threats to family honor. However, when Dutch cultural concerns such as autonomy and assertiveness were attacked, Dutch respondents reported more shame. These results indicate that shame is elicited in reaction to culture-specific concerns.

Although Wallbott and Scherer's (1995) large-scale cross-national survey found no cultural differences in shame intensity, other relevant differences were apparent. For example, shame-eliciting events reported by members of collectivistic cultures were less recent, of shorter duration, and were appraised as less expected, less immoral, and as having fewer negative implications for self-esteem and social relations. Shame was also characterized more by high body temperature (feeling hot, blushing), but low trophotropic symptoms (lump in throat, stomach troubles, crying –sobbing), and more often accompanied by laughter and smiling, but less often by verbal behavior in collectivistic cultures. Moreover, this typical shame profile was also prevalent in high-power–distance and high-uncertainty avoidance cultures. Interestingly, whereas shame was clearly distinct from guilt in collectivistic cultures, shame and guilt had more similar profiles in individualistic cultures.

In conclusion, it seems that collectivistic values are associated with the hypercognition of shame. For interdependent selves, shame is an important emotion because it serves to restore or retain social harmony and to preserve the social hierarchy. Shame therefore generally signifies an awareness of one's position in relation to others and serves an important social function in collectivistic cultures. In individualistic cultures, on the other hand, shame seems more associated with personal failure and therefore seems more difficult to acknowledge and express explicitly.

Anger and assertiveness

Anger is an important emotion in many cultures because it is considered potentially dangerous and destructive. For this reason, societies often develop strategies for avoiding or suppressing anger, or for releasing the emotion in a relatively safe manner. Despite its apparent universality, anger still seems to mean different things in different cultures, bringing different consequences for its expression and regulation.

According to several anthropological studies, collectivistic cultures tend to associate anger with aggression in contrast to the usual Western emphasis on assertiveness (see e.g., Averill, 1980 for an overview). This makes anger suppression a top priority. Probably the most famous ethnographic examples of this phenomenon are provided in Briggs' description of the life of the Utku in North Canada, as presented in her (1970) book *Never in Anger*. According to Briggs, suppressing anger helps the Utku to sustain interdependent relations among members of a tightly knit and isolated community in the face of various physical and economic hardships. It is not only angry expressions that are suppressed by the Utku, but also hostile and angry feelings and thoughts. Indeed, Utku people believe that thoughts carry a force that may literally kill. As a result, when individuals display verbal aggression, by scolding or even simply criticizing another person, everyone is embarrassed. In fact, Briggs noted only two genuine instances of anger among the Utku in the two full years that she lived among them. Perhaps unsurprisingly, her own American background meant that the Utku frequently accused her of *ningaaq*-ing (getting irritated) too easily.

Observations of Tahitian life also contained very few reports of angry behavior (Levy, 1973). Hardly any physical hostility (e.g., wife beating) was reported, and there were no displays of bad temper. Crime levels were also low in comparison with European standards. Tahitians have therefore been characterized as slow to anger, and soon appeased. If they do get angry, however, Tahitians' emotion is expressed dramatically through destructive action directed at physical objects rather than other people. For example, an angry person might set fire to coconut thatching lying at a safe distance from any houses, or throw very small stones near but not at someone else's feet. Underlying these emotional practices is the Tahitian conviction that anger leads to the serious possibility of extreme physical harm. As an informant in Levy's study remarked, "Tahitians could never play American football, they would kill each other; some women stayed away from the New Year's festival because they were afraid someone would get killed" (p. 284). Levy concludes that "the fear of the consequences of anger, of hostility, of violence—with little apparent experience of such consequences—is noteworthy" (p. 284).

Although Tahitians usually portray anger as a bad thing that is hard to control, it is also considered useful in small doses because it helps to overcome fear when someone has wronged you. When a person is angry, the wisest thing to do is to express it, preferably in words, not deeds, so that the emotion may be released. In the words of one of Levy's (1973) informants: "If you're angry at that man, don't procrastinate, go and talk to him, finish it. And afterward, things will be all right again between you" (p. 285).

Goddard's (1996) account of Malaysian emotions confirms that destructive tendencies are not a necessary characteristic of anger. Malaysian individuals who are *marah* (comparable to "anger") typically respond in a muted or restrained manner. Instead of the outburst of hostile words and physical symptoms characteristic of prototypical Western anger, there is a lingering period of sullen brooding, described by the verb *derajuk*. "This may last for days, weeks, or months before subsiding. In extreme cases it may culminate in the hysterical frenzy syndrome, *amuk*" (p. 437).

As may be inferred from these observations, the fact that anger is hardly ever expressed and thus seldom observed in some cultures neither implies that the emotion is absent (see Briggs, 1995), nor that is insignificant. On the contrary, anger may be hypercognized precisely because it is considered dangerous. Indeed, many cultures have elaborate scripts for how to deal with anger. Denial, as deployed by the Utku, is one possibility. For example, young Utku children are specifically trained in denial strategies. In adult conversations, Briggs never heard the expressions *uruklu(juq)* and *qiquq(tuq)* in the first person ("I am angry."), but only in the third ("He or she is angry."), suggesting an unwillingness to acknowledge its occurrence in the self.

Another popular strategy for regulating anger used among the Utku (and in other cultures) is substitution. For example, Utku children are explicitly taught to replace feelings of annoyance with amusement, and Briggs describes various occasions when irritated expressions were interpreted as "displays of funniness." A similar means of coping with angry outbursts is found on the Faeroe Islands (Gaffin, 1995), where children learn the appropriate way to suppress and replace their anger from an early age, as a result of their frequent experience of taunting and teasing by parents, peers, and teachers. Thus, children are trained not to take offense too easily and to develop an even temper.

A more direct coping strategy can be found on Santa Isabel, one of the Solomon Islands. Here, inhabitants believe that anger is very destructive, but that it can be handled through a special form of social control. When someone is angry, or has hostile feelings toward someone else, direct expression is forbidden. The only permissible way of venting anger is by talking about it in a formalized manner at a public meeting with family members and village mates. This ritual is known as "disentangling" (White, 1990), and permits the safe outlet of negative emotions that would supposedly cause illness and misfortune if they remained hidden. It is assumed that expressing one's anger in a public and organized way minimizes the chance of interpersonal confrontation and hostility.

Individualistic cultures also acknowledge anger's potentially destructive aspects. Indeed, many Western languages represent this emotion using the metaphor of a hot fluid in a container that may explode if the pressure increases too much (e.g., "boiling with anger," "blowing your top," or "flipping your lid," etc. [Kövecses, 1990, and see chapter 2]). Furthermore, many of the strategies for dealing with anger described above (e.g., venting, suppression, denial, substitution) are also used by members of many Western cultures. For example, many European and US children are taught at an early age to "count to 10" to allow themselves to calm down instead of getting angry (e.g., Tavris, 1983). Despite these similarities, anger does not seem to be represented solely in disruptive or destructive terms in individualistic societies, but is also seen as a means to emphasize one's rights, or to put right wrongs. Although anger can be defined as a socially disengaging unpleasant emotion emphasizing distance between oneself and others and breaking bonds between people (Markus & Kitayama, 1991; Markus, Kitayama, & Matsumoto, 1995), it also promotes an independent and powerful self, in accordance with the values of individualistic cultures. This reasoning suggests that anger may be more prevalent, more explicitly expressed, and better recognized in individualistic cultures, precisely because of these potential positive effects.

The idea that anger expression is more common and more acceptable in Western cultures is supported by Zahn-Waxler and colleagues' (1996) investigation of American and Japanese children's responses to conflict and distress situations. In this study, young children from both countries indicated their emotional responses to a series of written stories by selecting pictures of facial expressions. It was found that the American children chose the angry face more often, whereas the Japanese children chose the happy face more often.

Similarly, Scherer and colleagues (1988) found that adult Japanese participants reported weaker and less enduring anger than Americans (but not Europeans). Further, Japanese anger was more frequently evoked by strangers than was European or American anger, confirming the collectivistic emphasis on in-group harmony. By contrast, anger was more frequently directed at friends and family in individualistic cultures (Europe and the United States), perhaps as a way of showing honesty even about negative aspects of people with whom one shares a close relationship.

Cultural differences in the representation of anger functions were directly investigated by Ramirez, Andreu, and Fujihara (2001). They found that Japanese participants tended to emphasize the instrumental function of anger, whereas Spanish participants emphasized its expressive functions. Correspondingly, Japanese participants reported more physical aggression associated with anger, whereas Spanish participants reported more verbal aggression, hostility, and anger. Further, Ramirez, Santisteban, Fujihara, and van Goozen (2002) showed that the extent of action readiness for aggressive behavior was higher relative to felt anger for Japanese participants than for Spanish participants. In Japan, then, anger seems to be experienced as an aggressive state that is potentially damaging to in-group relations, but may serve practical functions when dealing with strangers.

The idea that anger may sometimes be experienced more strongly in collectivistic cultures has been investigated in several studies of the relation between anger, aggression, and honor. Cohen, Nisbett, Bowdle, and Schwartz (1996), for example, examined the role of culture-of-honor norms (see chapter 2) on anger and aggression. In three different studies, an accomplice of the experimenter bumped into participants from either the south or the north of the United States as he walked past them in a corridor, and called them an "asshole." Results showed that southerners (members of an "honor culture") were rated as more upset by observers, showed higher levels of cortisol in their saliva (indicating greater stress), greater preparedness for aggression, and were more likely to aggress in future insult situations. Southerners' higher levels of aggression, however, were only found in measures directly related to the specific insult, ruling out explanations in terms of constitutional irritability.

In conclusion, cultural variations in the experience, expression, and regulation of the supposedly basic emotion of anger seem to be quite pronounced. Anger appears to be hypercognized in most cultures, but in collectivistic cultures the negative consequences of its expression tend to be emphasized more strongly than in individualistic cultures. However, many of these variations also seem to be context-specific. The precise characteristics of anger, how it develops, and when and how it is expressed, apparently depend not only on general cultural values such as independence or interdependence and honor, but also on situational factors, including the status and group-membership of the person one is angry with, and the original reason for the anger.

Sadness, grief, and mourning

One of the most powerful elicitors of sadness is the loss of someone close. The experience of grief and the shedding of tears on these occasions seems to be almost universal among humans. Cross-cultural differences occur, however, in the ways in which people deal with sadness and death. Tahitian culture provides an extreme example of the extent of these variations. As we saw in chapter 2, sadness is so strongly hypocognized in their culture that the Tahitian language does not even contain a word for what English-speakers call "sadness" (Levy, 1973, and see chapter 2). Rather than experiencing responses to loss in terms of emotion, Tahitians seem to somatize their feelings as fatigue or illness. Further, the public expression of sadness is considered inappropriate across a wide variety of social contexts. For example, Levy (1973) reports that the entire family of the village-chief's wife and other villagers gathered around her on the occasion of her imminent death and proceeded to tell jokes incessantly. The apparently incongruous nature of this behavior is explained by the Tahitian belief that making a dying person laugh is good for them. Indeed, showing grief when someone is dying is considered to be bad because it makes it more difficult for their soul to leave the body. It is also believed that excessive mourning allows the transformed spirit of the dead person to gain power over you, resulting in sickness or even possession. Acting more casually thus frees the dying person from you, and you from them. However, the Tahitian joking ritual obviously does not rule out experiencing something similar to "sadness"; indeed, many tears were shed. Instead, it seems to provide a way of coping that emphasizes rebalance and restitution. Within this local meaning system, the bereaved husband's crying at his wife's grave was seen not as a natural expression of grief, but rather as a sign of his remorse for having wronged her.

At the opposite extreme, death for the Toraja (in South Sulawesi, Indonesia), is a highly significant event, and sadness is something to endure and elaborate on (Wellenkamp, 1988). Toraja funerals are lengthy, costly, and symbolically complex affairs. Chanting, singing, dancing, flute music, crying, and a great deal of wailing occur. However, after a funeral is concluded, the grief is also expected to dissolve, although it is recognized that some sad feelings may occasionally persist. On these occasions, a healer may be needed.

Similarly, Brison (1998) reports that the Kwanga (horticulturalists residing along the North West coast of New Guinea) spend a great deal of their time talking about illness and death. Their strong conviction is that death is a classic manifestation of sorcery, even though they are perfectly aware that people can die because of illness or age. The goal of funerals is to allow the people present to discuss their theories about the death, but also to identify the sorcerer responsible for it. The emotions of the bereaved are correspondingly mixed, including anger and the desire to punish the sorcerer, feelings of desertion, and appeals for pity. In other words, "displays of grief and rage are valued as ways of mobilizing support to restore equivalence" (p. 370).

Another different way of coping with losses is provided by the Awlad 'Ali, the Bedouin tribes living in the Western desert along the North West coast of Egypt (Abu-Lughod, 1986). These people deal with all kinds of pain, such as the unacceptability of romantic love, mistreatment by family members, or death, by writing poetry. According to Abu-Lughod, this helps the Bedouins to conceptualize their experience and maintain a positive image of themselves. However, sentiments, especially in response to death, are also expressed publicly, through ritualized funeral lament. At the news of a death, Awlad 'Ali women start a wordless wailing, and then they start crying in a way that is quite different from weeping: "It is a chanted lament in which the bereaved women and those who have come to console them express their grief" (p. 198).

Variations in crying, wailing, or weeping responses to bereavement are also found in other cultures. There may be a burst of desperate cries (Uaupes in Brazil), an alternation between loud sobs of loss and sustained shrill cries of joy (Yanoama of Brazil), repeated wailing of professional mourners (in Senegal), or just a restrained, silent shedding of a single tear, as observed at funerals in northwestern European countries. On Bali, funerals involve no crying at all, probably because they take place years after a person has died (Lutz, 1999).

In more individualistic cultures, crying is generally seen as a normal reaction to situations of loss, but an implicit cultural rule states that it should not be excessive, and that one should ultimately try to break away from a morbid fixation on the deceased and return to the normal course of life. Such norms are concordant with the view that an independent self is not completely reliant on others, and thus should be able to return to normal functioning quickly following the departure of someone close. In other words, one should grieve, but not for too long.

Some of the cross-cultural differences in grief, bereavement, and mourning practices may be a consequence of different religious beliefs about what happens after death held in different societies. Indeed, shared religious practices may help people to cope with their loss and to make sense of their suffering within a cultural script. For example, Schieffelin (1985) describes how the Kalulu (from the Papuan Plateau) reinterpret their loss as an attack from an enemy, and subsequently take vengeance on the attacker. Such action may prevent the bereaved from withdrawing from social activities and instead bring them back into the network of social relations, thus restoring social competence.

Emotional reactions to death are also related to the cultural belief system of Japanese people. In accordance with their collectivistic ideas, they take it for granted that a person's soul will always remain within the family. This conviction may help to explain why Japanese participants in Scherer and colleagues' (1988) study rarely mentioned the death of an intimate as an event that makes them sad, in contrast with European and American participants.

In summary, different cultures have different emotional reactions to the loss of a loved one. Further, any common emotional response to bereavement may take a variety of forms, depending on local beliefs and customs. Culture provides a system of representations for coming to terms with death and a set of practices for dealing with the event and the feelings it may evoke. Both of these make a crucial difference to how the emotional episode is played out over time at a personal and interpersonal level.

☐ Conclusions

In this chapter, we have questioned whether there are basic emotions that are experienced identically across all human cultures. Although biological constraints on emotional development clearly exist (e.g., Camras,

1992), and some of the components of emotion may be fixed by evolutionary pressures (e.g., Ortony & Turner, 1990), the evidence strongly suggests that pronounced cultural variations exist not only in how emotions are represented but also in the ways that people experience, express, and regulate them. Further, many of these differences seem to relate closely to corresponding differences in cultural beliefs and concerns. For example, collectivists experience other-oriented emotions differently in accordance with their conception of themselves as interdependent and the value they attach to in-group harmony.

How deep do these differences run? Some of the ethnographic evidence seems to suggest radically different emotional experiences that have no direct counterpart in Anglo-American life. Similarly, the direct comparisons between societies made by cultural psychologists seem to present a reasonably consistent pattern of contrasts between collectivistic and individualistic societies in particular. At first glance, one might be tempted to conclude that people from alien cultures really do live in different emotional worlds.

However, it is important to emphasize some of the limitations of the available evidence to temper this superficial conclusion. A central reservation relates to the reliance of our observations on systems of emotional meaning. This problem applies most obviously to questionnaire-based studies that use imprecise translations of emotion-related terms. Although investigators often present the results of such studies as demonstrations of differences in emotions themselves, in fact it may simply be that the different emotion words presented to members of the two cultures lead them to pick out different phenomena or different aspects of the same phenomenon. For example, imagine that members of culture A and culture B both experience two different forms of anger ("frustration" and "indignation") in identical ways, but that culture A's only word for anger actually means "frustration" and culture B's only word for anger actually means "indignation." The only option for a Western investigator analyzing anger across these two cultures would then be to use "frustration" as its closest possible translation in culture A and "indignation" as its closest possible translation in culture B. Thus, when answering the questions about their emotions, members of culture A and culture B will end up describing rather different situations, experiences, expressions, regulation strategies, and action tendencies, not because their emotional lives are really different, but because they have been directed to report on different aspects of identical emotional lives. In elucidating the causes of "anger," for example, participants from culture A may talk about goal blockage, whereas participants from culture B will talk about affronts to moral values. Although both groups may have experienced both frustration in response to goal blockage and indignation in response to affronts to moral values, they have no words to distinguish these experiences when describing them to the investigator.

To take this point further, even if a decent translation is available for an emotion word, differences in the cultural meanings attached to this word and in ethnotheories about the emotion it describes (see chapter 2) will also tend to change the way in which respondents answer the questions put to them. For example, when a Japanese man rates his readiness to aggress when angry at a higher level than a Spanish man (Ramirez et al., 2001), does this mean that the anger itself is different or merely that he perceives or indeed remembers it differently because of his preexisting cultural beliefs and sensitivities? Similar interpretational problems apply to many of the studies reviewed in the later sections of this chapter.

Ethnographic studies get around these issues to some extent by making more direct observations of the emotional phenomena in question. However, these observations are bound to be conditioned by the anthropologist's own cultural perspective. In identifying an emotional practice or experience as distinct from one that is more familiar in his or her culture of origin, there is always the danger of missing the point of what the aliens are actually doing. Informants and observees may be following different rules in their presentation of objects and events that are in reality more similar than they seem to the untrained eye. Of course, ethnography is not usually intended as a way of directly comparing cultures, but rather as a means of understanding their internal operation. Further, the ethnographer's guard against misperception and misconception lies in establishing how the many different aspects of cultural life fit together. From this angle, emotions observed in their articulated everyday context may be harder to misinterpret than those that are artificially abstracted from social life.

Another response to the practical problem of disentangling emotions and their representations is to acknowledge their interrelations. For example, a culture that develops a word for indignation but not for frustration presumably does so at least partly because differences already exist in the ways that the relevant emotions are valued, understood, and practiced. Further, differences in representation are unlikely to persist without making some corresponding differences in the processes they represent. As we have argued above, how we understand and evaluate emotion influences how we deal with it (in ourselves and in others). In short, languages and ethnotheories do not exist in some separate Platonic realm but reflect as well as affect emotional processes directly. Instead of trying to distinguish emotion from its representation, then, it might be better simply to accept that emotions are all about meaning in the first place. Not only do emotions mean something to the person experiencing them and to those who witness them, but they are also about things that have personal and interpersonal meaning. If an emotion means something different and relates to different event meanings in a different culture, then what grounds have we for claiming that it is the same emotion? Certainly there may be consistent aspects and components that allow us to make the comparison, but the overall package is still different, if only by virtue of the different meaning system from which it derives its identity.

In our view, emotions differ across cultures in a variety of interrelated ways. First, culturally specific practices present different occasions for the occurrence of emotion. For example, rituals have evolved to promote the experience of culturally sanctioned emotional responses to bereavement. Second, societal values provide criteria against which emotional events are appraised. For example, someone else's anger may be interpreted positively as assertiveness in one culture but negatively as aggression in another. Third, cultural socialization leads to different habitual bodily responses and modes of expression during emotion. For example, Elfenbein and Ambady (2002) posit culturally specific dialects of facial communication, and Levy (1973) proposes extreme somatization of sadness among Tahitians. Fourth, people regulate the presentation of their emotions to meet cultural standards. For example, the disentangling ritual on Santa Isabel changes the way islanders work on their anger (White, 1990). Finally, other people's interpretation and evaluation of emotion also depends on their cultural meaning system. Because the Utku disapprove of anger, for example, displays of apparent irritation are treated as childish and responded to with embarrassment (Briggs, 1970). This interpersonal response in turn may lead to regulation of the emotion itself. Indeed, repeated exposure to such interpersonal contingencies might have the effect of blending any incipient experience of what would otherwise be anger with the shameful anticipation of a negative response from others.

If culture permeates emotional life so thoroughly, does any aspect of it remain untouched by its influence? In our opinion, many of the microprocesses of the emotional syndrome and some of the forces shaping emotional development may indeed be fixed by biology. However, the way in which these come together to produce integrated emotional functioning in a fully socialized adult is largely a cultural affair. In chapter 8, these ideas will be developed in more detail. Next, however, we turn to an analysis of emotion at the group, rather than cultural, level.

Group Emotion

When people say that a mob is angry, an audience is enthusiastic, or a nation is grieving, what exactly do they mean? Is it just that each separate person is experiencing the same emotion at the same time or is it something more? And even if group emotions are simply collections of individual experiences, does it make a difference that people are having those experiences together?

On the surface, the notion that groups can "have" emotions seems paradoxical. Common sense and emotion theory both share the assumption that emotions are things that happen to individuals. What, then, is a "group emotion?" In this chapter, we shall use this term to refer to the fact that group membership can influence the ways in which people experience and express emotions. This influence manifests itself in the form of similarities in group members' emotional experiences or behaviors, similarities that would not be exhibited if the individuals concerned did not belong to the same group.

Several possible reasons exist for intragroup similarities of this kind. First, group members are more likely than randomly assembled sets of people to be exposed to the same kinds of emotional objects and events. Second, group members often interact directly with other group members and thereby exert mutual influences on each other's appraisals, emotions, and expressions. Third, group members are likely to share certain norms and values, and these will in turn promote similarities in the ways that they appraise emotional events and express or talk about their emotions. Fourth, under many circumstances, members are likely to define themselves at least partly as members of the group, meaning that their group membership constitutes a significant component of their identity. To the extent that members identify themselves as belonging to a common group, they are likely to have similar interpretations and evaluations of emotional events that have implications for the group as a whole. Finally, a set of people might actually define itself around the notion of expressing–experiencing a particular emotion, such that if an individual doesn't feel that emotion, he or she would not join the group or stay in it.

It may be helpful to start with some research examples of the sorts of phenomena that are typically classified under the heading "group emotion." Relevant evidence comes from studies finding that members of social groups tend to exhibit mood or emotion convergence, a phenomenon sometimes referred to as "group emotional contagion." For example, Totterdell, Kellett, Teuchmann, and Briner (1998) found significant associations between the reported moods of members of two kinds of workgroups (nurses and accountants). In a similar vein, Totterdell (2000) assessed the moods of members of two professional cricket teams 3 times a day for 4 days during a competitive match. Players' moods were more strongly correlated with the current aggregate mood of their own team than with the current aggregate mood of the other team or with the aggregate mood of their own team at other times. These correlations between player mood and team mood were also found to be independent of personal hassles, teammates' hassles, and the match situation between the two teams, effectively ruling out an explanation in terms of shared exposure to common situations.

Similar results were also reported by Bartel and Saavedra (2000). They argued that members of work groups experience "group moods" when their individual moods can be detected by other members. To test this argument they compared observers' judgments of work-group mood with the work-group members' own mood ratings for 70 separate groups. The predicted mood convergence was confirmed in eight different mood categories, and observers' judgments were positively correlated with the groups' aggregated self-report scores.

As a final example, Barsade (2002) examined emotional contagion in groups constructed in the laboratory that contained an accomplice of the experimenter who had been instructed to act in either a happy and optimistic, or an unhappy and pessimistic, manner. Participants in groups that included the happy confederate reported more pleasant moods than did their counterparts in groups that included the unhappy confederate. Moreover, the extent to which group members caught the confederate's mood seemed to determine levels of cooperation and conflict. In particular, dispersion of positive emotion apparently led to greater cooperation and reduced conflict in the group, whereas dispersion of negative emotion was associated with the opposite outcomes.

This evidence is consistent with the view that the moods and emotions of members of social groups are more similar than those of randomly assembled sets of individuals. However, it could be argued that the phenomena described in this section are due not to *membership of the groups* in question, but rather to simple proximity to other individuals. After all, the groups are ones that are involved in face-to-face interaction, and it may be that dispersion of emotion within the group arises from interpersonal contagion (see chapter 7) instead of group membership per se. To address this issue we need to consider more carefully what a social group is, and what group membership entails.

☐ Defining a Group

Social psychologists have proposed several definitions of group. Some (e.g., Lewin, 1948) have emphasized the *common fate* of group members as a defining attribute. Thus, the fact that Black Americans tend to be economically disadvantaged relative to White Americans and to be on the receiving end of prejudice and discrimination is something that binds them together as a social group. For other theorists (e.g., Sherif, 1966), the fact that a group is organized by *structural factors*, such as roles and status, is something that sets it apart from a mere aggregation of people, such as those waiting in line to be served. For still other theorists (e.g., Bales, 1950), the essential feature of a social group is that its members engage in *face-to-face interaction* on a regular basis. For a final set of theorists (e.g., Turner, 1982), the *self-categorization* of group members is the key attribute of group membership, in the sense that a group exists when its members regard themselves as belonging to the same social category.

Each of these definitions has something useful to offer, and they should not be seen as mutually exclusive. For example, the perception of a shared or common fate is something that is likely to promote self-categorization as members of the same social group. Likewise, repeated face-to-face interaction is likely to promote the structural attributes of role and status relationships, as individuals come to learn more about each other.

Brown (2000) argues that groups need to be considered not simply as entities in themselves but as entities in relation to other groups. He therefore extends the self-categorization approach of Turner (1982) by proposing that "a group exists when two or more people define themselves as members of it and when its existence is recognized by at least one other" (p. 3). Although Brown acknowledges that individuals who are bound together by common fate, who are interrelated in some social structure, or who engage in face-to-face interaction also constitute social groups, his argument is that these are sufficient but not necessary conditions for saying that a group exists. The self-categorization of common group membership, coupled with acknowledgement of this category by another nonmember, is the necessary condition.

☐ Top-Down Versus Bottom-Up Influence Processes

Brown's formulation implies that we can explain group formation by reference to the factors that lead people to categorize themselves and others as belonging to a common group. The self-categorization approach to group formation emphasizes the role of subjectively perceived intragroup similarities and intergroup differences in this process. Individuals have to perceive some people as like themselves but others as different before a group boundary is established. One possible source of these perceptions of interpersonal similarity and difference is emotion: To the extent that individuals' emotional reactions to a situation or event are the same as those of some people who are physically or psychologically present but different from those of others, they will be more likely to regard themselves as belonging to the same social category. In this way, shared (but distinctive) emotional reactions could be an important factor contributing to the group formation process.

Although this "bottom-up" influence of shared emotion on group formation seems theoretically plausible, to our knowledge no empirical evidence of its operation exists. Equally plausible is the corresponding "top-down" influence of group membership on emotion. The central idea here is that self-categorization as a group member implies associating oneself with attributes that are regarded as typical of that group. To the extent that particular appraisals and emotional expressions represent group-defining attributes of this kind, these too will be taken on by group members, thereby creating greater uniformity of emotion. Put simply, our groups memberships should influence our emotional experiences and behaviors in exactly the same way that they influence our perceptions, opinions, and nonaffective behaviors.

An alternative "bottom-up" process that may lead to shared emotional responses in a given situation and consequent group identification is contagion (Hatfield, Cacioppo, & Rapson, 1994; see also chapter 7). If emotion spreads from person to person, the resulting shared behaviors and experiences should encourage the perception that the affected people constitute a group. Similarly, appraisals may be negotiated between group members at an interpersonal level building into a common perception of group appraisal (see Table 4.1 for a summary of the possible top-down and bottom-up processes that might be involved in the coherence of group emotions). According to self-categorization theory, the resulting sense of groupness should in turn lead to top-down influences on emotional convergence. Again, however, little direct evidence exists for this line of theoretical argument.

To what extent do results of the studies of mood convergence cited at the start of this chapter provide support for the top-down influence of shared group identity on affect? Is it the case that members of work and laboratory groups exhibit increasing affective uniformity because of a general tendency to take on group attributes? Unfortunately, the studies in question provide no evidence of the specific processes resulting in increased similarity in mood. All of the possibilities specified in Table 4.1 therefore seem to represent viable explanations of the findings. A final possibility arises from the fact that members of the same group are more likely than random collections of persons to be exposed to the same settings and events. If so, at least part of the greater affective similarity among group members may depend on the similarity in the kinds of emotional stimuli to which they have been exposed. However, as noted earlier, Totterdell (2000) found evidence of mood linkage among sports team members even after controlling for the most obvious common external emotional stimulus, namely the state of the competitive match in which they were participating. It seems, therefore, that exposure to common events cannot be the sole explanation for affective convergence, and that one or more of the processes outlined in Table 4.1 also plays a role. Indeed, it seems likely that combinations of these processes work in concert to produce shared emotions in groups.

TABLE 4.1. Possible Bases for Emotional Coherence in Groups

	Directed at Appraisal	Directed at Expression
Top-down processes	Members orient to group norms about appraisal (e.g., feeling rules).	Members orient to group norms about expression (e.g., display rules).
Bottom-up processes	Individuals agree on common appraisals as a result of interpersonal negotiation.	Individuals adjust their expressions to match those of interaction partners.

☐ Defining Group Emotion

We define group emotion as emotion that influences and is influenced by an individual's membership of social groups. We assume that the primary way in which emotions *influence* group membership is through perceived similarity of emotional experience and expression, which enhances the likelihood that individuals categorize themselves as belonging to the same group. Correspondingly, the primary way in which emotions *are influenced by* group membership is via such self-categorizations, which in turn enhance the uniformity of experience and behavior among group members. However, we also acknowledge that group membership can influence emotion via processes that do not depend on self-categorization, as discussed above.

Relevant Theory and Research

In the remainder of this chapter, we focus on theory and research on emotions as experienced and expressed within social groups. Our general thesis is that group membership leads to shared ways of interpreting and evaluating potentially emotional events and to shared norms that govern the appropriateness of experiencing and expressing emotions in particular contexts.

Three lines of work will be examined in some detail. The first concerns group cohesiveness. Concepts like "group morale," *esprit de corps*, and "group solidarity" are central to understanding this phenomenon. We trace this work from its beginnings in Lewinian field theory (Festinger, Schachter, and Back, 1950), through research that operationalized cohesiveness as attraction to members of the group (e.g., Lott & Lott, 1965), to more recent studies that adopt a social identity or self-categorization approach (e.g., Hogg, 1992). The importance of cohesiveness to group emotion lies in the close relation between cohesiveness and conformity. To the extent that a group is cohesive, its members are more likely to be influenced by one another and to develop shared representations. They are therefore more likely to interpret emotional events in the same way. This shared frame of reference may be an important factor in explaining the phenomenon of group emotion.

The second line of research reviewed in this section focuses on what is sometimes referred to as "organizational culture" (e.g., Pettigrew, 1979) and sometimes as "emotional climate" (e.g., De Rivera, 1992). Recent research in work psychology has acknowledged the importance of emotions in creating and changing organizational cultures (e.g., Van Maanen & Kunda, 1989).

The third line of research concerns the ways in which the emotional styles of families influence the development of children's emotions. For example, do parents who have an "open" style in discussing and expressing their emotions socialize their children into having the same tendencies? Research by Halberstadt (e.g., 1986) and Saarni (e.g., 1990, 1999), among others, suggests that the prevailing emotional climate in a family has a lasting impact on how the children in that family experience and express emotion. We will consider different ways in which this impact might be mediated.

These three lines of research illustrate different aspects of the way in which groups and emotion are related. The research on group cohesiveness illustrates the central role played by social identity. A group is cohesive to the extent that its members are attracted to the identity implications of group membership, and this in turn has a bearing on how they construe events and settings that have implications for that identity. Thus, members of cohesive groups are especially likely to appraise events and settings in terms of their implications for group identity. The research on organizational culture illustrates how group norms, once established, can have far-reaching effects on the emotional behavior and experience of individual members. Finally, the work on family socialization of emotion shows how norms regarding the expression of emotion can be acquired in the context of one of the most influential groups to which many of us will ever belong.

☐ Group Cohesiveness

The concept of group cohesiveness has a long history in social psychology. The first systematic empirical examination of the phenomenon was provided by Festinger and colleagues' (1950) classic study of how informal social groups place their members under pressure to conform to group norms. In the study, group formation and functioning were investigated in two housing projects for married veterans at Massachusetts Institute of Technology (MIT). Group cohesiveness was defined as "the total field of forces which act on members to remain in the group" (p. 164). Two sets of factors were thought to shape group cohesiveness: the attractiveness of the group to its members ("the extent to which the group is a goal in and of itself and has valence," p. 165), and the extent to which members depend on the group for attainment of important goals (e.g., goals of interacting with other group members, or goals whose achievement requires cooperation from other group members). As later commentators (e.g., Hogg, 1992) have noted, Festinger and colleagues' approach to group cohesiveness focused mainly on interpersonal attraction. Thus, although the importance of the group in helping individuals fulfill goals was part of their theoretical framework, the way in which group cohesiveness was operationalized in their research was by asking participants which three persons living in one of two housing projects they spent the most time with socially. The larger the number of group members nominated, the more cohesive a particular group was thought to be.

From Festinger and colleagues' (1950) study onwards, researchers have found a link between group cohesiveness and conformity to group norms. Summarizing this substantial literature, Hogg (1992) noted,

> People in cohesive groups tend to agree with one another and behave in similar ways, and are thus relatively undifferentiated and homogeneous. Group behavior is characterized by conformity to group standards or norms. This aspect of solidarity ... is reflected in notions such as normative forces, unity of purpose, homogeneity of perceptions, attitudes and feelings, shared meaning structures, consensual representations, normatively bounded entities, and shared emotional connections. (pp. 80–81)

Normative Versus Informational Social Influence

Although the link between cohesiveness and conformity is well established, its explanation remains controversial. Traditional accounts focus on the notion of dependence: Individual group members are dependent on the group for social approval or for information about reality. These two types of dependence map to Deutsch and Gerard's (1955) well-known distinction between *normative* and *informational* social influence. Normative influence is based on what Abrams and Hogg (1990) call *pressure to comply*, whereas informational influence is based on what they call *reasons to agree*. Both types of social influence are likely to be greater in cohesive groups: If you are attracted to other group members and if you think that the group can help you achieve important goals, you are more likely to want to gain and maintain social approval from other group members, and therefore to feel pressured to comply with their apparent wishes and expectations; at the same time, you are also more likely to regard their thoughts, feelings, and behaviors as "valid," and therefore to bring your own thoughts, feelings, and behaviors into line with theirs.

Self-Categorization Theory

This dual-process model of social influence has been criticized by a number of authors, most notably Turner (e.g., 1991). The alternative generally offered by these critics is self-categorization theory (see Turner, Hogg, Oakes, Reicher, & Wetherell, 1987). As outlined above, this theory applies general principles of categorization (i.e., accentuation of within-category similarities and between-category differences) to group and intergroup behavior. By categorizing the self as belonging to an in-group, and others as belonging to an out-group, one accentuates both the similarities between self and other in-group members, and the differences between in-group and out-group.

This is not the appropriate place to review the intricacies of self-categorization theory; suffice it to say that a crucial way in which it differs from other theoretical perspectives is that it regards social influence as deriving from a single underlying process. Having categorized the self as belonging to an in-group and others as belonging to an out-group, the individual learns (or, in the case of a new group, helps to form) the in-group norms, and behaves in accordance with these norms to the extent that in-group membership is salient. The normative position for the in-group is one that simultaneously maximizes intergroup differences and minimizes intragroup differences.

Social Versus Personal Attraction

This leads to a different perspective on group cohesiveness. Proponents of a self-categorization approach argue that we need to distinguish between two forms of attraction to others: *personal attraction*, which is based on the idiosyncratic properties of the other person; and *social attraction*, which is based on the fact that the other person is a member of the in-group. Social, as opposed to personal, attraction therefore has nothing to do with other people's unique properties as individuals. Although these two forms of attraction can and do coexist (indeed, members of many small social groups are probably attracted to one another both socially and personally), it is important to keep the different bases of attraction conceptually distinct. I can be attracted to you because of who you are as an individual, or because we both share a group membership that is currently salient. According to self-categorization theorists such as Hogg (1992), it is only the latter form of attraction that is related to group cohesiveness.

Social Versus Personal Identity

The importance of the self-categorization perspective on group cohesiveness for present purposes lies in the central role accorded to the concept of *identity*. If I categorize myself as belonging to a particular group and that group membership is currently salient for me, I conceive of myself largely in terms of this group membership. This *social identity* is different from my *personal identity* (my sense of self as a unique individual, with specific interpersonal relationships), in that it describes and prescribes the attributes of a group member (i.e., any group member, not just me). If we further assume that a salient social identity is something to which individuals in cohesive groups are committed, then social identities have clear implications for "moral careers" (Greenwood, 1994). To respond emotionally to some event, I have to care about the implications of the event for those things that are of concern to me, and my social identity as a group member is of concern to me by definition if the group membership is salient.

Intrinsically Versus Derivatively Social Groups

Greenwood's (1994) distinction between "intrinsically social groups" and "derivatively social groups" is relevant here. Intrinsically social groups are characterized by a set of arrangements, conventions, or agreements that govern the behavior of group members (e.g., members of the Labour Party or fan clubs). Derivatively social groups have members who share a common attribute that is regarded by *others* as socially significant on the basis of certain arrangements, conventions, or agreements (e.g., illegal immigrants, BMW drivers). The importance of this distinction resides in the fact that membership of intrinsically social groups has implications for one's identity, whereas membership of derivatively social groups does not. The key issue here is whether or not membership of the group in question influences your own actions as opposed to other people's reactions to you. It is also worth noting in passing that derivatively social groups do not strictly fulfill Brown's (2000) definition of a group because their members do not define themselves as belonging to such groups.

To the extent that one can make a "moral career" out of being a member of a given group, that group is likely (a) to be an intrinsically social group, and (b) to have implications for one's identity. From the perspective of emotions and social groups, this is important because the emotions one experiences in the context of group memberships are often linked to one's identity as a group member. For example, the more significant being a supporter of a particular sports team is to your identity, the more joy you are likely to experience following the success of that team. A casual supporter might be fleetingly pleased at the success, whereas a die-hard supporter is likely to be euphoric. And the extent to which both give expression to these emotions partly depends on whether they are in the company of fellow-supporters, fans of a rival team, or people who do not care one way or the other.

Belonging to an intrinsically social group has consequences for emotions precisely because of the identity implications of group membership. You may aspire to be a member of a certain group because of the associated identity implications. Or you may belong to a certain group, and this carries with it a set of normative implications concerning your identity. Either way, it is the identity-implicating character of membership of intrinsically social groups that is important with respect to emotion.

Linking these considerations to a view of emotion as partly dependent on cognitive appraisals (see chapter 1) helps us to understand one of the foundations of group emotions. These emotions are ones that are experienced and expressed when social identities are at stake, and when events occur that challenge or support these identities. Thus, anger will be experienced to the extent that group goals are unjustly thwarted or threatened, sadness will be experienced to the extent that the group loses something that is important to its goals, pride will be experienced to the extent that the group's goals are achieved as a result of group members' own efforts, shame will be experienced to the extent that respect for the group is diminished as a result of group members' actions, and so on.

☐ Organizational Culture

The present section is concerned with theory and research on the emotional "climate" or "culture" of groups and organizations. The significance of this work in the present context is that it shows how groups and organizations shape the emotional lives of their members in the service of their collective goals.

Roles and Rules in Organizations

Much of the work on these issues has explicitly or implicitly made use of the constructs of "role" and "rule." The role one plays in a group or organization locates one's position relative to other members and includes some specification of what one should do within the group or organization. The rules one follows are equivalent to social norms: They prescribe what one should think, feel, or do. There is a clear relation between these two constructs: Rules vary as a function of the role one occupies in a group or organization.

Applying these constructs to the domain of emotion, some theorists have focused on the way in which group or organizational roles are associated with rules concerning the expression of emotion in various social settings (e.g., Goffman, 1967). As we saw in chapters 1 and 3, these rules are generally referred to in the literature as "display rules" (Ekman & Friesen, 1969). Other theorists have taken this argument one step further by suggesting that some roles carry with them prescriptions about which emotions it is appropriate to feel, and these rules are typically referred to as "feeling rules" (Hochschild, 1983; see chapter 6, this volume).

The Employee Role in Service Industries

The roles that have been most thoroughly investigated in this area are work roles. Indeed, much of the relevant research has focused on the impact of working in service industries on the expression and experience of emotion. The setting typically studied in such research involves social interaction with one or more clients. Examples are bank personnel who approve or reject loan applications, social workers who make decisions about whether or not a client is entitled to a benefit, physicians who have to deliver bad news about a patient's health, and teachers who have to deal with unruly or disrespectful pupils. As Parkinson (1995) puts it,

> Anyone whose institutional role defines their relationship with others (clients as well as colleagues) is subject to emotional control of some sort by the organization that surrounds them, which typically places lower as well as upper limits on the intensity of emotional expression and experience, as well as outlawing or encouraging specific kinds of emotion. (p. 204)

Parkinson (1995, pp. 204–205; see also Hochschild, 1979) specifically distinguishes two broad categories of rules governing emotional expression and experience in institutional settings of this kind: "restrictive prescriptions," which specify what *not* be expressed or felt in certain circumstances; and "expansive prescriptions," which specify what *should* be expressed or felt in certain circumstances. Crossing the display–feeling rules distinction with the restrictive–expansive prescriptions distinction, and adding a further distinction between rules that influence the *degree* of emotion experienced or expressed and rules that influence the *type* of emotion experienced or expressed yields the classification shown in Table 4.2.

The notion that one should restrict or expand one's emotional expressions or emotional feelings as a result of one's occupational role has come to be known as "emotional labor" (Morris & Feldman, 1996). The groundbreaking work on this issue was conducted by Hochschild (1983). She studied employees in two service occupations: flight attendants—who are encouraged to project pleasant affect even when passengers are being anything but pleasant; and bill collectors—whose job it is to be tough with delinquent debtors despite any sympathy they may feel for their plight.

TABLE 4.2. Possible Normative Prescriptions Concerning Emotion (adapted from Parkinson, 1995, p. 205)

Aspect of Emotion Affected	Type of Rule	Restrictive Prescriptions	Expansive Prescriptions
Degree of emotion	Display rule	Express less emotion (e.g., comportment conventions: English understatement)	Express more emotion (e.g., abandonment conventions: get into the party spirit)
	Feeling rule	Feel less emotion (e.g., don't get too involved with clients)	Feel more emotion (e.g., feel concern for clients)
Type of emotion	Display rule	Do not express a certain emotion (e.g., don't laugh in church)	Express a certain emotion (e.g., show respect for the dead)
	Feeling rule	Do not feel a certain emotion (e.g., don't get mad, get even!)	Feel a certain emotion (e.g., love thy neighbor)

Surface versus deep acting

Hochschild distinguished two different ways of fulfilling the emotional requirements of these occupational roles. In *surface acting*, employees modulate their expression of emotion to project the desired message to clients. The problem with this type of dissimulation is that clients may be inclined to interpret superficial displays of emotion as being required by the employee role, and may therefore discount them as nongenuine. Hochschild argued that employers attempt to overcome this problem by encouraging their employees to project the desired message in a more spontaneous and genuine manner. This is achieved by training employees to engage in *deep acting*. For example, flight attendants are explicitly taught to adopt new ways of thinking and feeling about their encounters with clients, such as seeing the airplane cabin as their own living room and the passengers as personal guests. Although this may help flight attendants to appraise troublesome passengers more benevolently than they otherwise would, Hochschild believes that costs are also attached to this strategy. In particular, employees may become so involved in the emotional needs of the job that they suffer from emotional burnout.

The value of Hochschild's research lies in her argument that work (and indeed other) roles can lead individuals to manage not only their expression of emotion, but also what they experience. However, her claim that emotional labor can be psychologically damaging has been called into question by subsequent theory and research. Although some investigators have found support for this prediction, the findings are by no means unequivocal. For example, Pugliesi (1999) distinguished between self-focused and other-focused emotion management, and assessed the relations between these constructs and measures of work stress, job satisfaction, and psychological distress in a sample of university workers. Both forms of emotional labor were found to be associated with negative effects on workers: Emotional labor increased perceptions of job stress, decreased satisfaction, and increased distress. By contrast, Wharton (1993) studied the psychosocial consequences of emotional labor among bank and hospital employees, and found that performance of emotional labor did not have uniformly negative consequences for workers.

One way of making sense of these apparently contradictory findings is by drawing on the concept of identity. Both Parkinson (1991) and Ashforth and Humphrey (1993) have suggested that a crucial moderator of the psychological consequences of emotional labor is identification with the work role. If the employee strongly identifies with the work role and the associated emotional prescriptions, he or she is less likely to suffer from the emotional labor entailed by proper performance of the role. In Rafaeli and Sutton's (1989) terms, there is a crucial difference between this kind of "faking in good faith" and the "faking in bad faith" that may be done when employees do not identify with the role requirements of their job. To take this further, the kind of emotion work that is performed when people feel a strong attachment to their role may not seem like work or faking in the first place.

Evidence consistent with this argument comes from Parkinson's (1991) interview study of trainee hairdressers, in which he found that trainees who rated their impression management style as less deceptive and who expressed more empathic concern for their clients also reported greater psychological well-being. Similarly, Schaubroeck and Jones (2000) reported that perceived demands on the employees of a survey research organization to express positive emotion were only related to negative health outcomes among those who identified less strongly with the organization and who were less involved in their jobs. An additional argument offered by Ashforth and Humphrey (1993) is that emotional labor might have a reciprocal impact on identification with the work role, by providing workers with information about the extent to which they are involved with their job. Thus, someone who finds it hard to put on a winning smile when confronted with an awkward client is less likely to feel involved in his or her work role than someone who finds it relatively easy. Further, effective deep acting may be treated by clients as genuine, leading to its desired emotional and instrumental consequences. This is likely to reinforce the practice of emotional labor and to lead to greater identification with the work role.

Another related factor that appears to determine whether or not the consequences of emotional labor are detrimental to psychological well-being is the extent to which the individual is aware of having to "put on a show" for the benefit of others. There is some evidence that it is what Hochschild called surface acting, rather than deep acting, that is associated with psychological decrements. For example, Morris and Feldman (1996) and Abraham (1998) investigated the experience of "emotional dissonance" (Hochschild, 1983), meaning the conflict between an experienced emotion and an expressed or required emotion. Both studies found that it was this aspect of emotional labor that was most strongly associated with variables (such as job satisfaction) related to psychological health. Findings from Parkinson's (1991) study of trainee hairdressers are also consistent with this argument. In this research, it was precisely those trainees who scored high in deceptive impression management who tended to have worse psychological health status. By contrast, those who reported expressing themselves naturally and spontaneously (high communicative "openness") had more positive scores on a measure of psychological health.

A final issue relating to emotional labor concerns the precise nature of the emotional dissonance experienced by those who are engaged in surface acting. Many researchers in this area appear to have adopted Hochschild's assumption that surface acting entails a conflict between "real" emotion and emotion that is "put on" for the benefit of others. An alternative account is provided by Parkinson (1995), who argues that the dissonance is not between "real" and "manufactured" emotion, or between "real" and "manufactured" expressions of emotion, but rather between the emotional requirements of two sets of roles, one being the work role and the other a nonwork role. A similar argument is also presented by Jansz and Timmers (2002), who found that schoolteachers report emotional dissonance when they experience an emotion that is at odds with their professional identity. Emotions that are consistent with the roles with which people are most identified presumably feel comfortable, whereas those that are consistent with roles with which they do not feel identified presumably create dissonance.

The difference between these two accounts is a very important one. In the view of Hochschild and others, such a thing as a "natural" emotion exists, an emotion that is appropriate for an individual in a given set of social and psychological circumstances. The fact that certain occupational roles make it difficult or impossible for the individual to express these natural emotions is the basis for arguing that emotional labor can be damaging to psychological health. The work reviewed above calls into question whether emotional labor is damaging to health, and therefore provides indirect support for the alternative theoretical perspective. According to this alternative account, emotions that feel more natural are simply those that reflect closer identifications. Thus, a critical variable determining felt conflict or dissonance is how strongly an employee identifies with his or her work role: The stronger that identification, the less difficult it should be for that person to engage in emotional labor. Psychological discomfort should be greatest for those employees who identify less with their work role and are therefore more likely to be more aware of the conflict between the emotional requirements of this role and the emotional reactions that they subjectively experience as natural, but which actually arise from identification with a nonwork role.

The importance of the difference is evident from the contrasting predictions that would be derived regarding the psychological consequences of deep acting. From Hochschild's perspective this is alienating and psychologically damaging, because it necessarily interferes with natural emotions. From the "role strain" perspective offered by Parkinson (1991) and by Ashforth and Humphrey (1993), deep acting—to the extent that it reflects high identification with the work role—should not be alienating, because it results in the work role-appropriate emotions being seen as natural. Although more evidence is needed before a firm conclusion can be reached, the current balance of evidence favors the role strain explanation.

The significance of the research on emotional labor is that it demonstrates the forces that operate on individuals to conform to the emotional requirements of roles within a group or organization. To the extent that most or all employees in the group or organization are subject to the same pressures to conform, it is likely that they will experience and exhibit greater uniformity of emotion than they would if they were not group members. This uniformity of emotional experience and expression is an obvious instance of group emotion.

Affective Team Composition

A different view of the role played by emotion in work groups is offered by Barsade and her associates (2000). These researchers build on prior work by George and her associates (e.g., George, 1989, 1990; George & Brief, 1992), in which mean affect (typically measured dispositionally, as a trait, rather than as a state) in a group was used to index "group affective tone," a term used to describe "consistent or homogeneous affective reactions within a group" (George, 1996, p. 77). This group affective tone has been shown to be related to outcomes such as absenteeism (George,

1989), prosocial behavior toward customers (George, 1990), and organizational spontaneity (George & Brief, 1992).

In keeping with this general approach, Barsade and colleagues (2000) stress the importance of the affective attributes that individual group members bring with them to group interaction, which help to shape the affective character (i.e., the emotional climate) of the group as a whole. In particular, Barsade stresses the importance of what she calls affective team composition—in other words, the combination of individual group members' affect: "Affective team composition examines how the emotions of individual group members combine to create group-level emotion, and how group emotion may be seen as the sum of its parts" (Barsade & Gibson, 1998, p. 88).

This clearly represents a relatively individualistic conception of group emotion. By contrast, much of the theory and research reviewed elsewhere in this chapter regards group emotion as *more than* "the sum of its parts." Group emotion may be seen as qualitatively distinct from individual emotion, in the sense that individuals are led to experience different kinds of emotion or express their emotions in different ways because of their group memberships. It is not simply that they bring the emotions that they experience as nonmembers to the group setting, where these emotions become integrated through some averaging (or weighted-averaging) process. This latter type of integration is nevertheless the conception of group emotion that has been pursued by Barsade and her associates.

Working within this individualistic perspective, the relation between individual member emotion and group emotion can be examined in different ways. Perhaps the most straightforward approach is to compute the average of the emotional dispositions of individual team members, to assume that this average represents the group emotion, and to examine how this average relates to other variables, such as group performance. An alternative approach is to examine the variance in emotional dispositions across group members, on the assumption that affectively homogeneous groups are likely to behave differently than affectively heterogeneous groups. A third possibility is to examine the impact of the group members with the highest or lowest score on the affective disposition of interest, with the idea that especially high- or low-scoring individuals will exert a disproportionate influence on group emotion.

Affective homogeneity versus diversity

A study by Barsade and colleagues (2000) illustrates the first and second of these approaches. These authors investigated the role of affective diversity in top management teams, focusing on what they term positive trait affect, or the degree to which an individual tends to be enthusiastic, energetic, mentally alert, and determined (see also Watson, Clark, & Tellegen, 1988; Watson & Tellegen, 1985). The affective heterogeneity of a group was operationalized in terms of the diversity of members' scores along the trait positivity dimension, and the group's general affective tone was assessed in terms of members' mean level of trait positivity. Affectively homogeneous groups were predicted to exhibit greater cooperation, less conflict, and better performance than affectively heterogeneous groups. These predictions were tested in the top management teams of 62 organizations in the United States.

No simple association was found between affective diversity, on the one hand, and cooperativeness, conflict, or (financial) performance. However, cooperativeness was higher, and conflict lower, for teams with higher mean positive trait affect. Further, affectively diverse teams that were low in positive trait affect tended to be less cooperative and higher in conflict than affectively diverse teams that were moderate or high in positive trait affect, whereas the level of positive trait affect made no difference in teams that were affectively homogeneous. Affective homogeneity was also weakly related to financial performance, such that more homogeneous teams tended to perform better.

One problem in interpreting these findings arises from its use of trait positive affectivity as a measure of emotion. It is well known (e.g., Larsen & Ketelaar, 1991) that this trait is highly correlated with the personality dimension of extraversion (e.g., Eysenck, 1967), which involves tendencies toward sociability and impulsivity as well as positive affect. Without controlling for these associated factors, it is difficult to evaluate the extent to which Barsade and colleagues' (2000) results reflect the influence of group affect per se, rather than more broadly conceived behavioral dynamics. For example, it would not be surprising if more sociable groups were also more cooperative, or if introverts tended to cooperate more if all other group members were similarly introverted than if other group members varied more widely in their levels of introversion. Of course, these effects themselves are not wholly unrelated to the phenomenon of group emotion. However, the specific mediation of trait effects by real-time emotional states needs to be more convincingly established.

Barsade's view that group emotion needs to take account of the affective composition of the group nevertheless provides a useful counterpart to other approaches to theorizing and researching group emotion. As Barsade and Gibson (1998) noted, most of the theorists and researchers who have considered group emotion adopt a "top-down" perspective, examining the ways in which normative forces in the group influence individual emotional responses. The approach championed by Barsade and her associates (2000) is, by contrast, "bottom-up," in the sense that group emotion is regarded as something that is shaped by the emotional attributes of individual group members.

Clearly this idea has some merit. For example, a group of clinically depressed persons seems likely to have a different type of emotional climate from a group of nondepressed persons. The challenge for the bottom-up approach, however, is to identify those individual-level emotional variables that have a bearing on the ways in which individuals codetermine the emotional climate of the group. Inevitably, this entails assessing trait-like constructs such as positive affectivity, and the problems of relating traits to behavioral outcomes are well known (see Ajzen, 1988). The fact that Barsade and her colleagues have demonstrated trait–behavior links despite these problems confirms the potential of the approach, but it is as yet unclear whether the findings can be extended beyond the trait of positive affectivity.

☐ Emotion in Family Groups

A crucially important type of social group to which virtually everyone has at some point belonged is the family. From the perspective of emotion theory, the family is doubly significant: It is both an arena in which emotions are socialized and a social group in which emotions are experienced and expressed. Families are social groups that are visited on us rather than sought out, but the dependence of the child on parents or other caregivers is such that the family is a highly significant social group.

Members of families are more likely to be exposed to similar events and circumstances than are persons who do not belong to the same family. Families are also undoubtedly characterized by shared norms that govern thoughts, actions, and, it will be argued, feelings. Further, there is typically some differentiation of the roles played by family members, with some (e.g., parents) being more influential than others (e.g., children). Finally, there are circumstances in which members of family groups are quite likely to define themselves in terms of their family membership. These observations provide ample reasons for supposing that the family is a group whose members will exhibit a greater degree of similarity in emotional experience and behavior than would otherwise be expected from individuals who differ from each other so markedly in other respects (e.g., age, occupation).

A growing body of evidence indicates that families play an important role in socializing children's emotions. Broadly speaking, this research can be divided into two related categories. First, work has been done on the influence of parents' responses to children's emotional behavior on the same children's subsequent emotional tendencies. An example is the study by Zahn-Waxler, Radke-Yarrow, and King (1979), who found that children tried harder to make reparations for social transgressions if their mothers had previously made efforts to explain to them what the consequences of their actions were for other people. Another example is Denham and colleagues' (1994) finding that a parent's style of responding to a child's emotions was associated with that child's ability to identify emotions. A second line of evidence focuses on family expressiveness and its influence on children's own expressive behavior (e.g., Halberstadt, 1983, 1984) and on their behavior toward or relationships with peers (e.g., Cassidy, Parke, Butkovsky, & Braungart, 1992; Denham, McKinley, Couchoud, & Holt, 1990).

An important distinction in these research areas contrasts "socialization instruction" and "socialization acquisition" (see Ratner & Stettner, 1991). The former refers to the messages sent by parents to children; the latter to what the child internalizes and subsequently incorporates into his or her behavioral repertoire. The point of the distinction is that the two aspects of socialization do not always overlap completely, although of course they often do. Evidence for the correspondence of instruction and acquisition comes from a number of studies. For example, it has been shown that mothers who respond calmly and reassuringly to their children's emotion tend to have children who are better in regulating their expressions (see Denham & Grout, 1993; Denham, Mitchell-Copeland, Strandberg, Auerbach, & Blair, 1997; Denham, Zoller, & Couchoud, 1994; Gottman et al., 1997). Similarly, research by Eisenberg and her associates (e.g., Eisenberg, Fabes, Schaller, Carlo, & Miller, 1991; Fabes, Eisenberg, & Miller, 1990) suggests that sympathetic parents produce sympathetic children.

Although many of these effects may be explained in terms of direct modeling, as suggested by Saarni (1999), parental influence also seems to have deeper effects. Indeed, some studies specifically suggest that children internalize parental norms about the appropriateness of emotional conduct. For example, Eisenberg and colleagues (1991) found that elementary school children whose parents reported restrictive attitudes to their children's emotional displays were more likely to express personal distress than sympathetic concern in reaction to another person's distress. The most obvious explanation is that these children had learned that showing emotion is a bad thing and makes others uncomfortable.

Although the evidence reviewed in this section suggests that parental reactions to children's emotional behaviors have an impact on children's subsequent emotional behavior, it is also possible that these reactions are partly shaped by the same children's previous conduct. Parents may learn to expect certain kinds of emotional behavior from particular children and adjust their expectations and responses accordingly (see Chapman, 1981). The implication is that whatever social influence is at work in the family arena does not only operate in one direction, with the child as passive recipient of parental indoctrination (see also chapter 8, this volume). Despite these ambiguities, we nevertheless regard these findings as consistent with the view that children internalize family norms and beliefs that are later manifested in their own emotional conduct.

Family Expressiveness

A related line of research on family influences is the work on how the expressive environment provided by the family relates to the child's own expressive behavior. Literature concerning this topic has been helpfully reviewed by Halberstadt, Crisp, and Eaton (1999). The straightforward hypothesis guiding much of this research is that a family environment that is high in expressiveness will promote high expressiveness in children who develop in that environment, whereas a family environment that is low in expressiveness will lead children to be low in expressiveness too. "Family expressiveness" refers in this context to "the predominant pattern or style of nonverbal and verbal expression found in the family" (p. 110). For present purposes, this "pattern or style" can be regarded as a norm concerning expressiveness that is established by the perception that other family members exhibit a degree of consistency in how they express emotion.

Total, positive, and negative family expressiveness

A distinction is often drawn between total family expressiveness (FE), positive FE, and negative FE. In Halberstadt and colleagues' (1999) review, 10 of the 13 studies examining the relation between total FE and "outcome measures" of child expressiveness found a significant positive correlation. Similarly, 18 of 20 studies that examined the relation between positive FE and children's positive expressiveness found positive associations. Finally, the 18 studies that examined the relation between negative FE and child expressiveness suggested that negative FE and child negative expressiveness were more strongly related for older children and adults than for younger children. This last finding apparently provides evidence for a delayed and gradual effect of FE that again cannot easily be explained in terms of direct modeling. Overall, there is a fair degree of support for the intuitively reasonable prediction that variations in FE are linked to variations in child expressiveness.

Accounting for Family Influence on Emotion Socialization

Probably the biggest challenge faced by researchers interested in the family's role in the socialization of emotion is the need to provide a coherent theoretical framework for explaining the observed associations. The prevailing theoretical assumptions are based in learning theory. An obvious way to account for the influence of parental reactions to children's emotional behavior is in terms of instrumental learning. If parents react to their children's emotional behavior in a rewarding or punishing way, such reactions could in principle have a reinforcing or inhibiting effect. Principles of social or observational learning can also be used to explain the influence of family expressiveness on children's expressiveness, the idea being that parents model behavior that is then imitated by their children.

There are several reasons for believing that such explanations are incomplete. First, they are too "top-down," in that they see influence as flowing exclusively from parents to children and not in the other direction. In fact, children probably play a key role in their own emotional socialization to the extent that their emotional behavior influences parental practices. Second, these conditioning and social learning explanations often fail to acknowledge the possibility that at least some of the observed associations have their basis in temperamental factors that have a heritable component. For example, extraversion, neuroticism, and emotionality are individual difference variables that are known to be related to expressiveness (e.g., Buck, Miller, & Caul, 1974), and are also known to be heritable (e.g., Zuckerman, 1991). Thus, the observation that parental expressiveness and child expressiveness tend to be positively associated may partly reflect genetic commonalities within families along relevant personality dimensions. Third, these learning explanations often fail to acknowledge any mediating role for internalized norms. If parents react to a child's emotional behaviors in a reasonably consistent way, or if they are openly expressive of their own emotional states, they are in effect passing on lessons about what is normative. An interesting aspect of norm-based explanations is their potential to do proper justice to the "group" character of the family. As Gordon (1989) has argued,

> Emotion norms of varying levels of generality are learned by children in different group contexts. Intimate interaction with family members and close peers exposes the child to *primary-group norms*. The rules are often idiosyncratic and apply mainly or exclusively to specific individuals (e.g., laugh at Daddy's jokes). As children's social worlds expand beyond the primary group, they become aware of more widely-accepted *societal norms* that apply equally to all, such as to not feel happy over anyone's death. From the broader social context children also acquire *status norms* that govern expression and feeling

between people in particular social positions, such as a rule to display interest and respect for teachers. . . . Most middle-class U.S. children . . . may not have to adjust their emotions according to status differences until they enter the more formal, impersonal relations of school. Thus primary group norms may retain a primacy or salience because of the early learning. (p. 334, emphases in original)

In other words, the first set of norms concerning emotion to which children are exposed are family norms, and these are unlikely to be modified or supplanted until the child enters formal education.

Injunctive Versus Descriptive Social Norms

Children learn a variety of norms that are relevant to their emotional conduct (see also chapter 8). For example, Cialdini, Kallgren, and Reno (1991; see also Cialdini, Reno, & Kallgren, 1990) make a useful and pertinent distinction between *injunctive* and *descriptive* social norms. Their argument is that injunctive social norms prescribe the way we ought to behave, whereas descriptive social norms reflect consistencies in actual social behavior. The way that parents and other caregivers react to children's emotional behavior is a likely source of knowledge of injunctive social norms, whereas the emotional behavior of parents and caregivers is a likely source of knowledge of descriptive social norms. Thus, a norm does not have to be overtly prescriptive to influence experience and behavior; mere consistency in the behavior of other group members will often be sufficient to create the perception of a norm, and thereby influence the individual. However, individuals probably need to identify with the group in question before consistency in other members' behavior has any impact on the way that they think, feel, or act.

Children's Normative Beliefs

Another relevant line of theorizing is the work by Guerra and colleagues (e.g., Guerra, Huesmann, & Hanish, 1995) on children's normative beliefs. They define normative beliefs as "an individual's cognitions about the acceptability or unacceptability of behaviors that regulate his or her corresponding behaviors" (p. 141). Broadening this definition to include emotions provides a social schema that has the potential to account for within-family commonalities in emotional behavior. These normative beliefs are presumably derived from injunctive and descriptive social norms.

How are such normative beliefs acquired? Guerra and her colleagues suggest that they are anchored in parental rules. Parents verbalize certain rules concerning behavior in the form of explicit injunctions to behave or not to behave in a certain way, and the child initially constructs normative beliefs on the basis of these rules. Rules regarding what should or should not be done can also be inferred from simple observation of behavior (descriptive social norms). Later in life, these normative beliefs will be influenced by individuals and social groups beyond the immediate family.

In Guerra and colleagues' (1995) view, normative information from different sources will influence the development of normative beliefs to the extent that the child identifies with these sources. Also entailed is a process of evaluation that includes an assessment of self-efficacy ("Can I perform—or refrain from performing—the behavior in question?"), of response-outcome expectancies ("What would happen if I did—or did not—perform the behavior in question?"), and of self-concept ("What kind of person am I?").

In Guerra and colleagues' (1995) conceptualization, then, normative beliefs are abstract knowledge structures that are in effect internalized social norms, derived from explicit injunctions and observed consistencies in significant others' behaviors. As Huesmann and Guerra (1997) put it, "Normative beliefs can be viewed as cognitive abstractions of knowledge acquired through observation, experience, and direct tuition" (p. 417).

Once these normative beliefs have been acquired, they have three types of effect on behavior. The first is to influence the salience and interpretation of situational cues: Cues that are relevant to normative beliefs are more likely to be attended to than ones that are irrelevant, and may be misinterpreted because of their relevance to normative beliefs. A second type of influence is on the retrieval of behavioral scripts: The existence of a normative belief makes it more likely that scripts consistent with that belief will be retrieved. The third sort of influence is on the regulation of behavior: Behaviors that are inconsistent with normative beliefs are likely to be inhibited.

Evidence of the impact of normative beliefs

Evidence that normative beliefs have an impact on behavior comes from longitudinal research by Huesmann and Guerra (1997). These authors developed a self-report measure of normative beliefs concerning aggression, administered this measure to 1,550 elementary school children (Time 1), retested 1,070 of these children 1 year later (Time 2), and took further measures on the remaining sample (N = 1,015) 2 years after the first wave (Time 3). In addition to normative beliefs, the researchers assessed peer-nominated aggression at Time 2 and Time 3.

Significant negative correlations between normative beliefs and peer-nominated aggression showed that children who disapproved of aggression less tended to be rated by peers as higher in aggression. This was true even for children in the youngest cohort. More important, normative beliefs about aggression as measured at Times 1 and 2 were a reliable predictor of peer-nominated aggression at Time 3 even after controlling for peer-nominated aggression at Time 2—but only for the older children in the sample. These findings therefore suggest that the internalization of norms may have delayed effects on emotional conduct that cannot be explained purely in terms of direct learning.

Interestingly, there was also some evidence that the youngest children's normative beliefs were influenced by their aggressive tendencies. In particular, aggression was a significant predictor of normative beliefs at Time 3 for this cohort, even after controlling for earlier (Time 2) normative belief and aggression scores. The most obvious explanation for this latter effect is that the younger children adjusted their still flexible beliefs to match their self-observed aggression for the purposes of justification or rationalization.

Summarizing the implications of these findings, Huesmann and Guerra (1997) conclude that:

> ... First graders develop normative beliefs on the basis of their own behavior and how it is reinforced; from observing others' behaviors; and from the direct tuition they receive from peers, parents, and others. Thus, their early normative beliefs are unstable, and their early behavior predicts their later beliefs. However, once their beliefs have become crystallized, they become resistant to change and thus more stable over time and less predictable over time from previous behaviors. At that point their beliefs predict their subsequent behaviors. (p. 417)

Generalizing these ideas and findings to the socialization of emotion rather than aggression, we suggest that parental reactions to children's emotional behavior, parental talk about emotion, and parental emotional expressiveness help children to develop normative beliefs about emotion and emotional behavior. These beliefs guide the children's later perceptions, evaluations, and actions in emotional settings.

Although children may explicitly reflect on their normative beliefs and respond to them in a deliberative way, more implicit and unselfconscious normative influences are also possible (see chapter 8). In this regard, Zelli, Huesmann, and Cervone (1995) found that aggressive people were more likely to make hostile attributions about nonhostile scenarios when they were under time pressure to make a judgment than when they were not. This finding may be explained by assuming that dispositional aggressiveness is associated with a spontaneous tendency to perceive the world as hostile that can only be suppressed in a controlled fashion when appropriate cognitive resources are available (Wegner, 1994). If these hostile perceptions are based on normative beliefs, the implication is that these beliefs typically aggravate aggression via a nonconscious route. More generally, normative beliefs about emotion may have the potential to influence children's own experience and expression of emotion without them necessarily being aware of this influence.

Norms and Emotion Socialization

The research on family socialization of emotion reviewed previously suggests that norms play an important part in the socialization process. It was suggested that through modeling and direct instruction, parents, siblings, and other family members can establish norms about what it is appropriate to feel or to express in emotional situations. Because families are the first social groups to which children are exposed, the norms they establish may be especially powerful ones. At the individual level, these norms may be conceptualized as normative beliefs—that is, internalized representations of appropriate and inappropriate feelings and behaviors. The implication is that family norms have the capacity to influence individuals even when other family members are not present, and when family membership is not salient.

However, to the extent that conflicting norms may be applicable in encounters with people from outside the family, there may also be some degree of flexibility in access to, and implementation of, these internalized norms. To some extent, their relative salience and appropriateness depends on the specifics of the current social situation. For example, aggression may be perceived as more acceptable when directed toward peers in a school playground than when expressed toward other family members while at home. However, the fact that family identities are often more longstanding, more habitual, and therefore less explicit probably means that the emotions that they shape are perceived as more natural and spontaneous. Again, any perception of emotional dissonance may reflect the relative priority of competing roles or the shifting salience of social identities.

Although this section has focused on norms that relate specifically to emotion, we do not wish to imply that these are the only family norms that have the capacity to influence the way in which individuals experience and express emotion. For example, children's appraisals of stimuli partly reflect the norms and beliefs instilled in a family context. Consistent appraisals within a family should in principle be associated with similar affective experiences, providing yet another example of group emotion.

☐ Conclusions

As we noted at the beginning of this chapter, the notion of a group emotion initially seems strange, because it conflicts with the commonsense assumption that the locus of emotional experience is the individual. However, in subsequent sections we have reviewed arguments and evidence in support of the view that the emotions experienced and expressed by individuals are influenced in important ways by their memberships of social groups.

Two concepts are central to understanding this influence of groups on the emotional lives of their members. The first is "identity." Membership of a social group offers individuals a basis for identity that extends beyond the self. If we accept Brown's (2000) idea that the essential prerequisite of a group is the self-categorization of individuals as group members and the recognition of this categorization by third parties, it follows that identity and identification are central to the group process. One first has to identify oneself as belonging to a certain group and, to the extent that such an identification is made, one's identity is colored by this group membership. In some circumstances, group memberships are likely to be especially important to the individual.

The more psychologically significant the group is for individuals, the more they will identify with the group, and the greater the impact of the group's norms on their thoughts, feelings, and behaviors is likely to be. However, we should not ignore the fact that the influence of a group on the emotional lives of its individual members is complemented by a reciprocal influence that individuals exert on the emotional character of the group. Indeed, the convergence of group affect is probably based on two complementary processes. The first involves group norms relating to emotion shaping each individual's feelings and expressions by a top-down process. The second involves the interpersonal influence of each group member on those with whom he or she interacts. The bottom-up coordination of emotion (working either by emotional contagion or the reciprocal negotiation of social appraisals; see chapter 6, this volume) consolidates lower-level interpretative, affective, or evaluative trends into shared group emotion. Of course, the relative priority of these two processes depends very much on the available modes of interaction between group members. In circumstances where communication is limited, the top-down normative influence of shared social identity is more likely to override any individual effervescence of affect.

Even when individual members do not identify strongly with a social group, the emotion norms espoused by that group are likely to exert some influence on their emotional experience and behavior, by helping to define what they should get emotional about and what the appropriate response is. As levels of identification increase, so too should the impact of the group on the individual. With high identification, the group's norms may become internalized so that they exert a more general, less situation-specific influence on experience and behavior. In particular, membership of what Greenwood (1994) calls intrinsically social groups should carry major implications for the emotional lives of their individual members because these groups specifically define their members' identity for them.

The second concept that is central to our understanding of a group's influence on its members' emotions is that of "norm." Thoits (2004) provides a comprehensive overview of evidence that emotions are governed by social expectations that both reflect and maintain the social structures in which they develop (see also chapter 8). One implication is that emotion norms vary not only in a "macro" way across time and cultural context (see chapter 2), but also in a "micro" way across social groups. Groups develop norms concerning the appropriateness of emotional experiences and expressions, and new members of social groups (such as children in families) are socialized explicitly or implicitly to observe these norms. However, the influence of these norms extends beyond the regulation of emotional expression and communication, and can penetrate to the experience of emotion. Here, too, identity has an important part to play, in that the impact of the normative requirements carried by (say) a work role are modulated by the extent to which the individual identifies with that role. If an employee identifies with her work role more strongly than with any other currently relevant identities, she should find it relatively easy to adopt the experiential as well as the expressive implications of that role. These are issues that we shall revisit in chapter 8.

Intergroup Emotion

As anyone who watches the news knows, relations between social groups often involve intense emotions. The most obvious examples are negative. In Northern Ireland, Catholics feel angry and resentful about their perceived mistreatment by Protestants. The present inhabitants of Gibraltar are fearful of Spain because they mistrust this powerful neighbor's intentions. Many Serbs in the former Yugoslavia felt contempt and hatred toward Muslims living in the same country. Of course, intergroup emotions with more positive implications are also possible. For example, Irish Americans might feel sympathy for Catholics in Northern Ireland because they identify with that group's suffering and regard it as unjust. Germans might feel guilty because of the despicable way that Jews were treated by their compatriots in the first half of the twentieth century. Supporters of a soccer team may feel happy about the achievement of another team if that success was achieved at the expense of a hated rival.

What all of these examples have in common is the fact that the feelings in question primarily depend on belonging to one group as opposed to another, and not on any individual disposition or behavior of anyone involved. Racists despise members of other racial groups not because they believe that any *individual* member of these groups has negative attributes or has done something reprehensible, but rather because they believe that *all* of them have these negative attributes or are prone to doing reprehensible things. People who feel guilty about their social group's behavior do not experience this guilt because of harm that they *personally* have inflicted on another group, but rather because they see members of their own group as having *collective* responsibility for the harm that has been done, and for making reparations.

☐ Defining Intergroup Emotion

In the interests of conceptual clarity, it may help to distinguish between the subject and object of an emotion, on the one hand, and whether the subject or object is an individual or a group, on the other. This results in the two-way table shown in Table 5.1.

The present chapter discusses emotions whose subject and object are both groups rather than individuals. Thus, we are clearly not concerned with emotions felt by individuals toward other individuals. Nor are the idiosyncratic emotions that a particular individual feels toward a social group relevant here. Emotions felt by groups toward individuals (e.g., the emotions felt by U.S. citizens toward Princess Diana) are group emotions like those discussed in the previous chapter but are no longer of concern in the present context. Rather, the emotions of specific interest in this chapter not only need to have their basis in this individual's membership of a group, but also need to take another group as their object. It is these collective emotions that are our current topic, and it is these alone that we are calling "intergroup emotions."

In reviewing theory and evidence concerning these intergroup emotions, our main contention is that they can only be understood by abandoning the notion that emotions are experienced by individuals because of things that have been done to them or by them as *individuals*. Rather, under certain conditions at least, emotions are experienced by individuals because of things that have been done to them or by them as members of *social groups*. In other words, the degree to which we define ourselves and others as group members, rather than as individuals, will play a major role in determining whether we experience an emotion, and in shaping what sort of emotion it is. As we shall see, emotions felt by members of one group toward members of another group have not always

TABLE 5.1. Interpersonal, Group, and Intergroup Emotions

Subject	Object	
	Individual	Group
Individual	Interpersonal emotions	Individual emotions directed toward a group
Group	Group emotions directed toward an individual	Intergroup emotions

been explained in these terms, although there is a gathering theoretical consensus that this is the most appropriate way of accounting for them.

Prejudice and Intergroup Hostility

There is substantial literature on the tendency to favor in-groups over out-groups (see Brewer, 2003). The present chapter is not concerned with those aspects of the literature that focus on in-group favoritism; rather, our focus will be on antipathy toward out-groups. Indeed, a preference for one's own group over another group can be explained in terms that have little or nothing to do with negative emotions felt toward that other group. However, there are also types of prejudice that are at least partly attributable to hostility directed at out-groups, and it is these that comprise the focus of the present section.

One type of emotion that is frequently aroused by the anticipation of interaction with out-group members is anxiety. Stephan and Stephan (1985) argued that the emotion experienced under these circumstances has the same cause as other types of anxiety, namely anticipated negative outcomes for oneself. These negative outcomes can range from simple uncertainty about how to behave when confronted with individuals with whom one cannot communicate smoothly or effectively (e.g., because they speak a different language or because they adhere to a different set of cultural practices or values) to a more profound lack of trust of the out-group's intentions.

A second type of emotion that is sometimes experienced in intergroup settings is anger, although most of the psychological research has tended to focus on just one of the ways in which this anger may be expressed, namely aggression. In its mildest form, this type of emotion may be experienced as little more than irritation or annoyance.

Emotions and Intergroup Attitudes

Evidence of the relation between emotions and intergroup attitudes comes from a study by Dijker (1987). He examined the emotions felt by indigenous Dutch people toward members of two ethnic minority groups: Surinamese and Turks–Moroccans. Using factor analysis, he found that these emotions could be grouped into four categories: anxiety, irritation, concern, and "positive mood." The anxiety category included fear, uncertainty, distrust, antipathy, and an action tendency involving keeping a distance from the out-group. The irritation category included annoyance, aversion, anger, contempt, and having unfriendly thoughts about the out-group. The concern category included worry and wishing that the out-group would move further away. Finally, the "positive mood" category included a range of pleasant emotions and feelings, including happiness, admiration, sympathy, liking, and an action tendency of seeking contact. Factor loadings were similar for both out-groups, and all four emotion categories were significantly associated with respondents' attitudes toward these out-groups, although positive mood was a somewhat stronger positive predictor of attitudes to Suri-namese, whereas irritation and concern were somewhat stronger negative predictors of attitudes to Turks–Moroccans.

Emotions and stereotypes

Fiske, Cuddy, and Glick (2002) have argued that there are two core dimensions of stereotype content, which they call competence and warmth, and that different combinations of competence–warmth appraisals result in different intergroup emotions. It is worth considering how Dijker's (1987) findings map onto Fiske and colleagues' hypothesized intergroup emotions. Fiske and colleagues propose that a unique intergroup emotion—contempt, pity, envy, or pride—will accompany each possible combination of high-low competence and warmth appraisals. Thus, groups stereotypically perceived to be low in competence and low in warmth (e.g., the homeless, the poor, welfare recipients) will arouse contempt emotions. Fiske and colleagues note that Dijker's finding that irritation emotions (which included contempt) were predictors of negative attitudes to Turks–Moroccans—but not to Surinamese—can be accounted for in terms of stereotypical perceptions of the Turks and Moroccans as low in both competence and warmth. Groups that are perceived as low in competence but high in warmth (e.g., the elderly, the mentally or physically disabled) will evoke pity. Although none of Dijker's categories maps cleanly onto this category, the one that comes closest is the positive emotions cluster, which included sympathy and seeking contact. The fact that these positive emotions were more predictive of attitudes to Surinamese than to Turks–Moroccans suggests that the former were perceived by at least some Dutch people as relatively high on the warmth dimension.

Groups that are perceived as high in competence but low in warmth (e.g., rich people) elicit envy. And groups that are perceived as high in both competence and warmth (e.g., middle-class Americans) arouse pride. Given Dijker's focus on Dutch attitudes to two ethnic minority groups, it is unsurprising that emotions reflecting high appraisals of competence were not observed in his study. It is interesting, however, to note that his anxiety and concern clusters do not map readily to Fiske and colleagues' analysis. We suggest that this is because Fiske and colleagues base their analysis on only two social structural variables, perceived relative status and perceived competition with one's own group. Perceived relative status determines how competent a group is seen to be, whereas perceived (lack of) competition determines how warm a group is seen to be.

What appears to be missing here is perceived power, in the sense of the ability of the out-group to threaten in-group concerns or values. In our view, variation on this dimension would shape perceptions of how threatening a group is regarded as being, which in turn should predict how much concern (low but nonnegligible perceived threat) or anxiety (relatively high threat) is aroused by the group. It is worth noting in this context that in Kramer and Jost's (2002) interesting analysis of "out-group paranoia" (high distrust and suspicion of another group), perceptions of threat and of (in-group) vulnerability are seen as playing a central role. It is the combination of dependence on the out-group and uncertainty about out-group trustworthiness that gives rise to these perceptions of vulnerability and threat, which in turn generate fear and anxiety.

Recasting prejudice as emotion

Dijker's (1987) study provides evidence that prejudice, a construct that is classically regarded as an *attitude*, can be recast in terms of emotion (see also Smith, 1993). The correlational nature of the data precludes firm conclusions about the causal relationship between experienced emotions and prejudiced attitudes. However, suggestive evidence arises from an analysis of the association between forms of contact with out-group members and the four emotion categories identified earlier. Certain forms of out-group contact were associated with more positive emotions and attitudes, especially in the case of the Surinamese. "Visiting each other," for example, was associated with more positive emotion, less concern, and a more positive attitude to Surinamese persons. By contrast, visiting was associated with more irritation and less positive attitudes to Turks–Moroccans. Dijker interpreted this differential pattern of associations in terms of cultural differences between the Dutch, on the one hand, and the two ethnic minority groups, on the other. Specifically, Surinamese persons living in the Netherlands are more likely to speak Dutch and to be closer to Dutch people on other cultural dimensions than are Turks or Moroccans. Drawing on theories of intergroup contact (e.g., Hewstone & Brown, 1986), Dijker suggested that increases in social interaction between members of two social groups are only beneficial under certain specific conditions.

Evidence consistent with this reasoning comes from a study of intergroup contact among Hindu and Muslim religious groups in Bangladesh, conducted by Islam and Hewstone (1993). In this research, the quality of contact between respondents and out-group members was related to reported feelings of anxiety during their intergroup interactions. More experiences of voluntary, pleasant, cooperative, and intimate contact with out-group members were associated with lower levels of anxiety. Additionally, lower anxiety was predictive of more positive attitudes toward the out-group. Applying these findings to Dijker's (1987) study, it seems possible that the magnitude of the cultural differences between Dutch and Turkish or Moroccan people meant that close contact with the latter was experienced as unpleasant (perhaps simply because of communicative difficulties), and thereby led to more negative attitudes to the out-group as a whole.

We will return to the relation between emotions concerning out-group contact and prejudiced attitudes later in this chapter. Our more immediate concern is with whether the emotions reported by Dijker's (1987) respondents were experienced primarily because of their own and others' group memberships. This is a matter that remained implicit in Dijker's study. Because the respondents were indigenous Dutch persons who were answering questions about two ethnic minority groups living in the Netherlands, it seems plausible that the social identities of the respondents and of minority group members were relatively salient. On the other hand, the respondents were told that the questionnaires were intended to assess the views different Amsterdam residents held about one another. It could be argued that this provided an inclusive social category (Amsterdam residents) that attenuated any tendency to categorize self (respondent) and target (Surinamese or Turkish–Moroccan) as members of different social groups.

☐ Self-Categorization and Intergroup Emotion

Smith (1993) has provided a theoretical analysis of prejudice as emotion that explicitly takes account of the extent to which self and target are treated as individuals or as group members. His starting point was self-categorization theory (SCT [Turner et al., 1987]), which holds that the relative salience of personal and social identity determines whether people see themselves more as individuals or as group members, respectively (see chapter 4). Factors that increase the salience of social identity include the presence (including the imagined presence) of an out-group, competition with that out-group, and the perception that attributes (e.g., opinions, physical characteristics, behaviors) covary with group membership. Exposure to these factors thus means that you will think of yourself not as a unique individual but as a member of the group whose social identity (e.g., as a lawyer, female, Spaniard, or supporter of a particular football team) has been made salient, and as having attributes that are typical for that group.

Once a self-categorization as a group member has been made, the individual will tend to perceive intragroup similarities and intergroup differences as greater than they objectively are, and also to think and act in ways that confirm the similarities within the in-group and its distinctiveness from out-groups. A natural consequence of defining your own identity in terms of a social group is that you will care more about what happens to the group and you will be more motivated to act on the group's behalf than you would if you had categorized yourself as an individual. Here lies the significance of SCT for group-based emotion: Self-categorization as a group member should promote the experience of emotions that are driven by appraisals and concerns that are *group*-based rather than *individual*-based (see also chapter 4).

Basking in Reflected Glory

If your personal identity is salient, the success or failure of a given football team is likely to have little impact on your emotion; however, if your social identity as a supporter of that football team is salient, the selfsame success or failure of that team may lead to exhilaration or crushing disappointment. A well-known study of the phenomenon of "basking in reflected glory" (Cialdini et al., 1976) showed that students at seven North American universities were more likely to wear clothing carrying insignia of their college or its football team on days following this team's victories than on days following defeats. Note that most of these football fans had played no personal role in their team's winning performance. Thus, the only possible explanation for their self-congratulatory feelings is that they defined themselves in part in terms of the team, so that the team's successes were also their own. Or, as Smith (1993) put it:

> We should . . . consider that when group membership is salient, the group functions as part of the self, and therefore that situations appraised as self-relevant trigger emotions just as they always do. Because the self is not limited by the skin, neither are emotions. (p. 303)

Group-Based Appraisals

Smith (1993) argued that combining conventional appraisal theories of emotion (see chapter 1, or Scherer, Schorr, & Johnstone, 2001 for a more comprehensive overview) with SCT provides a basis for predicting the kinds of emotions that members of a group are likely to experience. More specifically, he proposed that

> *to the extent that a self-categorization functions as a self-aspect, appraisals of events or situations with respect to that social aspect of identity will also trigger emotions.* Thus, in-group successes will lead to joy, threats to the in-group to fear, and injustices suffered by the in-group to anger. (p. 303, original emphasis)

Further, if these emotion-eliciting events (successes, threats, injustices) depend on an out-group's characteristics or conduct, then they will lead to intergroup rather than simply group emotions. Smith's (1993) translation of appraisal theory to the group level implies that intergroup emotions are the products of group-relevant appraisals of out-group events—such as the belief that public money is being unfairly spent on asylum seekers, thereby limiting the amount of money that is available for spending on the in-group. Such appraisals lead to negative emotions, such as anger. These emotions are in turn associated with out-group directed action tendencies that are also negative (e.g., aggressive actions against asylum seekers).

Testing Smith's Model

Smith's (1993) model was tested in three studies reported by Mackie, Devos, and Smith (2000). These researchers tested the hypothesis that in-group members would experience anger and report aggressive action tendencies toward out-group members if they appraised the in-group as strong relative to the out-group. In all three studies, strength was operationalized in terms of the perceived level of agreement in the broader society for the in-group's position on a group-defining issue of opinion ("collective support"). For example, a Labour party supporter might appraise her group's position as strong if she felt that most members of the general population also agreed with Labour policies.

In the first study, participants categorized themselves as members of one of two groups depending on whether they opposed or supported harsh punishment for users of illegal drugs. They then rated how strongly they identified with these two contrasting opinion groups, how much collective support they thought there was for the two groups, and the emotions and action tendencies they felt toward the out-group. The results showed that appraisal of collective support and group identification (i.e., how strongly participants identified with their own opinion group) together predicted both anger felt toward the out-group and willingness to take on members of the out-group by confronting, opposing, or arguing with them.

Studies 2 and 3 extended these findings by explicitly manipulating per-ceptions of collective support. In Study 2, participants categorized them-selves as being either in favor of or opposed to homosexual couples having equal rights to those of heterosexual couples, and in Study 3, they classified themselves as being for or against harsh punishment for users of illegal drugs. In both studies, perceived support for the in-group opinion on the issue in question was manipulated by presenting participants with newspaper headlines that were either mainly supportive of this position (strong support), or mainly unsupportive (weak support). Feelings of anger toward the out-group and associated action tendencies were found to be consistently greater for participants in the strong support condition, and anger was shown to mediate the effect on action tendencies.

A limitation of these studies is that only one aspect of appraisal was examined, namely the perception of in-group strength. According to Smith's (1993) extension of appraisal theory, however, five separate appraisals underpin the experience of anger as a social or group-based emotion. Not only must the out-group be perceived as weak relative to the in-group before anger is experienced, but its behavior must also be appraised as inconsistent with the in-group's goals, unfair, intentional, and as leading to consequences that are certain. The fact that Mackie and colleagues' (2000) studies only examined the first of these appraisal dimensions leaves the role of the other four dimensions unclear. Further, although the authors clearly believe that collective support influenced the *experience* of anger toward the out-group, an equally plausible inter-pretation of their results is that participants felt more willing to *communi-cate* their anger because they perceived that their audience would be more receptive. In other words, participants may have been less reluctant to say that the other group made them feel angry, displeased, and so on, and that they wanted to confront or oppose the out-group, when they knew that others were likely to agree with their position.

☐ Out-Group Images and Intergroup Emotions

A different but not incompatible approach to the issue of treating preju-dice as intergoup emotion has been offered by Brewer and colleagues (Brewer and Alexander, 2002; Alexander, Brewer, & Herrmann, 1999). Drawing on theory in the field of international relations, they examine the implications of having a certain *image* of the out-group. Boulding (1959) defined an "image" as a cognitive, affective, and evaluative structure, and suggested that "the images which are important in international systems are those which a nation has of itself and of those other bodies in the system which constitute its international environment" (pp. 120–121). Developing this concept further, Herrmann (1985) argued that images form as a consequence of strategic relationships between nations, and serve corresponding functions. Similarly, appraisals of the relationship between in-group and out-group may give rise to specific images of the out-group that justify and account for the in-group's affective and behavioral orientation toward that group.

The focus in image theory, then, is on the way in which perceptions of intergroup relations shape the image that the in-group forms of the out-group. This suggests that image theory should provide useful pointers regarding the sorts of appraisals that are relevant to the formation of out-group images, and the emotions that correspond to these appraisals. This is the line of reasoning followed by Brewer and Alexander (2002). They identify five images arising from different forms of in-group–out-group relationship. A summary of these images and their associated appraisals, action tendencies, and emotions is shown in Table 5.2.

The key idea underlying this application of image theory to intergroup emotion is that it is the character of the relationship between in-group and out-group (shown in the table as "appraisal pattern") that determines how members of the in-group want to act toward the out-group (shown in the table as "action tendencies"), what image they have of the out-group, and what emotions they feel toward out-group members.

TABLE 5.2. The Association of Images, Appraisals, Action Tendencies, and Emotions (adapted from Brewer & Alexander, 2002)

Out-Group Image	Appraisal Pattern	Action Tendencies	Emotion(s)
Ally	Goal compatibility Status equality Power equality	Cooperation	Trust Admiration
Enemy	Goal incompatibility Status equality Power equality	Containment or Attack	Anger
Dependent	Goal independent Status inferiority Power inferiority	Exploitation or Paternalism	Disgust Contempt
Barbarian	Goal incompatibility Status inferiority Power superiority	Defensive protection	Fear Intimidation
Imperialist	Goal independent Status superiority Power superiority	Resistance or Rebellion	Jealousy Resentment

Experimental Tests of Image Theory

This idea was initially tested by Alexander, Brewer and Herrmann (1999) in a series of three experiments. Participants were invited to imagine themselves in situations in which they were a member of an in-group in a situation that also involved an out-group. The relationship between the groups was varied by providing information about goal compatibility, relative status, and relative power. These appraisal manipulations were found to influence both the images that participants formed of the out-group and their action tendencies toward the out-group. The nature of these effects was consistent with what would be expected on the basis of Table 5.2. Moreover, when an implicit measure of image activation was used, there was evidence that appraisal patterns could influence images without the individual being aware of this influence.

A Field Test of Image Theory

In a field test, Brewer and Alexander (2002) examined whether image theory would be supported in a more concrete, everyday-life setting. They also took the opportunity to include measures of emotion in this study. The setting in which they conducted their research was an urban North American high school, and the intergroup issue at stake was the relation between Blacks and Whites. Appraisals of the intergroup relationship, images of the out-group, and emotions were assessed by means of a questionnaire completed by Black and White high school students. The two groups were agreed in seeing the goals of the groups as somewhat incompatible, and in regarding the status of Whites in the United States as higher than that of Blacks. However, there were somewhat divergent views of the power of the two groups. Blacks were more inclined to see Whites as having greater power than Blacks, especially power of the political and economic variety. Whites were more inclined to see Blacks as gaining power. According to image theory, these appraisals should have led Whites to perceive Blacks in terms of the barbarian image, and Blacks to perceive Whites in terms of the imperialist image. The results were consistent with these predictions. The pattern of reported emotions was also broadly consistent with image theory. In particular, the most distinctive out-group emotion reported by Whites was that of fear–intimidation, whereas the most distinctive out-group emotion reported by Blacks was anger–resentment. Further, correlational analysis showed that White respondents' perceptions that Blacks were gaining power were associated with greater endorsement of the barbarian image and greater fear of the out-group. Although there was a tendency for Black respondents' perceptions of relatively greater White power to be linked to endorsement of the enemy or imperialist images, there was no systematic relationship between out-group emotions and out-group images among Black respondents.

These are interesting findings that deserve to be extended by further research using different intergroup contexts and different methodologies. Although not all of the results are consistent with image theory, they mainly suggest that out-group emotions can be explained at least partly in terms of perceptions of the relationship between the two groups' goals, and their relative power and status. The most obvious limitation of the study is that the nature of the relationships between appraisals, images, and emotions remains unclear. The researchers explicitly assume that it is the appraisals that drive the other two variables, although they are less clear about the causal relation between images and emotions. Questions about the dependence of appraisals, images, and emotions on actual, rather than perceived, differences and changes in power (see chapter 8) are also worthy of further attention.

Images as studied by Brewer and Alexander (2002) can be seen as encapsulated patterns of appraisals, much like Lazarus' (1991a) "core relational themes." In the same way that Lazarus saw these themes as antecedents of emotional reactions, Brewer and Alexander would presumably want to argue that the evoked image of the out-group drives the emotion, rather than the other way around. A possible weakness with such an argument is that it assumes a rather rational view of intergroup emotions. Just as Sherif's (1966) "realistic conflict theory" regarded hostility toward out-groups as the product of perceived intergroup competition for a limited resource, image theory appears to be arguing that emotions felt toward the out-group are the product of perceptions of the quality of the intergroup relationship. Indeed, as in realistic conflict theory, these perceptions may even relate specifically to the question of whether the in-group's goals are compatible or incompatible with those of the out-group. The possibility that out-group emotions and images are established by means of a noncognitive route (such as classical conditioning), and that appraisals of the relationship between the two groups are shaped by these emotions or images, passes largely unacknowledged by image theory.

☐ Emotional Dialogue Between Social Groups

Another way of extending Brewer and Alexander's research would be to investigate the degree to which the emotions of in-groups and out-groups develop as a function of an intergroup "dialogue." In particular, it seems likely that emotions directed toward another group will provoke emotional reactions from that group and so on. If members of group A perceive themselves to be the object of group B's contempt, for example, this may well reinforce their feelings of resentment toward this out-group. In this way, the perceived emotion of the out-group may bolster its negative image in the eyes of the in-group. Positive dialogues are also conceivable, of course: Imagine that group B has previously felt resentful about group A's exploitative or paternalistic treatment of its members; now, however, group A expresses remorse and guilt for this behavior; these expressions of intergroup guilt might evoke forgiveness on the part of group B, which in turn elicits gratitude on the part of group A, and so on.

A theoretical approach to the study of intergroup emotion that is relevant to this possibility of "emotional dialogue" between groups is the one developed by Leyens, Demoulin, Desert, Vaes, and Philippot (2002). They argue that researchers need to take more account of how the expression and decoding of emotions is influenced by the intergroup context. They show, for example, that emotions are expressed differently to in-group and out-group audiences. When posing expressions, people believe that they provide clearer and more readable displays for an out-group audience, but in fact independent judges find that expressions delivered to an in-group audience reveal more about the intended emotion. To the extent that these findings are generalizable, they suggest that intergroup relations are likely to be permeated by emotional misunderstanding. People wrongly believe that their emotions should be highly transparent to out-group members, and when these out-group members fail to respond appropriately, this may generate frustration. Members of the first group will be inclined to attribute insensitivity to the out-group; members of the out-group will be inclined to regard such attributions as misplaced. Further, the out-group's emotional response will not get through to the in-group as intended either, leading to an exacerbation of the communication breakdown. As Leyens et al. (2002) put it,

> Such misunderstanding will lead to the fact that the interaction will not be pleasant, that the anxiety usually present in any relation with strangers will probably increase, that the members of the different groups will fear other interactions, and that they may avoid or refuse subsequent encounters. This cycle of consequences will contribute to reinforce existing prejudice and discrimination from both sides. (p.141)

Perceptions of other groups' emotions may also be influenced by our stereotypes about what their members typically experience, or are even capable of experiencing. In this regard, Leyens and colleagues (2001) have argued that people sometimes have a tendency to regard out-group members as somehow less human than in-group members, and as correspondingly lacking in distinctively human emotions such as sympathy, shame, and remorse. Thus, the "images" of a variety of out-groups might be distorted by the failure to fully appreciate their basic humanity: They might be seen not only as barbarians, for example, but also as barbarous animals. Coupled with the misperceptions of out-group expressions outlined above, this so-called infrahumanizing tendency might lead in-group members to overattribute animalistic emotions (fear, hate, etc.) to the members of other groups, and respond with retaliatory feelings and expressions of their own.

However, before we get carried away with such pessimistic implications, it is important to note that there are obvious limits to the reported effects of infrahumanization. For one thing, it is certainly not the case that all out-groups are treated as less than human under all possible circumstances. For example, men do not usually see women as less capable than themselves of finer feelings (Viki & Abrams, 2003). Further, questions remain about whether the preferential attribution of supposedly "human" emotions to in-groups can be seen merely as another instance of simple favoritism. If some emotions are considered to be signs of better character than others, it is perhaps not so surprising that, on average, we tend to see ourselves as having them to a greater extent than others. In none of the existing studies have participants gone beyond such relative judgments and explicitly stated that members of other groups are literally incapable of experiencing human emotions under any circumstances.

☐ Intergroup Anger

Relative Deprivation

As we have seen, one way of explaining the angry feelings of members of one social group toward members of another social group is in terms of appraisals of goal compatibility, relative power, and relative status. A long history of social scientific research on *relative deprivation* (RD) is relevant to this issue. Relative deprivation refers to the sense of injustice and the associated feelings of resentment and anger that arise from the perception that one has less than one deserves, relative to others. The important issue, then, is not how much one has in absolute terms, but how much one has relative to others.

As originally conceived, RD is a construct that applies at the individual level of analysis: What are my personal outcomes, relative to the outcomes of others? However, Runciman (1966) introduced the notion of *fraternal deprivation* to describe the perception that the outcomes of one's in-group as a whole are less than those of other groups. These two types of RD have come to be referred to as personal RD and group RD, respectively. It is, of course, group RD that is more relevant to the concerns of the present chapter.

The main focus of research on group RD has been to explain willingness to engage in collective behavior, such as protesting or going on strike. Relatively little attention has been paid to the feelings that are generated by a sense of group RD. In this regard, H. Smith, Pettigrew, and Vega (1994) reported a meta-analytic review of the RD literature in which they assessed how well the RD construct accounted for variations in collective behavior, individual behavior, and internal states. They found some evidence that group-level emotions play an important role. For example, measures of RD that included an assessment of feelings (e.g., anger and resentment) were better predictors of collective behavior, individual behavior, and internal states such as depression and self-esteem than were measures of RD that did not include any affect items. Although in one sense these are unsurprising results, given that group RD is defined partly as a sense of anger or resentment resulting from the comparison of in-group and out-group outcomes, they also suggest that the feelings generated by such comparisons play an important role in accounting for their effects. These comparisons can arouse anger and resentment, and when they do so they have a greater impact on the way that people think and behave.

Anger on Behalf of Other In-Group Members

Another perspective on intergroup anger is offered by Gordijn, Wigboldus, and Yzerbyt (2001). These investigators presented university students with written scenarios that described an out-group intentionally performing an action with unfair consequences for someone other than the self (a student from a different university). They predicted that more anger would be reported in such situations when the victims of the out-group's behavior are categorized as members of the respondent's in-group. Two experimental conditions were compared. In the first, participants were told that the study was an investigation of differences in impression formation between students at different universities, thereby rendering salient the *differences* in category membership of victims and perceivers. In the second, participants were told that the purpose of the research was to investigate differences in impression formation between students and professors, thereby rendering salient the *common* category membership (i.e., students) of victims and perceivers. A third, control condition, was simply described as a study of impression formation.

As predicted, perceivers were significantly angrier when similarity of category membership had been made salient. This suggests that perceivers' categorization of the victims as in-group members led them to regard the unfair and deliberate behavior of out-group members as "self-relevant," even though this behavior did not directly affect them personally. However, there was no direct evidence that it was this categorization process *per se* that was responsible for the observed differences between conditions. Another possibility is that the manipulation of similarity encouraged perceivers to empathize more with the plight of the victims, and that this difference in empathy in turn produced the variation in reported anger. In either case, the findings suggest that it is possible to feel angry about the behavior of a social group even if that behavior has no negative consequences for oneself.

Further support for such a conclusion comes from a study by Yzerbyt, Dumont, Gordijn, and Wigboldus (2000). Using a similar research strategy to the study described above, these researchers manipulated perceived similarity with the victims and also assessed the strength of identification with the social category to which participants and victims belonged (i.e., students). Participants then read what purported to be a newspaper article stating that the governing board of another Belgian university (Gent) had decided to make English the sole language of tuition for third, fourth, and fifth year students, and had done so in a way that was likely to arouse anger. Participants rated their anger as strongest when their similarity with the victims had been made salient, and when they identified closely with the student category. A similar pattern of results was obtained for self-reported action tendencies associated with anger, such as "moving against" the perpetrator. Although these findings fail to rule out an explanation in terms of differential empathy, they do show that identification with the victims' social category plays a role in shaping how one responds to actions committed against them, and thereby strengthen a theoretical account that is centered on shared social identity.

☐ Intergroup Guilt

Guilt Without Personal Responsibility

The notion that emotions can be experienced simply as a function of shared social identity was also studied in Doosje, Branscombe, Spears, and Manstead's (1998) research into the experience of intergroup guilt. These authors examined the impact on guilt feelings of increasing the salience of the in-group's history of exploiting another group. They succeeded in inducing different levels of group-based guilt by manipulating the past behavior of the in-group toward an out-group using both preexisting and artificially created groups. Study 1 used the minimal group paradigm (Tajfel, Flament, Billig, & Bundy, 1971) in which participants identify with a social category that is created *de novo* in the laboratory. In this case, participants were led to believe that they belonged to the category of "inductive thinkers," and were then invited to evaluate products that had supposedly been made either by the in-group or the out-group (i.e., "deductive thinkers"). They then learned that their in-group had displayed either a high or a low level of bias in these evaluations, and also that their personal level of bias was either high or low.

The critical condition, of course, was the one in which there was a high level of bias on the part of the group but a low level of personal bias. In this condition, collective guilt (measured using items such as "I feel guilty about the negative things inductive thinkers have done to deductive thinkers") was especially high. In other words, when participants were led to believe that they had not personally acted in a harmful way toward the out-group, but that their group had done so, they were especially prone to report group-based guilt. A similar pattern of effects was observed on a measure of the belief that it would be appropriate to compensate the out-group. Further, there was evidence that group-based guilt mediated the effects on this latter measure of the appropriateness of compensation. These findings therefore suggest that feelings of guilt arise from a group-based appraisal of collective responsibility for harming the out-group, and that this guilt is therefore appropriately described as a genuine "intergroup emotion."

The Importance of Identification

In their second study, Doosje and colleagues (1998) examined the collective guilt experienced by Dutch citizens as a result of how their own national group had treated an out-group (Indonesians) during the colonial era. Participants were asked to read a historical account of Dutch treatments of the Indonesians, which described how Dutch people had done good things, bad things, or a mixture of good and bad things. As might be anticipated, collective guilt was rated as higher when Dutch people's treatment of Indonesians was presented in negative terms than when it was presented in positive or mixed terms.

The central hypotheses of this study concerned the impact of participants' levels of Dutch national identification. Although group-based guilt must by definition depend on identifying with the relevant group of wrongdoers, high levels of identification may lead to a defensive denial that any wrong has been perpetrated in the first place. Thus, this study predicted that those who identified themselves most strongly with the Dutch national identity would report *less* collective guilt, but only when the historical treatment of the Indonesians by the Dutch was described in mixed positive and negative terms. If the information about their own group's history was unequivocally negative, both low and high identifiers should feel more guilty than when the information was unequivocally positive. In neither condition was there any ambiguity about whether treatment of the Indonesians was good or bad. However, when both positive and negative aspects of Dutch history were presented, there was more scope for selective interpretation. Here high identifiers should be more defensive than low identifiers, because the mixed information allowed them to attach more weight to its positive aspects. As a consequence, high identifiers should be less willing to accept group-based guilt than should low identifiers. This was precisely what was found in this study. Further, these effects on group-based guilt also mediated corresponding effects on perceptions about the appropriateness of compensating Indonesians for the ill treatment that they had received at the hands of previous generations of Dutch people.

Self-Focus Versus Other-Focus

The research reported by Doosje and colleagues (1998) suggests that an in-group's guilt leads to positive outcomes for a disadvantaged out-group because it strengthens their approval of compensatory action. A more skeptical assessment of the benefits of group-based guilt is offered by Iyer, Leach, and Crosby (2003). They studied "White guilt," the negative emotion experienced by European Americans who regard their own group as responsible for their unfair advantage over other ethnic groups, such as African Americans (Steele, 1990). Iyer and colleagues argue that collective guilt has three characteristics: First, it implies acceptance of responsibility for violating a moral standard; second, it involves a focus on the in-group rather than the out-group; and third, it engenders a desire to make restitution to the disadvantaged group(s), through apology or compensation.

Iyer and colleagues (2003) contrast this *self-focused* desire to make restitution with a more *other-focused* desire to offer practical help to members of the disadvantaged group(s), through programs such as affirmative action. The difference between these two orientations can be summarized as victim compensation, on the one hand, and equalization of opportunities, on the other. According to Iyer and colleagues, the latter orientation is most likely to be stimulated by sympathy, because this emotion focuses attention on the disadvantaged group's suffering, rather than on the advantaged group's responsibility. Focusing on an out-group's suffering is more likely to make in-group members want to make things better for that out-group.

Intergroup Guilt and Reparation

Iyer and colleagues (2003) report two studies that specifically addressed the issue of intergroup reparation. In the first, they examined whether White guilt is based on the belief that Whites are privileged (self-focus) or the belief that African Americans are disadvantaged (other-focus). In the second study they examined whether the self-focused belief that Whites discriminate elicits stronger White guilt and weaker White sympathy than does the other-focused belief that African Americans are the victims of discrimination. A further objective was to see whether White guilt was associated with support for compensation, and White sympathy with support for attempts to reduce inequality.

In Study 1, participants (who were all European Americans) answered questions concerning their beliefs about White privilege, attitudes toward discrimination against African Americans, strength of White guilt, and support for measures to compensate African Americans. The results confirmed the view of White guilt as a self-focused emotion, based on the belief that Whites are privileged. In particular, believing that African Americans are discriminated against did not predict White guilt. Further, White guilt was found to be a reliable predictor of support for compensatory action.

Study 2 manipulated whether participants focused on European American perpetration or African American suffering by adjusting the wording of questionnaire items assessing beliefs about present-day racial discrimination. For example, one item in the self-focus condition read, "Many White employers are racially biased in their hiring and promotion practices," whereas in the other-focus condition the equivalent item read, "Many Black employees face racial bias when they apply for jobs or are up for promotion." Participants also rated their levels of guilt, sympathy, and support for compensatory and equal opportunity forms of affirmative action. The results showed that self-focus led to greater feelings of guilt, whereas other-focus led to greater feelings of sympathy. Guilt predicted support for compensatory affirmative action, but not equal opportunity affirmative action, whereas sympathy predicted support for equal opportunity affirmative action and was a marginal predictor of support for compensatory affirmative action.

The authors were led to conclude that "White guilt motivates support solely for compensatory policy, and is overall a less consistent predictor of racial policy support than is group-based sympathy" (p. 125). This conclusion is consistent with Steele's (1990) argument that White guilt is a poor basis for support for affirmative action because it "makes the problems of Black students seem secondary to the need for White redemption" (p. 99).

Harvey and Oswald (2000) also report data suggesting that collective White guilt in and of itself is not a sufficient basis for support for Black programs. Indeed, their results showed that exposure to guilt-inducing material (a civil rights videotape) only led to an increase in such support when participants were allowed to engage in a self-affirmation task (see Steele & Liu, 1983) prior to the assessment of this support. The authors speculate that affirming positive qualities of personal identity may have served to individuate participants and to protect the personal self from the threat posed to the collective self, thereby facilitating prosocial behavior.

Group-based guilt as a basis for social action

McGarty, Pedersen, Leach, Mansell, Waller and Bliuc (in press) studied the extent to which group-based guilt can be a stimulus to social and political action. The context of this research was the relationship between non-Indigenous Australians and the Indigenous Australian people who have been mistreated over many years. A fierce debate has raged in Australia between supporters and opponents of the view that the Australian government should make a formal apology to Indigenous Australians for the harm done to them. Polling data cited by McGarty et al. show that in 2000 roughly 52% of the Australian population was opposed to an official apology. McGarty and his colleagues were interested in studying the predictors of support for such an apology.

In a first study they examined whether perceived in-group advantage and group-based guilt were related to support for an official apology by the federal government. They classified potential predictors into three groups: *distal* sociodemographic predictors, such as age and gender; *intermediate* predictors, in the form of perceived in-group advantage; and *proximal* predictors, in the form of group-based guilt. These variables were assessed in a sample of 164 residents of Perth, Western Australia. Support for a federal apology was regressed onto the three groups of predictors, which were entered hierarchically in the above order, from distal to proximal. Among the first block of predictors, men and those who supported right-wing political parties were less supportive of an apology. After taking account of demographic variables, it was found that perceiving non-Indigenous Australians as advantaged relative to Indigenous Australians was associated with greater support for an official apology. Finally, after taking both distal and intermediate predictors into account, group-based guilt was also found to be predictive of support for an apology, such that greater guilt was associated with greater support. Further analyses showed that the association between perceived in-group advantage and support for an apology was significantly attenuated when group-based guilt was also used as a predictor, although the mediation was partial rather than full. The association between gender and support for right-wing political parties, on the one hand, and less support for an official apology, on the other, was fully mediated by group-based guilt, suggesting that being a male and supporting a right-wing political party were predictive of less support for an official apology because they predicted less group-based guilt about the harm done to Indigenous Australians.

Consistent with the findings of Doosje et al. (1998), then, McGarty and colleagues found in this first study that guilt was strongly associated with support for an official government apology. In a second study, the researchers examined the antecedents of group-based guilt in predicting personal and collective apologies. Here they tested a "core model" in which they argue that the belief that harm has been done to an out-group, and that the in-group is responsible for this harm, give rise to group-based guilt on the part of in-group members, which in turn predicts support for apology. They also examined the extent to which group identification leads to avoidance of guilt, as found by Doosje et al. (1998, Study 2). Non-Indigenous Australians who are highly identified as Australians might feel less guilt and be less likely to support an apology because to do so would be threatening or embarrassing to the in-group. The authors also examined two other ways in which high identifiers might avoid guilt or they felt need to apologize: first, by attacking the idea of collective guilt, arguing that it is inappropriate to feel guilty about something for which you were not personally responsible; and second, by raising doubts about the wisdom of apologizing on the grounds that it might be very costly, in financial terms, because it may help to establish legal liability for the harm that was done.

These issues were examined in a sample of 116 non-Indigenous Australians living in the Australian Capital Territory. Analyses of their responses provided strong support for a slightly modified version of the researchers' core model. Believing that non-Indigenous Australians were responsible for the harsh treatment of Indigenous Australians was a significant predictor of group-based guilt, and this guilt was predictive of support for apologizing at both the personal and the governmental level. Strength of identification as Australian was not a predictor of group-based guilt or apology, although it was positively and significantly (albeit quite weakly in absolute terms) associated with doubts about group-based guilt and with the perceived cost of an apology, which in turn *were* predictors of group-based guilt and support for apology, respectively. In this second study, then, the researchers again found that group-based guilt was a powerful predictor of support for a government apology to Indigenous Australians. The authors note that the findings emphasize the importance of the role of group-based guilt as a predictor of behavioral intentions and political attitudes.

With regard to the role of identification, McGarty et al.'s (in press) second study raises some interesting issues. As we saw earlier, Doosje et al. (1998) found that high identifiers appeared to be more defensive in their interpretation of group history when the presented evidence about that history is ambiguous, and that this was reflected in lower feelings of group-based guilt. In McGarty et al's Study 2, strength of identification had no direct association with group-based guilt, although it was predictive of doubts about group-based guilt, which in turn did predict such guilt. In comparing these two sets of findings, certain issues are worth bearing in mind. First, McGarty et al. note that identification as Australian was on average quite high and had little variance. This raises the possibility that restriction of range may have limited the capacity of this measure to predict other variables. A second point, acknowledged by McGarty et al., is that national identification can mean different things across and even within different national contexts. For example, the meaning of being 'an Australian' may shift according to one's political and sub-cultural allegiances, such that both pro- and anti-apology respondents can equally strongly identify themselves as 'Australian' simply by focusing on different facets of national identity. A third point is that Doosje et al. only found that high identifiers reported less group-based guilt when the information about the history of the group relationship was ambiguous. When the information was unambiguous (whether it was favorable or unfavorable), there was no difference in guilt between high and low identifiers.

A comment on the limits of group-based guilt

As we have seen, there are apparently conflicting views about the extent to which group-based guilt is an emotion that is beneficial to the disadvantaged out-group. The findings of Doosje et al. (1998) and McGarty et al. (in press) suggest that there are benefits to the disadvantaged group, in that willingness to compensate the out-group for past wrongdoing and support for an apology to the out-group for past wrongdoing are both positively associated with group-based guilt. On the other hand, the findings of Iyer et al. (2003) and Harvey and Oswald (2000) suggest that group-based guilt is of limited benefit to the disadvantaged outgroup, in that it fails to predict support for Black programs such as affirmative action.

It is worth remembering that there are some important differences between the intergroup situations studied by Iyer and colleagues (2003) and by Harvey and Oswald (2000), on the one hand, and the one studied by Doosje and colleagues (1998) and by McGarty and colleagues (in press) on the other. Most obviously, Iyer and colleagues and Harvey and Oswald are concerned with current inequality, namely White–Black relations in the United States. The relations between these groups have deep historical roots, of course, but the point is that those who participated in these studies could in principle regard *themselves* as guilty of prejudiced attitudes and/or discriminatory behavior. Although the Dutch–Indonesian situation studied by Doosje and colleagues is one that continues into the present day, the focus of that study was on Dutch people's behavior during the colonial period that ended in 1949. For this reason, the participants in this study could not have regarded themselves as personally responsible for any of those actions. Furthermore, the minimal group procedure used in Doosje et al.'s first study manipulated group discrimination and personal discrimination independently, and found that group-based guilt was greatest when participants were led to feel that their group had behaved badly toward the out-group, even though they themselves had not done so. In the case of the McGarty et al. (in press) study, the government apology to Indigenous Australians that was the focus of the research is clearly in relation to past actions. Moreover, the measure of group-based guilt used in Study 2 refers to guilt about harm done to Indigenous Australians in the nineteenth century—although it is also worth noting that the guilt measure in Study 1 is less clearly focused on past wrongs.

It may well be that the self-focused and aversive nature of guilt is greater when members of an advantaged group think that they themselves could in principle be partly responsible for the disadvantages suffered by the out-group. When this personal responsibility is ruled out, as in the case of historical maltreatment by previous generations, group-based guilt may be less self-focused and less personally painful. Under these conditions, group-based guilt may be more likely to promote attitudes and actions that reflect a concern with improving the lot of the disadvantaged group, and not simply a need to unburden the negative affect of the advantaged group. Further work is needed in order to examine this possibility.

A final issue relating to the political consequences of group-based guilt is that there seems to be no simple relation between guilt and the precise form of reparation that is motivated. Doosje et al. (2004) examined how group-based guilt depended on the extent to which the dominant group has made financial compensation rather than apologized for its behavior. Low in-group identifiers felt less guilt when they were told that their government had apologized for the harm done to the out-group. High identifiers, by contrast, felt less guilt when they were told that their government had made a financial payment to compensate for past wrongs. These findings imply that the same state of group-based guilt motivated different types of reparation for high and low identifiers.

It is tempting to conclude that those who are most threatened by the negative aspects of their own group's past (high identifiers) are keen to find a way of repairing the damage that does not undermine the group's identity, and therefore favor financial compensation, which entails no admission of wrongdoing. On the other hand, those less threatened by an admission of wrongdoing (low identifiers) are keener on acknowledging this wrongdoing, presumably because apologies implicitly recognize and reaffirm the legitimacy of the moral standards that were violated, and thereby reduce the possibility of future violations of a similar kind. However, more research is needed before firm conclusions can be drawn about the consequences of group-based guilt.

☐ Intergroup Fear

As we have seen above, the role played by self-categorization as a member of a social group is central to the issue of intergroup emotion. To the extent that one classifies oneself as belonging to a group, one experiences emotions simply because of that classification. Without this self-categorization, the emotions would not make sense. Thus, one can feel guilty about the actions of others because one is associated with those others through common group membership. One can feel anger toward someone who acts unreasonably and to the detriment of others if one regards those others as fellow in-group members, despite the fact that no harm has been done to oneself. Precisely the same reasoning has been used by Dumont, Yzerbyt, Wigboldus, and Gordijn (2002) to analyze fear in relation to the events of September 11, 2001.

One week after the terrorist attacks on New York and Washington, DC, these investigators conducted two experiments, one in Belgium and the other in the Netherlands. In Experiment 1, identification with the victims of these attacks was manipulated by presenting the study as a comparison of the reactions to these atrocities of either Westerners and Arabs (in-group identification) or Europeans and Americans (no in-group identification). It was reasoned that categorizing the victims as members of an in-group rather than members of an out-group should increase feelings of fear. Self-reports of anger, sadness, and calmness were also collected, but it was expected that fear would be especially responsive to the categorization manipulation because the appraisal dimensions of negativity, unexpectedness, and uncertainty that are central to this emotion seem to apply so directly to the events of 9/11. As predicted, fear (but not anger, sadness, or calmness) was affected by the categorization manipulation, such that those who believed that the study was concerned with a comparison of Western and Arab reactions reported greater fear.

Participants in Experiment 2 were led to believe that the purpose of the study was to compare the reactions of Europeans and Americans, or those of Europeans and Arabs. Thus, the idea was that the same in-group would be seen in different terms depending on which out-group was the object of comparison. Comparing the in-group with an out-group (Arabs) that excluded the predominantly American victims should have encouraged participants to see the victims as part of the in-group, and thereby provoked stronger fear reactions. By contrast, comparing the in-group with an out-group (Americans) that included the victims should have encouraged participants to regard the victims as an out-group, resulting in weaker fear reactions. The results were consistent with these predictions, with fear (but not anger, sadness, or happiness) being significantly affected by categorization despite the implicit nature of this manipulation. Moreover, it was found that the effect of categorization on fear was mediated by feelings of being personally concerned by the terrorist attacks. Feelings of personal concern were greater when the comparison group was Arabs, rather than Americans, and controlling for these feelings reduced the effect of comparison group on fear to nonsignificance.

Although these two studies seem to provide consistent evidence that a rather simple, one-sentence manipulation concerning the ostensible purpose of the research had the theoretically predicted effect on self-reported fear, alternative interpretations are possible. For example, in both studies greatest fear was reported when Arabs were specifically mentioned in the instructions. It is therefore possible that the greater fear reported in these conditions was a simple result of rendering the ethnicity of the attackers salient. The results of Experiment 2's mediational analyses could also be accounted for in this way: When the attackers' ethnicity was made salient, participants felt more personally concerned, and this greater concern was responsible for their greater fear. What is missing in this research, as with the anger experiments conducted by Yzerbyt and his colleagues (2002), is compelling evidence concerning the mediating role of self-categorization.

A further interpretational problem concerns whether the fear reported in this study was genuinely group-based. Participants supplied with a social identity that included U.S. citizens as part of the in-group may, as a consequence, have felt afraid about possible future attacks that might threaten themselves and their loved ones as well as Americans. If so, the categorization manipulation may not have led participants to be afraid *on behalf of other group members* (U.S. citizens), but rather to see *themselves* as equally susceptible terrorist targets. The resulting fear would thus be interpretable as a personal reaction to perceived vulnerability to harm.

☐ Intergroup Gloating and *Schadenfreude*

There is often an understandable reluctance to dwell on the positive emotions that members of one social group may experience when they witness the suffering of another social group. However, there can be little doubt that such emotions can and do exist. Leach, Snider, and Iyer (2002) have argued that intergroup gloating is a feeling of malicious satisfaction at making a lower status out-group suffer. Intergroup *schadenfreude* is a closely related emotion: malicious pleasure at the suffering of members of another group. The key difference between these emotions is that of agency. In the case of intergroup gloating, the in-group is the agent responsible for the out-group's suffering; in the case of *schadenfreude*, the responsible agent is a third party.

Intergroup Gloating

In Leach and Spears' (2002) study of intergroup gloating, in-group members were told that either fellow in-group members or a third party had attacked and harmed an out-group. The out-group was either higher or lower in status than the in-group. Participants reported greater satisfaction when their fellow in-group members (i.e., Dutch people) had caused harm to lower status (Portuguese) others than when the same harm was inflicted on a higher status (German) out-group. They also expressed stronger intentions to gloat about the harm done by the in-group. When a third party (Spanish) caused the harm to the out-group, satisfaction was generally low and did not depend on the out-group's relative status.

How can this tendency to engage in intergroup gloating best be understood? Leach and Spears (2002) argue that such gloating is a malicious form of group bias, more pernicious than either the in-group favoritism that is so prevalent in intergroup situations (Brewer, 1979) or the out-group derogation that is observed when groups are threatened or feel insecure (e.g., Branscombe & Wann, 1994). The uniquely distasteful quality of intergroup gloating is of course the pleasure that is taken in the fact that the in-group has caused the out-group to suffer. As Leach and Spears observe,

Those in a position to gloat seem to show little regard for those of lower status and have little interest in helping them. Gloating can thus be seen as a forthright and unabashed assertion of group superiority that may encourage direct attempts at maintaining structural inequality and the oppression of those lower in status. (pp. 12–13)

However, it is worth noting that the evidence of intergroup gloating gleaned from Leach and Spears' experiment only reflected relative differences in satisfaction depending on out-group status when the in-group was the perpetrator. Satisfaction levels were not high in absolute terms, nor were intentions to gloat especially strong.

Intergroup Schadenfreude

In a related line of research, Leach, Spears, Branscombe, and Doosje (2003) have examined intergroup *schadenfreude*. More specifically, they focused on the pleasure taken by Dutch participants in the failure of rival national soccer teams. Drawing on Nietzsche's (1967) thinking, Leach and colleagues proposed that *schadenfreude* should be greater when (a) those who witness an out-group's setback are interested in that field of endeavor (e.g., are followers of the sport in question); (b) the witnesses are members of an in-group whose identity has been threatened in some respect (e.g., the group has itself suffered a recent setback); and (c) the expression of *schadenfreude* is in some way legitimated (e.g., by the fact that the failing out-group is not regarded as legitimately superior to the in-group).

In Study 1, Dutch participants' reactions to the elimination of Germany (by Croatia) in the 1998 soccer World Cup quarter-finals were assessed. To manipulate group threat, participants either were or were not reminded of the greater success of other national teams in successive World Cup competitions (chronic threat), and either were or were not reminded of the fact that the Dutch team had lost to Brazil in the same competition (acute threat). Interest in soccer was used as a third independent variable. Greater *schadenfreude* was reported by those with a high interest in soccer and by those exposed to either of the two forms of identity threat. More interestingly, the effects of chronic identity threat differed depending on the level of participants' interest in soccer. Those lowest in soccer interest expressed relatively high levels of *schadenfreude* when threatened, but expressed little *schadenfreude* when not threatened. Those with moderate or high levels of soccer interest, however, expressed relatively high levels of *schadenfreude*, regardless of identity threat. The authors argued that this pattern of findings suggests that Dutch people who show any interest in soccer may feel chronically threatened because the Dutch national team has a history of under-performing in the World Cup.

In Study 2, the researchers focused on Dutch participants' reactions to the elimination of Germany (by England) in an early round of the European soccer championship and the defeat of Italy (by France) in the final. This latter result was particularly significant because Italy had eliminated the Dutch team in the semi-final round in a close game that went to sudden-death overtime. Threat was manipulated by reminding some participants that their national team had lost to Italy in the semi-final. Interest in soccer again had a moderating influence on intergroup *schadenfreude*. Those with greater interest expressed more *schadenfreude* at the loss of a rival (Germany or Italy), and (as in the first study) were less influenced by group threat than were their less interested counterparts.

Study 2 also included a manipulation of the salience of either tolerance or honesty-directness norms, intended to influence the likelihood that *schadenfreude* would be expressed. When the honesty norm was salient, threat and identity influenced the *schadenfreude* expressed by participants with a low interest in soccer as predicted. For these participants, being reminded of the earlier Dutch loss to Italy increased expressed *schadenfreude* at the German defeat (as in the first study) but reduced expressed *schadenfreude* at the Italian defeat. This pattern of results suggests that emphasizing honesty as a goal released constraints on expressing pleasure about the German team's defeat, but inhibited the expression of pleasure about the Italian team's defeat. According to the authors, this differential effect may be explained by reference to the "reality constraint" engendered by the Italian side's legitimate intergroup superiority over the Dutch side as evidenced by the former's previous victory over the latter. Indeed, the honesty norm may have forced participants to confront this fact that the Italian side were genuinely better than their own team and this in turn may have reduced their pleasure about the Italians' defeat.

It might be wondered whether the participants were expressing positive emotion in reaction to the success of the winning team, rather than pleasure at the defeat of the losing team. It is not uncommon for neutral members of an audience at a sporting contest to be inclined to support the underdog. However, the measures used in the Leach and colleagues (2003) studies specifically asked participants how they felt about the target group's loss. Furthermore, the participants were not neutral observers; indeed, *schadenfreude* was greatest when group members were interested in soccer and learned of the defeat of a rival team. All in all, then, there are good grounds for thinking that these findings reflect the conditions under which malicious pleasure at the defeat of an out-group is experienced. The results of these studies suggest that *schadenfreude* is most likely to be expressed in domains that are important to the self, and that this emotion is exacerbated by threats to the in-group, but is sensitive to legitimacy concerns.

☐ Conclusions

Traditional theoretical accounts of intergroup conflict, such as realistic conflict theory (Sherif, 1966), social identity theory (Tajfel & Turner, 1986), and self-categorization theory (Turner et al., 1987) pay little attention to the role of emotion in such conflict. These theoretical accounts tend to regard the affective aspects of intergroup conflict as symptoms or outcomes of more fundamental processes, such as the perception that one's own group is competing with another group for a scarce resource, or the mere perception that two groups exist—"us" and "them."

Although these theories have done much to enhance our understanding of when and why conflict arises between social groups, they struggle to account for some of the phenomena associated with such conflict. The simple "in-group favoritism" shown when members of groups express preferences for their own group above other groups in a variety of ways is not especially difficult to explain in terms of the standard theoretical frameworks. However, the fact that members of groups often go further than this—sometimes much further—by engaging in actions that are explicitly intended to bring disadvantage and suffering to members of another group ("out-group derogation") is less easy to explain. Out-group derogation appears to be more driven, more motivated, by needs to right wrongs, to reduce or remove threat, or to express contempt or resentment. In short, it is difficult to account for the phenomenon of out-group derogation without taking proper account of its motivated, emotional character.

If out-group derogation is seen as a consequence of the anger or resentment that one group feels absout its treatment by another group, of the fear that one group feels in relation to another group's threatening actions, or of the contempt that one group feels for another group's values and practices, it becomes more intelligible, and in some ways more "reasonable." Here, then, is one way in which an account of intergroup relations that takes proper account of the intergroup emotions can make a real contribution to the understanding of social conflict.

Placing emotion at the theoretical heart of intergroup conflict also implies that any attempt to reduce or resolve this conflict needs to address the intergroup emotions that group members feel. As many commentators have observed, simply increasing contact between members of the two groups is insufficient to bring about any reduction in conflict (e.g., Allport, 1954; Hewstone & Brown, 1986; Pettigrew, 1998, *inter alia*). Indeed, increased contact between members of groups with a history of conflict may only serve to exacerbate the conflict. What is required is contact that serves to reduce the negative emotions and to enhance the positive emotions that members of each group feel toward members of the out-group. As Pettigrew (1986) noted nearly two decades ago,

> Affect is a central component of the phenomenon and definition of intergroup prejudice: an antipathy against groups accompanied by faulty generalization. . . . To treat intergroup contact as if it were dealing simply with cold cognition is to slight what makes the entire area of intergroup conflict problematic—its heat. (p. 181)

This is not to suggest that the research on intergroup emotion discussed in the present chapter is problem-free. Some of the problems that are specific to individual studies have been identified in the course of the chapter, but one or two more general issues remain.

First, although the research addresses issues that are real and important, the data that are collected usually consist of relatively trivial self-report ratings. Participants are simply asked to say whether they feel more or less happy, angry, guilty, and so on about an intergroup event and more or less prepared to engage in various emotional actions as a consequence. Although people's descriptions and presentations of their emotions certainly tell us something about what they genuinely feel and express, they are also often acutely sensitive to other aspects of the social and nonsocial context. To what extent are the findings of the studies reviewed above because of context-sensitive adjustments of word use rather than genuine differences in emotion?

For example, is it surprising that on average people say that they feel more "guilty" about their group's actions if their attention is drawn to those actions, or that they feel more "sympathy" if their attention is drawn to other people's suffering (Iyer, Leach, & Crosby, 2003, Study 2)? Isn't self-focus one of the connotations of the word "guilt," and other-focus one of the connotations of "sympathy?" Similarly, does the statement that you feel "guilty about the negative things inductive thinkers have done to deductive thinkers" (Doosje et al., 1998, Study 1) properly apply in situations when the relevant in-group has shown no bias against the out-group in question? And how likely would you be to say this kind of thing if you were *personally* responsible for bias along with other members of your group? In the latter case, wouldn't such a statement carry the unwanted implication that you were denying personal responsibility? Although we do not believe that all of the evidence concerning intergroup emotions can be dismissed as semantic artefact in this way, inclusion of other kinds of measures such as psychophysiological, behavioral, expressive, and implicit indices would certainly bolster the conclusions of this research. As things stand, we cannot always conclude that relative differences in ratings of questionnaire items reflect corresponding differences in actual emotion.

Second, virtually all of the studies in this area have involved only two groups and assessed the emotions that one of these groups feels toward the other. In everyday life, matters are typically more complex. It is at least sometimes the case that the intergroup context consists of multiple groups. As well as constituting different targets for intergroup emotion, these multiple groups can be regarded as different audiences for the emotions expressed by any one group toward another group (cf. Fleming, 1994). Further, in-group members also represent another potential audience for these emotional communications. In our view, then, some intergroup emotions are likely to be conditioned not only by the appraised attributes or behaviors of members of the target out-group, but also by the actual and anticipated reactions of members of other out-groups and fellow in-group members.

Third, some of the research reviewed here has a tendency to treat emotion as a simple outcome variable—a direct product of appraisals of relations between groups. Although it is clearly interesting to see how such appraisals relate to the emotions felt toward out-group members, the real value of studying intergroup emotion is surely to increase our understanding of how emotion affects intergroup relations. In this case, emotion needs to be cast in the role of an independent, mediating, or moderating variable, as well as a dependent measure (see chapter 8).

Finally, much of the research reviewed here would be greatly enriched by incorporating a longitudinal dimension. Studying intergroup emotions over time would enable researchers to examine the extent to which intergroup dynamics are shaped by (or simply reflect) changing patterns of intergroup emotion, and also how those changing patterns can be seen as components of an emotional dialogue.

6

Moving Faces in Interpersonal Life

In the everyday business of interpersonal interaction, faces do a lot of the important work. As well as carrying their own specific meanings, they set the tone for whatever else is happening, ironizing the surface content of a sentence or drawing attention to hidden semantic subtleties. A criticism delivered with a smile or wink, for example, has a quite different effect from one accompanied by scowls. Being face-to-face also makes obvious and inescapable differences to how we engage with one another. Catching someone's eye is often a prerequisite to starting a conversation, and the course of the ensuing dialogue is directed and redirected by the exchange of looks, yawns, and grimaces. As we interact, we seem to be acutely responsive to the slightest twitch or contraction of facial muscle.

Why do people devote so much attention to faces? The obvious answer is that important information can be derived from them. But that is only part of the story. Our looking also conveys our engagement. The act of collecting information provides information collected by the other person in a corresponding act. We see each other collecting information and coordinate our perspectives (or arrive at opposing positions, or break away from the interaction). More generally, facial movements (including looking) not only serve to provide information for someone else to decode, but also play a more direct role in the performance of interpersonal action.

This chapter reviews psychological thinking about faces as sources of information and as vehicles for action. We try to broaden the usual perspective on facial conduct by looking not only at faces in isolation but also at their dynamic coordination in the context of ongoing interactions (and joint actions). Our aim is to illustrate how faces, especially faces conveying emotional meaning, are best understood not as individual movements or expressions but as part of an unfolding interpersonal context. We start with a consideration of the range of information that faces might carry.

☐ Varieties of Facial Meaning

Faces mean a lot to us. Their movements seem to reveal all kinds of details about what a person is thinking and feeling. We can't help reading things into them. Exactly what faces might convey, however, has been more controversial than might be imagined. Here are a few of the possibilities:

1. *Personality:* Some of the earliest studies attempted to divine information about personality and character from faces (e.g., Aristotle, tr. 1984). Even now, and even though we know it may often be misleading, we often find ourselves drawing conclusions about what someone is like on the basis of their facial appearance. Of course, our first impressions often change radically as we get to know a person better, undermining our confidence in their reliability. One of the reasons why we read character into facial configurations despite these doubts may reflect their emotional connotations. People with wide eyes may seem temperamentally more timid or anxious, for example (cf. Berry & McArthur, 1985). Although some theorists believe that faces really do reflect temperament or personality, it is generally accepted that many popular intuitions about facial character are off the mark. The fact that people can be wrong about the implications of facial appearance despite substantial experience calls into question some of the other common inferences about their meaning—for example, how accurately they indicate emotion (Russell, 1994).

2. *Attractiveness:* We like some faces more than we like others. Further, people tend to agree about which faces are most appealing (e.g., Langlois et al., 2000). Although beauty is usually attributed to structural and static aspects of faces, it also seems obvious that certain facial movements and positions are less attractive than others. A face contorted in a grimace is often hard to look at. This latter observation may go some way to explaining why "emotional" faces can contribute to processes of social influence. For example, if a certain facial movement

(e.g., one connoting pain or distress) tends to induce uncomfortable feelings, then those exposed to it may take steps to escape the offending stimulus (by removing the cause of suffering, comforting the sufferer, or simply leaving the situation [cf. Cialdini, 1991; Piliavin & Piliavin, 1972]). Correspondingly, Rolls (1999) suggests that smiles may serve as primary positive reinforcers that facilitate social learning and attachment behavior (see also Dimberg, 1990).

3. *Femininity:* The shape of a face and the size of its features determine our recognition of gender as well as our judgments about the masculinity and femininity of its owner (e.g., Bruce et al., 1993). For example, angular faces are perceived as more masculine than rounded faces, and large eyes and lips are perceived as more feminine than small eyes and lips (Keating & Doyle, 2002). Interestingly, the perceived femininity and attractiveness of female faces seem to be more closely related than the perceived masculinity and attractiveness of male faces (O'Toole, Edelman, & Buelthoff, 1998). It may also be the case that certain facial *movements* are more closely associated with perceptions of femininity than with masculinity and vice versa.

4. *Status and dominance:* Just as gender-typical facial features are seen as indications of the extent of femininity or masculinity at a dispositional level, age-related facial features are perceived as indicating a person's level of maturity. For example, submissiveness is also perceived in so-called "baby-faced" appearance, when eyes are positioned relatively low in the face and the forehead is large (e.g., Berry & McArthur, 1986). People also make inferences about relative position in a social hierarchy from facial movements and positions. For example, Tiedens (2001) found that "angry expressions" led people to impute status to others. The fact that the expression of anger is often seen as more typical for men than for women further suggests that there may be intriguing links between perceptions of gender typicality, status, and emotion.

5. *Distinctiveness:* Despite their superficial physical similarities, we seem to be able to pick out faces of people we know even from crowds of other faces. This easy and immediate recognition is not substantially impaired when faces are seen from different perspectives. Many researchers believe that these observations suggest that purpose-built hardwired neural systems subserve the process of face recognition (e.g., Ellis, 1975; Farah, O'Reilly-Randall, & Vecera, 1997). Although neuropsychological evidence is also consistent with this possibility (e.g., Leonard, Rolls, Wilson, & Baylis, 1985; Rolls & Baylis, 1986), the fact that we pay so much attention to faces from an early age (a fact that may also reflect genetic preprogramming) suggests that we are also

well-equipped to learn to distinguish faces accurately. Similar arguments also apply to the recognition of specific facial movements, some of which may correspond to emotions. Indeed, evidence exists that angry faces stand out from a crowd just like faces of people we know (Hansen & Hansen, 1988; Ohman, Lundqvist, & Esteves, 2001).

6. *Direction of visual attention:* One of the reasons for looking at other people's faces is to see what those other people are looking at (and sometimes they are looking at our faces for the same reason). Indeed, if we see anyone staring intently in a particular direction, it is often difficult to stop ourselves from casting a glance there too. All kinds of conclusions about a person's mental state are deducible from the information conveyed over time by shifts of visual attention (including looking away from things as well as looking at them [e.g., Rutter, 1987]).

7. *Intensity of visual attention:* We can also tell how much attention someone is paying to something from their face (or at least how much attention they want us to think they are paying to it). This kind of information may be especially important during conversation to check whether someone else is following our reasoning or train of thought.

8. *Other sensory uptake:* As well as showing where and how hard the person is looking, the face contains other sensory organs whose orientation can be discerned relatively directly. We can usually tell whether someone is sniffing at something, listening to something, sucking or chewing on something, and so on.

9. *Liking:* Attention also carries affective implications. An intent gaze toward someone or something and a forward tilted orientation can convey liking (attraction), and a deflection of visual attention tends to imply dislike (e.g., Argyle, 1967). Mixed patterns of gaze which do not stay fixed on any point are often read as disinterest or distraction. Similarly, listening, sniffing, sucking, and touching movements are informative about the perceived pleasantness of stimuli in other modalities.

10. *Turn-taking:* Facial movements also help to regulate the flow of conversation. For example, conventional facial signals exist (particularly relating to gaze direction and aversion) that are used to indicate a desire to interrupt someone, or to show that one wants to stop speaking or continue (see, for example, Goodwin, 1980 1981; Kendon, 1967)

11. *Backchannelling:* People often provide a kind of running commentary on what they are saying or hearing using facial movements (e.g., Brunner, 1979). For example, we may pull a face to show that our report of what someone else said is not to be equated with our own opinion (see Birdwhistell, 1970; Ekman, 1979). Further, appropriately timed indications of thoughtfulness from the other suggest that they know that

what we are saying demands thought and that they are engaged enough in what we are saying to cooperate.

12. *Understanding and rapport:* Other people's faces can convey that they are in tune with your perspective not only in conversation but also more generally. Smiles and displays of pertinent discomfort (e.g., Bavelas, Black, Lemery, & Mullett, 1986) can evidence emotional attunement, empathy, or sympathy.

13. *Deception:* Many people believe that they can tell whether somebody is lying or telling the truth by observing their face. For example, people who divert their gaze are sometimes seen as shifty and untrustworthy. However, much of the evidence suggests that the facial movements that we believe are symptomatic of deception bear no necessary relation to the veracity of a presentation (e.g., Zuckerman, DePaulo, & Rosenthal, 1981). For example, contrary to stereotypes, people often maintain eye contact while they are lying to someone else.

14. *Intentions and motives:* Faces can give an indication of what people are about to do, as happens when we get ready to hit or kiss someone (cf. Fridlund, 1994, and see discussion following).

15. *Alertness:* Tension of facial muscles and wide-opened eyes can reveal whether someone is fully awake and attentive, tired, or asleep (e.g., Russell, 1997).

16. *Thinking:* As Scherer (1992) argues, the idea that facial movements can reveal that someone is thinking goes back at least as far as the Ancient Greeks. For example, Bell (1844, p. 137) wrote that the muscle that wrinkles the brow (corrugator supercilii) "unaccountably, but irresistably, conveys the idea of mind" (cited in Darwin, 1872/1998, p. 219). According to Wierzbicka (1999, p. 205), one of the semantic primitives underlying the universal meaning of raised eyebrows is "I'm thinking now." Further, certain eye movements that are unconnected with the movements of physical objects or the constant gaze undirected at anything in particular characterizing a "distant" look, strongly convey absorption in private thought.

17. *Emotion:* Most people believe that faces are particularly useful in indicating someone's current feelings, though we also know that sometimes these feelings can be disguised or dissimulated. Although this final aspect of facial meaning is a central focus of the present chapter, it is important to recognize that emotional information is conveyed alongside several other streams of interpersonal data, providing a wider context for any attribution of emotion. Further, it turns out that very few of our everyday faces primarily serve the function of emotion communication in the first place. Raising eyebrows, sneezing, coughing,

blinking, yawning, and twitching, for example, are all things that faces do in both nonemotional as well as emotional situations.

In conclusion, the meanings that we read into faces are diverse and of varying clarity. Some of our interpretations seem to be relatively straight-forward and direct (direction of attention, coordination), whereas others may be more subject to error (character, attraction). How then does the facial expression of emotion fit into this picture? Some commentators believe that emotion can be perceived directly from the face under some circumstances, at least (e.g., Ekman, 1975, 1997; Izard, 1994), whereas oth-ers believe that the process is often more inferential and subject to error (e.g., Hebb, 1946; Russell, 1997). One thing at least should be clear: Faces do not always, only, or exclusively provide emotional information. Indeed, emotional communication may sometimes be simply a side-effect of the other kinds of work that faces are doing in interpersonal interaction.

In the next section of the chapter, we will consider some of the most influential psychological theories and studies of the meanings and func-tions of facial expression. The initial emphasis is on factors that underlie the production of facial movements and their interpersonal basis. For example, we address the question of whether faces express emotions or communicate social motives (or both). In subsequent sections, we turn our attention to the effects of facial movements, in terms of their per-ceived meaning and their more direct impact on interpersonal interac-tion. How, for example, do facial signals contribute to processes of social appraisal? Finally, we discuss how faces operate as part of dynamic dia-logues between people and how they help to constitute the unfolding emotional context for interpersonal conduct.

☐ Facial Movements as Expressions of Emotion

The scientific respectability of attributing emotion to expression derives from the influential work of Darwin (1872/1998), who exorcised religion and cosmology from the commonsense explanatory framework. Dar-win's focus was on a little-studied scientific question: Why does the expression of any emotion take its particular distinctive form? For exam-ple, why should it be that the corners of our lips tend to point upwards in a smile when we are happy, but downwards when we are sad? Why do we sometimes grit our teeth when angry, and why does our mouth often drop open when we are surprised? Before the time of Darwin, most West-ern theories of facial morphology (and of representational visual art) had converged on the conclusion that facial muscles were put there specifically by God to reveal people's emotions (e.g., Bell, 1844; Duchenne, 1862/1990). The central explanation offered for the specific connections between facial movements and particular feeling states was that they corresponded to the Creator's own expressions; though quite why the corners of His mouth should have turned upwards to denote happiness remained something of a mystery. Darwin's aim was to provide explanations for expression-emotion associations without recourse to myths of divine origin.

The first and most important of these explanations ("the principle of associated serviceable habits") was that facial movements that are read as expressive of emotion had, at some point in our evolutionary history, served direct adaptive functions in specific emotion-related situations. For example, he pointed out that closing the eyes or turning away serves to shut out an unwanted stimulus. Over time, this same set of movements became associated not just with stimuli that actually required literal rejection but also with situations in which rejection-related feelings were experienced, such as disagreement with someone else's views during a conversation. Thus, movements that originally served some direct purpose also came to occur in situations where their primary functions were no longer relevant.

Darwin's second "principle of antithesis" proposed that movements "opposite" to those that were originally serviceable on the basis of the first principle somehow become associated with contrasting feeling states. For example, if baring teeth serves purposes in antagonistic situations, covering them may come to be associated with situations in which animals experience decidedly nonantagonistic feelings. Although Darwin wavers about the explanation for antithesis, he does give some hints about its potential communicative functions. In particular, he describes how animals facing potentially dangerous assailants adopt a submissive attitude that is maximally distinctive from an aggressive posture. Instead of "erecting its hair, thus increasing the apparent bulk of its body, ... showing its teeth, or brandishing its horns" (p. 57), the animal will cower, make itself appear smaller, and cover its fangs (see Figure 6.1).

The point is apparently to show the antagonist that no challenge is presented. Similarly, many human facial movements may serve to indicate to other people what is not, rather than what is, about to happen. Despite mentioning "the power of intercommunication" (p. 63) in this context, Darwin's central claim once more is that the movements are no longer "serviceable." Subsequent evolutionary accounts have been less reluctant to attribute adaptively relevant communicative functions to facial movements (see, e.g., Andrew, 1963; Burkhardt, 1985; Fridlund, 1992, and discussion below).

FIGURE 6.1. Submissive and angry dog

The starting assumption of Darwin's account is that faces express emotions. He attempts to explain why this should be so by reference to historical adaptive pressures rather than present functions (Tooby & Cosmides, 1990). Further, emotions are said to be associated with expressions not because of their intrinsic qualities, but because of the situations in which they occur (as "serviceable habits") or their antithesis to other emotions (or in the case of his third "principle of action of the nervous system," as a consequence of their physiological side effects). In this sense, Darwin does not seem to believe that facial movements give a direct and natural expression to an inner state of emotion. Instead, they have come to connote emotional meaning for extrinsic reasons. Similarly, Tomkins (1995, pp. 90–91) argues that in explaining what the face does, "communication of affect is a secondary spin-off function rather than its primary function." For neither theorist did facial movements originally evolve specifically to convey emotional meaning.

Darwin's explanation of how movements that are no longer directly functional come to be inherited as expressions of emotion is in terms of Lamarckian use-inheritance. The idea is that humans learned to associate facial movements with the emotional experiences that tended to co-occur with the survival-relevant situations that prompted these movements, back when the movements still served their direct functions. People came to turn up their nose, for example, not only when something really smelled bad, but also when they experienced feelings similar to those they had experienced when they smelled something bad. Having made this association, the experience-expression connection was then passed down through the generations. However, as we now know, acquired dispositions cannot be inherited in this manner, leaving Darwin with no easy explanation for why nonfunctional expressions of emotion should not simply die out or be extinguished.

One possible resolution of this problem is to accept that facial movements continue to serve practical or communicative functions, thus explaining why they have not been selected out. Indeed, many more recent evolutionary approaches treat facial movements as ritualized displays that inform other animals about the displayer's future conduct (e.g., Andrew, 1963). Ritualization occurs when a movement provides adaptively (or reproductively) relevant information to other animals, thus making its progressive exaggeration beneficial. Correspondingly, perceptual sensitivity to the same informative movements is likely to enhance the probability of gene survival.

Although some aspects of facial morphology and movement may have developed specifically for communicative purposes, in most cases, the muscles used in displays probably started out serving some other function (e.g., control of sensory input, respiration, eating, etc.) and were later co-opted to serve communicative purposes too. For example, widening the eyes serves a direct purpose when a novel stimulus requires attention, but if the movement is made in a clearly visible way (or if other animals are attuned to its presence), it also tells others that something worthy of attention has happened. Along these lines, it has been argued that eyebrows evolved partly to underline attentive movements of this kind (see Buck, 1984). Thus, the practical and communicative functions of facial movements are often perfectly compatible with each other.

☐ Facial Movements as Conduct

Dewey: Facial Movements as Practical Actions

Instead of starting from the assumption that facial movements express emotion, John Dewey's pragmatic approach led him to emphasize instead Darwin's ideas about the direct functional significance of some facial movements in carrying out actions. For example, shutting one's eyes or turning away can be genuinely part of an act of rejection, rather than being evolutionary remnants of an ancestor's movements that happen to be associated with feelings of rejection. Perhaps the practical functions of facial movements continue to be relevant as explanations of their present origins.

One of the aims of Dewey's (1894) theory of emotion was to combine the insights offered by Darwin's principles of explanation for facial expression of emotion with William James's (1884) ideas about the causes of emotion itself (see chapter 1). According to James, facial movements (like other bodily changes) were not a consequence of being emotional, but rather direct reactions that were then internally perceived as emotion. We do not smile because we are happy, in this view; instead, we feel happy partly because we are smiling. If James's feedback theory is correct, then Darwin's notion of facial movements expressing preexisting emotions must be misconceived.

However, Dewey also noted a corresponding theoretical problem with James's explanation of the bodily reactions that produce the emotion. James argued that these were elicited by the "perception of the exciting fact," but failed to specify exactly what made the fact exciting in the first place. Confronted by a bear, for example, how does the body know what responses to produce to generate an appropriate fear reaction? The obvious solution seems to be to suggest that the bear is already perceived as a frightening bear, before any bodily changes are felt (cf. Ellsworth, 1994; Smith & Lazarus, 1993). But perception of a bear as frightening seems to imply that an emotion is present prior to the bodily changes, thereby undermining James's basic contention that the reaction precedes the emotion rather than vice versa.

According to Dewey, Darwin's explanation of the functions of expressive behavior helps to solve this problem. Rather than seeing the bear at once as frightening, we are simply impelled to run away from it. More accurately, we are pursuing practical actions to which the bear is an impediment and we adjust our conduct accordingly. The so-called expression of emotion is part of this adjustment, and the emotion itself also emerges in parallel with its development: "the mode of behavior is the primary thing and ... the idea and the emotional excitation are constituted at one and the same time" (Dewey, 1895, p. 18).

What is inherited according to Dewey's theory is not a connection between an emotion and a distinctive pattern of facial movement, but rather a set of movements that serve direct practical functions: "All so-called expressions of emotions are, in reality, the reduction of movements and stimulations originally useful into attitudes" (pp. 568–569). For example, leaning forward, directing one's visual attention toward the antagonist, and tightening one's muscles involve useful movements when preparing to attack someone. The fact that many of our practical actions and their associated facial movements are specifically directed toward other people (when we attack, comfort, or help them, for example) adds an interpersonal dimension to Dewey's analysis.

Mead: Facial Movements as Communicative Acts

Darwin's central principle for explaining facial movements emphasized their original practical functions in dealing with environmental problems, and he failed to follow through the insight that these same movements also serve to influence other animals' conduct. The central point here is that if preparation for action results in visible facial movements, then these movements will come to serve as useful indications of future behavior.

Mead (1934) extended Darwinian ideas of the functions of gestures by explicitly considering their social impact, seeing them as a primitive form of the kind of "significant symbol" that permits the distinctively human characteristics of self-conscious mental life. His recurrent example is that of the dog fight, in which two animals may circle one another, face-to-face, each apparently adjusting its posture in response to the antagonist's changing stance. Here, Mead sees a rudimentary form of intercommunication. Because the first dog's movements of leaning forward, tensing muscles, and baring teeth are part of a more extended action sequence that often results in attack, the second dog is able to anticipate such an attack when these movements are made and may therefore adjust its own stance accordingly (either by backing off or adopting a confrontational posture). Further, the first dog registers the second dog's response to the preparatory movements and may ultimately learn to use these movements precisely to achieve this reaction. Baring teeth, for example, may become a way of warning the antagonist that force will be met with counterforce. In short, the "meaning" of the preparatory movements for the first dog comes to be defined by the movements that they "call out" in the second dog. The upshot is that the dogs are able to size each other up by registering the effects of threatened attack or withdrawal before any kind of fight actually occurs. Thus, postural and facial movements allow mutual coordination in the development of an ongoing sequence of action.

To the extent that human facial movements are also involved in more articulated action sequences, it is clear that a similar meaning-manufacturing process may operate in interpersonal life. My staring at an object that I am about to take hold of, for example, carries obvious information about my current intentions that is available to any onlooker. It would be surprising if exposure to these interpersonal contingencies did not ultimately result in my recognition that looking at something tells others something about what I am about to do. As a consequence, I may come to use looking not only to fix on an object that I am about to take hold of, but also to inform others about this intended action.

In summary, Mead's account implies that the original meaning of emotional actions and expressions arises from their functional role in ongoing practical encounters. However, these movements acquire communicative value as means of social influence because of the courses of action they come to stand for. Thus, adopting a leaning forward position with eyes fixed on the other person and with fists clenched is "recognized" as the beginnings of an aggressive line of action by both parties and thus often calls out the response required.

☐ Facial Movements as Displays

Fridlund's (1991, 1994) ideas about facial displays share Mead's assumption that movements of the face are primarily oriented to others, but Fridlund diverges in attributing their origins more to natural selection than to social and cultural pressures. He argues that Darwin's insistence that expressions of emotion are vestigial and of no service has led to an underemphasis on the continuing communicative functionality of facial movements. Facial displays, in his view, have evolved precisely because they provide adaptationally relevant information to other animals. Correspondingly, sensitivity to these displays has coevolved to ensure that they properly serve their communicative purpose.

From the point of view of evolutionary economy, Fridlund argues that it would be counterproductive to show one's emotional state uncontrollably in all circumstances. For example, it is pointless to waste energy by displaying that one is about to run away unless another conspecific is nearby to pick up the message. Further, information about emotional state is worthless to other animals unless it tells them what the displaying animal is actually about to do. Thus, natural selection should have provided a mechanism for conveying behavioral intentions (or more broadly social motives) to others rather than for expressing emotions regardless of context. Furthermore, this mechanism would need to be sensitive to the nature of the current audience for this communication of intention, because this determines whether it is advantageous for the signal to be transmitted.

In Fridlund's view, displays do not map one-to-one to emotions because the same emotion may under different circumstances be accompanied by quite different social motives (anger may result in a desire to aggress physically, to withdraw, or to undermine the other more subtly, and the associated displays will be different in each case). Thus, the prototypical "anger" face identified by Ekman (1973) and others occurs on some occasions when people are angry, but only if an overtly hostile intention exists, and if a suitable audience is available to receive the message. Even here, the face does not express the emotion itself, but rather the intention to aggress.

☐ Audience Effects on Smiling

Evidence for Fridlund's claim that facial conduct depends on the availability of suitable addressees comes from a variety of studies concerning "audience effects." Perhaps the most famous of these was conducted by Kraut and Johnston (1979). Observers recorded when players smiled during a game of ten-pin bowling. One observer took a concealed position behind the pins and could therefore record smiles that occurred in response to a positive emotional event that was nonsocial (no one else could see the bowler's face when the pins fell). A second observer watched the bowler from behind the bowling pit, and was thus able to record any smiling that was specifically directed to fellow bowlers. The results were clear-cut. Smiling was relatively rare when bowlers faced the pins (less than 5%), even when bowlers had scored a strike or a spare (only one of the 26 strikes or spares observed produced a smile from the bowler while facing the pins). However, smiling was much more common when bowlers turned to face their friends even when only a few pins had fallen. This suggests that smiling depends more on the presence of an addressee to pick it up than it does on an individual's emotional state.

Similar effects were obtained by Jones, Collins, and Hong (1991) among 10-month old prelinguistic infants. Each infant was left in a room that was laid out so that attention could either be directed toward their mother or some attractive toys. Substantially more smiles were made toward the mother than toward the toys when mothers were attentive to the child, whereas smiling was equally directed at the toys as to the mother when mothers sat reading a magazine and paying little attention to the infant. Smiles oriented at mothers usually started before infants turned around, suggesting that they were displays relating to the toys rather than emotional reactions to the mother's presence. Further, Jones and Raag (1989) found no evidence that 18-month-old toddlers' *enjoyment* of play depended on their mother's attentiveness even though *smiling* clearly depended on her availability as an addressee.

One way of dismissing the above evidence would be to point out that no strong emotional reactions were involved in the investigated events. Fernandez-Dols and Ruiz-Belda (1995) corrected this problem by examining facial conduct at moments when people were undergoing some of the most intensely positive experiences of their lives. These investigators analyzed close-up footage of faces from TV coverage of the 1992 Olympic games. Comparisons were made between gold medalists' facial movements during three phases of the awards ceremonies. In Stage 1, the medalists waited behind the podium while the organizers took their positions, and engaged in very little face-to-face interaction. In Stage 2, the athletes stood on the podium to receive their awards, conversed with the authorities, and were highly visible to the public. In Stage 3, the winners' National Anthem was played and they were facing their country's flag. Again, there was little or no interpersonal interaction during this stage, and although the medalists were clearly visible to the public, their attention was supposedly focused on the flag.

If smiling depends on happiness, we would expect it to occur throughout these three stages, because the athlete's world-beating victory was still a very recent event. Indeed, an independent group of gold medalists rated levels of happiness at more than 9 on a 10-point scale and all negative emotions at less than 1 on a 10-point scale for all three stages of the ceremony. However, smiles were rare except during Stage 2 when the competitors were actively interacting with other people. These results suggest that intense happiness is not a sufficient condition for the facial movements often considered to be its natural expression. Further, it would be hard to explain the lack of smiling in Stage 1 as reflecting a suppression of spontaneous emotional expression because of display rules about appropriate demeanor (e.g., Ekman, 1973, and see chapter 1, this volume) because the most salient audiences for any display would be likely to condone rather than disapprove of smiling. In any case, the medalists were unobserved during this period (except, of course, by the constantly present TV cameras). Thus, the results again suggest that smiling depends on the presence of a suitable audience.

The Happiness–Smiling Link as Optical Versus Artistic Truth

The reason why these audience effects seem surprising is that we usually assume that smiling is intrinsically related to happiness. But why do we think that? When someone else wants to show that they are happy, they may very well smile. But if their face remains neutral, we may never find out whether or not they are experiencing pleasure. We assume that people are happy when they smile, but not when they don't, often without recourse to any other kind of evidence. In short, our sampling of other people's smiling and other people's happiness is biased and we may infer illusory correlations (e.g., Chapman & Chapman, 1967; Hamilton, 1981) on the basis of our knowledge that smiles can be used to convey happiness. Similar arguments about the limitations of interpersonal feedback were made by DePaulo and Pfeifer (1986) in connection with people's apparently mistaken beliefs about the nonverbal signals that reveal deception. DePaulo and Pfeifer point out that many well-delivered lies may pass unnoticed. Correspondingly, only an unrepresentative selection of poorly prepared or misconceived lies are ever immediately recognized as such. Thus, we may perceive associations between lying and facial cues that relate not to lying per se, but rather to lies that are about to be discovered (partly because they are so transparent). Similarly, smiles are seen as reflecting true happiness, when in fact they may only relate to people wanting to communicate that they are happy.

Of course, it might be argued that the true meaning of smiling is also obvious from self-observation. When we feel happy, surely we can tell if we are smiling or not. In fact, available evidence suggests that we are often simply mistaken about what is visible on our own faces. Barr and Kleck (1995), for example, showed that people often believe that their expressions are more pronounced and obvious than they actually are, unless they are explicitly trying to communicate their feelings. At any rate, more systematic and careful retrospection should temper the conclusion that smiling and happiness always go together, even discounting the operation of display rules. For example, most of us can think of intensely happy moments in congenial company when we didn't smile at all (maybe we cried or punched the air and made a victorious cry of "yes" instead). To contend that these nonsmiling pleasant episodes involve emotions that are subtly different from simple happiness seems a plausible argument but smacks of circularity. If smiles did indeed reflect the emotion of happiness (rather than particular happy situations) then they should be observed across the whole range of happiness-inducing incidents.

According to Fernandez-Dols and Ruiz-Belda (1997), the emotion-expression linkage represents an artistic truth rather than an optical one. In movies, for example, an actor's face indicates feelings that might be expressed quite differently in everyday life (cf. Carroll & Russell, 1997). We all know that we can clearly convey happiness with a smile, but that doesn't necessarily mean that we usually smile when we are happy. And, of course, we sometimes smile when we are not happy at all.

Smiling, Gender, and Power

Hecht and LaFrance (1998) explored the effects of power and gender on smiling in interpersonal situations. Their basic idea was that women as well as people with relatively less influence tend to feel obligated to smile rather than simply smiling because they are happy. Participants assigned the role of an interviewer in a simulated job application procedure did not smile any more than their interviewees, but their smiling was more closely associated with their self-reported positive affect. By contrast, smiling by the interviewees, who had relatively less power in this situation, was more closely associated with their desire to please the other person (a more explicit social motive). This latter association applied even to Duchenne smiles involving the eyes as well as the mouth (see chapter 3 and Figure 3.3), which Ekman and Friesen (1982), among others, believe are uniquely diagnostic of authentic happiness.

Gender was also found to influence levels of both Duchenne and non-Duchenne smiling (smiles involving an upturned mouth but not crinkling of the eyes, see Figure 3.3), but only in conditions where participants had an informal conversation to get acquainted with one another and therefore did not differ in assigned power levels. When one interactant took on a higher-power role than the other (interviewer), the effects of this power apparently overrode any impact of gender. The fact that independent effects were obtained for both power and gender suggests that women do not smile more or smile for different reasons simply because of their relatively lower power in society (e.g., Henley, 1977; see Hall & Friedman, 1999 for further counterevidence).

These findings make the important point that it is not simply the presence of another person that makes a difference to smiling, but also that other person's relative degree of influence on what is happening, as well as their socialized gender role. Clearly, smiles are not just switched on in direct response to the appearance of another human being. Instead, they take into account our specific relationship to that other person and are shaped by learned interpersonal motives.

Audience Effects on Other Facial Movements

Although most of the audience effects research has focused on smiling, a few studies have also reported concordant results for other kinds of expression. For example, Bavelas and colleagues (1986) staged an incident in which a male experimenter dropped a television monitor on his already bandaged finger in full view of the participant. In one condition, the experimenter was facing the participant; in the other, he was side-on and turned away to face someone else after the apparent accident. Participants winced more often in response to the accident when facing the experimenter. Those winces that did occur in the in the side-on condition soon dissipated when no eye contact was forthcoming from the injured experimenter. It seems therefore that people were wincing to demonstrate sympathy to the other person rather than as a direct empathic emotional reaction to another's pain.

Similarly, Chovil (1991) found that the facial conduct of participants listening to stories about close calls (when a serious unpleasant event was only just averted) contained significantly more empathic displays when the stories were delivered face-to-face than in other less directly interactional situations.

Of course, Fridlund's theory does not predict that the presence of others will lead to increases in all kinds of facial displays under all circumstances. For example, several studies have shown that it makes a difference who the other person is (e.g., Hecht & LaFrance, 1998, and see earlier discussion). In particular, facial movements seem to be more readable in the presence of friends than strangers (e.g., Hess, Banse, & Kappas, 1995; Wagner & Smith, 1991). Further, the different effects of friends and strangers may also depend on the specific character of the motives that are being expressed, and these motives may vary depending on the emotional qualities of the stimuli being shown (cf. Buck, Losow, Murphy, & Costanzo, 1992; Jakobs, Manstead, & Fischer, 2001). Indeed, some messages are more appropriate for some audiences than others. As Chovil and Fridlund (1991) argue:

> Facial displays are a means by which we communicate with others. Like words and utterances, they are more likely to be emitted when there is a potential recipient, when they are useful in conveying the particular information, and when that information is pertinent or appropriate to the social interaction. (p. 163)

☐ Display Rules Versus Social Motives

Fridlund's view of how interpersonal factors influence facial conduct is rather different from that implied by Darwinian accounts such as Ekman's (1973) neurocultural theory. According to Ekman, people disguise their spontaneous facial expressions when others are present in accordance with culturally specific display rules (see chapters 1 & 3). In other words, an impulse to express emotion may be either suppressed or exaggerated depending on who else is present and what society dictates is appropriate. Instead, Fridlund sees all displays as being shaped by social requirements from the outset. If facial messages are already directed at specific audiences, people do not usually also need to regulate them after the fact. However, under some conditions, we may have incompatible intentions, or more than one social audience for our displays may be simultaneously present, producing a kind of conflict in what shows on our face. But this need not mean that natural urges are pit against cultural prescriptions. Instead, each potential message may reflect the equally authentic or inauthentic demands of different kinds of addressees.

For example, when we show a supposedly "masked" smile at a funeral, both the smile and its apparent masking may be displays of conflicting social motives. On the one hand, we may be showing our respect for the other mourners; on the other hand, we may be aligning ourselves with other real or imagined addressees. We may be thinking of someone else who always made fun of the deceased or carrying on an unrelated conversation in our heads. In this view, the social context does not lead us to disguise the natural expression of a spontaneous emotion, but rather provides the social motives that shape our nonverbal conduct in the first place.

Direct evidence for Ekman's alternative idea that spontaneous expressions are inhibited depending on the interpersonal and cultural context is limited. Until recently, an unpublished but often cited experiment by Friesen (see, for example Ekman, 1973; Fridlund, 1994, and chapter 3, this volume) was the only available study of cross-cultural differences in spontaneous facial displays among adult participants. In this study, Japanese and U.S. students watched stress-inducing films (depicting surgical procedures, etc.) alone and then again while being interviewed by a researcher about their content. Facial expressions were described as equivalent across the two "cultures" when the film was viewed alone, but Japanese participants showed fewer "negative" expressions and more "positive" ones in the interview situation. Ekman (1973) concluded that Japanese participants' unpleasant reactions to the films were masked in response to a cultural display rule. For example, this rule may have discouraged them from expressing unpleasant emotions in the presence of authority figures.

However, some serious ambiguities of interpretation arise First, as Fernandez-Dols and Ruiz-Belda (1997) point out, the equivalence of facial conduct even in the alone condition is questionable, because it depends on a relatively coarse distinction between positive and negative expressions, whereas more fine-grained analysis suggests differences in specific movements at a micro level. Regardless of whether the initial solitary movements were identical across cultures, the arrival of the interviewer brings a variety of consequences in addition to its supposed effects on the motivation to conceal emotion. In particular, unlike American participants, Japanese participants may not have perceived the interviewer as a suitable addressee for communications about the negative aspects of the film, but rather as someone for whom respectful messages were more appropriate. Their displays need not have been related to the film at all but instead may have been oriented to the interpersonal relations inherent in the situation.

Of course, the U.S. students were unlikely to have been insensitive to the interpersonal context, but may have read it as requiring symbolic communication of the film's negative content to the interviewer. Thus, neither group's facial movements need have been directly in response or counter-response to the content of the film. Instead, they may have reflected alternative perceptions of the interview situation, with Japanese students being more sensitive to its authority implications, and U.S. students being more attentive to the film and its emotional impact as the topic of conversation.

A subsequent extended replication of Friesen's study by Matsumoto and Kupperbusch (2001; also see chapter 3, this volume) complicates the picture still further. For example, participants who scored higher on a collectivism scale presented more negative faces while pleasant films were shown in the presence of a professor than when watching them alone, but more positive faces when unpleasant films were shown in his presence. This pattern of findings seems to suggest that if display rules are operating, they dampen the expression of positive as well as negative feelings (see chapter 3). However, high-collectivist participants also apparently intensified rather than dampened their positive or negative displays when watching the correspondingly valenced film clips alone after they had been told that the experimenters wanted to ask them some questions about these clips. One possible interpretation of this latter finding is that these participants were now displaying appropriate expressions to an imagined audience that was interested in their emotional reactions. Perhaps, then, people with more other-oriented values are simply more attuned to the differential requirements of interpersonal situations.

Unlike Friesen, Matsumoto and Kupperbusch (2001) also collected self-report data about emotional reactions. This allowed them to assess the correspondence between experience and expression more directly. Even though their facial displays were affected, it was found that high-collectivists did not report less intense emotional reactions to the film clips after watching them while observed by the professor. At first glance, this finding seems to support Ekman's notion that expression of emotion is being explicitly suppressed.

However, problems of interpretation exist here, too. First, emotion was reported after rather than during the film clips, whereas facial movements were recorded while the films were still showing. As argued previously, the facial communications to the professor may not always have been about the film clips in the first place and would not therefore be expected to reflect the overall emotional impression produced by them. Further, like facial communications, self-reports of emotion may also be closely attuned to the perceived interpersonal context, especially for people with collectivistic values. It is possible, therefore, that these participants' reports of emotions reflected the perceived demands of an enquiry about their specific reactions to the films as much as their actual emotional feelings during all aspects of the procedure (including their interaction with the professor). Psychophysiological measures were also recorded during film-viewing, but Matsumoto and Kupperbusch (2001) fail to report the results of their analysis.

Although these studies provide only limited evidence for Ekman's notion of display rules, the idea still has a strong intuitive appeal because most of us can readily think of situations where we felt an urge to express something but tried to control it. Fridlund's alternative interpretation that this depends on conflicting social motives (or conflicting demands of different audiences) seems less satisfactory because the impulse to express something often seems to come from a source that is somehow deeper inside us than the need to suppress this impulse. Of course, this sense of primacy (or "control precedence" [Frijda, 1986]) may derive from our prior socialization into romantic ideologies, but it doesn't usually feel that way. Alternatively, it is possible to argue that our deeply felt urges reflect our closer identification with the relevant identity positions or roles rather than any natural origins (Parkinson, 1995; cf. Sarbin, 1986).

However, the implication that one set of motives come from a different and more personally felt (or identity relevant) place would still take us close to an interpretation of these motives as specifically emotional ones. To permit distinctions between motives and intentions on the basis of either their priority or proximity to personal or social identity opens the door for a two-factor analysis not too dissimilar from Ekman's where emotional expression urges are controlled by culturally determined regulation strategies.

A few studies have attempted to uncover separate effects of display rules and social motives. For example, Zaalberg, Manstead, and Fischer (2004) used confederates to tell either good or bad jokes to their participants and assessed their social motives, conformity to display rules, and facial movements. Good jokes produced more Duchenne smiling and were associated with the desire to share pleasant feelings. Participants who experienced unpleasant emotions in response to the joke (e.g., embarrassment) showed more non-Duchenne, or "polite" smiles, and reported "prosocial motives" relating to not wanting to offend the other, wanting to reassure them, and not wanting to appear disloyal. Further, differences in smiling between conditions were apparently mediated by these social motives and display rules. These results seem to suggest that the expression of true happiness is mediated by a sharing motive, explaining audience effects on smiling, whereas the camouflaging of negative emotion is mediated by conformity to display rules. Although this study attempted to manipulate social motives and display rules by varying joke quality, in fact non-Duchenne smiles were not confined to conditions in which the bad joke was delivered but also depended on the gender of the joke-teller. In particular, when a woman told the joke, this led to more "polite" smiling regardless of how good or bad the joke was. Clearly, then, the possibility exists that other unmeasured kinds of gender-relevant social motives explained this effect rather than the display rules that were explicitly assessed. More generally, "display rules," "social motives," and even "emotions" do not always seem to represent mutually exclusive categories of phenomena that can easily be manipulated independently of one another.

Solitary Smiling

An obvious problem for an exclusively communicative account of facial movements is the undisputed fact that our faces are not static when no one is around to observe our displays. Indeed, some people seem to cry more in private than in public, and it is certainly true that we may smile, frown, blush, or show surprise in situations that involve no direct interpersonal interaction. Fridlund's response is to question whether sociality is something that can ever be totally absent from a situation. Like Mead, he argues that even private actions are conducted with someone else in mind, even if that someone is simply a generalized other. With respect to facial movements, our displays may be oriented to imagined audiences, our parents, absent lovers or friends, antagonists, heroes or heroines.

Although at first blush the notion of imagined audiences seems to make Fridlund's contention that displays are always interpersonally oriented unfalsifiable in principle, an ingenious experiment successfully established the viability of his concept of *implicit sociality* (Fridlund, 1991). In this study, participants watched a humorous film alone, but with others more or less present either physically or in their imagination. Facial movements were most pronounced when participants believed that an acquaintance who had arrived with them was watching the same film in a separate room, weaker when the acquaintance was described as performing a different task, and weaker still when the participant had arrived at the laboratory alone. Fridlund's explanation of these findings is that we direct private displays at imagined others, and those others are more available in imagination when they are sharing a similar experience.

Subsequent studies using a similar procedure have shown that the emotional power of the film also makes a difference to facial movements, and concluded that displays depend on both emotion and social context (e.g., Hess, Banse, & Kappas, 1995). However, it might equally be argued that different films elicit different social motives and different affiliative tendencies (e.g., Chovil & Fridlund, 1992).

It is not only the intensity of the emotion provoked by a film that may affect social motives (or display rules), but also its quality. For example, Jakobs, Manstead, and Fischer (2001) found that facial displays while watching sad films were influenced by the sociality of the setting, with more smiles and "sadness" displays when the film was watched with a friend than when a stranger viewed the same film in a separate room. Correspondingly, "fear" displays were least common in the coviewing friend setting. The authors interpret these results as being broadly consistent with the behavioral ecology view, but point out the anomaly that "sad" faces were most common in the alone condition when sociality was apparently at a minimum. However, they also acknowledge that this last finding might be explained by solitary viewers' imagining an idealized audience to whom they can address their appeals for comfort during the presentation of upsetting material (Jakobs, Manstead, & Fischer, 2001).

☐ Conclusions

A major distinction between accounts of faces concerns whether referential meaning of faces is prior to or dependent on their role in pragmatic action. Ekman (1973), for example, sees faces as symptoms of emotion that are then subsumed for purposes of conversation. Fridlund (1991, 1994), on the other hand, sees the communicative role of displays as primary. Furthermore, he argues that what displays communicate is something intrinsically social. And, despite his emphasis on evolutionary origins, Fridlund is also willing to acknowledge that part of the development of facial displays may depend on learning and socialization. In all three senses, then, Fridlund's theory elevates the importance of interpersonal factors.

However, Fridlund's account remains restrictive in a number of ways. In particular, his emphasis on facial displays as indicators of social motives tends to give the impression that facial movements can never express emotions. However, the simple fact that people often interpret faces in emotional terms makes it highly likely that they will also come to use them to convey this kind of meaning. Rather than claiming that facial movements display social motives instead of expressing emotions, then, it is possible to conclude that they communicate both kinds of information in different circumstances (see, e.g., Zaalberg, Manstead, & Fischer, 2004).

A second limitation of Fridlund's account is that he does not explicitly differentiate the various possible roles of other people in modulating facial conduct. The emphasis is on audience effects, wherein the presence or absence of other people determines whether or not a display is given. However, other people don't only serve as audiences for facial movements, but also as their direct targets. For example, an aggressive face may serve as a threat directed toward an antagonist (target) as well as a display of power to other onlookers. Facial conduct is likely to be influenced by the characteristics of both of these other parties to the exchange. To make things even more complicated, targets and onlookers will often be engaging in facial conduct themselves, bringing their own influence to the ongoing episodes. Further, existing relations, respective roles, and social identity positions are likely to make a difference to how each party to an interaction acts and reacts (e.g., Hecht & LaFrance, 1998; Hess, Banse, & Kappas, 1995, and see chapter 5, this volume).

Similarly, Fridlund's theory may acknowledge the other-orientation of facial movements, but it underestimates the variety of pragmatic functions that they serve. Signaling in Fridlund's terms implies a transmission of semantic meaning (telling the receiver something about the sender) rather than an exertion of pragmatic effects (influencing others directly as in Dewey's and Mead's theories). Faces don't only communicate information about social motives; they can also perform corresponding interpersonal acts of blaming, persuading, asking for help, and so on.

A final problem concerns Fridlund's treatment of facial displays as relatively time-limited signals. He gives little attention either to the temporal structure of facial movements or their mutual responsivity over time. Faces aren't just directed at others; they are attuned to their reciprocally attuned faces. "Displays" don't just flash on to provide a single message. They unfold to develop meaning in context.

☐ Interpersonal Consequences of Facial Conduct

In previous sections of this chapter, we have considered how the nature of the interpersonal context affects facial movement. Our conclusion is that faces may perform a variety of practical and communicative acts that are specifically oriented to other people. One implication is that the meaning of faces derives partly from their effects, particularly their effects on other people.

To the extent that facial movements are expressions, their consequences are in terms of other people's recognition of the meaning of these expressions. To the extent that faces convey pragmatic meaning, their effect is the influence they exert on others. To the extent that faces move as part of practical actions, their effects reflect their direct contribution to the outcome of the action. Assuming that all three of these effects operate to some degree, faces can impact the interpersonal context by providing information about a person's emotional state, by indicating what that other person is about to do, and by directly influencing the interpersonal situation. In the following subsections, we will focus on some of the possible effects of facial movements on other people's behavior.

Facial Mimicry

One of the most obvious interpersonal effects of facial movements is on other people's facial movements. For example, it has often been observed that people show a tendency to mirror or copy the postures and expressions of people with whom they are interacting (Lipps, 1907). I lean forward to share an intimacy, you lean forward to receive and acknowledge it. You grimace at the memory of an embarrassing moment, and I grimace in sympathy, imagining the experience myself (cf. Chovil, 1991). At a less explicit level, we make mutual adjustments to our demeanor as the conversation proceeds, often barely noticing how our faces are changing in response to each other.

Of course, faces don't always respond to other faces by matching their position, otherwise we'd all quickly end up wearing the same expression. It is clearly possible, for example, that you resist my attempt at intimacy and move away from me instead of closer. More generally, sometimes people copy other people's faces, sometimes they make corresponding or complementary facial movements, sometimes they show contrasting facial positions, and at other times, their faces either bear no relation to other faces, or fail to react at all. What then determines whether or not facial positions are copied during interaction?

According to Hatfield, Cacioppo, and Rapson (1994), mimicry is a basic automatic process that runs off in response to attended facial stimuli, as long as contrary impulses or regulatory mechanisms do not counter its effects. In effect, mimicry will happen unless something else gets in its way. For example, our dislike of someone may lead us to express emotions or display social motives that override our natural tendency to match the other person's facial movements. Alternatively, when intimacy reaches too high a level, corrective processes are brought into play to restore interpersonal equilibrium resulting in a decrease in mimicry (cf. Argyle & Dean, 1965; Patterson, 1996). Similarly, we may deliberately stop ourselves from mimicking if the costs are too great.

Part of the reason for assuming that mimicry reflects a primitive reaction comes from evidence relating to its ontogenetic origins. For example, Meltzoff and Moore (1977) showed that neonates tend to copy many adult facial movements, and Haviland and Lelwica (1987) found that this includes emotionally relevant facial movements. These findings are usually seen as offering support for an innate sensitivity to human faces (cf. Fantz, 1965), and a predisposition to associate these stimuli with prewired motor programs for facial muscles. Infants are equipped with appropriate neural machinery ensuring that they quickly enter into an intersubjective relationship with an appropriate caregiver (cf. Trevarthen, 1984).

However plausible this may be, it is also true that infants' attention is explicitly directed to human faces from birth, as a consequence of caregivers' attempts to engage them in interaction. Further, these faces are usually set in an appropriate position and at an appropriate distance for visual focus, and are acutely responsive to any nascent movement from the baby. Arguably, any suitably complex dynamic object at the centre of the perceptual field, whose movements are precisely timed to match those of the infant (e.g., Beebe, Jaffe, Feldstein, Mays, & Alson, 1985) would soon become the target of manipulation attempts. However, because the muscle movements registered (from the adult) correspond to the muscular output (from the infant, cf. Meltzoff and Borton's (1979) evidence for active intermodal mapping), symmetrical movements become possible from both sides, allowing a convergence of mutual action. Caregiver attention means that any relevant movements from the infant will attract exaggerated response. Thus, regardless of the specifics of the underlying neurobiology, the conditions are in place for a rapidly developing mutual shaping of facial conduct (see Fogel et al., 1992). Over time, structured sequences of nonverbal dialogue emerge, providing the basis for coordination of perspectives. In many ways, relationships between infants and caregivers may produce the interdependence of their behavior, rather than prewired interdependences resulting in the relationships. The interaction of caregiver and infant constitutes a higher-level system within which joint actions can be formulated.

Over the course of development, responsiveness to others' faces presumably becomes more flexible. Faces start to be used not only to maintain mutual attention, but also to redirect the course of interaction. This increasing sophistication results in a more selective deployment of mimicry in response to particular interpersonal contingencies. For example, Bavelas and colleagues (1986) presented evidence that wincing in response to another's apparent pain reflects an interpersonally-oriented strategy for communicating empathy (see earlier discussion). In particular, facial movements are precisely timed to permit their perception by the other. This seems to reflect a more context-sensitive form of mimicry than that postulated by Hatfield and colleagues (1994). Here, the underlying process is not a basic link between perception of a facial stimulus and a motor program, but rather a strategy specifically designed to match unfolding circumstances. Indeed, it seems likely that people also sometimes mimic in an entirely intentional and deliberate way, and this ability may reflect a developmental articulation of the low-level processes proposed previously. In most real-life circumstances a complex interplay probably exists between these different kinds of process.

Even the most basic forms of imitation seem to reflect a more active process than the primitive emotion contagion account implies. Newborn infants do not simply respond automatically to someone else's movement but rather seem to deploy their movements selectively in anticipation of specific responses from others (e.g., Nagy & Molnár, 2003; Uzgiris, 1984). Indeed, Trevarthen, Kokkinaki, and Fiamenghi (1999) propose that imitation specifically serves communicative motives from the outset. For example, an infant may copy the form of an adult's action or its temporal structure to convey his or her interpersonal engagement.

Countermimicry

If mimicry becomes more context-sensitive over the course of development, what happens when individuals are not matching one another's faces? In many circumstances, of course, we are not attuned to each other in the slightest degree, but carry on independent lines of facial action. However, there can also be circumstances in which facial interaction does happen, but the two parties' movements do not match but complement or even counter one another. These processes too may have early developmental origins. To take a simple example, looming objects (including faces) induce withdrawal and eye closure. At a more articulated level, attempts to engage an infant's attention using appropriate facial movements may be resisted when the infant is pursuing a different line of action. Similarly, de Rivera (1977; de Rivera & Grinkis, 1984) argues that a primitive form of anger consists in the infant struggling against an over-restrictive embrace (see also Camras, Campos, Oster, Miyake, & Bradshaw, 1992). Corresponding interpersonal dynamics may also underlie facial dialogues in which approach leads to withdrawal from the other, attack leads to escape, or activity is matched by quiescence. If infants always matched their caregiver's facial movements, facial warnings of punishment ("anger expressions") would be less effective regulators of behavior, and interactions with babies would be smoother and duller than they are.

Further, infant facial movements may be more actively attuned to those of interactants than any directly reactive account might imply. For example, in a study by Murray and Trevarthen (1985), a mother's transition from facial responsiveness to impassivity did not provoke similar impassivity, but rather visual attention followed by distress faces. Infants aren't just sensitive to facial position but to the temporal correspondence of facial movements to their own activities. In this regard, a related study by Murray and Trevarthen showed that identical facial movements recorded from an earlier part of a dialogue via closed circuit TV had different effects when reshown in playback, presumably because the movements were no longer in tune with those of the infants.

Regardless of the developmental origins of countermimicry, it is clear that it is a relatively common occurrence in adult interactions. Lanzetta and colleagues conducted a series of experiments showing that whether facial movements match or contrast with those of interactants depends on the specific nature of the interpersonal context. For example, Englis and Lanzetta (1984, cited in McHugo, Lanzetta, Sullivan, Masters, & Englis, 1985) showed that in-group facial movements are often copied, whereas out-group facial movements tend to produce less differentiated facial responses (cf. chapters 5 and 6, this volume). Further, Lanzetta and Englis (1989) found that anticipation of competitive tasks tends to result in countermimicry, whereas anticipation of cooperative activities is more likely to lead to mimicry. The explanation offered for these effects is that facial positions serve as conditioned stimuli for emotional outcomes. In other words, people learn that other people's positive faces are not always associated with pleasant outcomes but sometimes predict punishment or withdrawal of rewards. Correspondingly, their negative faces may sometimes predict withdrawal of punishment or reward. We thus come to react with counter-empathy when interpersonal cues appear indicating a competitive rather than cooperative context.

Most accounts of mimicry and countermimicry assume that facial movements are expressions of underlying affective states. For example, Lanzetta and Englis (1989) argue that faces move concordantly or non-concordantly with others depending on the rewards signaled by those other faces, which in turn elicit internal feelings that ultimately appear on the face. However, countermimicking as well as mimicking facial movements may also be more directly and intrinsically embedded in unfolding conduct. For example, nonmatched facial positions may be used as part of a strategy for influencing the course of an encounter. Just as people winced to establish an empathic relation in Bavelas and colleagues' (1986) study, they may acknowledge the force of an attack (complementary withdrawal), resist an evolving formulation of a relationship (countermimicry), or simply blank the other. In each case, these moves may be carefully orchestrated to fit the evolving tempo of the encounter.

Social Referencing

Faces don't only respond to other faces, but also to other stimuli in the social and nonsocial environment. The information that they convey about these stimuli may then help to influence someone else's reactions. In other words, if we are not sure how to make sense of what is happening, we may look around at others' faces to clarify things (e.g., Latané & Darley, 1968). A clear example of this phenomenon is provided by Sorce, Emde, Campos, and Klinnert's (1985) study of infants' reactions to the "visual cliff" (Gibson & Walk, 1960). One-year-olds were separated from their mothers by a 30 cm deep chasm covered with clear Plexiglass™ that was actually quite safe to cross. It was found that most of these infants ventured over the visual cliff toward an attractive toy if their mothers was smiling or displaying interest from the other side, whereas almost all of them stayed firmly put if their mothers showed a "fear" or an "anger" face. Sorce and colleagues concluded that infants appraise uncertain situations partly on the basis of information derived from facial signals from their primary caregiver. In this study, the infants explicitly sought information by looking toward their mothers for guidance about how to proceed. However, unsolicited expressions can also shape behavior, as when a sudden shriek deters a child from continuing a dangerous course of action (see also Feinman & Lewis, 1983).

From the present point of view, this kind of social referencing (Campos & Stenberg, 1981) is another, more developed manifestation of coordination of mutual activity. Not only are infants equipped to register their caregivers' responses to them, they are also able to calibrate their perspectives on objects and activities in the current environment. Although social referencing may seem like a one-way process of information transmission from caregiver to infant, it is also probable that caregivers adjust their faces in response to their perception of the infant's developing reaction. Indeed, adult faces can provide a guiding commentary on the infant's emerging behavior.

An example of this kind of mutual coordination is provided by Stern and colleagues' (Stern, 1985; Stern, Hofer, Haft, & Dore, 1985) research into affect attunement. This phenomenon occurs when caregivers spontaneously produce movements that match the temporal parameters (or "vitality contours") of infants' actions. For example, imagine a baby struggling to push a square block into an appropriately shaped hole. The task is achieved after a final effort. Under such circumstances, the watching caregiver moves her face or gives a spoken commentary whose onset, development, and offset correspond closely to the rise and decay of effort by the infant and the transition from frustration to relief. She might say something like: "Oo-ooh, ye-es, now you've done it," and release the tension in her face just as the block is finally eased through. According to Stern, such occurrences are part of the establishment of communion between interactants, and serve the function of drawing attention to abstract features of an experience that are not dependent on modality of information. They thus permit the shared formulation of a common focus of activity in a way that goes beyond any simple mimicry.

For adults too, others' facial movements can regulate action and interpretation. For example, Manstead and Fischer (2001) outline processes of social appraisal involving us taking other people's perspectives and potential reactions into account when interpreting and evaluating the emotional significance of a situation. To the extent that facial movements express emotions or signal probable future actions, they will provide one of the central inputs to such a social appraisal process.

☐ Interpersonal Dynamics

Previous sections of this chapter have treated facial movements as inputs or outputs of an interpersonal process. Indeed, the usual emphases of psychological research fall on what the face reacts to and how its reactions are read. The idea seems to be that isolated snapshots of facial behavior provide iconic images of emotional state that are then read (or misread) by someone else. Of course, in everyday interactions, all senders are also receivers, and part of what they are reacting to is the reaction of the other. Faces are part of the interpersonal context as well as what this context shapes, and this context is by no means fixed or static.

Some research into nonverbal conduct goes part way toward acknowledging this impact of the dynamic interpersonal context. For example, Bernieri, Reznick, & Rosenthal (e.g., 1988) emphasize the continuous interplay between nonverbal movements of parties to interaction, including processes of mimicry, complementarity, and synchronization. From such perspectives, it becomes possible to view emotional meaning as an emergent phenomenon arising from an unfolding conversation of gestures (cf. Mead, 1934).

Bernieri and colleagues (1988) have shown how rapport is not sensed purely on the basis of positivity of expressive conduct but also on the mutual temporal coordination of the parties to an interaction. People get in tune with each other without realizing that this is happening. This leads to an important lesson: The study of what faces do and what influences faces should not restrict itself solely to preconceptions about what faces tell us. Even when examining their social role, it is important to remember that part of the interpersonal impact of faces is not mediated by any kind of conscious reflection about what the face means.

Temporal interdependence of facial movements need not be restricted to different levels of synchrony, however. Instead, there may be a more complex internal dynamic structure to the unfolding of interpersonal encounters. For example, Grammer, Kruck, and Magnusson (1998) used a computerized search algorithm to detect hierarchically patterned synchronies between the movements of interacting men and women. Romantic interest between the two parties to the conversation led to articulated interpersonal sequences of exchange with consistent time structure. The particularities of these patterned rhythms, however, did not generalize across couples, suggesting that a more creative process of relationship development may be at work. Despite the limitation that verbal conduct was not analyzed in this study (leaving open the possibility that some of the internal structure reflected the course of the verbal dialogue [cf. Wagner & Lee, 1999]), the research represents a very promising approach to the dynamics of real-time nonverbal interaction.

☐ Toward an Interpersonal Theory of Facial Movement

Faces seem to play such diverse roles in interpersonal interaction that a unifying theory capable of accommodating them all may seem beyond our grasp. However, some researchers have risen to this challenge. For example, Patterson (1996) has developed a functional model of nonverbal exchange that attempts to articulate the parallel processes of perception and action underlying interactive conduct at an individual level. The basic assumption is that both strategic and reactive elements control non-verbal conduct. On one level, interactants are pursuing a variety of possible goals, and modulate their behavioral presentations accordingly. For example, if we are concerned with making a good impression on someone, we will attempt to monitor our metaperceptions of how they are evaluating us, and adjust our performance to correct any problems in this regard. The extent of cognitive capacity devoted to this task will detract from the performance of any other effortful tasks.

These strategic processes are in constant interaction with lower-level reactive processes. For example, levels of intimacy are automatically regulated within interactions by compensating for changes in contact from the other person. A classic example of this phenomenon is provided by Argyle and Dean's (1965) research showing that induced spatial proximity between interactants leads to reduction of other signals of intimacy. Thus, smiling and eye contact might occur less when someone else gets too close to you. One of Patterson's (1996) important insights is that these low-level regulatory processes may be overridden when higher-level goals become relevant. For example, the desire for a closer relationship with someone who gets closer to you may lead you to intensify rather than diminish your expressions of intimacy.

Patterson's model explicitly restricts itself to an individualistic level of analysis, and this clearly excludes the effect of goals or functions that are not somehow represented in the minds of single interactants. However, it is also possible that emergent functions arise because of the nature of the relationship between two people. For example, couples with relationship problems tend to adopt a tit-for-tat strategy in which disapproval from one party tends to be met by disapproval from the other, whereas satisfied partners tend to respond to negative communications with positive ones (Gottmann, 1994). These interpersonal processes presumably do not directly reflect the simple intentions of either party, nor do they arise from the automatic regulation of their intimacy behaviors. Instead, interactants get locked into patterns that neither of them can easily control. More generally, theories of nonverbal interaction need to consider processes that address the mutual contingency and interdependence of entities rather than exclusively working upward from constituent events.

☐ Final Words

The words normally used to describe facial movements carry strong implications about their functions. "Expression" implies an outpouring of something that was inside, whereas "display" implies putting on a show for others. Both words imply that faces carry meaning: semantic or referential meaning in the first case, and pragmatic meaning in the second. In this chapter, we have argued that all of these implications are restrictive. Faces do other things, in addition to expressing or displaying meanings, and the meanings that they express or display are not exclusively emotional in the first place. Examining facial conduct in interpersonal context facilitates a better appreciation of the dynamic complexity of the phenomenon, and gets us closer to the processes underlying the real-time production of emotion in everyday social life.

Interpersonal Emotions

Someone does something to offend you. You get angry. The other person gets angry back (or perhaps feels appropriately guilty). Emotions often unfold like this as a consequence of somebody else's actions or emotions. And they rarely simply fizzle out without having any further impact on the interpersonal world. Indeed, it is usually hard to ignore other people's emotions. Just as an outstretched finger tends to direct attention wherever it points, a witnessed emotion encourages us to take account of its implied perspective on events.

The fact that the interpersonal arena is one of the key venues for the interplay of emotions is hardly controversial. Cinematic, theatrical, and narrative representations of emotional episodes typically rely on social interaction to exert their dramatic effect. Attraction, betrayal, self-sacrifice, rejection, redemption—all these are themes worked out in encounters between people at various stages of their developing relationships.

Despite emotion's evident connections to interpersonal processes, however, its central essence is usually considered to be private. Indeed, the intrapsychic aspects of emotion are also routinely emphasized in Western popular narratives. Many of the most poignant works of fiction work from the premise that a powerful emotion can be hidden or suppressed. Few things are more moving than seeing someone facing impossible problems but refusing to give in to despair, or even to acknowledge it openly. Unexpressed inner turmoil somehow seems more powerful than the vented variety. Furthermore, it is patently true that emotion can be experienced when one is alone, for example, in a darkened cinema, or when a loved one has departed.

In this chapter, we will propose that in spite of their internal aspects, many emotions make most sense when put into interpersonal context. Our focus will fall on theory and research concerning the impact of other people on emotions and of emotions on other people. Although interpersonal factors might be seen as extrinsic to the real individual business of what emotions do, we believe that, like facial movements, emotions are often fundamentally other-oriented processes. Indeed, many of the theoretical principles used to explain facial conduct have similar application to the understanding of emotion itself.

A recurrent theme of this chapter is that a key function of many emotions is to bring about interpersonal effects (Parkinson, 1995, 1996). We get angry to draw attention to the unfairness of our predicament; we become sad or frightened to solicit different kinds of social support; we fall in love so that we may redefine our relationship, and so on. Further, these interpersonal projects are not always privately formulated in the individual minds of coineteractants but instead often emerge from the process of interaction itself, resulting either in mutuality of feeling or the establishment of antagonistic boundaries. For instance, emotions tend to come in matching or contrasting pairs over the course of a dialogue, with anger leading to another's anger or guilt, love begetting love or disdain, and so forth. Our emotional attitudes to one another are part of the continual redefinition of ongoing relationships.

☐ Interpersonal Processes

How does emotion relate to the interpersonal world? In this section, we review some of the possible ways in which other people affect and are affected by our emotions. We focus in particular on three kinds of processes. The first involves the direct transmission of emotion from one person to another, implying that affect may spread like a virus through the interpersonal world (emotional contagion [Hatfield et al., 1994]). In the second, emotions are seen as oriented to other people's apparent evaluation and interpretation of the current situation (social appraisal [Manstead & Fischer, 2001]). For example, whether we find a joke amusing may partly depend on other people's reactions to its content (i.e., whether or not they seem to find it offensive). The final kind of process operates when other people's emotions motivate our own behavior more directly, by conveying congratulation, blame, and serving as rewards or punishments for what we have done (interpersonal reinforcement [cf. Keltner & Haidt,

1999]). Thus, one of the incentives for taking a course of action may be our anticipation of other people's positive emotional reactions to its outcome. In subsequent sections of the chapter, we will turn our attention to the interpersonal causes and effects of specific emotions, but for the moment our focus will be on more general processes.

Emotion Contagion

Other people's emotions often directly influence our own. For example, the emotions of team members sometimes converge with one another (e.g., Totterdell, 2000, and chapter 4, this volume). When people spend a lot of time together they may end up sharing similar feelings. One possible process underlying this kind of interpersonal influence is primitive emotion contagion (see also chapter 6, this volume). According to Hatfield and colleagues (1994; see also Lipps, 1907), automatic mimicry involves the transmission of feelings as well as expressions of feeling. In particular, internal feedback from the postural and gestural movements induced by others is thought to also produce corresponding emotional experiences. As in James's (1884) theory, the idea is that perceptions of bodily changes provide the substance of emotion. Thus, even a copied smile might induce happiness.

Neumann and Strack (2000) present evidence that listening to someone reading in a happy, sad, or neutral voice tends to induce corresponding emotional states. Their explanation is that motor impulses to vocalize in matching tones are automatically elicited by the sound of another person's voice, and these impulses are in turn associated with affect. Alternatively, the sound of a happy voice may simply be more pleasant than that of a sad voice, just as a smile is usually perceived as more attractive than a grimace (cf. Rolls, 1999 on smiles as potential positive reinforcers, and see discussion following). In either case, these findings suggest that people do not need to physically mimic someone else to catch their mood.

The usual interpretation of emotion contagion is that one person's affect influences another's in a one-way, one-shot process. However, emotions clearly function as causes as well as effects (Hess, Philippot, & Blairy, 1999). Therefore, one person's emotion may influence another's, that other person's emotion may in turn influence the first person's, and so on. If this kind of mutual contagion operated automatically and without correction, emotion would rapidly escalate between people in a seemingly unstoppable process. For example, my anxiety about an impending event would intensify yours, which in turn would increase mine still further, with no apparent end to the rising panic developing between us. In fact, the kind of mass hysteria implied by this account seems to be a relatively rare phenomenon. One possible reason why interpersonal emotions do not lead to resonance catastrophes of this sort is that deliberative control processes may override contagion. For example, Argyle and Dean's (1965) account of intimacy regulation (see chapter 6) suggests that when people get too close (or start matching us too precisely), we tend to withdraw from them in some way.

If imitation is an active rather than automatic process in the first place (e.g., Trevarthen, Kokkinaki, & Fiamenghi, 1999, and see chapter 6, this volume), then this fact too might help to explain why contagion does not run wild through the interpersonal world. In particular, seeing mimicry as a communicative act (e.g., Bavelas et al., 1986) rather than a reflex-like reaction implies that the capacity to copy someone else is deployed flexibly and with sensitivity to the specific characteristics of the present interpersonal context. In effect, we may only adjust our expressions to match those of people who are either physically or psychologically close to us in some way.

Along similar lines, Hatfield and colleagues (1994) argue that one set of factors determining whether mimicry occurs concerns the nature of the relationship interactants have with one another (during a particular interaction [see Cappella & Planalp, 1981]). In particular, it is proposed that liking facilitates mimicry and contagion, and that people who are relatively less powerful are more likely to copy the movements of those who are more powerful. Unfortunately, the processes underlying these differential effects are not usually specified in the emotion contagion literature. Obviously, both liking and power can influence emotions independently of contagion processes, so the question arises of whether any effects are specifically mediated by mimicry and feedback.

Taking first the case of liking, we obviously care more about what happens to friends than strangers. For this reason, their expressed happiness also makes us happy and we share their sadness when they seem blue. However, this kind of interpersonal process seems to bypass mimicry because it is not the movements that change our affective state but their meaning in the context of our relationship. Of course, it is also true that we tend to pay closer attention to the conduct of those who are near to us, making it more available as a stimulus for copying. But the reason for our attention is again that we already care. Similar arguments apply to putative effects of power on contagion. The feelings of more powerful people matter to us partly because they have the wherewithal to make our lives better or worse, and that is primarily why we are affected by them.

A final reason for the limited consequences of contagion is that postural and facial feedback seems to have only a small effect on experienced emotion. Most studies suggest that expressive movements at best modulate the power of an existing reaction. For example, Strack, Martin, and Stepper (1988) found that holding a pen between the teeth (thus encouraging

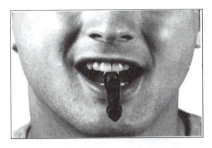

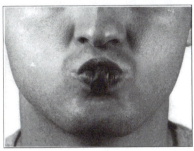

FIGURE 7.1.   Strack et al.'s technique to induce participants to smile or not to smile, without their awareness (from Strack et al. 1988, p. 771). Copyright Fritz Strack and APA.

smiling, see Figure 7.1) led to ratings of greater amusement than holding a pen with the lips (encouraging more of a sad face).

However, this marginally significant effect was smaller than the effect of differences in the humorous cartoon slides designed to provoke amusement in the first place. Feedback effects are not always obtained in the most carefully controlled studies (Tourangeau & Ellsworth, 1979), and when they are, their size is rarely impressive. At face value, these data seem to imply that feedback-mediated emotion contagion would make much less difference to experienced emotion than other aspects of the emotional situation. If so, it would be hard to explain how emotions get effectively transmitted via such a route. Any alteration of affect induced by feedback would be quickly swamped by the emotional power of other aspects of the unfolding situation.

On the other hand, it might be argued that experiments rarely produce the complete, accurate pattern of postural and facial feedback required to induce full-blown emotion, whereas real-life interactive situations typically do (cf. Tomkins, 1981). Evidence to support such a view would be hard to come by, however, because producing the veridical emotion manifestation inevitably implies also producing the emotion itself (Ellsworth & Tourangeau, 1981). Another way of reconciling observations of weak feedback effects with stronger contagion effects is to suggest that people catch each other's emotion by other processes (e.g., exposure to a shared situation, social appraisal [Manstead & Fischer, 2001], normative influence, and so on; see chapter 4 of this volume for discussion of these alternatives).

Despite these reservations, we do not want to rule out any role for emotion contagion processes in interpersonal life. Sometimes it certainly seems true that the tone of an interaction can be influenced by subtle indications of affective state, conveyed not only by the face, voice, and body, but also by the rhythm and tempo of the exchange, its enmeshment, and the way different parts relate to each other. However, we do not believe that the emotional aspects of these phenomena are produced purely as a function of direct individual sensory feedback. People read their emotional states not only from observation of their own reactions, but also from the reactions of others who reflect it back to them. We tend to feel happier when smiling mainly because others often smile back, and their apparent happiness makes us feel better. In other words, interpersonal rather than intrapsychic feedback may mediate many examples of real-life emotion contagion.

Social Appraisal

Work on emotion contagion suggests that other people's emotions may affect our own because of the physical characteristics of the responses they elicit. Alternatively, it may be the contextual meaning of their emotional presentation that is more important. For example, someone else's fear tells us that there may be something in the current situation to be afraid of, and someone else's anger may direct us to an otherwise unnoticed injustice. More generally, our emotions are attuned not only to others' emotions but also to their apparent evaluations and interpretations, even when these are expressed in nonemotional terms. Other people's emotional and nonemotional conduct can provide information that modifies or otherwise elaborates the emotional meaning of what is happening to us.

What makes an insult insulting, for instance, is not always the words themselves, nor even our private interpretation of their meaning, but rather the way in which other people are apparently responding to it. Their sudden silence or catching of breath underlines the affective significance of what is happening, in addition to making them appropriate addressees for any reparatory communicative attempt. In other words, we may get angry not only to show an antagonist that we deserve more respect, but also to restore our status in the eyes of others who might be present. This section provides a general discussion of how other people's reactions may magnify or minimize the emotional power of events.

Chapter 6 introduced the phenomenon of social referencing, whereby infants check adults' emotional responses to ambiguous situations to clarify how they should respond. In adult life, too, the definition of what is happening at an emotional level is often interpersonally formulated. For example, mutual congratulation may build into a celebratory mood in cohesive groups (cf. Totterdell, 2000; Totterdell et al., 1998; chapter 4, this volume), whereas sharing niggles about an unfavorable outcome may make people more depressed than they were before. In short, our emotions do not depend solely on the intrinsic character of their intentional object but also on how others' reactions frame the focal event (Manstead & Fischer, 2001).

When infants engage in social referencing, they actively seek a definition of the current transaction by checking their parents' apparent emotional response. Similarly, adults may attempt to engineer or locate specific interpersonal situations that help to clarify meaning or preserve a favored interpretation of what is happening. For example, Schachter (1959) found that people anticipating electric shocks in an unfamiliar situation preferred the company of another person awaiting a similar fate to that of someone in a different and more pleasant predicament. One of the participants explained this preference in the following terms: "I wanted to wait with other people to see how they would react while waiting for the experiment" (p. 41). According to Schachter, we seek emotional clarity by engaging in social comparisons with relevant others.

Social comparison can also determine the strength and character of our emotions more directly. Upward social comparison with someone who is better off tends to make us less happy, whereas downward social comparisons can be reassuring. Indeed, in many competitive sports, what makes an outcome a success or failure does not reflect the intrinsic quality of the performance, bur rather whether it exceeds or falls short of the performance of others. According to research by Medvec, Gilovich, and Madey (1995), obtaining a bronze medal often feels better than obtaining a silver one because the latter invokes comparisons with the winner, whereas the former invokes comparisons with competitors who failed to obtain a medal at all. Needless to say, the institutions surrounding competitive activity also provide part of the cultural context for our achievement-related attributions, appraisals, and emotions in the first place (see chapters 3 & 8).

Our emotional responses to others' reactions also depend on our specific relationship with them. For example, we may be inclined to adopt stances toward an emotional object that correspond to those of our friends and allies but contrast with those of our enemies (see chapter 5). Further, we may adopt complementary emotional positions on the basis of predefined role positions. For example, in a study by Zillmann,

Weaver, Mundorf, and Aust (1986), male students rated a horror movie as more enjoyable when their female companion was distressed, but female students had a better time when their male companion showed "mastery." Of course, such stereotypical reactions may have invoked a traditional date-movie scenario that had positive connotations for participants of this age group. In different cultural or subcultural settings, it is likely that different effects would be observed.

In addition to influencing the course of the appraisal process, other people also help to constitute the focus and content of appraisal. For example, one of the things that I am upset about may be the fact that you are upset too. Thus, the transmission of emotion from one person to another may depend on empathy rather than primitive emotional contagion. Of course, if two people have an antagonistic relationship they may be pleased about, rather than sympathetic toward, the other person's distress (as happens in experiences of *Schadenfreude* [e.g., Ben Ze'ev, 2001, and see chapter 5, this volume]).

A final way in which interpersonal factors may influence the appraisal of an object relates to their perceived implications for the coping process. According to Lazarus (1991a), for example, situations that we feel able to deal with have less of a negative impact than those about which we can do nothing. One of the factors determining coping ability is clearly the presence or availability of others who might help. Indeed, social support is widely acknowledged to be a central coping resource (e.g., Saltzman & Holahan, 2002). In addition to shaping appraisals about perceived coping potential, enlisting social support may actually help more directly with the practical task of addressing the emotional situation (*problem-focused coping*) and the feelings associated with it (*emotion-focused coping*). To take this further, it is possible that one of the central functions of many negative emotions is precisely to enlist the cooperation of others in addressing current concerns.

Interpersonal Reinforcement

The literature concerning social appraisal suggests that other people's emotions influence our own by virtue of their informational content. For example, fear conveys danger and threat, whereas happiness conveys safety. Missing from this account is the obvious fact that witnessing other people's emotions can be a pleasant or unpleasant experience prior to interpretation of their meaning. For example, we all know how uncomfortable it feels to hear a baby crying, and how pleasant the sound of their laughter can be. Further, we don't like it when someone shouts at us not only because of the implications of their anger but also because of the raw intensity of the noise. Thus, the pleasure or pain induced by others' emotions may derive directly from the inherent reward or punishment value of their physical manifestations rather than from mimicry-induced internal feedback (as outlined above). For example, Rolls (1999) proposes that smiles may be innately defined positive reinforcers for good evolutionary reasons. Similarly, Keltner and Buswell (1997) imply that the distinctive dynamic presentation of embarrassment may serve as a strategy for deflecting attention (see following discussion). Because witnessing another's discomfiture is painful for us, we tend to look away or otherwise divert attention from their conduct.

So-called social referencing effects may also be interpreted in accordance with such an account. In particular, Klinnert, Campos, Sorce, Emde, and Svejda (1983) document how the adult's expression of emotion regulates the infant's behavior as it approaches a visual cliff. But does the mother's smile represent a safety signal or rather a simple reward for proceeding forward? Does the fear display convey a warning about danger, or represent an unpleasant interpersonal stimulus that the infant wants to terminate? Of course, the truth probably lies somewhere between these two extreme formulations of cognition or conditioning. Although it is certainly possible that some patterned expressions are primary reinforcers, their reward value is likely to change as a function of experience over the course of interpersonal development. For example, a parent's display of anger toward an infant represents a reliable predictor of shouting and possibly worse, and thus becomes a conditioned stimulus for the affective reaction to loud noises and direct punishment. An angry frown may soon accrue its meaning as a warning because of the interpersonal routines within which it predictably occurs. Nevertheless, some of the more direct effects of emotional presentations (pitch and modulation of voice, intensity of volume or movement) probably persist throughout development and into adult life.

Summary

In this section, we have reviewed evidence that three kinds of process underlie emotion's relations to the interpersonal world. The emotional contagion concept implies that our emotions influence those of others by virtue of the *bodily changes* that they evoke. Interpersonal affect spreads because of the internal experiences that it induces. By contrast, the idea of social appraisal is that the *information* conveyed by others' reactions helps to define emotional significance. Finally, interpersonal reinforcement processes suggest that others' emotions have inherent *motivational* properties that underlie their regulation of our behavior. Clearly these possibilities are not mutually exclusive. You may catch my smile and experience similar feelings because of mimicry, evaluate the situation more positively as a consequence of my implied evaluation, and also be motivated to repeat whatever action provoked my smile because of its reinforcing properties. Further, your reaction to my smiling may reward me for engaging in this particular emotional attitude in the first place. As a consequence of repeated experiences of this kind, I may well learn to use emotion as a way of inducing exactly the kinds of interpersonal effect implied by contagion, social appraisal, and interpersonal reinforcement. In short, emotion soon may come to be a mode of strategic interpersonal influence that systematically regulates the reactions of other people. In later sections of this chapter, we shall explore this possibility more explicitly.

☐ Social Emotions

In the previous section, we focused on general processes whereby the interpersonal world might influence (and be influenced by) emotional processes. Now we shall apply some of these general principles to specific emotions. Most of the relevant research has focused on uncontroversially social emotions such as guilt, shame, and embarrassment. In this section, then, we shall present some of the key research findings concerning these emotions before broadening our analysis in the next section to cover the interpersonal causes and consequences of less obviously interpersonal emotions. In each case, our focus will be on an emotion's interpersonal causes, effects, and functions. More specifically, we attempt to show how the emotion in question is oriented to the real and anticipated reactions of others rather than depending solely on appraisal of a social or nonsocial object. Indeed, we shall also argue that many social emotions emerge at an earlier stage of ontogenetic development than the articulated cognitive representations that are often assumed to underlie them. Further, we believe that even so-called "basic" emotions have interpersonal origins and develop in close attunement with social relations. The final recurrent theme is that emotions are not necessarily defined by the quality of the associated feeling state but may instead derive their identity from the interpersonal dynamics that provide the context for their subjective aspects (cf. Russell, 1979, 2003; chapter 2, this volume).

Embarrassment

Is it possible to feel embarrassed without even imagining a social situation? Indeed, if no one could conceivably witness our *faux pas*, would it be a cause for embarrassment? Would it even be a *faux pas* in the first place? In a study by Tangney, Wagner, Hill-Barlow, Marschall, and Gramzow (1996), about 98% of reported experiences of embarrassment occurred in the presence of other people. Psychologists who study embarrassment usually take its fundamentally social nature for granted, disagreeing mainly about what its precise interpersonal causes and functions are.

Keltner and Buswell (1997) compare and contrast "social evaluation" and "awkward social interaction" accounts of the occasions for embarrassment. According to the first view, people get embarrassed when they believe that others may evaluate them negatively because of some social transgression. In support of such a notion, Miller (1995) found that people scoring higher on personality measures assessing social evaluation concerns (e.g., fear of social exclusion, need for approval) also tended to be more prone to embarrassment.

The alternative "awkward interaction" account sees embarrassment as a social lubricant that smoothes out and glosses over disruptions in interpersonal interaction. The key occasion for embarrassment, in this view, is an interruption of the orderly performance of social action. For example, Parrott and Smith (1991) found that this kind of flawed conduct is one of the most commonly reported embarrassing situations. You get someone's name wrong, accidentally knock over his or her drink, or choke on your food when trying to speak. To repair your relation to the other, you need to distance yourself from the apparent implications of these mishaps and show that the conduct in question was just a temporary aberration. Embarrassment serves to communicate that you are not the kind of person who normally does this kind of thing, and that you are acutely aware that this is not the way things are supposed to be done. Indeed, the remedial function of embarrassment is evidenced by more positive evaluations of people who display appropriate discomfiture following social gaffes (e.g., Semin & Manstead, 1982). We are more willing to overlook a *faux pas* if it is accompanied by appropriate discomfiture. Further, Leary, Landel, and Patton (1996) have demonstrated that embarrassment persists until its communicative function has been served. In their study, participants who had just recorded their own rendition of the schmaltzy song "Feelings" rated their embarrassment as higher if the experimenter had apparently not interpreted their blushing as a sign of embarrassment. People will apparently continue to be embarrassed until the message conveyed by the emotion has been received and acknowledged by its intended recipient.

In Keltner and Buswell's (1997) presentation, both "social evaluation" and "awkward interaction" are primarily *interpersonal* factors that have an effect on individual emotion. Goffman (1956), however, develops an account that situates these effects within a broader *institutional* frame. His argument is that organizations sometimes carry contradictory norms about interpersonal conduct. For example, implicit rules about equality of status in certain settings (the coffee machine or elevator) may be pit against the more rigid hierarchies of power that operate in other contexts. Individuals sometimes find themselves in situations where the consequent prescriptions for conduct are brought into conflict, producing embarrassment (e.g., social obligations to converse with a social inferior as an equal on an extended elevator ride). These observations should remind us that interpersonal adjustments are tightly embedded in broader networks of social arrangements (chapters 2, 4, and 8, this volume). Goffman also pinpoints an important interpersonal function of embarrassment based on this analysis. Showing embarrassment is a way of avoiding a failed performance when one's position would be untenable. However, it serves as a commitment to the norms that one is failing to live up to and a promissory note that more successful performance is possible in the future. As such, it functions to preserve personal status as well as the contradictory social structure surrounding it (cf. Averill, 1980).

The accounts of embarrassment reviewed so far certainly capture many of our everyday intuitions about when embarrassment occurs. Indeed, much of the supportive evidence derives from participants' reports of embarrassing incidents, and so presumably reflects their prototypical representations of what should count as a good example of this emotion (cf. Parkinson, 1999). However, it remains an open question whether either beliefs about others' evaluations or flawed social performances are necessary conditions for the occurrence of this emotion when nontypical cases are also considered. For example, embarrassment sometimes occurs when people are praised in public (e.g., Parrott & Smith, 1991), or more simply when other people's attention is directed at them (e.g., Sabini, Siepmann, Stein, & Meyerowitz, 2000). Neither of these seem to imply negative evaluations, and, although there may be uncertainty about how to respond, awkwardness in interaction hardly seems inevitable. Lewis (2000), for example, reports that while lecturing he often tells students that he is going to point at one of them randomly. He then closes his eyes and stretches out his arm in an arbitrary direction. The hapless victim reliably shows embarrassment. A minimal condition for this emotion therefore seems to be public attention (of certain kinds)—being put on the spot. Of course, this may well then lead to concerns about how to present oneself, but these seem to be secondary to the initial reaction. If this analysis is correct, the function of embarrassment may not be strictly appeasement (as suggested by Keltner & Buswell, 1997), but rather a deflection of this unwanted attention. Situations involving negative evaluations or awkward interactions are just some common examples of occasions where attention is unwanted and its deflection is desired.

Such an account suggests that embarrassment does not depend on "beliefs about others' evaluations" but rather on the direct detection of interpersonal attention. As such, the emotion might have plausible pre-cursors during early infancy. Indeed, Reddy (2000) observed "coy" smiles accompanied by gaze aversion when 2-month-old infants interacted with parents or were held in front of a mirror (see Figure 7.2).

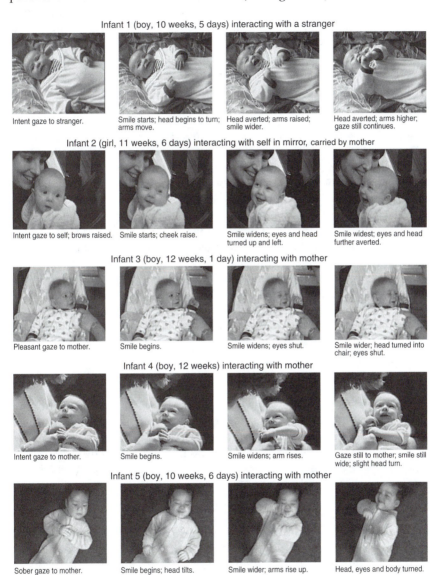

Infant 1 (boy, 10 weeks, 5 days) interacting with a stranger

Intent gaze to stranger.

Smile starts; head begins to turn; arms move.

Head averted; arms raised; smile wider.

Head averted; arms higher; gaze still continues.

Infant 2 (girl, 11 weeks, 6 days) interacting with self in mirror, carried by mother

Intent gaze to self; brows raised.

Smile starts; cheek raise.

Smile widens; eyes and head turned up and left.

Smile widest; eyes and head further averted.

Infant 3 (boy, 12 weeks, 1 day) interacting with mother

Pleasant gaze to mother.

Smile begins.

Smile widens; eyes shut.

Smile wider; head turned into chair; eyes shut.

Infant 4 (boy, 12 weeks) interacting with mother

Intent gaze to mother.

Smile begins.

Smile widens; arm rises.

Gaze still to mother; smile still wide; slight head turn.

Infant 5 (boy, 10 weeks, 6 days) interacting with mother

Sober gaze to mother.

Smile begins; head tilts.

Smile wider; arms rise up.

Head, eyes and body turned.

FIGURE 7.2.   Coyness in early infancy (Reddy, 2000)

Further, Draghi-Lorenz, Reddy, and Morris (in press) found that students attributed coyness, shyness, or embarrassment to these movements significantly more than for control movements in similar contexts. As an example of early discomfort of this kind, a parent in Draghi-Lorenz's (2001) study reports that her 10-month-old boy looked embarrassed when a friend praised him for having just started to crawl. The infant immediately buried his face in the carpet and stopped crawling. Whether particular situated actions of this kind reflect *bona fide* embarrassment is largely a matter of definition. However, it is clear that something very like adult manifestations of this emotion emerge from early interpersonal interactions, and therefore do not seem to depend on articulated cognitive representations of self in relation to others. Indeed, it seems possible that the development of self-consciousness depends on the experience of affective reactions to others' attention (cf. Barrett, 1998). Later in development, social norms and rules about the proper occasions for embarrassment may be superimposed on these more basic elicitors (see following discussion).

In summary, embarrassment is typically caused by unwanted interpersonal attention, and its manifestations serve to deflect this attention. Further, a more articulated form of this emotion plays a role in the maintenance of social order in cultures and institutions where status is not a permanent possession across all possible interpersonal situations. In the following sections, we analyze the interpersonal causes, effects, and functions of other emotions along similar lines, emphasizing their origins in early developmental interaction and their role in coordinating relational positions between people.

Shame

Like embarrassment, shame seems to be an emotion that is oriented to others' reactions. In fact, some theorists believe that shame is simply a stronger and more enduring form of embarrassment (e.g., Borg, Staufenbiel, & Scherer, 1988). Many languages do not even distinguish these two emotions, or treat the words for each of them as synonyms. At least in the English speaking world, however, shame seems to imply something more than intense embarrassment. According to many theorists, other people must be seen as negatively evaluating your *intrinsic character* and not merely your *temporary behavior* before shame can occur (e.g., Babcock & Sabini, 1990). For example, Keltner and Buswell (1997) found that reports of embarrassing incidents were associated with violations of social conventions, whereas reports of shame concerned the failure to live up to central standards of conduct. People reported shame when they had failed to meet parents' or important others' expectations, hurt others' feelings, or performed poorly in consequential ability-relevant tasks, but reported embarrassment mainly after minor accidents and mistakes. Direct interpersonal attention also seems less crucial to shame than it does embarrassment, although it may still intensify the emotion. As a 9-year-old in Harter and Whitesell's (1989) developmental study remarked: "I might be able to be ashamed of myself if my parents didn't know, but it sure would help me to be ashamed if they were there" (p. 96).

The interpersonal function of shame also seems rather different from that of embarrassment. In embarrassment, the person simply wants to deflect others' attention or change its character, but in shame there seems to be a deeper need to withdraw from interaction, hide, or disappear completely, signaling to others that one is not worthy, and communicating appropriate deference (e.g., Barrett, 1995; Frijda, 1986).

Although the Anglo-American adult notion of proper shame implies various articulated appraisals about lack of worth with respect to social standards, this kind of self-consciousness may not be required for the early elicitation of this emotion. Indeed, the use of shame induction as a key mode of socialization in many cultures (Barrett, 1995, cf. Benedict, 1946, and see chapter 3, this volume) may initially work not by directly changing the child's appraisals but by clearly conveying others' response to their conduct. Children are often made aware that they ought to be ashamed of themselves by a nonverbal presentation of contempt as well as by explicit verbalizations.

Adult shame too may not always depend on perceiving that one's conduct reflects badly on oneself. For example, self-reports from a study by Terwijn (cited in Frijda, 1993) include the case of a Dutch girl who felt shame when others laughed at her for having a boy's name (Jonny), something that in no way reflected on her character. In such instances, shame seems to be a direct response to social exclusion or ridicule rather than depending on complex cognitive appraisals concerning self-worth (Frijda & Mesquita, 1994). If so, the characteristic gaze aversion and social withdrawal may simply reflect attempts to escape from aversive disapproval from others. To take this further, some theorists see the occurrence of shame in early life as one of the ways in which self-consciousness is constructed rather than one of its later consequences (Barrett, 1995). The child's impression of the interpersonal situation during shame can be translated into something along the lines of "Someone thinks I am bad. Everyone is looking at me" (p. 43). The convergence of social attention on the child as an object and the child's affective reaction to it may contribute to her growing appreciation that she represents an object in the social world, rather than depending on that appreciation already being present.

Guilt

Guilt is the third in a triad of sociomoral emotion. Like embarrassment, it tends to focus on a particular incident rather than a more general moral failing. Like shame, the object of the emotion is not something that can easily be made light of or shrugged off. Keltner and Buswell's (1996) participants reported failures of duty and transgressions as common occasions for guilt. With regard to action tendencies, guilt seems to involve attempts to repair social relations and make amends for the perceived sin or omission.

According to appraisal theory, guilt depends on the perception that the self is accountable for a motivationally incongruent outcome (e.g., Smith & Lazarus, 1993), or detection of incompatibility between one's behavior and relevant social norms (Scherer, 2001). In either case, the idea is that a blameworthy action is the key elicitor of the emotion. What one blames oneself for, what one's motivations are, and what norms one uses for comparison may obviously depend on socialization to a large extent, but the proximal process generating the emotion is usually seen at an individual level.

However, examples exist of apparent guilt that do not fit easily with this appraisal model. For example, many of us can probably remember times at school when the teacher berated the whole class about a misdemeanor committed by one of its as yet unidentified members. Even knowing that you are in no way responsible for the sin doesn't stop you from feeling guilty when blamed. Similarly, a participant in a study by Parkinson (1999) reported feeling guilt when a "friend had a go at me over something she accused me of telling someone else that should have remained confidential," when in fact she "hadn't said anything" (pp. 377–378). In a subsequent unpublished study by Parkinson, participants were explicitly asked to report their emotions in response to recalled incidents when others blamed them for something that was not their fault. Several remembered feeling guilty but rated their personal accountability as very low. For example, one female student described intense guilt when her brother revealed his feeling that their parents were proud of her but not him, although she had never before recognized this possibility.

Further evidence of dissociations between guilt and responsibility appraisals comes from a study by Kroon (1988, see Frijda, 1993), which showed that only 28% of participants describing strong experiences of guilt considered themselves to have caused the event that provoked the emotion. Finally, McGraw (1987) reports a negative correlation between perceptions of having intended a victim's misfortune and intensity of guilt feelings. People apparently felt less rather than more guilty when they had hurt someone else deliberately, perhaps because their reasons for wanting to hurt them made them feel less bad about it. Similarly, the often-reported phenomenon of victim guilt suggests that people perpetrated against feel guilt in addition to perpetrators.

In short, for guilt to occur, it doesn't seem necessary to feel personally responsible for an event, only for someone else to have been affected badly. More specifically, the other person is typically someone who is perceived as having the right to demand an apology from you. Indeed, the earliest forms of guilt in development probably arise from direct accusations rather than individual appreciations of self-blame. Of course, there may also be examples of moral guilt where no obvious victim is present, and nobody but God to whom one should apologize. However, even here it may be that the guilt relates to rituals of confession, or beliefs about final reckonings in which all one's sins are revealed. Some children, for example, imagine judgment day as an extended cinema show during which the most intimate and regretted moments of their lives will be played back for everyone else to see.

Support for the idea that guilt depends on other people's anticipated reactions is provided by studies that separately assess own and others' expectations. For example, Millar and Tesser (1988) found that estimated guilt after lying about a transgression was independently predicted by the perceived expectations of the target of the lie, after having controlled for own expectations.

Baumeister, Stillwell, and Heatherton (1994) proposed that guilt serves three interpersonal functions. The first is that the emotion helps to repair relationships by equalizing the extent of unpleasant feelings of transgressor and victim. For example, I may not feel as hurt by your insult if you are obviously suffering as a consequence of having delivered it. Similarly, O'Malley and Greenberg (1983) found that female participants allocated smaller fines to motorists who expressed remorse after a hypothetical accident.

The second interpersonal function of guilt is that it encourages actions that maintain relationships, including apologies and other forms of reparation. Guilt thus motivates people to stay on good terms with one another. Third, guilt induction serves as a way of influencing another's conduct from a relatively powerless position. For example, assuming that you care about my feelings, I can enlist your help by emphasizing your many unfair advantages over me. Research into guilt-induction strategies confirms that people have ready and accessible knowledge about many of the interpersonal causes of this emotion (Miceli, 1992; Vangelisti, Daly, & Rudnick, 1991), allowing them to deploy them for personal advantage.

Just as embarrassment can be seen as a response to unwanted attention, and shame as a response to ridicule, guilt may be a response to a close other's accusation, especially when the other person is perceived to be suffering. However, we do not mean to imply that these emotions are always direct and automatic responses to simple interpersonal stimuli. Indeed, occasions arise when attention is ignored or accepted rather than deflected, when ridicule is met by defiance rather than shame, and when accusations are met by counter-accusations and reciprocal anger instead of guilt. What determines these particular responses concerns the nature of preexisting relations between the parties to the exchange as well as the current state of the developing interaction between them. In particular, presentation of a sociomoral emotion may be seen as a communicative strategy designed to exert specific effects on particular others.

Jealousy and Envy

Both jealousy and envy refer to negative reactions to someone else's good fortune (Ben Ze'ev, 2000), and both have an obvious interpersonal basis. Which of these words is applied depends on the particular nature of the other's good fortune and one's own relation to that good fortune. Envy depends upon social comparison and involves one person's bad feelings about another person's desired qualities, predicament, or possessions. Jealousy, on the other hand, relates to a situation when you have something and are afraid of losing it (or when another person has something desirable that you once had yourself). More specifically, jealousy usually applies to a three-person situation in which another person is involved with someone who is or was involved with you. Parrott and Smith (1993) have outlined some of the important distinctions between the two kinds of experience or episode along similar lines.

According to Hupka and colleagues (1985), *jealousy* and *envy* are not names for specific and distinct emotions, but rather "compound emotion words" that describe a range of different affective reactions associated with the particular interpersonal predicaments embodied in the concepts in question. Similarly, we would contend that the cultural scripts that people use to represent these emotions may not specify a particular quality of subjective experience (see chapter 2, this volume) but rather a class of events that provoke a variety of affective reactions (cf. Frijda & Mesquita, 1994).

If this is correct, then research attempting to uncover the intrinsic differences between the two emotions can be reinterpreted as semantic investigations. Their avowed purpose of distinguishing two separate psychological conditions instead becomes a struggle to uncover people's interpretations of the specific situations in which these words should be applied (and in some languages the distinction is not made in the first place). Indeed, Salovey and Rodin (1986) were unable to find consistent differences in the thoughts and feelings associated with the two supposedly different states. Although jealousy and envy may often feel different to us, perhaps not everyone experiences the differences in the same way. Further, maybe different instances of jealousy and different instances of envy also feel different from one another. Parrott (1991) helpfully distinguishes different forms of each emotion along these lines. For example, non-malicious envy involves wishing you had what someone else has without also wishing that they didn't have it, whereas malicious envy involves both kinds of wish. How many subcategories are necessary before we get to the roots of the underlying phenomena is an open question.

As with the sociomoral emotions of embarrassment, shame, and guilt, the consensus in developmental theory is that jealousy and envy only emerge after articulated representations of self in relationship have been attained. However, Draghi-Lorenz (2001) demonstrated that even 5-month-olds reliably showed distress when their caregivers paid attention to other infants (see also Hart, Field, & Del Valle, 1998). Further, their distress was consistently preceded by looks directed at this other baby rather than the mother who was now ignoring them. Parents witnessing such incidents in more naturalistic situations seem perfectly prepared to attribute jealousy to their offspring. For example, one mother in Draghi-Lorenz's study conducted an informal experiment to convince her partner that their youngest child "Daisy" was jealous of attention directed to an older sibling: "Her dad didn't believe me so I said 'put Alison down' and she was like 'coo-coo' ... Then I said 'now pick her up again' [and she was like,] 'Grrr!'" (p. 116). Parents also reported that they often reacted to such displays of apparent jealousy by supplying attention to the excluded infant, or by including him or her in joint activities. A possible social function of jealousy, therefore, may be to communicate being left out and thereby to solicit reintegration into interpersonal interaction.

Few of the parents in Draghi-Lorenz's (2001) study used the term "envy" rather than jealousy to describe their infants' actions. However, they often noted that the infants experienced a form of distress when another infant had possession of something (e.g., a toy) that their child apparently wanted. Clearly, displays of this kind may serve to direct other people's attention to a prior claim on a desired object, just as "jealous" displays assert rights in purely interpersonal relationships.

Love

Regardless of their cultural origins, people consistently rate love as one of the most prototypical examples of the category of emotions (e.g., Fehr & Russell, 1984; Shaver, Wu, & Schwartz, 1992; chapter 2, this volume). With some notable exceptions (e.g., Averill, 1985; Solomon, 1981; Shaver, Morgan, & Wu, 1996), however, the attention this emotion has attracted from emotion researchers (as opposed to researchers interested in relationships, see Hatfield & Rapson, 2001) has been disproportionately slight. One of the problems facing potential investigators is that many conventional usages of the word *love* are not strictly or purely emotional. Saying that you love someone is often a statement about the perceived status of a relationship or a promise of commitment rather than simply a description of a transient state or process. Correspondingly, feelings of love (like those of envy and jealousy) may be quite diverse in character, sometimes positive and exciting, sometimes painful, sometimes calm and serene. Indeed, Chinese participants in Shaver and colleagues' (1992) study included some love-related words in a "joy" category but others in a distinct "sad love" cluster (see chapter 2, this volume). What we talk about when we talk about love is not any one easily isolated kind of object or event (see Solomon, 1981, *inter alia*). For this reason, it may be a mistake to look for the essence of love in either the mental or interpersonal world.

What is certainly clear, however, is that love is commonly directed toward other people. It also seems to be the case that the quality of the experience depends on the specific nature of your relationship to these other people and on how they react to its expression. Unrequited love is different to reciprocated love but both are constituted as a function of an interactive process rather than pure individual calculation or perception.

Averill (1985) argues that the specific Western variety of romantic love arises from the tension between cultural norms and social reality. On the one hand, individualistic values promote the worth and value of each person in his or her own right. On the other hand, the market economy leads to intensive competition for resources, often leaving little space for the pure expression of individuality. The culturally sanctioned idealization of romantic partners permits a partial resolution of this conflict by setting up a specific interpersonal arena in which self is valorized. Even if nobody is quite as special in absolute terms as they are made to feel they ought to be, at least one context apparently offers the potential for fuller appreciation of personal qualities and idiosyncrasies: "I may not be best at anything else, but no one else loves me like you do (and I don't love anyone else like I love you)."

A clear illustration of cultural specificity in the practices surrounding loving relationships concerns how partners are selected for marriage in different societies. The Anglo-American romantic notion that you should marry mainly because of "love" has its counterpart in the Indian valuation of arranged marriages. Here, parents and relatives agree on a suitable partner, often to achieve financial security or alliances between families. Loving relationships thus develop from social obligations and endorse interdependent values rather than representing a celebration of individualistic desire. Indeed, when asked whether they would marry someone they did not love but who possessed all the other qualities they desired, participants from India, Pakistan, or Thailand were significantly more likely to say "yes" than those from other countries (Levine, Sato, Hashimoto, & Verma, 1995).

Fago

The emotions considered so far are all relatively common and recognizable to Westerners. Many of them probably also occur in other societies, although their specific representation and articulation may differ (see chapter 3). However, culturally more specific emotional syndromes also exist with obvious interpersonal aspects. We will consider just one of these to avert the impression that Western emotions should be treated as some kind of gold standard against which alien experiences should be measured. (Other relevant examples of culturally specific interpersonal emotions such as *amae*, *dapdaphada*, *litost*, *Schadenfreude*, *ququq*, *utsungu*, and *verguenza ajena* are discussed in chapter 2, this volume).

According to Lutz (1988), the Ifaluk emotion word *fago* may be translated as compassion–love–sadness. *Fago* represents a kind of concern for other people when they are alone, ill, or, by contrast, exhibiting qualities of interpersonal sensitivity and social intelligence. The emotion therefore seems to combine what Westerners might call sympathy and respect. In either case, *fago* is clearly oriented to interpersonal relations and occurs most commonly when close others are suffering, dying, about to leave the island for a long period, or simply demonstrating their attunement to people's feelings. *Fago* therefore serves to maintain tight and mutual social bonds either when these bonds are threatened, or when attention is otherwise drawn to their value. Indeed, parents explicitly invoke *fago* when their young children are being aggressive to emphasize that interpersonal connections should override any antagonism. For example, Lutz reports that a mother's response when her son raised a piece of coral rubble and aimed it threateningly at a 2-year-old was "Don't you *fago* your 'brother'?"

Although socialization practices endorse the attitude of *fago* from an early age, Ifaluk ethnotheory assumes that children below the age of about 7 cannot experience this emotion because they lack the appropriate sensitivity to others' feelings. However, once this sensitivity has developed, *fago* is thought to be a direct and automatic reaction to the perception of someone else's needs. For the Ifaluk it is a natural sign of maturity to *fago* others in appropriate circumstances. Like its Anglo-American counterparts, love and sympathy, then, part of what is called *"fago"* presumably reflects unselfconscious adjustment to existing social arrangements and part represents explicitly sanctioned modes of response that modify these prior tendencies. Young Ifalukians probably exhibit forms of *fago* before its fully articulated practice emerges and certainly prior to the acquisition of internalized cultural scripts representing this emotion.

This chapter's earlier descriptions of "Western" emotions may sometimes have given the misleading impression that interpersonal dynamics somehow represent intrinsic and determinate aspects of their operation. However, the case of *fago* serves to remind us that the cultural practices that crystallize around emotion are a crucial part of how they come to be defined and enacted in everyday social life (see chapter 8). Even emotions that seem more natural to us in a Western context take their specific form partly as a function of local cultural factors.

Grief

When mourning, people experience emotions ranging from numbness to anger, anxiety, and depression. Nothing about the intrinsic nature of the sufferer's affective condition seems to identify it as grief, but if it is experienced as a consequence of the death of someone close it counts, almost by definition, as an example of this emotion. Like jealousy, envy, and possibly love, then, grief might be a syndrome of responses represented by situational and relational scripts rather than the name for any particular emotion. In fact, grief's time course suggests that it may involve a concatenation of states and episodes characterized by a variety of shifting feelings and thoughts about the lost loved one.

The functions of grief are often discussed from an attachment perspective. Classic work by Bowlby (e.g., 1951, 1956, 1973) argued that the emotion arises as a consequence of an adaptive mechanism for ensuring the availability and maintenance of protective social relationships. The idea is that loss of contact with caregivers constituted a common survival-threatening situation for our ancestors, and natural selection therefore led to emotional responses to abandonment that reduced its probability. In particular, an abandoned human infant initially emits protest signals, and subsequently complains when reunited with the caregiver as a punishment for abandonment. Grief represents a negative side-effect of this normally effective interpersonal system (e.g., Archer, 1999). When reunion with a key support-provider is no longer possible, the complaint finds no suitable recipient and despair sets in.

According to the traditional attachment account, the purpose of the private rumination and personal redefinition of "grief work" is ultimately to sever connections with the departed. Whether coming to terms with loss is wholly a private and cognitive process has been disputed, however, by Stroebe and Stroebe (1987), who emphasize the establishment of alternative relationships to replace parts of the social identity, and instrumental and emotional support once provided by the lost loved one. In a related vein, Klass, Silverman, and Nickman's (1996) "continuing bonds" perspective suggests that relationships with the deceased persist long after death and that bereavement is therefore not about breaking ties as claimed in the original attachment model. However, according to Fraley and Shaver (1999), Bowlby did not imply that the process of "detachment" meant that the loved one was completely forgotten and abandoned after death, but simply that the relevant relational bonds required reconfiguration.

Stroebe and Schut (1999) argue that two kinds of functions are performed by different forms and phases of grieving. The first is loss-oriented and involves confronting the reality of absence of the loved one. As in the traditional conception of grief work, the ultimate task is to come to terms with loss and possibly to find positive meaning in the experience of bereavement. This process may involve conducting conversations with real or imagined others (Pennebaker, Zech, & Rimé, 2001). To the extent that these imagined others include the departed person him- or herself, this is also consistent with a continuing bonds perspective. However, according to Stroebe and Schut (1999), bereaved people occasionally need to take "breathers" from this continued focus on often depressive concerns, and therefore also engage in restorative behaviors, including avoidance of thoughts about the departed. For Stroebe (2001), the key issues for bereavement research are not whether grief involves "breaking bonds or breaking hearts" (Stroebe, Gergen, Gergen, & Stroebe, 1992), nor whether avoidance or confrontation is the most appropriate regulation strategy. Instead, we need to acknowledge that the multifaceted dynamic process of adjustment involves phases in which all of these aspects feature to a greater or lesser extent. To some degree and in some ways, relationships with the bereaved are maintained after death, in a manner that may seem to reflect avoidance. However, outright denial of absence may be maladaptive at some phases of grieving (Bonanno & Field, 2001). Working through also has its place, but not if practiced exclusively and without respite.

In sum, grief is an emotional complex that has clear interpersonal origins, and is worked through in the interpersonal sphere. Although withdrawal and privacy are common during many phases of the syndrome, these may serve as ways of preserving an imagined, sometimes idealized, relationship with the loved one, rather than as a total break with any kind of interpersonal relationship.

☐ Nonsocial Emotions?

The interpersonal basis of the emotions considered so far is widely accepted. Everyone agrees that love, envy, and grief have social causes and effects, for example. However, none of these emotions consistently appears on lists of "basic emotions," and most are seen as emerging relatively late in ontogenetic development. Indeed, many theorists believe that social and self-conscious emotions represent secondary elaborations of more primary biological processes. According to such an analysis, emotions initially arise as individual, genetically determined states that later get linked up either with cognitions about the social world or other basic emotions to constitute more articulated states. For example, Johnson-Laird and Oatley (2000) suggest that Western "embarrassment" is actually fear coupled with an unfavorable appraisal of other's attention to oneself. Similarly, some psychologists argue that infants start out with a palette of primary emotional colors that are only later blended with one another and given different textures as a function of their cognitive articulation (e.g., Izard, 1978). It is commonly supposed, for example, that pride, guilt, and shame depend on the development of cognitive capacities unavailable at an early age, such as being able to see oneself as others do (e.g., Lewis, 2000, and see following discussion).

Of course, it is generally accepted that so-called "basic" emotions can serve interpersonal functions, too. It also seems likely that in their developed form, even these primary emotions represent complex and articulated modes of practical and social action that are not simply reducible to preset programs of individual response. In this section, we will consider the interpersonal causes, effects, and functions of two emotions that are often considered to be basic. The first of these is anger, whose interpersonal implications are obvious, but is nevertheless an emotion that is not usually interpreted from a primarily social perspective (for exceptions, see Averill, 1982). The second is fear, which is usually treated as a response to physical rather than interpersonal threats, and whose functions are supposed to be dictated by practical considerations relating to survival. In our view, the interpersonal basis of both of these emotions has often been underestimated. We also discuss the role of social factors in the origins and maintenance of clinical conditions of depression, relating to a third putatively basic emotion: sadness.

Anger

Anger is a basic emotion that often takes an interpersonal object. For many appraisal theorists, it depends on blaming someone else for motivationally incongruent events (Lazarus, 1991a; Smith & Lazarus, 1993). It involves action tendencies relating to antagonism or retaliation directed at others (e.g., Frijda, 1986; Roseman, 1996). We get angry with other people for things they have said or done (or not said and done), and we want to get back at them in some way. All this seems self-evident. However, in this section we want to argue that this ready consensus about the role of social factors in anger is partly mistaken, and that although the social world is centrally implicated in this emotion, its role is not the one that is conventionally supposed in ordinary language or appraisal theory.

One problem with explaining anger in terms of other-accountability is that our anger is often directed at nonhuman objects. Most of us can think of times when we have shouted at our cars or computers, for example. Certainly it might be argued that we are treating these objects as if they had human-like agency, but this begs the question of why we should do this in the first place. What functions would it serve to become antagonistic toward things that cannot respond in any way to this antagonism apart from getting damaged? Another possibility is that these examples don't reflect true anger, only frustration, but it is hard to see what is different about the states and actions involved except the fact that no other person is directly involved. If it is decided that an emotion counts as anger only if it is focused on another person, then the connection between anger and human objects is a tautology rather than a matter of empirical fact.

One of the reasons why anger is often considered to be a basic emotion is that it seems to appear very early in infant development. For example, something looking very like anger occurs in 5-month-old children from a variety of cultures whenever their movements are physically restricted (Camras et al., 1992; Watson, 1929). Further, Lewis, Alessandri, and Sullivan (1990) observed angry facial movements and intensified actions at an even earlier age. In their study, 8-week-old infants first learned that pulling on a string led to the appearance of a slide showing a baby's smiling face and the Sesame Street signature tune being played. When this contingency was removed, the infants tugged harder on the cord and showed "anger" faces.

These infant examples of apparent anger are reconcilable with the usual appraisal account only if we assume that a primitive sense of blame or illegitimacy is perceived from physical obstruction or lack of contingency. Alternatively, we might assume that blame and illegitimacy are subsequent cognitive articulations of more simple perceptions that are at the core of anger. For example, Frijda (1993) argues that anger can arise simply from "acute goal interference" (see also Berkowitz's [e.g., 1990] discussion of the frustration-aggression hypothesis). When the frustrating situation is an interpersonal one, what may provoke the anger instead is a breakdown in power relations between parties.

Even adult anger does not always seem to involve blame appraisals, but simply the presence of some resistance that stops us getting through. This might be physical resistance, as when a door stays resolutely jammed however hard we push against it, refusing to cooperate with our need to get indoors, or it may be social resistance when someone just won't listen or acknowledge our point (when we can't "get through" to them, to coin an appropriate metaphor). Indeed, a study by Stemmler (1989) used exactly this kind of manipulation to generate "real-life" anger for the purpose of assessing its physiological correlates:

> Anagrams were displayed for 5s, and the first 15 items were solvable. Then unexpectedly, the task was interrupted, "Listen, we can hardly understand you, although the amplifier's volume is already turned up to maximum. It would be best if you could speak louder!" The following anagram was solvable. Then in a brusque voice, a second interruption, "Louder, please!" The next anagram was unsolvable. After the subject's answer, it was aggressively insisted, "Can't you speak up?" (p. 622)

Although the other person is clearly in some ways blameworthy during this episode, what seems to be fuelling the anger is their continuing unresponsiveness to escalating communications. Similarly, Parkinson (2001) argues that one of the reasons we are more prone to anger while driving than in other situations is that the usual channels of communication are disrupted. Because of the relative interpersonal distance and the insulation provided by your vehicle, you are slower to notice my subtle indications of disapproval, and I am slower to register the fact that you are acknowledging them. We both therefore intensify our displays before we are aware of them getting across. One implication of this analysis is that anger depends not only on characteristics of the prior situation but also on the ongoing potential and actual responsiveness of others. Just as facial movements are oriented toward potential addressees according to Fridlund's (1994) account (see chapter 6, this volume), so too are broader aspects of unfolding presentations of emotion.

Fear

Although anger is usually taken to be a basic emotion, few would deny that it often takes a social object. Academic discussion of fear, on the other hand, usually refers to physical threats. The standard evolutionary account locates the origin of this emotion in the struggle for survival in a hostile, often predatory environment (e.g., Cosmides & Tooby, 2000). We see the bear and our consequent fear mobilizes the necessary cognitive and physiological resources for flight.

But is it really the case that even savannah-inhabiting hunter-gatherers first experienced fear in response to exposure to heights or wild animals? Did they really need prewiring to cope with threats for which their caregivers could much more effectively prepare them? In ontogenesis, the most primitive fear is likely of abandonment, lacking guidance and comfort in an uncertain environment. The typical response is not to run or even to hide, but to seek solace, comfort, and protection. Even running in fear is not only running away from, but also running toward. Toward safety, toward some haven, ideally toward someone who can protect us. None of this should be taken as a denial that certain nonsocial objects (spiders, snakes, heights) easily acquire fear-arousing properties, suggesting some level of biological preparedness for phobia. However, the basic function of the emotion may not be purely to escape such objects but also to solicit a certain kind of help in dealing with them (cf. Fridlund, 1994). After all, if these objects are first confronted during infancy, the frightened individual has few personal resources to deal with them on a practical level in the first place.

Although fear is sometimes directed at nonsocial objects, then, this does not mean that it lacks interpersonal content. As with anger, early manifestations of this state in an appropriate context are likely to enlist rapid caregiver responses such as comforting or removal of the fear-inducing object. The function of enlisting help or support therefore soon becomes ingrained in the interpersonal meaning of this basic emotion.

It is also clearly true that we are often afraid of other people and of specific kinds of interpersonal events. For example, agoraphobia is an apparently irrational fear of public places. A rich account of the historical development of this clinical syndrome is provided by de Swaan (1981), who argues that its origins lie in the increasing urbanization arising from the industrial revolution. Because people from all social classes were brought into direct contact in the burgeoning cities of the time, fears developed both about the unpredictability of interpersonal encounters and about the loss of valued status distinctions. Bourgeois women in particular were encouraged to stay at home to demonstrate that their husbands had the necessary resources to support them and keep them from the world of work. Contemporary agoraphobia is thus seen as a kind of recapitulation of nineteenth century family values, expressed as the wife's fear of being out in public and often reinforced by the husband's urge to remain in control of her movements. The associated anxieties take an interpersonal object (public spaces, the marketplace), and serve relational functions deriving from a broader sociocultural context (see chapter 8).

Depression

Depression is used to describe both a specific emotion and a clinical condition involving persistent and debilitating bouts of this emotion. However, most of the available evidence concerns its clinical manifestations and it is on those that we focus here. Clinical depression is usually diagnosed on the basis of one person's "symptoms," and the treatment typically involves changing that individual's physiology with antidepressants and/or working on his or her subjective beliefs and interpretations of the external world. Despite the individualistic focus of therapy, it is clear that many of the events that precipitate this emotional disorder are interpersonal ones. For example, Brown and Harris (1978) found that many of the major negative life events preceding depression involved loss or separation—in particular, loss of or separation from someone close, or loss of a job and its associated role and social contacts. A common cause of depression, then, is a negative change in social relationships.

Further, positive relationships can often alleviate or guard against depression. For example, Brown and Harris found that the chances of experiencing a depressive episode following a negative life event were greater than one in three for women who were not involved in a supportive intimate relationship, but only one in ten for women who had close confidants. Indeed, the vast literature on "social support" contains many demonstrations that other people make a vital difference to our overall psychological well-being, not only by providing practical help when we have a problem (*instrumental* and *informational* support), but also by offering condolence (*emotional* support) and changing the way that events are framed (*appraisal* support [see Barrera, 1986; Cobb, 1976; Cohen, Mermelstein, Kamarck, & Hoberman, 1985 inter alia for distinctions between different varieties of social support]). As well as altering the emotional reaction to a separate stressor ("buffering" [Cohen & Wills, 1985]), positive social interactions (or the availability of a social network) can, under some circumstances, directly lead to happiness (e.g., Tennant & Bebbington, 1978), as we all know from our usual response to other people's compliments.

Coyne and Downey (1991) suggested that much of the apparently beneficial impact of social support can be explained in terms of the implied absence of negative social factors. People with good social support networks tend not to suffer from discord in close relationships, and it may be this latter factor that makes them less likely to become depressed. In other words, it is not that people who are equipped with social support are more psychologically healthy as such, but rather that those reporting a lack of social support tend to be those who are involved in psychologically unhealthy relationships. Consistent with this analysis, the available evidence confirms that marital discord is a common factor in many depressive episodes. For example, a survey by Paykel and colleagues (1969) found that the life event that best predicted depression was a recent increase in the number of arguments between husband and wife. A subsequent study found that "being married and being unable to talk to one's spouse" was associated with a whopping 25-fold increase in the odds of becoming depressed (see Coyne & Downey, 1991).

Interpersonal life, then, forms the context for the onset of depression, as well as affecting how well individuals cope with depressing events. Further, it may be that other people's ongoing responses to the expression of depressed feelings sustain the condition. Coyne (1976a) proposed that people close to depressed people react to them in ways that often perpetuate the problem. Depressives are commonly worried that specific other people are beginning to reject them, and therefore express sadness in an attempt to solicit comfort and reassurance. However, because any expression of support is produced only in specific response to a demand, it is perceived as unconvincing. To clarify things, requests for emotional succour are renewed until the other person starts to feel burdened by their persistence. Solidarity then starts to be expressed more ambiguously, and the depressed person feels even less convinced by its reliability. Unfortunately, the typical response is to re-intensify interpersonal demands (or to break off completely, closing down any channels of potential support). Thus a vicious interpersonal spiral soon develops.

Support for the idea that other people can react negatively to someone's depression is provided by Coyne's (1976b) naturalistic study of interactions with depressed women. The results showed that talking to a depressed woman on the telephone made people feel more depressed themselves and led them to be more rejecting of their interaction partner. Clearly, then, some of the interpersonal consequences of emotions may be unwanted side effects of their intended function.

Coyne's theory implies that the expression of depression within a relationship may serve to sustain negative patterns of interaction. Similarly, wives in Biglan and colleagues' (1985) study apparently used expressions of sadness to reduce their husbands' anger in the short term. Their emotional presentation presumably served to draw their partners' attention to their helplessness in a process of social appraisal. However, husbands also apparently used anger to blame wives for situations that they were sad about. Thus, again a vicious spiral of increasingly negative emotions might develop between parties to a relationship leading to increased levels of sadness and depression especially in the least powerful party. In a related vein, Gottman (1979) showed that a tit-for-tat interaction style where expressions of negativity from one party were met with negativity from the other indicated a negative prognosis for a relationship. If interactants instead adopted complementary emotional stances, offering comfort instead of complaint in response to the presentation of problems, both parties unsurprisingly ended up feeling happier about the relationship (cf. Tiedens & Fragale, 2003).

The lesson from this research is that emotions like sadness and depression may be maintained by their interpersonal consequences and oriented to anticipated or desired interpersonal effects. Where cognitive therapists attribute emotional disorder to distorted individual thought patterns (negative schemata, depressogenic attributional styles), Coyne's (1976) interpersonal approach suggests that depressed people may be interpreting interpersonal cues accurately, but making interpersonal responses more negative than they need be with their own ineffectual cries for help. One implication is that the site for intervention in cases of depression should be the interpersonal system of the family or relationship rather than the cognitive apparatus of the depressed individual (Gottlib & Colby, 1987). Of course, even cognitive therapy contains interpersonal manipulations in terms of how its experiments change the nature of social life, and how the relationship with the therapist may provide direct support for the client.

☐ Emotional Development in Interpersonal Context

The preceding sections of this chapter have discussed a variety of emotions that seem to depend on interpersonal processes, and that have corresponding effects on interpersonal life. Further, we have proposed that many of these emotions originate from interpersonal experiences at an early stage of ontogenetic development. In the present section, we will attempt to draw together our conclusions about how interpersonal emotions emerge or are acquired in the first few years of an infant's life, and to make some proposals about their subsequent articulation. Our proposal is that many of the pragmatic effects of emotion consolidate prior to internalization of mental representations, but that more strategic functions may be subsequently superimposed on these as a function of explicit socialization. If so, there may be two possible modes of interpersonal influence arising from adult emotions, one implicit and direct, the other more articulated and tactical.

Ontogenetic Development of Emotions

As we have noted, many developmental psychologists delineate a subset of emotions that are socially oriented. These are usually seen as emerging later in development than primary emotions (such as anger and fear), partly because they depend on the availability of particular cognitive capacities. For example, Lewis (e.g., 2000) argues that self-conscious emotions such as empathy and envy first appear around the age of 18 months, after toddlers acquire the ability to see themselves from another's point of view. Self-conscious *evaluative* emotions (e.g., pride, guilt, shame) develop even later (at around 30 months) when children can compare their conduct against internalized goals and standards. According to this view, babies start out with a small set of emotions or undifferentiated affective states that subsequently get articulated as a function of development and experience. "Basic" emotions are treated as the foundations for the construction of more complex emotional structures.

The evidence usually presented to support such a developmental sequence involves demonstrating that the appearance of a particular emotion is contingent on the possession of a specific cognitive capacity that only emerges relatively late in infancy. For example, pride, embarrassment, and other self-conscious emotions are more commonly observed after babies first start trying to remove a lipstick mark from their foreheads on seeing their own reflection in a mirror (e.g., Lewis, Sullivan, Stanger, & Weiss, 1989), supposedly indicating that they have attained a representation of the self as an object. In fact, although the emotions in question apparently become more obvious or more frequent following these developmental milestones, evidence of their earlier occurrence is growing (see Draghi-Lorenz, Reddy, & Costall, 2001).

The case for developmental primacy of so-called basic emotions partly depends on their association with distinctive iconic facial expressions (e.g., Ekman, 1992a, 1992b), so that a straightforward criterion for their occurrence is easily defended. Anger, fear, happiness, sadness, disgust, and surprise are thus attributed to infants as soon as the supposedly diagnostic display appears. On the other hand, no single facial configuration has consistently been identified as characteristic of guilt, pride, or shame. It is therefore easy to deny their occurrence in infants who cannot tell you what they are feeling directly.

When something resembling one of these supposedly nonbasic emotions does arise, it is often treated as a more basic state that has fortuitously occurred in connection with the appropriate occasion for the more articulated emotion (Draghi-Lorenz et al., 2001). An infant who smiles after first managing to stand up, for example, is seen as happy for other reasons, and an infant who looks uncomfortable when exposed to social attention is treated as afraid rather than embarrassed or shy. Indeed, it often seems as if the only justification for denying the presence of the supposedly more complex emotion is the apparent lack of the cognitive capacities that are assumed to underlie it. Smiling after success cannot reflect pride because the infant has no internalized standards of comparison for performance, for example. Of course, it may be that apparent displays of nonbasic emotions are actually responses to aspects of the complex situation other than those that would constitute proper occasions for the emotion in question. For example, infants may smile following achievement simply because of the positive attention they receive rather than because of its implications for personal competence. Indeed, it seems plausible that this is one of the ways in which children are socialized into experiencing appropriate pride in the first place. The question that then arises is: When does smiling because someone else is apparently pleased with you become genuine pride? Perhaps pride could be seen as a direct response to perceived congratulation rather than an internalized representation of oneself as worthy (cf. Draghi-Lorenz et al., 2001).

According to many appraisal-based accounts, social emotions are social at one remove. Embarrassment is not a reaction to the attention of others; it is a consequence of representing yourself as subject to their attention. Guilt is not about someone else's relative misfortune; it is about representing oneself as responsible for this misfortune. Pride is not a response to praise but a recognition that action is praiseworthy, and so on. In our view, by contrast, the dynamics of interpersonal interaction may produce emotion without the internal cognitive representation of those dynamics. All that is required is a basic perception of self in relation to others, which may well be present at a very early age (e.g., Trevarthen, 1984). The representation-based version of events may seem commonsensical because we often seek recourse to our particular view of events rather than the events themselves when justifying our reactions. However, accounting for emotions in interpersonal contexts is not always the same as identifying their true causes for the purposes of scientific explanation.

In many respects, debates about precisely when particular emotions first appear during infant development simply boil down to squabbles over semantics (cf. Barrett, 1998). For example, if emotions are defined in terms of articulated appraisals (e.g., Ortony, Clore, & Collins, 1988), then no conceivable evidence could rule out their dependence on cognitive representational capacities. On the other hand, if we are willing to attribute emotion to infants on the basis of dynamic expressive behavior occurring in attunement to its appropriate context, then early appearances of pride, jealousy, and so on seem uncontestable (e.g., Draghi-Lorenz, 2001). There is no need to get embroiled in such definitional disputes here. Indeed, we can all agree that babies exhibit conduct that is similar to adult emotional behavior in some respects but not in others. The implication is that emotions don't spring into life fully formed but are shaped, pruned, and cultivated over the course of ontogeny. What is inherited, then, need not be seen as an intact basic emotion (see Ortony &

Turner, 1990), but rather some of the conditions for its emergence (e.g., Camras, 1992). Other conditions are not directly prewired but are specified in the typical reactions of caregivers, and the cultural conditions that give these their context (including available modes of representation; see chapter 2).

For example, it may be that infants start out with innate sensitivity to others as dynamic and responsive aspects of their environment. The earliest and most basic human emotions then emerge from the intersubjective relationship with caregivers as movements of joining and separation (de Rivera, 1984, and see following discussion). Nonhuman objects attain their emotional meaning as part of mutually constituted projects and rituals surrounding feeding and other bodily functions. At some later point, instrumentality begins to appear in the infant's actions, bringing the potential for frustration and satisfaction. The child sucks on things, touches or reaches for them, and learns the consequences. Right from the outset, some of these consequences are reflected in caregivers' reactions. Some objects are forbidden, for instance, whereas others are the proper focus of attention. Thus, aspects of the physical environment become charged with emotional power as a function of an intrinsically relational process.

Before the child has any capacity for language, it is subjected to an already codified set of emotional conventions manifested in practical reactions. More explicit verbally mediated indoctrination of emotional rules and norms follows at a much later stage, bringing further complications to emotional life. Children are taught when and where it is proper to experience and express anger, fear, shame, guilt, and so on. The fact that this explicit instruction takes place ought to warn us that the way emotions are represented in the discourses of prohibition, justification, and encouragement do not always match the unmanipulated occasions for their occurrence. Emotions clearly don't only happen when they are supposed to. However, this does not mean that a kind of biological energy pours out when sociocultural barriers are released. Instead, we would contend that contradictions are inherent in some of the interpersonally situated practices of emotion socialization. The way we learn to be emotional at an implicit level does not fully mesh with our explicit culturally derived knowledge about when an emotion should occur (or how emotion works; see chapter 8). Indeed, we sometimes become very extremely angry even when we know that anger is not completely justified. Nevertheless, explicit emotion representations may themselves be productive of new forms of emotion (cf. Averill & Nunley, 1992). In the next chapter, we shall develop and formalize these ideas about the cultural and interpersonal constitution of emotions.

Ontogenetic Development of Relational Temperament

For much of this chapter, our emphasis has fallen on immediate interpersonal situations as occasions for and consequences of emotion. However, developmentally prior interpersonal processes also help to constitute the present relational context. Just as interactions between people are conditioned by their cultural and intergroup context, earlier experiences of relationships also leave their traces on our emotional dispositions. Currently, the most influential theoretical perspective on such developmental influences is attachment theory.

Like the supposed critical periods for the acquisition of perceptual and cognitive faculties and skills (e.g., Blakemore & Cooper, 1970; Lenneberg, 1967), attachment theory postulates time windows early in life during which styles of emotional interaction and regulation are ingrained. Following influential work by Bowlby (e.g., 1951, 1956, 1973), psychologists have been increasingly interested in the process of caregiver-infant attachment, during which basic working models of how relationships work are apparently laid down. The fundamental idea, familiar from the psychodynamic literature, is that the mode of interaction between parent and baby sets the tone for subsequent relationships into adult life, giving context for the emotions that later emerge.

Control programs underlying attachment behaviors are supposed to be inherited because of their adaptive value. Solitary infants would not survive for long in a predatory environment and therefore need to enlist the support and protection of caregivers. Caregivers in turn need to be sensitive to infants' requirements, and their sensitivity presumably coevolves with infant characteristics and conduct to solicit help. Although the constitutional foundations for parenting relationships are preset by genetics, the specific patterns of interaction characterizing any caregiver-infant pair may still vary considerably (partly reflecting previous attachment experiences of caregivers, and partly temperamental differences in infants [O'Connor & Croft, 2001]).

Initial distinctions between attachment responses of infants were drawn by Ainsworth (e.g., Ainsworth, Blehar, Waters, & Wall, 1978) on the basis of her "strange situation" test. This involves the parent leaving the infant with a stranger, returning again, then leaving the infant completely alone before the stranger, and finally the parent, return. The infant's reaction to separation and reunion (with parents and others) are carefully recorded as manifestations of underlying modes of attachment. For example, a child who is upset when the parent leaves, but quickly reassured when the parent returns, shows *secure* attachment, whereas a child who seems unaffected by the parent's departure but looks away or avoids the parent on return is deemed *avoidant*. Of course, it is questionable whether the contrived and restricted nature of the aptly-named strange situation is representative of more general dispositional tendencies (see, for example, Clarke-Stewart, Goossens, & Allhusen, 2001; Vaughn et al., 1994), and whether it has universal validity across cultures (Takahashi, 1990). Nevertheless, studies using this procedure certainly provide a vivid demonstration not only that interpersonal events have a potent effect on young infants, but also that the nature of these reactions varies as a function of prior interpersonal experiences.

Moving on from Ainsworth's work, four contrasting adult attachment styles are often distinguished in the current literature, on the basis of whether internalized "working models" of self and other are viewed positively or negatively (Bartholomew & Horowitz, 1991). A *secure* attachment style involves a positive working model of both self and other, a *dismissing* attachment style involves a positive model of self but a negative model of the other, a *preoccupied* attachment style reflects a negative model of self, but a positive model of other, whereas a *fearful* attachment style involves negative models of both self and other. Possession of a particular style predisposes the individual to show characteristic modes of emotional response in relational contexts. For example, securely attached people have rewarding relationships with others, whereas fearfully attached individuals tend to be anxious about relationships and socially avoidant.

Obviously, the four-way categorization is still relatively crude and fails to do justice to the range of interpersonal dynamics characterizing relationships. For example, recent research using the adult attachment interview identifies a *disorganized* style, similar but not identical to the anxious style, arising from frightened or frightening parental behavior, leading to conflicting representations of the caregiver as a source of both security and threat (see Hesse & Main, 2000). More generally, the four categories previously considered fail to take into account the nature of negativity or positivity in working models of self and other. In this regard, the labeling of the self-evaluation dimension as "anxiety" seems to preclude being led to feel ashamed of the self, angry with the self, ambivalent about the self, and so on. However provisional its classifications, attachment theory does at least represent a first step toward acknowledging differences in relational contexts as possible determinants of subsequent emotional life. The extent to which the primary attachment relationship leaves lasting cognitive or emotional traces has been disputed, however. For example, Lewis, Feiring, and Rosenthal (2000) found no evidence that attachment style at 12 months predicted attachment style at age 18. It therefore seems likely that experience of a wide range of relationships throughout life has a continuing influence on evolving attachment behaviors.

Attachment theory has attributed particular importance to the relationship between the mother and infant in shaping internalized working models and the course of future relationships. More recent work has begun to acknowledge the range of early interpersonal contacts. For example, Steele, Steele, and Fonagy (1996) have investigated the effects of father-infant as well as mother-infant interactions. Steele and Steele (2001) conclude, in partial accordance with popular stereotypes, that mother-infant attachment is related to the subsequent understanding of emotional life, whereas father-infant attachment better predicts functioning in peer relationships (see also Steele, 2002). Clearly, nothing is inevitable about the gender distribution of emotional labor implied by these findings. Different cultural practices involving more extended families or more collective child care are likely to produce different associations. Regardless of these variations, the research leads to the conclusion that allegiances and conflicts are intrinsic to early relations because no care-giving dyad exists in an isolated bubble. The basis for social identifications is laid down quickly after birth. Studies investigating effects of daycare (e.g., NICHD, 1997) or divorce (e.g., Page & Bretherton, 2001) on attachment offer further evidence that specific social arrangements may have a direct impact on how emotional life develops (e.g., True, Pisani, & Oumar, 2001). Further, to the extent that experience of early relations helps to establish a blueprint for later ones, including those with progeny, traditions of attachment interactions may become established over time, ultimately crystallizing into standard cultural practices.

☐ Interpersonal Theories of Emotion

In preceding sections of this chapter, we have presented evidence that emotions play a central role in interpersonal life, and that their development, causes, effects, and functions are clarified by reference to their broader social context. For many theorists, these interpersonal aspects of emotion are secondary to their subjective and private core. It is commonly believed, for example, that emotions are essentially individual responses to personal meanings whose interpersonal implications are merely a side-effect of their primary function. By contrast, we believe that interpersonal factors may be closer to the heart of emotion than such approaches imply. In the present section, we briefly present two theories that see emotions as fundamentally interpersonal processes.

Emotions as Relational Phenomena

The central argument of de Rivera's (1984) theory is that emotions are located between, rather than inside, people, and function as adjustments of their current relations. According to this view, each individual emotion derives its particular meaning not from its subjective character but rather from the movements it implies toward or away from others (or from objects whose meaning directly derives from interpersonal activities). Indeed, de Rivera and Grinkis (1986) point out that emotions are not only felt by those who are expressing them but also by the person they are directed toward: that is, "*I* may feel the 'heat' of *your* anger" (p. 352, emphasis in original).

In particular, de Rivera argues that emotions start out as movements that pull others closer or push them back. Primitive love, for example, involves the baby entering a state of merger or communion with the caregiver, whereas hate implies an opposite trajectory. Different interpersonal emotions are subsequently mapped out by reference to two basic dimensions concerning whether the underlying movement is one of extension or contraction, and whether this movement achieves approach (toward positive others) or withdrawal (away from negative others). Extension toward a positive interpersonal object is an act of giving to the other and is characterized as love, tenderness, or gratitude, whereas contraction with respect to a positive object expresses attraction. Table 7.1 organizes some familiar interpersonal emotions according to de Rivera's classification.

De Rivera also specifies the movements characterizing a set of self-directed emotions including sadness, embarrassment, and pride that cannot be characterized simply as relationships with others. However, his argument is that each of these self-directed emotions derives from a corresponding other-directed one:

> In every case, there is an *implicit* other and the person is behaving as *though* he or she were the object of this other's emotion. Thus, it is *as if* the depressed person is subject to another's anger, the ashamed person is subject to another's contempt, the secure person is subject to another's love. (de Rivera & Grinkis, 1986, p. 367, emphasis in original)

Similarly, we have argued above that the primary ontogenetic cause of so-called self-conscious emotions is the caregiver's evaluative action. In other words, guilt starts out as a response to blame from others, and pride as a response to praise. Subsequent internalization of the rules for

TABLE 7.1. Differentiating Interpersonal Emotions (adapted from de Rivera & Grinkis, 1986)

	Extension	Contraction
Positive (approach)	*Giving to other:* Love, affection, gratitude, respect, sympathy	*Attracted to other:* Desire, admiration, fascination, awe
Negative (withdrawal)	*Pushing other away:* Anger, disrespect, contempt, hate, resentment	*Pulling back from other:* Fear, shock, aversion, oppression

appropriate experience and expression of these conditions allows them to occur in less obviously interpersonal situations.

Regardless of whether de Rivera's specific interpretations of particular emotions are correct, it seems clear from the evidence presented above that emotions often do achieve exactly this kind of reconfiguration of relative positions in interpersonal space. As a consequence of emotion, we may end up closer to others or further away, higher or lower in respective status, redeemed or condemned in their eyes.

Emotion as Communication

Nobody would deny that emotions often serve to communicate messages to other people. The fact that I am angry shows that I take exception to something, and the fact that you are shocked by my anger implies that you don't share my perspective on whatever that something might be. All this seems self-evident. However, are these communicative effects spin-offs of the individual appraisals that provoked the emotional reaction in the first place, or could the appraisals simply be meanings attached to an already communicative emotion after the fact instead? Along the latter lines, Parkinson (1996) contends that emotion does not necessarily depend on a private apprehension of the personal significance of events, but rather represents a way of making a claim about significance to others. In particular, anger serves to blame others or recruit allies in resistant situations, fear is a way of enlisting support, and so on. Obviously, in order for emotional communication to serve its purpose it must be partly sensitive to the specific nature of the prevailing context, and sometimes this depends on a prior cognitive apprehension of the particular nature of its significance. We may blame someone else by getting angry because we have interpreted their action as blameworthy, for example. However, at other times, mutual positioning occurs as a function of interpersonal negotiation, of pushing and pulling against the social forces that prevail, with intrapsychic representations playing only a secondary role. We sometimes just get backed into emotional corners by the force of interpersonal events.

If emotions are communications, what relation do they have to other, more familiar, forms of language? One answer is that we resort to emotion when the common ground of everyday verbal interaction begins to give way. Most of our statements make sense within a shared frame of reference that is constructed between people during dialogue (e.g., Clark, 1996). For example, I make assumptions about what you already know and tailor my messages to fill in gaps (Grice, 1975). I presume that we see things from compatible perspectives. However, at certain times, these basic suppositions are harder to sustain. Occasions arise when our relative identity positions (what you are assuming about me, and what I am assuming about you) need realignment. For example, a higher status becomes defensible in a publicly obvious way and I become proud in order to reinforce the consequent change in relations. Emotions, according to such an account, reconfigure respective interpersonal positions when their viability is called into question.

Other occasions when a common frame of reference is elusive occur in multiple-audience situations (e.g., Fleming, 1994). The greater the range of interpersonal projects of the various parties to an exchange, the higher the chance that two or more of them will be incompatible. Emotion then emerges as a way of excluding or including individuals or subgroups. For example, polite conversations between groups of strangers can easily be disrupted when remarks are made that have implications for salient identities of some of the interacting individuals. Emotions remind us that the veneer of easy consensus is something that is achieved partly by actively negotiated omissions and exclusions (cf. Billig, 1999).

□ Concluding Remarks

As we have seen, emotions can take interpersonal objects, exert effects on interpersonal life, and serve broadly interpersonal functions. One possible way of integrating these observations is to interpret emotions as moves in an ongoing dialogue. One person has an emotion that affects someone else who may then respond with another emotion and so on, just like the back-and-forth exchange that characterizes much verbal conversation. Further, we have argued that part of the purpose of the first person getting emotional may be to produce a reaction in the second one, thus implying that emotions aren't just like descriptive statements concerning an appraised object but are more performative and pragmatic, oriented to actual and anticipated responses from others (cf. Spackman, 2002).

However, this analysis in terms of turn-taking may itself fail to acknowledge the full extent of interrelation between people during most interactions. Emotions develop over time in attunement or complementarity to others' emotions. Indeed, one of the advantages of emotion communication is that it can set or alter the tone of an exchange on line as the interaction develops. Emotions are often about feeling a way through unfolding encounters. I start to push a little at your opinion, you begin to give way and I push a little harder, or you offer resistance and I draw back or intensify my presentation. A shift in tone of voice, a glance away, or leaning forward all serve as adjustments in the fluctuating mood of our developing relationship.

This analysis of emotions arising from online adjustments in ongoing interactions is compatible with our previous discussion of ontogenetic origins. The earliest appearance of interpersonal emotion during development seems to involve reconfiguration of relations between infants and caregivers (and subsequently between infants, caregivers, and objects of shared activity). Much later, more articulated and strategic emotions begin to emerge from these more primary modes of influence.

But interpersonal influence of the tactical or strategic kind does not operate in a social vacuum. The process of mutual emotional adjustment even in the primary intersubjective context depends on negotiating a shared field of joint activity that is already mapped out by cultural practices and group allegiances. Similarly, the meanings later attached to emotional movements derive from preexisting representational resources. Your response to my outburst, for example, partly depends on whether you have been socialized to view anger as an aberration, a legitimate means of expressing power, or as some form of spirit possession. Because anger brings about different interpersonal effects depending on the sociocultural context, its interpersonal functions are transformed, too. In particular, anger will not encourage you to take my concerns more seriously if it is considered an immature and childish response in the first place (e.g., Briggs, 1970). It is harder to push my way through if cultural obstacles are already in the way. Further, some of the realignments achieved by emotions concern social rather than personal identity, and these too are constrained by culturally derived bases of social classification. Our task in the next chapter is to explore some of the many ways in which interpersonal, group, and cultural processes interact and interlock in the unfolding of emotion, and to begin to put these three realms of social life back together.

8

Interconnecting Contexts

How does emotion fit into the social world? Earlier chapters of this book have addressed this question in a number of ways, and at a number of levels. As we have seen, what counts as an emotion of a particular type partly depends on our cultural background. When and how it is regulated depend both on what society recommends and on what resources it provides for the task of regulation. Moving from the cultural to the group level, emotions are attached to objects of collective as well as individual concern, contributing to intragroup solidarity and intergroup differentiation. Other groups affect our group's emotions, and our group's emotions affect other groups, just as at the interpersonal level, other individuals affect our emotions and our emotions affect them. But how do these different kinds of social influences, effects, and functions interlock? What is the big picture? In this chapter, we sketch our impression of its basic shape.

Our aim is to provide an integrative overview of the ways in which cultural, group-level, and interpersonal factors influence one another, and set the context for the experience, communication, and regulation of emotion. We start by considering how cultural factors shape social processes that might impact emotion at the group and interpersonal level. In particular, we attempt to set out the range of societal influences that may be worthy of psychological attention. Having delineated these social structural factors, we turn to the questions of when and where they might exert their impact on emotion. By what processes do societal variables impact emotion, and what mediates their influence? Our argument is that the interpersonal and intergroup processes that set the immediate relational context for emotions are directly and indirectly affected by cultural meanings, artefacts, and practices. Finally, we present a relational approach that accommodates not only the impact of social structures on emotion, but also the reciprocal influence of emotion on the interlocking social networks that surround it.

☐ Cultural Influences and Their Operation

Putting something into context implies zeroing in from a wider perspective. The present project of putting emotion into social context thus involves framing relevant group and interpersonal processes within the broadest possible cultural perspective. The basic idea is that we can understand emotion better by seeing how it works as part of more inclusive systems, much as the significance of a heart beating is clarified by considering the circulatory processes it regulates and the surrounding mechanisms of bodily metabolism. Whereas it is relatively straightforward to trace the flow of blood around veins and arteries, mapping out the ramifications of emotion for social life presents less tractable problems.

Nonetheless, a good starting point is provided by Markus and Kitayama's (1994) model of how societal features shape behavior and experience (see Figure 8.1). The basic assumption of this model is that individual action and emotion are embedded in overlapping social contexts that can be specified at increasingly inclusive levels. At the broadest and most abstract level, the core values and ideas of a culture, together with structural features relating to economics, ecology, and politics, shape institutional customs and practices. These customs and practices in turn constrain or facilitate the ongoing interpersonal interactions that form the immediate context for the subjective experience of emotion.

Similarly, this chapter presents intergroup, intragroup, and interpersonal processes as operating within the framework of societal systems. Although we place more emphasis than Markus and Kitayama on differences between various kinds of social processes, many of the central principles are similar. The following sections present our own parallel attempt to explain how societal factors shape the intergroup and interpersonal settings that provide the immediate context for emotions. We start by reexamining the content of the "societal features" box specified in Figure 8.1, considering more carefully what aspects of cultures might exert their impact on emotional processes at the group and interpersonal levels. After having discussed the sources of societal influence, we review the general

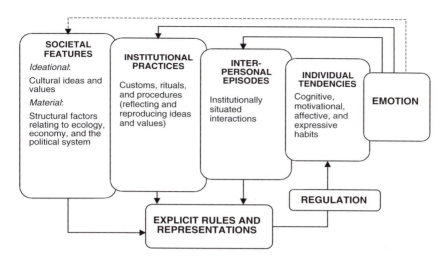

FIGURE 8.1.   Cultural construction of psychological reality (adapted from Markus & Kitayama, 1994)

processes underlying their operation, the more local contexts on which their effects are exerted, and finally their impact on individual emotions.

Ideational and Material Sources of Influence

Which features of society make a difference to our emotional lives? What are its active ingredients? If we assume that emotions are private events occurring within the confines of individual minds, then culture somehow has to get inside the mental system before it can influence them directly. Perhaps for this reason, psychologists often tend to explain societal influences on emotion in terms of rules and representations (*ideational* or cultural factors) that are internalized over the course of socialization. Thus, society teaches us how to interpret what is happening and what to do about it.

Such an approach is compatible with the anthropological conception of cultures as systems of meanings (e.g., Geertz, 1973; Lutz, 1988; Rohner, 1984). Indeed, the ethnographic approach is usually concerned either with the symbolic function of cultural practices, or more directly with the rules and representations deployed within a society. There is less focus on any direct effects of the practices themselves.

Markus and Kitayama also see collective reality as containing cultural ideas and values that may influence emotion (*ideational factors*, in our terms). In particular, their model focuses on independent and interdependent representations of the self arising from individualistic and collectivistic ideologies. Because emotional events are interpreted and evaluated in accordance with these cultural models, certain patterns of emotion are more likely to occur in one culture than another. In particular, socially engaged emotions such as shame and respect have higher prominence in Japan than the United States, whereas socially disengaged emotions such as pride and anger feature more strongly in the United States (e.g., Kitayama, Markus, & Kurakawa, 2000, and see chapter 3, this volume). Similarly, some emotions are the central focus of cultural representations because of their relationship to the "focal concerns" (Frijda & Mesquita, 1994) of a society (hypercognized emotions), whereas others attract less social attention (hypocognition). Not only do these differences change the way that emotional events are appraised in the first place, but they also affect the regulatory practices that attempt to bring emotional reactions into line with cultural rules and norms (*prescriptions*).

But the social world is not a purely symbolic realm, as Markus and Kitayama acknowledge. Although not a central focus of their analysis, ecological, sociopolitical, and economic factors are also specified as structural features (*material factors* in the present terminology). From the present perspective, these material factors may shape the intergroup and interpersonal processes underlying emotions. For instance, envy may arise among the lower classes as a consequence of inequitable distribution of wealth (relative deprivation [Runciman, 1966]), even if it is less likely to be communicated as envy in societies where unequal power distribution is culturally sanctioned.

At the ecological level, society constructs the very objects that require negotiation and the available routes around or between them. The buildings we live in, the roads we travel, and the food we eat take a form that reflects our social history. Thus, emotional interaction always takes place within a social context that is set not only by socialized ideology or sociopolitical reality but also by physical constraints that are often literally concrete. These too are clearly material factors.

Indeed, ideologies are implemented and made manifest in material culture. For example, the confession booth as used by the Catholic Church provides a technology for shaping modes of communication. Its architecture systematically restricts the possibilities of nonverbal influence and identification in ways that are bound to alter the style and course of any unfolding emotion that is expressed within its confines. For example, the semiprivacy of the setting and the lack of visibility afforded to participants combine to encourage confessions of guilt instead of expressions of embarrassment. Of course, this socially constructed aspect of the material environment is also bound up with a range of institutional practices with emotional consequences (the second box in Figure 8.1). Similarly, the psychiatrist's couch, the entry-phone, and the Internet partly embody prescriptive and representational ideologies and convert them into practical constraints on emotional conduct.

Markus and Kitayama (1994) point out that because cultural ideas and values are crystallized in specific artefacts and the practices surrounding them, members of a society may be influenced by these ideational factors without being explicitly aware of their meaning (this implicit mode of influence is represented by the overlap between successive boxes in Figure 8.1). People simply respond to a manufactured world that is already ideological. For example, someone engaging in the ritual of confession does not need to understand the motivation underlying the specific construction of the booth to be influenced by the material setting in ways that conform with the original intentions of its designers. More generally, the structures guiding interpersonal and intergroup interaction do not need to be interpreted as expressions of ideology to exert their effects.

The examples presented in the last few paragraphs illustrate how material culture can *reinforce* ideological effects. However, the development of material artefacts and their combination in practical settings often does not wholly reflect the prior intentions of their individual or collective inventors. Adjustments are made in the implementation of design to meet contextual requirements as well as the competing demands of different interest groups. Further, conventions of design and manufacture are often applied in settings other than those for which they were originally intended. For all these reasons, the material features of a society can exert influences on human interaction and conduct that are partly independent of ideology.

For example, buildings not only reflect a society's aesthetic values (and scientific understandings of what is possible), but also the specific climatic and geographical constraints of the location. If extremes of weather occur, people build different structures than they do when the climate is consistently temperate. Resulting variations in room size, penetrability of boundaries, and social density have direct implications for the kinds of interpersonal contact and conduct that arise. For example, people who are physically distant from one another need to use different channels for emotional communication from those who are constantly in close proximity with one another (cf. Munroe, Munroe, & Winters, 1996; Parkinson, 2001a).

As well as setting the context for human action and its interpretation, society also provides *tools* for addressing individual and social concerns. The physical characteristics of such technologies tend to facilitate certain modes of interaction at the expense of others. For example, telephones require a relatively quiet environment, so we tend to make our conversations using them more private. However, mobile telephones can be used even in public settings where noise levels are high, as long as their users are willing to shout. This may lead not only to miscommunication of emotion to the person at the other end of the line, but also to emotional reactions from those who cannot help overhearing conversations that would otherwise be intimate. Here again, the material elements shaping emotion develop a life of their own, imposing effects on psychological functioning that are not entirely explicable in ideological terms.

Not only do our interactions with technology have general consequences for our emotional life, either by freeing our time or by presenting frustrations of their own, but they can also provide means for specifically dealing with emotions themselves. For example, Prozac™ and Valium™ have obvious and relatively direct effects on depression and anxiety.

Table 8.1 summarizes the active ingredients of culture and social structure. In this table, we draw a distinction between ideational and material factors, both of which may vary in content from one society to the next. By *ideational*, we mean factors that relate to how the world is interpreted and evaluated: representations that provide some putative descriptive mapping of reality (cultural representations), and prescriptions that supply guidance about how one ought to move through the terrain (cultural values and rules). By contrast, *material* factors refer to physical rather than mental structures, including technologies and manufactured objects in addition to the more abstract economic, political, and ecological factors emphasized by Markus and Kitayama.

In fact, sociocultural reality does not divide up neatly into its ideational and material aspects. As we have seen, ideology exerts much of its impact via its expression in material practices (e.g., Cole, 1996; Foucault, 1970, *inter alia*). Objects are constructed in accordance with representations, just as representations adjust to match constructed objects.

TABLE 8.1. Sources of Societal Influence

	General	Emotion-Specific
Ideational		
Prescriptions	Values, norms, rules	Feeling and display rules
Descriptive representations	Scripts, schemata, mental models	Emotion scripts Ethnotheories about emotions
Material	Resources	Emotional capital (e.g., role-conferred power, status, gender)
	Settings	Venues for emotion (e.g., temples, stadia, bars, homes)
	Tools	Emotional technologies (e.g., prayer beads, stress aids, mood-altering drugs)

Nevertheless, distinguishing material from ideational factors helps to draw attention to aspects of societal influence that have often been neglected in previous theory and research.

A second distinction is drawn in Table 8.1 between the general manifestations of ideational and material factors and those that are specifically targeted at emotion. Clearly, the latter represent the primary focus of our discussion. However, by setting the context for emotion, defining its intentional objects, and defining possible modes of relation between social actors, the former sources of influence also play an important role. As an illustration of this distinction, Delta airline's regulation of flight attendants' emotions is achieved not only by prescribing appropriate emotions in feeling rules, but also by providing concordant representations of the audience and setting for emotional performance (Hochschild, 1983, and see chapter 5, this volume). As noted earlier in this volume, Delta cabin crew are specifically encouraged to view passengers as guests in their living room and treat them accordingly. At the material level, too, societies not only set the physical context for emotional conduct (freeways, yashmaks, truncheons), but also provide specific venues for emotional experience and tools for manipulating it (e.g., cinemas, tranquillizers, teddy bears).

Socialization and Real-Time Processes

In the previous subsection, we focused on the sources of cultural and structural influence. Now we turn to the general processes underlying the effects of these active ingredients of society. Like many psychologists, Markus and Kitayama assume that culture influences action mainly via the medium of socialization. In particular, individuals learn over the course of development to adapt to the cultural environment with consequent effects on thought, feeling, and action. This influence can operate in at least two ways, one explicit, the other more implicit. In Figure 8.1, the explicit influence process is indicated by the boxes and arrows at the bottom of the diagram: Societal features, institutional practices, and interpersonal episodes all provide explicit rules and representations that guide each person's active regulation of his or her individual tendencies. The implicit influence process is illustrated by the overlap between the boxes representing the intersecting contexts for individual tendencies, the idea being that the less inclusive contexts partly reflect adjustments to higher-level constraints and affordances.

At the explicit level, children are overtly schooled in societal values, and these values may in turn motivate more deliberative control processes. For example, at home and in school, individuals are directly instructed to conform to display rules as well as normative appraisals of emotional events (see the "explicit rules and representations" box in Figure 8.1). Westerners are taught that "big boys don't cry" or to count to 10 when feeling angry. Thus, cultural representations affect interpretation of events and also determine the strategies used for dealing with these events.

However, long before any of us is able to decode the meanings of cultural messages explicitly, we accumulate a vast store of practical expertise in the local workings of emotion at an implicit level. In the course of individual development, knowing *how* to respond to culturally constituted objects clearly precedes knowing *that* these objects have the attributes specified by the cultural representation. For example, Shweder, Mahaptra, and Miller (1987) detail the adult Oriya conception of menstruation (*mara*) as a potentially contaminating condition. Although children have no clear understanding of this meaning at an explicit level, they witness, participate in, and are affected by practices surrounding menstruating women. They are told not to touch their mothers during menstruation and observe them sleeping separately and refraining from food preparation whenever *mara* is present. Thus, values, rules, and representations with their associated emotional implications (e.g., developing disgust about menstruating women) become attached to the phenomenon, not as a result of deliberate inculcation, but simply as a function of participation in everyday social practices.

According to Markus and Kitayama (1994), then, a second, implicit process of emotional socialization involves individuals learning to adjust and conform to the social customs and practices of their society (the second box in Figure 8.1—the implicit influence of these practices on interpersonal episodes is indicated by the overlap between the second and third box). In later sections of this chapter, we will have more to say about the implicit and explicit processes underlying the cultural socialization of emotion and their interactions.

In addition to their effects on the *ontogenetic* development of emotional habits, we believe that social processes also directly influence the course of emotions *in real time*. Cultural meanings, norms, and values do not always need to be internalized within an individual mental system before they can exert their effects on emotional life. Indeed, to the extent that representations are embodied in cultural artefacts and practices at a material level, they may exert a relatively direct influence on current emotional conduct (e.g., the impact of the confession booth discussed earlier).

Like cultural socialization, real-time cultural forces may shape emotion at a more or less explicit level. For example, someone getting married for

TABLE 8.2. Processes of Societal Influence

	Explicit	Implicit
Past (socialized effects)	Emotion regulation in accordance with internalized rules/values	Emotion determined by habitual appraisals
Present (real-time effects)	Emotion regulation in accordance with formalized procedures	Emotion shaped by currently operative cultural forces

the first time may deliberately work up appropriate emotions at key moments of the ceremony. Moreover, if the person is from a remote culture and has not been schooled in the relevant conventions, then these reactions may seem less natural and more scripted. Supplementing this explicit regulation process, however, are the more direct effects of the formalized events. The ornate yet somber setting of the church, the organ music playing, the sequencing of scenes, and the congregation's conventional reactions together serve to orchestrate emotional responses at a more implicit level. When it is time to make the vows, it may be necessary to summon up the emotional response demanded by the priest's words, but the intonation with which those words are delivered and the facial expression that accompanies them help the process on its way. Thus, institutional practices operating within a socially constructed material setting can directly shape ongoing affective experience. Table 8.2 summarizes the processes whereby societal factors may have an effect on emotions.

Group and Interpersonal Mediators

Having delineated the sources of cultural and structural influence and the general processes underlying their operation, we turn to the issue of how they shape the more immediate social context for emotion before addressing more directly where their influence falls. According to Figure 8.1, cultural values are embodied in institutional practices that guide the course of the interpersonal episodes within which emotion unfolds. Thus, society's influence on psychological functioning is mediated by processes operating between people. Such an account is entirely compatible with our previous discussion of how culturally constituted material factors constrain and facilitate emotional interaction. However, we view this interaction in intergroup as well as interpersonal terms. In this section, then, we consider how the intergroup and interpersonal processes relevant to emotion are influenced by ideational and material factors (as specified in Table 8.1) over the course of socialization and in real time (see Table 8.2).

The most obvious way in which society influences interpersonal and intergroup emotional conduct is by providing explicit rules (*prescriptions*, Table 8.1) about how individuals and groups should conduct themselves in social life. For example, display rules not only prescribe what and how much emotion individuals *in general* should express to others, but also specify the appropriate expression and demeanor for members of *specific* social groups ("Big boys don't cry," "It's not your place to answer back," "You're too young to be in love"). Indeed, many societies expect women to display more fear, sympathy, and happiness than men, but less anger.

However, much of the socialization of group and interpersonal norms proceeds at an implicit rather than an explicit level (see Table 8.2, and the previous discussion). Members of different groups are treated differently at a practical level from a very early age and quickly learn the consequences of their emotional behavior. For example, if a cultural premium is placed on women expressing happiness (cf. LaFrance & Hecht, 1999), their smiles are likely to bring more positive consequences from others. Girls then may learn to smile not only because they know they are supposed to, but also because smiling gets them better treatment from other people who have internalized the relevant cultural stereotype.

A similar variety of prescriptive influence on group and interpersonal life clearly also operates in the *real-time* regulation of emotional conduct. If others implicitly subscribe to a smiling norm, then emerging frowns may be met immediately with frowns and thus be turned quickly back into smiles. We pick up culture- and group-sanctioned modes of emotional conduct not only over the course of socialization but also as part of our continuing adjustment to the ongoing responsiveness of our interaction partners. In either case, the impact of cultural prescriptions on emotional conduct seems to be mediated by its effects on intergroup and interpersonal processes.

It is not just cultural rules specifically relating to emotion that can influence emotional life at the intergroup or interpersonal level. Society also dictates more general modes of comportment and conduct for different categories of individuals (see Table 8.1), and these too can affect emotion (albeit less directly). For example, until relatively recently, the age of consent for sexual intercourse in the United Kingdom was higher for homosexuals than for heterosexuals. Breaking this rule brought clear emotional consequences both for transgressors (e.g., guilt, defiance) and for certain out-group members who became aware of the transgression (e.g., anger, sympathy). Indeed, it might be argued that the legal basis for the discriminatory practice helped to legitimate homophobia and even gay-bashing in less formal contexts. One of the reasons why we hate, fear, or are angry with other people is because of rules attached to the social categories applied to these people within a broader cultural system of meanings.

As well as responding to more or less explicit rules about emotional and nonemotional conduct, members of a society also acquire conventional *descriptive representations* (see Tables 8.1 & 8.2) of different social groups and individuals and of possible relations between them. In particular, cultures provide the categories defining in- and out-groups, and attach evaluative meanings to each. We are born into families, social classes, and groups characterized by race, faith, and gender, rather than undifferentiated societies. Further, we are socialized into appraising events from subject positions that derive their significance partly in relation to other subject positions. The emotional significance of another's actions or outcomes depends crucially on whether they are part of your group or outside it (and on the relative cultural status of the out-group in question). For example, a positive outcome experienced by an in-group member may lead to collective pride, whereas a similar outcome experienced by an out-group member may either be ignored or lead to unpleasant emotions whose specific nature depends on the nature of existing intergroup relations (see chapter 5, this volume).

The nature of our emotional reactions to out-groups also depends on how we represent their power and status with respect to our in-group. In particular, Mackie and colleagues (2000) found that relatively higher levels of perceived support for the in-group's position on key issues tend to be associated with greater anger, thus confirming the notion that appraisals concerning group power lead to antagonistic tendencies. Along similar lines, Fiske and colleagues (2002) found correlations between perceived group status and felt warmth (see chapter 5).

Societies not only attach *representations* concerning power and status to social categories, but also provide *material resources* to some groups and withhold them from others. Indeed, one of the main reasons why some groups are perceived as powerful is because they genuinely have the means to influence outcomes. Similarly, Fiske and colleagues (2002) argue that social stereotypes are shaped by structural forces relating to status and competition. An out-group with high status tends to be perceived as competent, whereas one that does not compete for common resources elicits warmth. Different combinations of competence and warmth in turn produce distinct emotional responses (see chapter 5). For example, welfare recipients in American society have few resources and are in competition with nonrecipients of welfare for whatever resources they have. Thus the low-warmth, low-perceived competence reaction to them is one of contempt.

Power and status are also clearly relevant to emotions operating at the interpersonal level. In Kemper's (e.g., 1978, 1991, 2000) terms, power is a relational condition in which one actor forces another to act in a certain way, whereas status reflects the willing cooperation of another actor. He argues that emotions are related to levels of power and status and to experienced or anticipated changes in these levels. In particular, high power and high status lead to feelings of security and satisfaction, respectively, whereas anticipated loss of power and status produces a combination of pessimism and lack of confidence experienced as hopelessness, despair, or depression. Further, temperamental differences arise from the differential use of power or status to reward or punish a child during the socialization process. For instance, a disposition to experience shame may arise from punishment routines involving the withdrawal of status. Clearly, child-rearing regimes of this kind may derive partly from the resources provided to parents by the wider society (as well as internalized rules and external sanctions for disobeying these rules).

Although some individuals are specifically granted resources because of their specific roles (e.g., inherited titles), more commonly, it is a person's social position as a member of a more inclusive group that determines relative power in a given interaction. For this reason, we believe that the impact of social-structural factors on interpersonal processes is often mediated by group membership. However, it is also certainly true that power and status can be acquired over the course of individual development and even on a moment-by-moment basis in an interpersonal interaction. The ways in which lower-level processes of this kind can lead to changes in structural factors will be considered in the final section of this chapter.

Another set of structural features that influence intergroup and interpersonal relations concerns modes of interaction. In particular, opportunities for contact and available channels of communication determine when and how groups and individuals clash or combine forces. For example, the physical demarcation of Catholic and Protestant areas of Belfast and their separate schools and institutions tend to reinforce emotional divisions between the groups (e.g., Hewstone & Greenland, 2000). Of course, this does not mean that ending segregation would automatically lead to intergroup harmony in the absence of broader political change. However, it seems clear that removal of the possibility of positive interaction makes a difference to how emotional positions are staked out. At a more extreme level, the incarceration of criminals and their isolation in separate cells clearly makes a difference to the emotional quality of the intergroup and interpersonal relations that can develop. In some circumstances, society can quite literally put, and keep, us in our place.

A society's material practices not only constrain or facilitate interpersonal and group conduct in real time, but also over the course of socialization. For example, obvious differences exist in the extent to which child-rearing is communal or personalized. We need only compare the kibbutz with the extended family, the nuclear family, or the lone parent to appreciate the magnitude of the differences in socialized group identification.

More generally, teams of adults may work together on the upbringing of groups of children in some collectivistic societies, whereas individual parents or nannies may devote their attention to each infant in isolation in some individualistic societies. Throughout the schooling process too, children may or may not be divided into groups, which may or may not be encouraged to compete with one another directly. The boundaries between these groups may be either physical or symbolic (walls or neckties, territories or badges) and may artificially impose categories (different "houses") or reinforce and amplify existing social divisions (boys and girls, those good or bad at mathematics or games). In either case, the selection of demarcation criteria for groups has the effect of emphasizing differences that would otherwise have been less salient. Thus, children may learn to see the world as more or less structured in terms of groups that are more or less arbitrary depending on their cultural background.

Structure is imposed *within* these groups, too. Individuals are elected or otherwise allotted specific roles as leaders, treasurers, secretaries, and so on, or are assigned specific tasks in the everyday business of the team. The extent to which this stratification occurs and the particular positions that it defines vary from society to society. Whether individuals are granted the opportunity to work their way up through the hierarchy or are simply expected to know their place sets clear constraints on the kinds of relational influence that they exert (cf. Hirschman, 1970 on "exit" and "voice" strategies). Power and status conflicts may be less of an issue when the surrounding structure permits little movement up or down a social hierarchy.

In summary, society presets the range of possible interpersonal and intergroup positions and the relations between them at both an ideational and practical level. Indeed, it would be impossible to take on the role of a shaman, doctor, member of the Labour party, or web-site designer in a society not organized to facilitate the associated practices. Furthermore, the specific resources attached to these roles and group allegiances depend on their place in a wider social network. Nevertheless, the parts we play are not always held tightly in place by structural constraints but may be reworked by actors using whatever representations, materials, and alternative practices at their disposal (see discussion following).

Individual Effects

Having considered how social structures can influence the intergroup and interpersonal practices and interactions within which emotion occurs, we now directly address their consequences for emotion at an individual level. On what aspects of the emotion process do the effects of social structures fall? The usual answer is that culture influences both appraisal and the regulation of emotion (see chapter 1). Internalized descriptive representations define what counts as a relevant occasion for emotion (e.g., Ellsworth, 1994; Mesquita & Frijda, 1992; Roseman et al., 1995), whereas internalized prescriptive representations dictate how situations ought to be appraised (feeling rules [Hochschild, 1983, and see Gross, 1998]) and when it is permissible to express your reaction (display rules [e.g.,. Ekman, 1973, Matsumoto, 1990]). Similarly, individual regulation might be applied to the actions that an emotion may provoke (e.g., aggression) and to the situations that provoke the appraisals (e.g., avoiding hostile encounters).

The above discussion suggests a number of ways in which this analysis might be extended. First, as argued in the previous section, the impact of culture on individual emotions may be mediated by intergroup and interpersonal processes. For example, we may follow a cultural display rule not because we personally have internalized the associated norms but because other members of our in-group are currently following them (e.g., emotional contagion [see chapters 4, 6, & 7]) or because our caregivers have reacted negatively to rule-breaking expressions in the past. Second, it is not only the ideational culture of a society that shapes emotion but also its material structures and practices. For example, I cannot express my anger directly at my boss if his secretary regulates access to his office and I have to arrange to make a later appointment to see him. I do not have sufficient *emotional capital* (Cahill, 1999, and see Table 8.1) within this organization to give free rein to my feelings under all circumstances. Third, as this example also demonstrates, cultural and structural influences do not need to be internalized over the course of socialization; they can also exert real-time effects on emotional processes. Finally, it is not only emotion-specific representations, rules, and practices that shape emotional life, but also the more general structures making up our social lives. We get emotional about culturally defined objects in culturally constituted settings from culturally specified subject positions.

Social structure not only influences appraisal but also what exists to be appraised in the first place. In societies where the death penalty is not a legal option, for example, people are less often afraid of dying as a result of state-sanctioned execution, and less often excited by the prospect of a public hanging. More generally, differences in the probability of relational events can result in differences in the probability of the associated emotions.

We have also argued that appraisal itself can be an interpersonal process that takes account of others' perspectives (social appraisal [see chapter 7]), or can be oriented to normative evaluations specified by group membership (cf. Smith, 1993). Similarly, the process of regulation often operates in a socially distributed manner. I check my expression against yours, especially if I strongly identify with the group to which you belong. I watch how you react when I smile or frown. Thus, social structure not only shapes when and how we regulate emotions, but also what the consequences of this regulation are for ourselves, our group, and for other people. The ongoing responsiveness of these others continually redirects the unfolding process of interpersonal and intergroup emotion.

Figure 8.2 summarizes some of these proposed social influences on emotion. The basic idea is that emotion develops in tandem with the evolving situation (see also Parkinson, 2001b). Social and nonsocial events occurring within this situation are shaped by the characteristics of the physical setting, which may be partly a product of societal forces, and by the institutional practices that apply to that setting. Further, an important aspect of even non-social events is how other individuals and groups are reacting both to them and to how we ourselves are reacting. Their reactions as well as ours are influenced by rules and representations supplied by the culture. Finally, the model does not view emotion or its expression as simple outcomes. Not only is expression seen as communicating an appraisal that in turn influences the social world, but emotions may also be preparatory stages for subsequent practical action that can directly alter the situation. In short, emotion performs operations on the social worlds in which it is embedded, and therefore changes those worlds to constitute a different context for subsequent emotion. In the final sections of this chapter, we will clarify the social functions and effects of emotion and present our own analysis of emotions as relational processes.

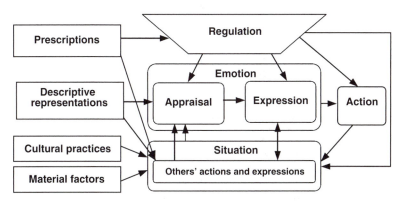

FIGURE 8.2. An extended model of social influences on the emotion process

☐ Marking Out the Territory of Cultural Psychology

Given their particular domain of expertise, it is perhaps not surprising that psychologists tend to focus on individual and intrapsychic processes. In cultural psychology, too, many researchers look specifically for influences exerted at the level of information processing or symbol manipulation, focusing on how the context is perceived, evaluated, and interpreted in culturally socialized ways, thereby de-emphasizing practical constraints and affordances of the real social arrangements themselves. Unfortunately, such an approach often seems to leave us, like Tolman's proverbial rat, buried in thought, unable to move. The hunt is on, therefore, for suitable excavation equipment that may help us dig our way out.

In our view (see also Markus & Kitayama, 1994), cultural psychology's relative neglect of practical and material influences on specifically emotional processes tends to sustain an artificial separation of experience and context. If it is only ideas and values that make a difference and only interpretation and self-control are affected, then it clearly makes most sense to articulate connecting processes in exclusively cognitive and cybernetic terms. By contrast, we propose that social and emotional processes intertwine more intimately in real time, with the unfolding practical and interpersonal situation continually shaping and reshaping the course of emotional action itself.

Of course, social factors not only influence emotion on line, but also have more remote consequences for subsequent emotion. For example, experience educates attention to focus on certain aspects of the emotional landscape at the expense of others. Parents and other adults impart habits of appraisal, expression, and regulation either by explicit training or implicit example. The usual interpretation of these and similar phenomena is that social relations are internalized as mental structures that control future emotional conduct. For example, children learn feeling and display rules that are later implemented on cue. In short, society is again seen as exerting only a top-down interpretative influence on emotion. Despite the evident validity and success of such an approach, our view is that experience also leaves other kinds of traces on affective processes. Unfortunately, however, the impact of social constraints and affordances on the bottom-up development of patterns of emotional response has typically attracted less research attention (but see Fogel, 1993).

If social factors can have an effect on emotion by virtue of their practical and material embodiment, their effects need not be imposed by overarching ideational structures, but instead by processes of lower-level adjustment. For example, if resistance is always met with intensified constraint, habits of struggling probably alter just as quickly as any internal representation of the situation. Anger consistently followed by disapproval and consequent guilt changes its character long before we learn the moral norms underlying that disapproval. The resulting emotion ultimately becomes a strategy that needs to be deployed more selectively and in different ways. In the following section, we develop this account of how emotions come to serve their social function as modes of relational activity over the course of development.

☐ Emotions as Relational Processes

Our discussion so far has often treated emotion as the endpoint of a causal chain leading from social structures via intergroup and interpersonal processes to the individual response itself. We may have given the misleading impression that individuals are hemmed in on all sides by interlocking social structures, both close and remote, and that their emotions are passive inescapable reactions to whatever is happening in these concentric contexts. However, as the arrows feeding back from the emotion box in Figure 8.1 indicate, Markus and Kitayama propose that individual conduct also exerts a reciprocal influence on its social context. Their argument is that controlled emotional responses may work to unsettle rather than reproduce established social practices, and to call their ideological basis into question. In our view, too, societal structures not only exert a top-down influence on emotional processes, but are also reshaped by the bottom-up pressures and tensions arising from interpersonal and intergroup interaction. Emotions are not simply things that happen to us, but things that we engage in actively, and that have consequences for the other people around us and for the wider settings for our conduct. In this section, then, we start to work outward from emotion to the lives and worlds that it affects.

Our basic assumption is that emotions are ways of aligning and realigning interpersonal and intergroup relations. This is achieved by two possible routes. First, emotions regulate interactions by redirecting others' action and attention on line (e.g., pushing away and pulling toward [de Rivera, 1984, and see chapter 7, this volume]), adjusting moment-by-moment to the changing social forces that guide them. However, this direct and implicit process is supplemented by a second process of explicit influence. In this second mode, emotions communicate more articulated appraisals to others and thereby influence their conduct (e.g., anger as a way of conveying blame). Any particular instance of emotion may involve either of these modes in isolation, or, more commonly, a combination or concatenation of both implicit and explicit processes. The specific interconnections and commonalities between the two emotion modes are best explained by a consideration of the course of ontogenetic development. In the following sections, then, we extend our analysis of emotion socialization, before considering more directly how emotions serve to reconfigure social networks in real time.

☐ Primary Intersubjectivity

Where in development do emotions begin? For some theorists, a small set of basic emotion programs lie dormant in babies' brains even before birth, waiting for their opportunity to emerge (e.g., Izard, 1978, and see chapter 7, this volume). Later, some of the resulting basic emotions get attached to more articulated cognitive representations, allowing more complex states to emerge. We, too, believe that the origins of emotion occur very early in life and that the developmental process can be seen as having two or three stages. However, our view of the nature of early emotions and of the process of articulation differs from the basic emotions view.

In our opinion, an infant's engagement with the very first interpersonal interactions already carries an emotional quality. In particular, babies are born with innate affective sensitivity to others and experience relationships with their parents and siblings in terms of attractions, aversions, and tensions (*primary intersubjectivity* in Trevarthen & Hubley's [1978] terms). Rhythms of contact and withdrawal are quickly established. The caregiver typically provides an amplified running commentary on the infant's movements, making exaggerated movements and sounds that the infant continually tracks. Mutual attunement and coordinated affective exchange occur from the outset.

Infants also play an active role in initiating and sustaining interaction. For example, they specifically imitate others' movements partly as a way of displaying their engagement in the interpersonal dialogue (e.g., Uzgiris, 1981; Nagy & Molnár, 2003). Because the specific movements that are copied are often shaped (at least partly) by societal and group-based influences, this process represents one of the first ways in which the broader social context influences emotion, and culture is acquired (e.g., Trevarthen, Kokkinaki, & Fiamenghi, 1999).

How do discrete emotions emerge from the ebb and flow of nonverbal interaction and communion between babies and others? At the most basic level, they seem to involve movements and activities that serve to sustain, reinstate, modify, or interrupt interpersonal rhythms. For example, 2- and 3-month-old infants in Murray and Trevarthen's (1985) study first reacted with a stare and then distress when their mother's faces no longer responded to their own faces' movements (see also Tronick, 1989; Weinberg & Tronick, 1996). These displays may begin as simple adjustments to an apparent alteration in the pattern of interaction. Indeed, interpersonal synchrony is not an automatic accomplishment but needs to be kept in place by cooperative activities in which each party tracks the looks and movements of the other. Changes in tempo or melody need to be negotiated nonverbally. Thus, the infant's distressed face is an intensification of a movement that would normally interlock with a counter-response to maintain the momentum of the interpersonal rhythm.

A similar analysis may be applied to some of the earliest ontogenetic forms of "anger" (e.g., Camras et al., 1992), although in this case the infant is physically adjusting to the constraints of the adult's flesh, rather than modulating mutual attention and communication. If a caregiver's embrace tightens, the baby may initially respond by stiffening and starting to struggle. Under normal circumstances this leads immediately to a loosened grip from the other. However, if the hug is maintained despite the baby's attempt to work against it, his or her struggle may intensify. The muscular tension associated with this physical struggle also shows on the child's face and the focused attention is apparent from his or her gaze. The overall pattern of relational movement may be seen as a rudimentary version of anger focused on the restraining arm as its object.

Up to this point, although the infant is active in negotiating the course of interpersonal events and helps to maintain and alter their rhythms, control processes are distributed between the two parties to the exchange (*coregulation* in Fogel's [1993] terms). What transforms this pattern of coregulated activity into a socially recognizable emotional stance? One possibility is provided by Vygotsky's (e.g., 1986) theory.

In Vygotsky's view, the child's actions are given meaning by the caregiver's reactions. For example, if a baby reaches toward something, the observing parent may infer that she wants it, and consequently move it to within the baby's reach. The infant thus learns that reaching for something can not only directly change her relationship to an object, but can also induce another person to act in ways that bring it closer. In other words, the perceptible interpersonal effects of a movement or gesture may change its functional character (cf. Mead, 1934, and see chapter 6, this volume).

Although Vygotsky's account of the development of pointing clearly underestimates the extent to which infants appreciate the interpersonal implications of their movements from birth (e.g., Rönnqvist & van Hofsten, 1994), the general principle may still apply in other contexts. In particular, the child's primitive struggle to get free in rudimentary frustration may already be interpersonally directed, but its specific communicative meaning may still depend on the restrainer's (or anyone else's) reaction to it as an indication of a certain desire or action tendency. Something that was originally oriented to the immediate interpersonal situation comes to be used as a way of exerting a predefined communicative effect. At this stage, anger stops being simply a struggle against resistance, or even a direct show of resistance, and becomes a request for release ("Let me go!" or "Get me out of this!"). Such an account would explain why younger infants respond to arm restraint with frustrated faces that are oriented toward the arm that is restraining them, whereas 7-month-olds start to direct their angry gaze at the face of the person who can release them (Campos, Campos, & Barrett, 1998). Direction of visual attention thus shifts from the *object* of practical action to the addressee of the communicative attempt (the *target* of the emotion).

Vygotsky's account suggests that it is the caregiver's *interpretation* of a child's impulsive movements that shapes their emerging function. To the extent that this interpretation can vary from one society to another, culture can also enter into the development of emotions at this early stage. An apparently angry baby, for example, may be perceived as being frustrated in legitimate desires or as expressing unjustified willfulness. In the first case, anger is likely to crystallize as an effective means of interpersonal influence; in the second, it may be more a source of conflict to be expressed only when others would not disapprove (cf. Evers et al.'s [submitted] account of gender-related norms for anger expression).

In addition, the way that caregivers deal with the perceived predicament of their charges depends on the tools that society provides. Even if the baby's frustrated desires are conceived as legitimate, for instance, there may not be appropriate resources available to fulfill them. Correspondingly, even a child perceived as acting willfully may be indulged if the caregiver knows of no other way to calm him or her. Thus, culture affects the early consolidation of emotional responses at both an ideological and practical level.

According to the Vygotskian account, infants adapt to a preexisting social world, but do not simply soak up its influences like sponges. Instead, they negotiate ways of making practical or communicative use of whatever cultural resources are at hand. Socialization is partly a process of coming to arrangements with others about how to proceed, given the constraints and opportunities of the current and anticipated social setting. Although Vygotsky emphasized the role of culturally competent adults in pulling infant development forward, more recent evidence (e.g., Selby & Bradley, 2003; Vandell, Wilson, & Buchanan, 1980) suggests that interaction with peers can also lead to the social production of emotional meaning. Indeed, the process whereby movements attain their social significance sometimes seems to operate on a tighter time scale than implied by Vygotsky's analysis of internalization.

For example, research by Selby and Bradley (2003) investigated the interactive behavior of infants who were arranged facing one another in groups of three. Actions such as foot-holding, vocalization, and arm-stretching changed their apparent function over the course of the interaction as other infants responded to them in real time (e.g., by copying them in modified form, or withdrawing or redirecting their attention). For example, in one interaction, 8-month-old Paula started to hold her foot soon after her mother left the room, apparently as an attempt to reestablish a secure base after an attachment figure left the scene. However, one of the other infants, Esther (7 months old) was looking intently at Paula while she held her foot and repeatedly copied the movement. Eventually, when Paula had stopped her foot-holding, she responded to one of Esther's overtures by looking back at her and copying the already copied action of holding her foot. From this point on, Paula came to use the foot-holding movement along with looks to initiate interaction with Esther (see Figure 8.3).

These examples of imitative behavior clearly seem to involve attempts at communication rather than passive mimicry (see also Nagy & Molnár, 2003; Trevarthen, Kokkinaki, & Fiamenghi, 1999, and chapter 6, this volume). Indeed, their precise timing and repetition and its orientation toward the other's responses is hard to read as simply reactive. Further, the communicative significance of foot-holding developed very quickly as a function of the interpersonal response that it elicited.

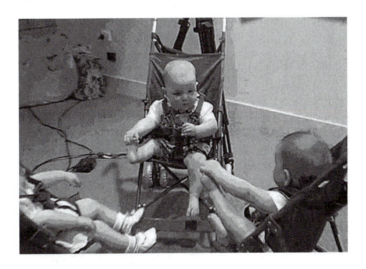

FIGURE 8.3.   Esther and Paula foot-holding together

FIGURE 8.4.   Ann and Joe playing footsie

During another interaction recorded in the same study, two 9-month-old infants, Ann and Joe, played footsie, while the younger Mona (6 months) looked on (see Figure 8.4). After a time, Mona started to rub her own feet then stretched one toward Ann while whining loudly—an action that the investigators interpreted as an attempt to get herself included in the game ("What about me?"). The other babies both looked at her and then back at each other. When Mona finally managed to stretch her leg far enough that her foot touched Ann's, Ann pulled her feet back from both other infants and touched them together before reestablishing contact with Joe but keeping her other leg well clear of Mona. From this point, Ann devoted her attention almost exclusively to Joe, while frequently pointing at him with both her hands. On one occasion, she turned to Mona, sneered, and raised the back of her hand in her direction with the index finger outstretched, a gesture that gives the appearance of being overtly rejecting (see Figure 8.5). Joe's reaction was to smile intently at Mona, inducing a bout of crying from Ann.

It is hard not to impute at least rudimentary interpersonal emotions to the three infants participating in this interaction (see also Draghi-Lorenz, 2001 and chapter 7, this volume). A little drama of jealousy, rejection, and sympathy seems to unfold before our eyes. Further, it is clear that the infants' various movements and noises served direct functions in realigning their interpersonal relationships over the course of the exchange. What is particularly interesting about these examples, however, is that they show that infants are able to manage interactions between more

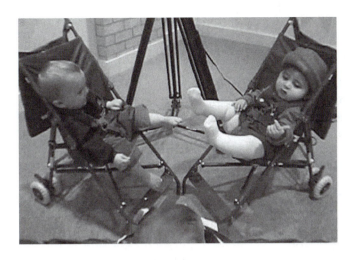

FIGURE 8.5. Ann's gesture to Mona (From Selby, J. M., & Bradley, B. S. (2003). Infants in groups: A paradigm for the study of early social experience. *Human Development, 46* , 197–221. Copyright Karger Publishers.)

than one other party simultaneously, even when those other parties are not adults who can provide appropriate "scaffolding" for the meanings being constructed (e.g., Vygotsky, 1978). Indeed, Selby and Bradley (2003) argue that even young infants are already equipped with the intersubjective resources necessary for participation in group as well as interpersonal life. Of course, because these infants were old enough to have already picked up various interpersonal skills from their earlier experiences with siblings and parents, their interpersonal flexibility need not be entirely innate. However, the study certainly demonstrates that babies learn at a very early age how to negotiate with others at an emotional level.

☐ Secondary Intersubjectivity

In the early months of a child's first year of life, he or she seems capable of managing interactions with other children or adults, and with objects in the environment. Early signs also exist of the corresponding person- or object-directed emotions such as anger, affection, and anxiety. Toward the end of the first year, however, a new capacity seems to emerge that involves an appreciation of the relationship between persons and objects (*secondary intersubjectivity* [Trevarthen & Hubley, 1978]), of how other people stand with respect to things that are the focus of mutual attention. In Selby and Bradley's (2003) study, some of the infants already seem to be developing this capacity. In particular, Joe's conciliatory reaction to Ann's apparent attempt to exclude Mona from the triad suggests some recognition of Mona's frustrated desire to interact with Ann. An even clearer example of infants involved in three-way relations is provided by the phenomenon of social referencing (see chapters 6 & 7, this volume). For instance, Hornik, Risenhoover, and Gunnar (1987) found that 12-month-old infants spent less time playing with a toy if their mother had shown a "disgust" expression toward it than if she had smiled or shown a neutral expression. In other words, the toddler is able to appreciate someone else's stance toward an object rather than just relating to the person or the object independently of one another.

The usual interpretation of social referencing is that the caregiver's emotional reaction provides a template for the child's appraisal of the object. Clearly, if the caregiver is appraising the object in a culturally appropriate way, then the child also picks up its cultural meaning and evaluation as a consequence. However, here too, the child's active role in the process may have been underestimated. In most circumstances, the adult's emotional expression is not a once-and-for-all definition of what something means, but rather an ongoing modulated response to how the child is proceeding with respect to that object. Correspondingly, the child may be actively seeking an understanding of what the caregiver currently thinks about what she is doing with the object ("How clever—or how reckless—do you think I am being?") to manipulate the interpersonal and practical situation more effectively (cf. Trevarthen, Kokkinaki, & Fiamenghi, 1999). Ordinarily, the meaning of what both parties are doing with respect to a third object is negotiated between them rather than imposed from either side.

Another aspect of secondary intersubjectivity is the infant's growing fascination with time-patterned interaction rituals, including games such as peek-a-boo and songs with accompanying actions such as "This Little Piggy Went to Market" and "Round and Round the Garden Walked the Teddy Bear." Both cases involve predictable cyclical sequences of building tension and release that follow quite precise temporal contours (see Stern, 2000). The child quickly learns not only to focus on a joint activity and to anticipate its outcome, but also to modify its parameters in collaboration with the caregiver. We see here some of the origins of active emotion regulation as well as the development of affective reactions that are not exclusively directed at the other person in a dyad. Further, although the temporal pattern and structure of routines such as these is universal among humans, their specific content varies more widely. Infants playing these games learn cultural-specific emotional meanings as well as more general strategies for expectation and control. In short, affect is invested in objects that are accommodated within these dyadic routines.

The kinds of emotion that emerge during periods of secondary intersubjectivity include those that are not simply directed at other people or at objects, but are also more directly concerned with other people's positions with respect to other people or objects. Children are now not just frustrated with someone or something, but also angry with someone for what they are doing with something. Further, rudimentary forms of jealousy on the basis of perceived relations between others and pride occasioned by others' stance toward something done by the self begin to emerge (Draghi-Lorenz et al., 2001). As proposed by Barrett (1995), however, these early emotions need not depend on prior cognitive apprehension of the significance of person-object or person-person relations. Instead, the affective experience of these relations may be a factor in establishing a subsequent appreciation of their meaning. Emotions can drive development rather than being simply symptoms of the current level of mental functioning. For example, an early version of "guilt" may emerge in direct reaction to a caregiver's unfolding accusatory presentation (see chapter 7), and repeated exposure to such contingencies may attune the developing child to the potential blame that may be attached to his or her actions by others.

☐ Articulation

Although infants are active in adjusting two-way and three-way relations in the intersubjective stages, and can modulate their emotion presentations in response to actual and anticipated feedback, there is little sense that they have an explicit representation of what they are doing. The emotions that they present emerge moment-by-moment from the course of coregulated events and have relatively immediate effects on what is happening. Indeed, the objects and events that are the focus of emotional actions mostly exist either in the here-and-now or at some earlier or later point of a routinized sequence of encapsulated events (e.g., peek-a-boo). However, children ultimately learn to organize sequences of emotional action that are oriented to more abstract features of episodes. What gets them to this stage of being able to articulate emotions?

After secondary intersubjectivity, the next major landmark in emotional development is the ability to use objects, gestures, and ultimately words as symbols. This is part of what we mean here by articulation: the capacity to represent meanings symbolically, to articulate something to someone else or oneself. According to Mead (1934; see also Hobson,

2002), this capacity emerges as a consequence of the ability to take another person's perspective on events. With secondary intersubjectivity, the infant comes to appreciate other people's relations to objects. The next step is to understand that people can have different relations to the same object, and that objects can therefore be made to mean different things by changing one's perspective on them.

The central capacity on which symbolic functioning depends is the ability to treat something as a representation of something else (Hobson, 2002). A piece of paper becomes a pretend blanket or a Lego brick takes on the role of a car. Further, the child begins to see that within a shared framework of practical activities using these pretend objects, perspectives become interchangeable. I can use a stick as a play sword and you may treat it equivalently. This forms an initial point of entry into the language games that underlie adult communication (Wittgenstein, 1953). When I use a word, I know that it picks out the same meaning for you as hearer as it does for me as the speaker. And I know that you know that I know this, and so on (Mead, 1934). Now I am able to use the common symbol to influence any other person who shares the relevant linguistic conventions.

Mead assumes that humans who share a common language occupy a kind of ideal speech community where meanings are transparent to all members. Whether or not such a situation is ever fully achieved, an initial step in this direction probably involves the child's appreciation that the person with whom he or she is currently interacting is using a symbol in a compatible way. "Let's both pretend that this stick is a magic wand!" Subsequently, this sense of mutual agreement may extend to more broadly defined in-groups. Thus, the trajectory of socialization works outward from the interpersonal to the group level, and ultimately toward the reproduction or transformation of a more broadly defined society (see also Gordon, 1989). Although what happens in the earliest interpersonal and group contexts is clearly shaped by societal structures, the potential also exists for the negotiation of new meanings. Indeed, certain kinds of idiolect only ever remain mutually meaningful for delimited sets of people within the wider society. Consider, for example, the rapid changes in the words used by youth subcultures to express positive evaluations. In some eras and social contexts, "bad" can mean "good," "hot" can mean "cool," and "wicked" can mean something else entirely.

The onset of the symbolic function has two kinds of consequences for emotional conduct. First, the objects of emotion are no longer restricted to the current situation but may represent more abstract or anticipated aspects of the child's predicament. Because events can have symbolic meanings, what is happening now can be indicative of a more general class of episode. Now, it is not just seeing a parent cuddling another child that provokes a jealous response, for example, it is also the prospect of friends going off to play together, a party invitation that arrives for a sibling but not for oneself, and so on. In short, it is not only things that directly have an effect on current relations that provoke emotions, but also events that signify changes in relations even when those changes are temporally remote. Indeed, explicit and increasingly abstract representations of the situations that produce different emotions soon develop as the child learns to speak (e.g., Harris, 1983, 1989; Wellman, Harris, Banerjee, & Sinclair, 1995).

Various societal factors can affect this process of symbolic abstraction at the material and ideational level (see Table 8.1). What gets abstracted partly depends on the specific objects and practices that are provided by society, and how abstraction proceeds partly depends on the available linguistic categories for representing these objects and practices. For example, in societies where material possessions are used as ways of expressing individuality (cf. Dittmar, Beattie, & Friese, 1996), emotional concerns may develop around the relative quality and quantity of toys that a child personally owns. Further, media representations may attach specific value to certain kinds of merchandise as a function of product placement in the latest movie or TV show. Children do not even need to be directly exposed to this propaganda for the cultural message to filter through to them through social networks, shaping their desires and satisfactions. Furthermore, the stickers, badges, costumes, and play-figures that are purchased for them convey messages about group membership that also carry emotional power. Nevertheless, we should not present children as cultural dupes who blindly appropriate everything that society provides. Instead, they are able to make use of the available resources in ways that suit their own negotiable or coregulated projects.

Another important way in which young children acquire culturally loaded emotional representations and values is through family conversations (e.g., Brown & Dunn, 1996; Dunn, Bretherton, & Munn, 1987). Whether or not the lessons learned in these less public contexts endorse or conflict with wider ideologies, they certainly contribute to the child's practical and moral understanding of how the world works. Parents and siblings thus convey cultural messages about the emotional implications of events that apply not only to individual children but also to others who share their developing social identity. Here again, however, this is not a simple inculcation process. Rather, children play an active role in negotiating the prescriptions and interpretations that are relevant to emotional conduct.

It is not only emotion-relevant situations that attain conventional meanings during the development of the capacity for articulation, but also the various aspects or components of emotions themselves (see Table 8.1). A smile or frown from someone else, for example, is no longer only something that entrains my own expressive movements in real time. It is now also something that signifies something about the status of our relationship or respective social identity, something that is appraised as appropriate or inappropriate to how things stand with us. Further, knowledge of these communicative meanings also allows me to use *my own* expressions to convey these shared meanings to others. *My* smile too stops being simply a way of regulating the responses of a specific person with whom I am interacting directly, and begins to be recognized as having a shared meaning across a variety of people. Now when someone has a tight grip on my arm, or when I am having problems pushing a block through a hole, I can use a cross look as a general appeal to potential onlookers ("Someone should be doing something about this!"). It is but a short step from here to the habitual use of conventionalized expressions in adult emotion communication.

As a consequence of their continuing selective exposure to cultural meaning systems in the media and their conversations with others, children ultimately come to organize their growing understanding of how emotions unfold into more articulated representations (acquisition of *emotion scripts* [Fischer, 1991]). This brings us to a second meaning of "articulation": Not only do emotions carry symbolic meaning, but their representations also imply temporal organization and allow us to structure and coordinate our emotional responses and responses to emotions over extended interactions.

Emotion scripts not only specify the situations in which emotions typically occur, but also the thoughts and feelings that are associated with these situations, and the nature and time course of the person's responses (Nelson, 1993; Wellman et al., 1995). Further, they contain prescriptive as well as descriptive features, dictating how emotions are supposed to be played out, not just how they usually happen. Although the child had previously picked up implicit messages about the appropriateness of her emotional expressions from others' reactions, she is now taught explicit rules about what to show or feel, and when and how to show and feel it (display and feeling rules) depending on abstractly defined features of situations. Emotion is now clearly perceived as action in a moral as well as practical universe. In particular, children are taught that the intensity of an emotional presentation should be proportionate to the seriousness of the precipitating event (primary appraisal) and that different varieties of emotion are appropriate to different kinds of transaction (secondary appraisal).

For example, in Anglo-American cultures, anger is seen as justified when someone else is responsible for deliberately acting in a way that conflicts with your own rights in more than a trivial way. Different societies have different rules and representations of emotions that are otherwise comparable to this kind of anger. Although having this particular articulated representation makes a difference to how anger is regulated, it is not the case that recognizing that the situation conforms to the required core relational theme is necessary or sufficient for anger to occur (as apparently assumed by Lazarus, 1991b and some other appraisal theorists; see Parkinson, 1999). Indeed, although Anglo-Americans may work themselves up into a state of indignation when they see someone else as to blame, they also experience and show something that looks very like "anger" when events frustrate them in more basic ways. In our view, the kinds of anger-inducing interactions experienced by infants at the stages of primary and secondary intersubjectivity continue to exert their emotional power even when the more explicit and articulated representation of anger becomes available. We don't learn how to get angry in the first place by following cultural rules, even if those rules are applied to our anger after the fact.

However, cultural representations are not entirely divorced from reality, either. One reason is that implicit cultural influences have already had a concordant influence on emotional action prior to the stage of explicit articulation. Infants quickly learn whether or not an angry expression elicits help or disapproval from culturally competent others, for example. Second, some modes of emotional action emerge from recurrent practical and interpersonal contingencies regardless of cultural conditions. For example, a frustrated response to arm restraint occurs in infants across a variety of societies (Camras et al., 1992). Given a basic motive for movement and the configuration of human musculature, this pattern of bodily and facial movement is an almost inevitable consequence of early learning. Relatively primitive action complexes such as this may form part of the basis for many of a culture's articulated emotion concepts.

For both these reasons, many of the culturally sanctioned occasions for anger in which someone else is to blame for something bad happening also involve frustration of the less articulated kind, leaving little conflict between the articulated angry role and the emergent feelings for which this role provides structure. In other words, the unfolding interpersonal situation generates implicit emotions that are compatible with our explicit representations and control processes. Indeed, it would be surprising if a society developed a representation of a mode of emotional action that bore no relation to its spontaneous manifestations. However, because ideologies of emotion provide a selective or biased perspective (indeed, this is exactly their point), the emergence of the spontaneous version of anger does not always match the cultural requirements. Occasions also arise when the angry role needs to be adopted more deliberately, or when an apparently unjustified outburst must subsequently be justified according to the cultural rules.

The availability of cultural scripts for anger and other emotions (depending, for example, on their hyper- or hypocognition within a culture [Levy, 1973, and see chapter 3, this volume]) also facilitates a more strategic form of regulation. Like the words that we use to convey anger, certain unfolding patterns of facial expression acquire a conventional meaning and can be used without thinking as ways of influencing others' conduct. For example, because other people in our society know that getting angry implies that somebody else is to blame, the emotion may be used explicitly as a strategy for conveying blame. This development has parallels with the earlier Vygotskian process of internalizing interpersonal meanings. Here too, people register the effects of their emotional presentation and learn lessons about how it may be used to influence others. The difference is that the effects are not direct but are based on a system of shared meanings, and the control processes are correspondingly more explicit. Of course, the strategic use of anger to convey blame to others may ultimately become habitual, too.

It is perhaps misleading to see articulation as a single, well-defined stage of ontogenetic development. Instead, the emergence of this capacity is gradual and leads to a series of progressively more complex competencies. Ultimately, individuals not only learn how to represent and regulate emotional situations and experiences in a culturally sophisticated manner, but also to deploy their representational and regulatory competencies in a flexible manner depending on the current interpersonal and group context. Further, they may even come to question the basis of existing cultural representations and to reformulate them creatively in collaboration with others. Thus, interpersonal and intergroup dialogue concerning emotions and emotional objects may lead to the production of new articulated emotional meanings (see discussion following).

☐ Summary

We have argued that many emotions emerge developmentally from basic relational processes (also see chapter 7). According to this view, "anger" as conceived in Anglo-American societies is a cultural articulation of a more fundamental mode of interaction. A baby struggles against any restriction, but a socialized individual in the Western world is only supposed to get angry when someone else is to blame for imposing the restriction. The tendency, then, is to account for our anger in terms of this articulated cultural model, even if something very like anger still occurs in the simpler ways (cf. Parkinson, 1999). Our culturally constrained categories do not always map easily to the implicit relational emotions that sometimes occur.

This admittedly simplified outline of the development of emotion presents their emergence in overlapping stages. First comes primary intersubjectivity when the infant is oriented and attuned to her relationship with others, and experiences emotional engagements and disengagements in ongoing interpersonal dialogues. Here, cultural practices intrude by providing the initial modes and patterns of caregiver engagement to which the infant accommodates. Secondary intersubjectivity comes later with the capacity to respond (emotionally or otherwise) to relations between a person and object (which may be another person). At this stage, culturally manufactured objects and culturally defined relationships set the format for these three-way exchanges. Finally, and much later, children learn how to symbolize their emotions and find out what explicit rules are applied to them within their culture. Different kinds of emotion arise during each stage (see Table 8.3 for a summary of this model).

However, the later modes of functioning do not entirely supersede earlier ones. Primary intersubjective emotions are not replaced by secondary emotions, which then become obsolete when articulated emotions are possible. Instead, the emotional competencies achieved at each stage are superimposed on earlier capacities, resulting in a complex of

TABLE 8.3. Stages of Emotional Development

	Types of Emotion	Orientation	Relevant Cultural Factors
Primary intersubjectivity	Emotions aligning direct relations with persons or objects (e.g., affection, repulsion, frustration)	Persons or objects	Child-rearing practices, material settings for interaction
Secondary intersubjectivity	Emotions operating on relations between persons and objects (e.g., jealousy, pride)	Relations between persons and objects (or other persons)	Manufactured tools and objects, caregivers' internalized representations and rules relating to emotions and emotional objects
Articulation	Emotions directed at abstract objects, scripted emotions, strategic emotions	Relational meanings	Explicit display and feeling rules, emotion scripts

interlocking relational processes operating sometimes in parallel, sometimes in interaction with one another, and also occasionally in mutual conflict. Such conflicts are precisely the basis for the experience of inappropriate or unreasonable emotion (e.g., Parkinson, 1999), which may therefore be subject to deliberate regulation. For example, simple exclusion from a dialogue may directly provoke a jealous reaction (cf. Selby & Bradley, 2003), but Anglo-American cultural (and interpersonal) prescriptions do not sanction this emotion unless intentional betrayal occurs by someone with whom you share a close relationship. Under these circumstances, you will tend to feel something that you know you should not feel, and may try to do something about it either by redefining the situation or by working on your feelings.

Our distinctions between these three stages and varieties of emotion bear some resemblance to those proposed by Leventhal and Scherer (1987). Their theory specifically differentiated the sensorimotor, schematic, and conceptual processes that are supposed to underlie emotional responses. Further, these authors imply a similar developmental sequence of processes, in which children first react to innately specified emotional stimuli, then learn to generalize their emotional responses to other stimuli (e.g., by classical conditioning), then finally develop articulated representations of their emotions (including rules, scripts, and ethnotheories). However, important differences of emphasis also distinguish the two accounts. We stress the interpersonal basis of early emotional experience, whereas many of Leventhal's examples of sensorimotor emotions are reactions to physical stimuli such as tastes, sights, and sounds. Further, our view is that emotions are never purely reactive states in the first place. Instead they are relational moves that regulate the respective positions of the emotional person and the people or objects with which he or she is interacting. Finally, we see the articulated "conceptual" processes associated with emotion not just as another equally valid route to the same emotional outcome, but rather as often pitting themselves against the coregulated, bottom-up processes that characterize the more basic relational modes. Our culturally derived ideas about emotion do not just represent useful practical knowledge about their workings, but also selectively bias our attention and regulatory conduct.

☐ Adult Relational Regulation in Real Time

Our account of emotional development suggests a dichotomy between emotions that are implicitly oriented to unfolding interactions in the here-and-now, and those that address more abstract, symbolic meanings.

In practice, adult emotions usually combine both kinds of process, although the balance between them can shift. In some cases, tension exists between the implicit and emergent properties of our emotional presentation and its more explicit meaning for ourselves and others. However, harmonization of emotion modes is probably more common. For example, the spontaneous attunement of our developing smiles may also be reflected in our overt articulation of the current status of our interaction, relationship, and shared group identity. Alternatively, it may be that I know that I should not be getting so close to a person like you.

The symbolic meanings that are attached to our real-time emotional presentations mainly derive from cultural ideas and values or from considerations relating to social identity. At the societal level, they may reflect concerns relating to an abstract notion of self as independent or interdependent. For example, pride may serve to mark either a collective or personal achievement (see chapters 2 & 3, this volume). At the group level, emotions communicate claims relating to social identity as defined by group membership. My affiliative emotions may be an expression of group solidarity, for instance (see chapter 4, this volume). More specific forms of emotional inclusion or exclusion depend on the particular relations that exist between and within groups, for example with respect to relative power or status (e.g., Fiske et al., 2002; Mackie et al., 2000). Thus, my contempt may be a way of implying your lower standing along a salient dimension of comparison, as well as a move to push you into the position of an out-group member.

We have argued that emotions may emerge implicitly from ongoing interactions or may be controlled by more explicit processes. Similarly, another person may respond to your emotions at the implicit or the explicit level. Further, the way that others respond to your emotions may or may not be concordant with the processes that caused them in the first place. Four basic alternatives are possible. First, a person may explicitly orient emotion to the identity aspects of the relational situation but the emotion's target may respond only to its direct interpersonal implications. For example, my smile may be a polite acknowledgement of our shared group membership, but you react only to its approach aspects. Second, and conversely, an emotion may emerge from interpersonal dynamics but be read as a symbolic message about identity. Your smile is an adjustment to my approach but I read it as an expression of polite respect for my status, for instance. Third, my symbolic presentation of an emotion may be read by you at a corresponding symbolic level. Fourth, an interpersonal emotion may only have direct interpersonal effects with no symbolic significance attached to it by either party to the exchange. However, it would be surprising if the deeper symbolic meanings of our emotional presentations in either words or gestures did not also carry deeper symbolic meanings concerning roles, social identities, and selves at some point in any extended adult encounter.

Appraisal theory's central idea is that because emotions carry implications about the meanings of transactions, individuals have to arrive at these meanings to become emotional (Lazarus, 1984). In other words, our minds only know that they should output an emotion when they have recognized the personal significance of what is happening. However, meaning and significance are often secondary consequences of becoming emotional rather than its specific antecedent. Earlier, we suggested two ways in which emotion can occur without any direct apprehension of the relational meaning that is supposed to be at its heart. First, emotions may be actions that emerge from, and operate on, unfolding relations with other people and objects. A baby held too tightly increasingly adjusts its posture to loosen the other's grip. No sense of other-accountability or blame characterizes this pattern of movements, although both may be attributed to the movements by caregivers after the fact. Much later, children learn more explicitly when they should get angry. As a consequence they may ultimately use anger as a way of conveying blame even when they do not believe at any level that the other person is responsible for what is happening.

Rather than seeing emotions only as reactions to interpretations and evaluations, we view them as moves that adjust relations in ways that produce and convey these interpretations and evaluations. Of course, this does not mean that our appraisals are not associated with our emotions, nor even that they are never part of their cause. Indeed, the appraised meaning of an event may be an articulated representation of a subset of the relational contingencies that lead to emotions at the implicit level, or it may represent one of the reasons for getting emotional at the more articulated level. As an example of the latter phenomenon, you may realize after thinking about it that what someone else did was an intentional attempt to interfere with your plans, and this may lead you to convey your blame using anger. Of course, this need not be a wholly intentional or deliberate process because the articulated meanings of anger-inducing events are apprehended by a process of automatic skilled perception and the angry actions and expressions have become habitual.

Although appraisals may provide descriptions of the relational contingencies that produce implicit emotions, or capture the relational meaning conveyed by emotion in the articulated mode, in neither case do they represent sufficient conditions for experiencing emotion. With regard to implicit emotions, the reaction is shaped on line by the unfolding encounter with the social environment rather than by any central registration of the event's meaning. Further, even when appraisals explicitly convey an articulated appraisal that derives from prior interpretation and evaluation of what is happening in a transaction, we believe that there also needs to be a potential addressee for the appraisal that is to be conveyed (cf. Fridlund, 1991). Although people certainly get emotional in an articulated mode when no one else is around, their emotions under these circumstances are oriented not only to the perceived meaning of what is happening but also to someone for whom they would like this meaning to be clear: I feel angry that you don't understand what I am telling you, and my anger is part of my attempt to make you understand.

Our view of the relational functions of emotions can also be extended to emotional language. Just as appraisal theory focuses on the representational meaning of emotional events, most accounts of emotion representation look for the situational and personal events that emotion words are supposed to describe (see chapter 2, this volume). However, emotional language does not provide a neutral description of the transactional world, but instead represents a practical resource for emotional influence. Saying "I love you," "I hate you," or "I am angry with you" is never simply a reflection of an underlying state of mind; it always also serves as a pragmatic move that realigns relational positions. The words are not descriptions of emotion; they are its expressions (Coulter, 1979; Wittgenstein, 1953). Thus, emotion words, like the articulated emotions that they express, convey appraisals rather than representing them (cf. Spackman, 2002).

So far, we have argued that emotions influence social relations at an implicit or explicit level, but have said relatively little about how this happens. What, then, are the specific relational functions of adult emotions in the implicit and explicit mode? First, emotion draws someone else's attention to an object of emotional concern either by making it the direct focus of orientation or action (implicit mode) or by symbolic emphasis (explicit mode). In particular, topics are made salient and their significance is amplified by an emotional presentation or message, thus discouraging indifference from others (cf. Tomkins, 1962 on the intrapsychic rather than interpersonal amplifying function of emotions). Second, emotion conveys a stance or attitude toward the object either directly because of the specific form of orientation or action (withdrawal or approach, sustained focus or aversion of gaze, etc.), or by conveying a conventional appraisal. Finally, and in the explicit mode only, presentation of an emotion restricts the normative range of responses that are available to its targets.

How do articulated emotions serve this last function of setting conventional parameters for the other's reactions? In this regard, we would suggest another parallel between emotional and linguistic pragmatics. Like verbal utterances, emotions come in adjacency pairs with preferred and dispreferred responses. In everyday conversations, a request may be met with unqualified acceptance but not by unqualified refusal. For the sake of politeness (Brown & Levinson, 1987), when asked for a favor, we are expected to provide an excuse if we want to say no. Similarly, in the emotional rather than linguistic realm, anger serves as a request for an apology that is best delivered as an appropriate expression of guilt. However, to avert this interpersonal demand, we may show reciprocal anger ourselves as a way of demonstrating that we do not accept the basis for the other's claim on us. Needless to say, all of this depends on cultural conventions and representations of when and where anger and guilt are appropriate.

☐ Bottom-Up Influences of Emotion on Social Structures

If emotions act on relations between individuals and groups, their consequence will often be a change in these relations. Because society is partly constituted from social relations, this influence may also permeate more widely with deeper implications for so-called structural factors. Like the proverbial flapping of a butterfly's wing, an interpersonal realignment may lead to catastrophic shifts in more inclusive dynamic systems.

Some of the most consequential emotional relations occur in early ontogenetic development as a caregiver responds moment-by-moment to the child's unfolding movements and expressions (Halberstadt, 1986; Saarni, 1999, and see chapter 4, this volume). The infant's participation in this dialogue is active from the start, and improvisations around established themes soon emerge. By selective imitation, families may develop their own idiolects of emotional expression, adjusting group and cultural norms to suit present relational purposes.

Although parents tend to think of their responses to infants as entirely natural and spontaneous, they are also constrained by local practices and material conditions. Awareness of alternative ways of relating as practiced in different cultural settings (see chapters 2 & 3, this volume) may extend the possibilities of emotional contact with children and attune parents to different aspects of their sons' and daughters' presentations of affect. Indeed, seeing emotions as active as well as reactive may also effect immediate changes in the emotional stances adopted by parents. These adjustments in turn could potentially be consolidated in the temperament of later generations.

However, it is not necessary to speculate about such remote intergenerational consequences to appreciate how the effects of emotional actions can trickle back up the social system. Indeed many of the wider implications of emotions are apparent in real-time encounters. At the most basic level, emotions link people together or divide them. For example, think of 9-month-old Ann's sneer and gesture directed at 6-month-old Mona in an apparent attempt to exclude her from a developing relationship (Selby & Bradley, 2003; see Figure 8.5). Correspondingly, Joe's subsequent smile can be seen as a countermove establishing a new alliance. Out of such tiny emotional movements, groups can grow (see chapter 4, this volume).

In adult multiperson exchanges, subtle negotiations about the appropriateness of claims to power or status go on all the time. Influence is exerted on others partly via the medium of nonverbal expression as well as by invoking more explicit representations of emotion. For example, if the appropriate tone of righteous anger can be maintained against detractors' counter-claims, blame may be diverted, and reputation defended. The outcome of such interactions can have real consequences for resistance or the granting of authority.

In more commercial settings, the increasing tendency of U.K. consumers to express irritation about perceived inadequacies of products and services has led to various changes in company practices (e.g., the institution of more elaborate "customer care" procedures). The consequent positive reinforcement for irritated conduct has also arguably been a factor both in the development of a "complaint culture," and in the wider prevalence of anger (trolley rage, road rage, flatpack rage, etc.) outside the immediate sphere of economic consumption. Routinized interpersonal and institutional responses to outbursts of the latter variety are also beginning to develop.

The phenomenon of emotional contagion (or communicative imitation) also suggests that emotions may disperse more widely through social networks. Many people believe that a charismatic leader can infect followers with enthusiasm for a cause, or more generally enhance the positive feelings of a group (e.g., Barsade, 2002; George, 1995). Given congenial circumstances, such effects might resonate into a pervasive cascade of affect throughout an organization, even a society. Economists argue that the feel-good factor is crucial in maintaining consumer confidence and market investment in capitalist societies. Perhaps, then, emotions can have more profound material consequences than is usually acknowledged.

From where do such changes in the emotional climate (e.g., de Rivera, 1992) of an organization or nation originate? It seems unlikely that single individuals spontaneously adopt new emotional positions of their own accord, and then lead others by example. However, exposure to other cultures may enhance appreciation of the contingency of our own emotional practices and representations. Indeed, the assertion of consumer rights in the United Kingdom may partly reflect the experiences of visitors to the

United States, or the observation of the successful complaints of U.S. tourists in British shops, hotels, and restaurants.

Scaling up to the intergroup level, a consistent presentation of group emotion may lead to others shifting their position to accommodate its implied perspective on events. Moscovici (1976) sees such processes of minority influence as one of the engines of social change. Thus, pressure groups often use emotional tactics to bring topics to the political agenda. Clearly, emotional dialogues can occur between groups as well as individuals, and their resolution can involve merger or fractionation, accommodation or rejection.

To the extent that society can be seen as a network of intergroup and interpersonal relations, the low-level adjustments of respective position effected by group and individual emotions also reconfigure the broader social system. Depending on where movement occurs in the network, its consequences may be slight or revolutionary. According to Averill (1980), articulated, scripted emotions serve precisely as strategies for reconciling conflicting ideological prescriptions, ways of papering over the cracks as the structure threatens to crumble. Anger, for example, represents a short-term social role that is adopted to resolve the discrepancy between pacifistic and retributive cultural values in situations where someone is thought to have done you wrong, and yet you must not hurt them deliberately in retaliation. Getting angry is a way of conveying the blame without premeditation. If Averill is correct in seeing emotions as operating at the points of ideological tension, then any adjustment of their conventional enactment (e.g., as a function of emotional creativity [Averill & Nunley, 1992]) might unsettle the entire edifice. If emotions are represented as articulated roles, then someone somewhere can begin to rework their scripts, and social actors can improvise around the new themes that emerge. The consequence might be a resurfacing of repressed cultural contradictions, potentially leading to a more widespread reconfiguration of ideas, values, and practices.

For example, Averill (1985) analyzes romantic love as a specific reaction to an ideological conflict between the rights of the individual and the needs of society (see chapter 7, this volume). Although individualistic cultures encourage everyone to pursue their own goals and express themselves to the utmost, in practice, insufficient resources exist for everyone to be completely fulfilled. The role of being in love allows a specific interpersonal arena in which one is granted the highest possible value by one other person at least. One strand of the countercultural movement in the United Kingdom and the United States during the 1960s was precisely to question the proprietorial basis for exclusive loving relationships of this kind. Exponents of "free love" actively worked on their feelings of jealousy and involvement as part of their broader purpose of changing society. Of course, the system has its own mechanisms for resisting such emotional deviance (Thoits, 2004), and arguably the forces of conservatism ultimately won out in this particular ideological battle. However, the free love experiment has certainly left its traces on current representations of the family unit and its role in society.

Similarly, the avowed equality of opportunity for Black people in U.S. society has long been contradicted by their relatively lower power and status in comparison to White people. In some sense, subscription to the American Dream may have led earlier generations of Blacks to experience shame that they apparently did not deserve the promised heights of achievement. The Black Pride movement of the 1960s was partly designed to correct this kind of false consciousness. By feeling themselves to be worthy and entitled, Blacks asserted their rights and called into question some of the tenets of the U.S. Constitution. Structural adjustments were made partly to accommodate the new collective expression of emotion, even if there is still some way to go before full equality is achieved.

All of these examples suggest that despite appearances, cultures are not fixed and monolithic structures whose effects permeate down to the nuts and bolts of individual emotional conduct, but instead are partly responsive to the outcomes of that conduct. Societies do change, even if the change is usually gradual, and often resisted. Although it is tempting to regard cultural evolution as working to a higher design, and to search for corresponding functional explanations for any structural shifts, in fact there may be more local and contingent reasons for the specific forms of social object that they shape and define. Just as biological characteristics do not always directly reflect the straightforward logic of natural selection (Gould & Lewontin, 1979), so too there may be cultural "spandrels" that arise as side-effects of lower-level processes. In our view, some of these lower-level processes depend on interpersonal and intergroup emotions. As a consequence of reconceiving and reworking these emotions, then, there is at least a faint chance that society may also change accordingly.

References

Abraham, R. (1998). Emotional dissonance in organisations. *Leadership and Organisational Development Journal, 19*, 37–146.

Abrams, D., & Hogg, M. A. (1990). Social identification, self-categorization, and social influence. In W. Stroebe & M. Hewstone (Eds.), *European review of social psychology*, (Vol. 1, pp. 195–228). Chichester, UK: Wiley.

Abu-Lughod, L. (1986). *Veiled sentiments. Honor and poetry in a Bedouin society.* Berkeley, CA: University of California Press.

Ainsworth, M. D. S., Blehar, M. C., Waters, E., & Wall, S. (1978). *Patterns of attachment: A psychological study of the strange situation.* Hillsdale, NJ: Erlbaum.

Ajzen, I. (1988). *Attitudes, personality, and behavior.* Milton Keynes, UK: Open University Press.

Alexander, M. G., Brewer, M. B., & Herrmann, R. K. (1999). Images and affect: A functional analysis of out-group stereotypes. *Journal of Personality and Social Psychology, 77*, 78–93.

Allport, G. W. (1954). *The nature of prejudice.* Reading, MA: Addison-Wesley.

Andrew, R. J. (1963). Evolution of facial expression. *Science, 142*, 1034–1041.

Archer, J. (1999). *The nature of grief: The evolution and psychology of reactions to loss.* Florence, KY: Taylor and Francis/Routledge.

Argyle, M. (1967). *The psychology of interpersonal behaviour.* Harmondsworth: Penguin.

Argyle, M., & Dean, J. (1965). Eye-contact, distance and affiliation. *Sociometry, 28*, 289–304.

Aristotle (1984). *The complete works of Aristotle: The revised Oxford translation.* (Jonathan Barnes, Ed.) Princeton, NJ: Princeton University Press.

Arnold, M. B. (1960). *Emotion and personality, Vol. 1, Psychological aspects.* New York: Columbia University Press.

Ashforth, B. E., & Humphrey, R. H. (1993). Emotional labor in service roles: The influence of identity. *Academy of Management Review, 18*, 88–115.

Averill, J. R. (1974). An analysis of psychophysiological symbolism and its influence on theories of emotion. *Journal for the Theory of Social Behavior, 4*, 147–190.

Averill, J. R. (1980). A constructivist view of emotion. In R. Plutchik & H. Kellerman (Eds.), *Theories of emotion* (pp. 305–340). New York: Academic Press.

Averill, J. R. (1982). *Anger and aggression: An essay on emotion.* New York: Springer.

Averill, J. R. (1992). The structural bases of emotional behavior: A metatheoretical analysis. In M. S. Clark (Ed.), *Review of personality and social psychology, 13: Emotion* (pp. 1–24). Newbury Park, CA: Sage.

Averill, J. R., & Nunley, E. P. (1992). *Voyages of the heart: Living an emotionally creative life.* New York: Macmillan.

Ax, A. F. (1953). The physiological differentiation between fear and anger in humans. *Psychosomatic Medicine, 15*, 433–442.

Babcock, M. K., & Sabini, J. (1990). On differentiating embarrassment from shame. *European Journal of Social Psychology, 20*, 151–169.

Bales, R. F. (1950). *Interaction process analysis: A method for the study of small groups.* Chicago: Chicago University Press.

Barr, C. L., & Kleck, R. E. (1995). Self-other perception of the intensity of facial expressions of emotion: Do we know what we show? *Journal of Personality and Social Psychology, 68*, 608–618.

Barrera, M. Jr. (1986). Distinctions between social support concepts, measures, and models. *American Journal of Community Psychology, 14,* 413–445.

Barrett, K. C. (1995.) A functionalist approach to shame and guilt. In J. P. Tangney & K. W. Fischer (Eds.), *Self-conscious emotions* (pp. 25–63). New York: Guilford Press.

Barrett, K. C. (1998). A functionalist perspective on the development of emotions. In M. F. Mascolo & S. Griffith (Eds.), *What develops in emotional development?* (pp. 109–133). New York: Plenum.

Barsade, S. G. (2002). The ripple effect: Emotional contagion in groups. *Administrative Science Quarterly, 47,* 644–677.

Barsade, S. G., & Gibson, D. E. (1998). Group emotion: A view from top to bottom. In D. Gruenfeld, B. Mannix, & M. Neale (Eds.), *Research on managing groups and teams* (Vol. 1, pp. 81–102). Stamford, CT: JAI Press.

Barsade, S. G., Ward, A. J., Turner, J. D. F., & Sonnenfeld, J. A. (2000). To your heart's content: An affective diversity model in top management teams. *Administrative Science Quarterly, 45,* 802–836.

Bartel, C. A., & Saavedra, R. (2000). The collective construction of work group moods. *Administrative Science Quarterly, 45,* 197–231.

Bartholomew, K., & Horowitz, L. M. (1991). Attachment styles among young adults: A test of a four category model. *Journal of Personality and Social Psychology, 61,* 226–244.

Baumeister, R. F., Stillwell, A. M., & Heatherton, T. F. (1994). Guilt: An interpersonal approach. *Psychological Bulletin, 115,* 243–267.

Bavelas, J. B., Black, A., Lemery, C. R., & Mullett, J. (1986). "I show how you feel": Motor mimicry as a communicative act. *Journal of Personality and Social Psychology, 50,* 322–329.

Beebe, B., Jaffe, J., Feldstein, S., Mays, K., & Alson, D. (1985). Interpersonal timing: The application of an adult dialogue model to mother-infant vocal and kinesic interactions. In F. M. Field & N. Fox (Eds.), *Social perception in infants* (pp. 249–268). Norwood, NJ: Ablex.

Bell, C. (1844). *The anatomy and philosophy of expression, as connected with the fine arts* (3rd edition). London: George Bell.

Benedict, R. (1946). *The chrysanthemum and the sword.* London: Routledge and Kegan Paul.

Ben Ze'ev, A. (1992). Pleasure-in-others'-misfortune. *Iyyun, The Jerusalem Philosophical Quarterly, 41,* 41–61.

Ben Ze'ev, A. (2000). *The subtlety of emotions.* Cambridge, MA: The MIT Press.

Berkowitz, L. (1990). Biological roots: Are humans inherently violent? In B. Glad (Ed.), *Psychological dimensions of war: Violence, cooperation, peace* (pp. 24–40). Thousand Oaks, CA: Sage Publications.

Bermond, B., Nieuwenhuyse, B., Fasotti, L., & Schuerman, J. (1991). Spinal cord lesions, peripheral feedback, and intensities of emotional feelings. *Cognition and Emotion, 5,* 201–220.

Bernieri, F., Reznick, J. S., & Rosenthal, R. (1988). Synchrony, pseudo-synchrony, and dissynchrony: Measuring the entrainment process in mother-infant interactions. *Journal of Personality and Social Psychology, 54,* 243–353.

Berry, D. S., & McArthur, L. A. (1986).Perceiving character in faces: The impact of age-related craniofacial changes on social perception. *Psychological Bulletin, 100,* 3–18.

Berry, D. S., & McArthur, L. Z. (1985). Some components and consequences of a babyface. *Journal of Personality and Social Psychology, 48,* 312–323.

Besnier, N. (1990). Language and affect. *Annual Review of Anthropology, 19,* 419–451.

Besnier, N. (1995). The politics of emotion in Nukulaelae gossip. In J. A. Russell, J. M. Fernandez-Dols, A. S. R. Manstead, & J. Wellenkamp (Eds.), *Everyday conceptions of emotion* (pp. 221–350). Dordrecht, NL: Kluwer.

Biehl, M., Matsumoto, D., Ekman, P., Hearn, V., Heider, K., Kudoh, T., & Ton, V. (1997). Matsumoto and Ekman's Japanese and Caucasian Facial Expressions of Emotion (JACFEE): Reliability data and cross-national differences. *Journal of Nonverbal Behavior, 21,* 3–21.

Biglan, A., Hops, H., Sherman, L., Friedman, L., Arthur, J., & Osteen, V. (1985). Problem-solving interactions of depressed women and their husbands. *Behavior Therapy, 16,* 431–451.

Billig, M. (1999). *Freudian repression.* Cambridge: Cambridge University Press.

Birdwhistell, R. L. (1970). *Kinesics and context.* Philadelphia: University of Pennsylvania Press.

Blakemore, C., & Cooper, G. F. (1970). Development of the brain depends on the visual environment. *Nature, 228,* 477–478.

Bonanno, G. A., & Field, N. P. (2001). Examining the delayed grief hypothesis across 5 years of bereavement. *American Behavioral Scientist, 44,* 798–816.

Bond, M. H., & Tedeschi, J. T. (2001). Polishing the jade: A modest proposal for improving the study of social psychology across cultures. In D. Matsumoto (Ed.), *The handbook of culture and psychology* (pp. 309–325). Oxford, UK: Oxford University Press.

Borg, I., Staufenbiel T., & Scherer, K. R. (1998). On the symbolic basis of shame. In K. R. Scherer (Ed.), *Facets of emotion: Recent research* (pp. 79–98). Hillsdale, NJ: Erlbaum.

Boucher, J. D., & Carlson, G. E. (1980). Recognition of facial expressions in three cultures. *Journal of Cross-cultural Psychology, 11,* 263–280.

Boulding, K. (1959). National images and international systems. *Journal of Conflict Resolution, 3,* 120–131.

Bowlby, J. (1951). *Maternal care and mental health: A report prepared on behalf of the World Health Organization as a contribution to the United Nations programme for the welfare of homeless children.* Geneva: World Health Organization.

Bowlby, J. (1956). Mother-child separation. In K. Soddy (Ed.), *Mental health and infant development. Vol. I. Papers and discussions* (pp. 117–112). Oxford, UK: Basic Books.

Bowlby, J. (1973). *Attachment and loss: Vol. 2. Separation: Anxiety and anger.* London: Hogarth Press.

Bowlby, J. (1980). *Attachment and loss: Vol .3. Loss: Sadness and depression.* London: Hogarth Press.

Branscombe, N. R., Doosje, B., & McGarty, C. (2002). Antecedents and consequences of collective guilt. In D. M. Mackie & E. R. Smith (Eds.), *From prejudice to intergroup emotions: Differentiated reactions to social groups* (pp. 49–66). New York: Psychology Press.

Branscombe, N. R., & Wann, D. L. (1994). Collective self-esteem consequences of outgroup derogation when a valued social identity is on trial. *European Journal of Social Psychology, 24,* 641–657.

Brewer, M. B. (1979). In-group bias in the minimal intergroup situation: A cognitive-motivational analysis. *Psychological Bulletin, 86,* 307–324.

Brewer, M. B. (2003). *Intergroup relations* (2nd edition). Philadelphia, PA: Open University Press.

Brewer, M. B., & Alexander, M. G. (2002). Intergroup emotions and images. In D. M. Mackie & E. R. Smith (Eds.), *From prejudice to intergroup emotions: Differentiated reactions to social groups* (pp. 209–225). New York: Psychology Press.

Briggs, J. L. (1970). *Never in anger: Portrait of an Eskimo family.* Cambridge, MA: Harvard University Press.

Briggs, J. L. (1995). The study of Inuit emotions: Lessons from a personal retrospective. In J. A. Russell, J. Fernandez-Dols, A S. R. Manstead, & J. C. Wellenkamp (Eds.), *Everyday conceptions of emotion. An introduction to the psychology, anthropology, and linguistics of emotion* (pp. 203–221). Dordrecht, NL: Kluwer.

Brison, K. J. (1998). Giving sorrow new words: Shifting politics of bereavement in a Papua New Guinea village. *Ethos, 26,* 363–386.

Brown, G. W., & Harris, T. (1978). *Social origins of depression.* London: Tavistock Press.

Brown, J. R., & Dunn, J. (1996). Continuities in emotion understanding from 3–6 yrs. *Child Development, 67,* 789–802.

Brown, P., & Levinson, S. C. (1987). *Politeness: Some universals in language usage.* Cambridge: Cambridge University Press.

Brown, R. J. (2000). *Group processes* (2nd edition). Oxford, UK: Blackwell.

Bruce, V., Burton, A. M., Hanna, E., Healey, P., Mason, O., Coombes, A., et al. (1993). Sex discrimination: How do we tell the difference between male and female faces. *Perception, 22,* 131–152.

Brunner, L. J. (1979). Smiles can be back channels. *Journal of Personality and Social Psychology, 37,* 728–734.

Buck, R. (1984). *The communication of emotion.* New York: Guilford Press.

Buck, R., Losow, J. I., Murphy, M. M., & Costanzo, P. (1992). Social facilitation and inhibition of emotional expression and communication. *Journal of Personality and Social Psychology, 63,* 962–968.

Buck, R. W., Miller, R. E., & Caul, W. F. (1974). Sex, personality, and physiological variables in the communication of emotion via facial expression. *Journal of Personality and Social Psychology, 30,* 587–596.

Burkhardt, R.W., Jr. (1985). Darwin on animal behavior and evolution. In D. Kohn (Ed.), *The Darwinian heritage* (pp. 327–365). Princeton, NJ: Princeton University Press.

Buss, D.M., & Craik, K. H. (1980). The frequency concept of disposition: Dominance and prototypically dominant acts. *Journal of Personality, 48,* 379–392.

Cacioppo, J. T., Berntson, G. G., Larsen, J. T., Poehlmann, K. M., & Ito, T. A. (2000). Biological and neurophysiological approaches to emotion. In M. Lewis & J. M. Haviland-Jones (Eds.), *Handbook of emotions* (2nd ed., pp. 173–191). New York: Guilford Press.

Cahill, S. E. (1999). Emotional capital and professional socialization: The case of mortuary science students (and me). *Social Psychology Quarterly, 62,* 101–116.

Campos, J. J., Campos, R. G., & Barrett, K. C. (1989). Emergent themes in the study of emotional development and emotion regulation. *Developmental Psychology, 25,* 394–402.

Campos, J. J., & Stenberg, C. (1981). Perception, appraisal, and emotion: The onset of social referencing. In M. E. Lamb & L. R. Sherrod (Eds.), *Infant social cognition: Empirical and theoretical considerations* (pp. 273–314). Hillsdale, NJ: Erlbaum.

Camras, L. (1992). Expressive development and basic emotions. *Cognition and Emotion, 6,* 269–283.

Camras, L. A., Campos, J. J., Oster, H., Miyake, K., & Bradshaw, D. (1992). Japanese and American infants' responses to arm restraint. *Developmental Psychology, 28,* 578–583.

Cannon, W. B. (1927). The James-Lange theory of emotions: A critical examination and an alternative theory. *American Journal of Psychology, 39,* 106–124.

Cantor, N., & Mischel, W. (1977). Traits as prototypes: Effects on recognition memory. *Journal of Personality and Social Psychology, 35,* 38–48.

Cappella, J. N., & Planalp, S. (1981). Talk and silence sequences in informal conversations: III Interspeaker Influence. *Human Communication Research, 7,* 117–132.

Carroll, J. M., & Russell, J. A. (1997). Facial expressions in Hollywood's protrayal of emotion. *Journal of Personality and Social Psychology, 72,* 164–176.

Carroll, J. M., Yik, M. S. M., Russell, J. A., & Feldman Barrett, L. (1999). On the psychometric principles of affect. *Review of General Psychology, 3,* 14–22.

Cassidy, J., Parke, R., Butkovsky, L., & Braungart, J. M. (1992). Family-peer connections: The roles of emotional expressiveness in the family and the children's understanding of emotions. *Child Development, 63,* 603–618.

Chapman, L. J., & Chapman, J.P. (1967). Genesis of popular but erroneous psychodiagnostic observations. *Journal of Abnormal Psychology, 73,* 193–204.

Chapman, M. (1981). Isolating causal effects through experimental changes in parent-child interaction. *Journal of Abnormal Child Psychology, 9,* 321–327.

Chovil, N. (1991). Social determinants of facial displays. *Journal of Nonverbal Behavior, 15,* 141–154.

Chovil, N., & Fridlund, A. J. (1991). Why emotionality cannot equal sociality: Reply to Buck. *Journal of Nonverbal Behavior, 15,* 163–167.

Church, A. T., Katigbak, M. S., Reyes, J. A. S., & Jensen, S. M. (1999). The structure of affect on a non-Western culture: Evidence for cross-cultural comparability. *Journal of Personality, 67,* 505–534.

Chwalisz, K., Diener, E., & Gallagher, D. (1988). Autonomic arousal feedback and emotional experience: Evidence from the spinal cord injured. *Journal of Personality and Social Psychology, 54,* 820–828.

Cialdini, R.B. (1991). Altruism or egoism? That is (still) the question. *Psychological Inquiry, 2,* 124–126.

Cialdini, R. B., Borden, R. J., Thorne, A., Walker, M. R., Freeman, S., & Sloan, L. R. (1976). Basking in reflected glory: Three (football) field studies. *Journal of Personality and Social Psychology, 34,* 366–375.

Cialdini, R. B., Kallgren, C. A., & Reno, R. R. (1991). A focus theory of normative conduct. In L. Berkowitz (Ed.), *Advances in experimental social psychology* (Vol. 24, pp. 201–234). San Diego, CA: Academic Press.

Cialdini, R. B., Reno, R. R. & Kallgren, C. A. (1990). A focus theory of normative conduct: Recycling the concept of norms to reduce littering in public places. *Journal of Personality and Social Psychology, 58*, 1015–1026.

Clark, H. H. (1996). *Using language.* Cambridge, UK: Cambridge University Press.

Clarke-Stewart, K. A., Goossens, F. A., & Allhusen, V. D. (2001). Measuring infant-mother attachment: Is the strange situation enough? *Social Development, 10*, 143–169.

Cobb, S. (1976). Social support as a moderator of life stress. *Psychosomatic Medicine, 38*, 300–314.

Cohen, D., & Nisbett, R. E. (1994). Self-protection and the culture of honor: Explaining southern violence. *Personality and Social Psychology Bulletin, 20*, 551–567.

Cohen, D., & Nisbett, R. E. (1997). Field experiments examining the culture of honor: The role of institutions in perpetuating norms about violence. *Personality and Social Psychology Bulletin, 23*, 1188–1199.

Cohen, D., Nisbett, R. E., Bowdle, B. F., & Schwarz, N. (1996). Insult, aggression and the southern culture of honor: An "experimental ethnography." *Journal of Personality and Social Psychology, 70*, 945–960.

Cohen, S., Mermelstein, R., Kamarck, T., & Hoberman, H. M. (1985). Measuring the functional components of social support. In I. G. Sarason & B. R. Sarason (Eds.), *Social support: Theory, research and applications* (pp. 73–94). The Hague, NL: Martinus Nijhoff Publishers.

Cohen, S., & Wills, T. A. (1985). Stress, social support, and the buffering hypothesis. *Psychological Bulletin, 98*, 310–357.

Cole, M. (1996). *Cultural psychology.* Cambridge, MA: The Belknap Press.

Cole, P. M., Bruschi, C. J., & Tamang, B. L. (2002). Cultural differences in children's emotional reactions to difficult situations. *Child Development, 73*, 983–996.

Conroy, M., Hess, R. D., Azuma, H., & Kashigawa, K. (1980). Maternal strategies for regulating children's behavior. *Journal of Cross-Cultural Psychology, 11*, 153–172.

Cornelius, R. R. (1996). *The science of emotion.* Upper Saddle River, NJ: Prentice Hall.

Cosmides, L., & Tooby, J. (2000). Evolutionary psychology and the emotions. In M. Lewis & J. M. Haviland-Jones (Eds.), *Handbook of emotions* (2nd ed., pp. 91–115). New York: Guilford.

Coulter, J. (1979). *The social construction of mind: Studies in ethnomethodology and linguistic philosophy.* London: Macmillan.

Coyne, J. C. (1976a). Toward an interactional description of depression. *Psychiatry, 39*, 28–40.

Coyne, J. C. (1976b). Depression and the response of others. *Journal of Abnormal Psychology, 85*, 186–193.

Coyne, J. C., & Downey, G. (1991). Social factors and psychopathology: Stress, social support, and coping processes. *Annual Review of Psychology, 42*, 401–425.

Crespo, E. (1986). A regional variation: Emotions in Spain. In R. Harré (Ed.), *The social construction of emotion* (pp. 209–218). New York: Basil Blackwell.

D'Andrade, R. (1984). Cultural meaning systems. In R. A. Shweder & R. A. LeVine (Eds.), *Culture Theory: Essays on Mind, Self, and Emotion* (pp. 88–119). Cambridge, UK: Cambridge University Press.

D'Andrade, R. (1987). A folk model of the mind. In D. Holland & N. Quinn (Eds.), *Cultural models in language and thought* (pp. 112–148). Cambridge, UK: Cambridge University Press.

Darley, J. M., & Latane, B. (1968). Bystander intervention in emergencies: diffusion of responsibility. *Journal of Personality and Social Psychology, 8*, 377–383

Darwin, C. (1872). *The expression of the emotions in man and animals.* London: John Murray.

Davitz, J. R. (1969). *The language of emotion.* New York: Academic Press.

De Rivera, J. (1977). *A structural theory of emotions.* New York: International Universities Press.

De Rivera, J. (1984). The structure of emotional relationships. In P. Shaver (Ed.), *Review of personality and social psychology 5: Emotions, relationships, and health* (pp. 116–145). Beverly Hills, CA: Sage.

De Rivera, J. (1992). Emotional climate: Social structure and emotional dynamics. In K. T. Strongman (Ed.), *International review of studies on emotion* (Vol. 2, pp. 197–218). Chichester, UK: Wiley.

De Rivera, J., & Grinkis, C. (1986). Emotions as social relationships. *Motivation and Emotion, 10,* 351–369.

De Souza, R. (1987). *The rationality of emotion.* Cambridge, MA: MIT Press.

De Swaan, A. (1981). The politics of agoraphobia: On changes in emotional and relational management. *Theory and Society, 10,* 359–385.

Denham, S. A., & Grout, L. (1993). Socialization of emotion: Pathway to preschoolers' emotional and social competence. *Journal of Nonverbal Behavior, 17,* 205–227.

Denham, S. A., McKinley, M., Couchoud, E. A., & Holt, R. (1990). Emotional and behavioral predictors of preschool peer ratings. *Child Development, 61,* 1145–1152.

Denham, S. A., Mitchell-Copeland, J., Strandberg, K., Auerbach, S., & Blair, K. (1997). Parental contributions to preschoolers' emotional competence: Direct and indirect effects. *Motivation and Emotion, 21,* 65–86.

Denham, S. A., Zoller, D., & Couchoud, E. A. (1994). Socialization of preschoolers' emotion understanding. *Developmental Psychology, 30,* 928–936.

DePaulo, B. M., & Pfeifer, R. L. (1986). On-the-job experience and skill at detecting deception. *Journal of Applied Social Psychology, 16,* 249–267.

Deutsch, M., & Gerard, H. B. (1955). A study of normative and informational influences upon individual judgment. *Journal of Abnormal and Social Psychology, 61,* 181–189.

Dewey, J. (1894). The theory of emotion I: Emotional attitudes. *Psychological Review, 1,* 553–569.

Dewey, J. (1895). The theory of emotion II: The significance of emotional attitudes. *Psychological Review, 2,* 13–32.

Diener, E., Oishi, S., & Lucas, R. E. (2003). Personality, culture and subjective well-being: Emotional and cognitive evaluations of life. *Annual Review of Psychology, 54,* 403–425.

Dijker, A. J. M. (1987). Emotional reactions to ethnic minorities. *European Journal of Social Psychology, 47,* 1105–1117.

Dimberg, U. (1990). Facial electromyography and emotional reactions. *Psychophysiology, 27,* 481–494.

Dittmar, H., Beattie, J., & Friese, S. (1996). Objects, decision considerations and self-image in men's and women's impulse purchases. *Acta Psychologica, 93,* 187–206.

Doi, T. (1973). *The anatomy of dependence.* Tokyo: Kodansha International.

Doise, W. (1986). *Levels of explanation in social psychology.* Cambridge, UK: Cambridge University Press.

Doosje, B., Branscombe, N. R., Spears, R., & Manstead, A. S. R. (2004). On being perpetrator or victim of immoral intergroup behavior: The role of ingroup identification. In N. R. Branscombe & B. Doosje (Eds.), *Collective guilt: International perspectives* (pp. 95–111). New York: Cambridge University Press.

Doosje, B., Branscombe, N. R., Spears, R., & Manstead, A. S. R. (1998). Guilty by association. When one's group has a negative history. *Journal of Personality and Social Psychology, 75,* 872–886.

Draghi-Lorenz, R. (2001). *Young infants are capable of "non-basic" emotions.* Unpublished Ph.D. thesis. University of Portsmouth, UK.

Draghi-Lorenz, R., Reddy, V., & Costall, A. (2001). Rethinking the development of "nonbasic" emotions: A critical review of existing theories. *Developmental Review, 21,* 263–304.

Draghi-Lorenz, R., Reddy, V., & Morris, P. (in press). Young infants can communicate shyness, coyness, bashfulness, and embarrassment. *Infant and Child Development.*

Ducci, L., Arcuri, L., Georgis, T., & Sineshaw, T. (1982). Emotion recognition in Ethiopia: The effect of familiarity with Western culture on accuracy of recognition. *Journal of Cross-Cultural Psychology, 13,* 340–351.

Duchenne de Boulogne, G. B. (1862/1990). *The mechanism of human facial expression.* New York: Cambridge University Press.

Dumont, M., Yzerbyt, V., Wigboldus, D., & Gordijn, E. H. (2003). *Social categorization and fear reactions to the September 11th terrorist attacks.* Personality and Social Psychology Bulleetin, 29, 1509–1520.

Dunn, J., Bretherton, I., & Munn, P. (1987). Conversations about feeling states between mothers and their young children. *Developmental Psychology, 23,* 132–139.

Edwards, D. (1997). *Discourse and cognition.* London: Sage.

Eisenberg, N., Fabes, R. A., Schaller, M., Carlo, G., & Miller, P. A. (1991). The relations of parental characteristics and practices to children's vicarious emotional responding. *Child Development, 62,* 1393–1408.

Ekman, P. (1971). Universals and cultural differences in facial expressions of emotion. In J. Cole (Ed.), *Nebraska Symposium on Motivation* (pp. 207–283). Lincoln, NE: University of Nebraska Press.

Ekman, P. (1973). *Darwin and facial expression.* New York: Academic Press.

Ekman, P. (1975). Face muscles talk every language. *Psychology Today, 9,* 35–39.

Ekman, P. (1979). About brows: Emotional and conversational signals. In M. von Cranach, K. Foppa, W. Lepenies, & D. Ploog (Eds.), *Human ethology: Claims and limits of a new discipline* (pp. 169–202). New York: Cambridge University Press.

Ekman, P. (1989). The argument and evidence about universals in facial expressions of emotion. In H. Wagner & A. S. R. Manstead (Eds.), *Handbook of social psychophysiology* (pp. 143–164). Oxford, UK: Wiley.

Ekman, P. (1992a). An argument for basic emotions. *Cognition and Emotion, 6,* 169–200.

Ekman, P. (1992b). Are there basic emotions? *Psychological Review, 99,* 550–553.

Ekman, P. (1994). Strong evidence for universals in facial expressions: A reply to Russell's mistaken critique. *Psychological Bulletin, 115,* 268–287.

Ekman P. (1997). Should we call it expression or communication? *Innovation, 10,* 333–344.

Ekman, P. (Ed.) (1998), Darwin, C.: The expression of the emotions in man and animals (3rd ed.). London: Oxford University Press.

Ekman, P., & Friesen, W. V. (1969). The repertoire of non-verbal behavior: Origins, usage, and coding. *Semiotica, 1,* 49–98.

Ekman, P. & Friesen, W. V. (1971). Constants across cultures in the face and emotion. *Journal of Personality and Social Psychology, 17,* 124–129.

Ekman, P., & Friesen, W.V. (1982). Felt, false, and miserable smiles. *Journal of Nonverbal Behavior, 6,* 238–252.

Ekman, P., Friesen, W. V., & Ancoli, S. (1980). Facial signs of emotional experience. *Journal of Personality and Social Psychology, 39,* 1125–1134.

Ekman, P., Friesen, W. V., O'Sullivan, M., Chan, A., et al. (1987). Universals and cultural differences in the judgments of facial expressions of emotion. *Journal of Personality and Social Psychology, 53,* 712–717.

Ekman, P., & Heider, K. G. (1988). The universality of a contempt expression: A replication. *Motivation and Emotion, 12,* 303–308.

Ekman, P., Levenson, R. W., & Friesen, W. V. (1983). Autonomic nervous system activity distinguishing among emotions. *Science, 221,* 1208–1210.

Ekman, P., Sorenson, E. R., & Friesen, W. V. (1969). Pan-cultural elements in facial displays of emotion. *Science, 164,* 86–88.

Elfenbein, H. A., & Ambady, N. (2002). Is there an in-group advantage in emotion recognition? *Psychological Bulletin, 128,* 243–249.

Ellis, H. D. (1975). Recognizing faces. *British Journal of Psychology, 66,* 409–426

Ellsworth, P. C. (1991). Some implications of cognitive appraisal theories of emotion. In K. T. Strongman (Ed.), *International review of studies on emotion* (Vol. 1, pp. 143–161). New York: Wiley.

Ellsworth, P. C. (1994). Sense, culture, and sensibility. In S. Kitayama & H. R. Markus (Eds.), *Emotion and culture: Empirical studies of mutual influence* (pp. 23–50). Washington, DC: American Psychological Association.

Ellsworth, P. C., & Tourangeau, R. (1981). On our failure to disconfirm what nobody ever said. *Journal of Personality and Social Psychology, 40,* 363–369.

Englis, B. G., & Lanzetta, J. T. (1984). *The effects of group categorization on observers' vicarious emotional responses.* Paper presented at the annual meeting of the Eastern Psychological Association, Baltimore, MD.

Evers, C., Fischer, A. H., & Manstead, A. S. R. (submitted). Sex differences in anger: the role of social appraisal.

Eysenck, H. J. (1967). *The biological basis of personality.* Springfield, IL: Charles C. Thomas.

Fabes, R. A., Eisenberg, N., & Miller, P. A. (1990). Maternal correlates of children's vicarious emotional responsiveness. *Developmental Psychology, 26,* 639–648.

Fajans, J. (1983). Shame, social action, and the person among the Baining. *Ethos, 11,* 166–180.

Fantz, R. L. (1965). Visual perception from birth as shown by pattern selectivity. *Annals of the New York Academy of Sciences, 118,* 793–814.

Farah, M. J., O'Reilly-Randall, C., & Vecera, S. P. (1997). The neural correlates of perceptual awareness: Evidence from covert recognition in prosopagnosia. In J. D. Cohen, & J. W. Schooler (Eds.), *Scientific approaches to consciousness. Carnegie Mellon Symposia on cognition* (pp. 357–371). Hillsdale, NJ: Erlbaum.

Fehr, B., & Russell, J. A. (1984). Concept of emotion viewed from a prototype perspective. *Journal of Experimental Psychology: General, 113,* 464–486.

Feinman, S., & Lewis, M. (1983). Social referencing at ten months: A second-order effect on infants' responses to strangers. *Child Development, 54,* 878–887.

Fernández-Dols, J. M., & Ruiz-Belda, M. A. (1995). Are smiles a sign of happiness? Gold medal winners at the Olympic Games. *Journal of Personality and Social Psychology, 69,* 1113–1119.

Fernández-Dols, J. M., & Ruiz-Belda, M. A. (1997). Spontaneous facial behavior during intense emotional episodes: Artistic truth and optical truth. In J. A. Russell & J. M. Fernandez-Dols (Eds.), *The psychology of facial expression* (pp. 255–294). Cambridge, UK: Cambridge University Press.

Festinger, L., Schachter, S., & Back, K. W. (1950). *Social pressures in informal groups.* New York: Harper & Row.

Fischer, A. H., & Rodriguez Mosquera, P. M. (2001). What concerns men: Women or other men? A critical appraisal of the evolutionary theory of sex differences in aggression. *Psychology, Evolution, and Gender, 3,* 5–25.

Fischer, A. H. (1991). *Emotion scripts: A study of the social and cognitive aspects of emotion.* Leiden, NL: DSWO-Press.

Fischer, A. H. (1993). Sex differences in emotionality: Fact or stereotype? *Feminism and Psychology, 3,* 303–318.

Fischer, A. H., & Manstead, A. S. R. (2000). The relation between gender and emotion in different cultures. In A. H. Fischer (Ed.), *Gender and emotion: Social psychological perspectives* (pp. 71–94). Cambridge, UK: Cambridge University Press.

Fischer, A. H., Manstead, A. S. R., & Rodriguez Mosquera, P. M. (1999). The role of honor-based versus individualistic values in conceptualizing pride, shame, and anger: Spanish and Dutch cultural prototypes. *Cognition and Emotion, 13,* 149–179.

Fischer, A. H., Rodriguez Mosquera, P. M., van Vianen, A. E. M., & Manstead, A. S. R. (2004). Sex and culture differences in emotion. *Emotion, 4,* 87–94.

Fiske, S. T., Cuddy, A. J. C., & Glick, P. (2002). Emotions up and down: Intergroup emotions result from perceived status and competition. In D. M. Mackie & E. R. Smith (Eds.), *From prejudice to intergroup emotions: Differentiated reactions to social groups* (pp. 247–264). New York: Psychology Press.

Fleming, J. H. (1994). Multiple audience problems, tactical communication, and social interaction: A relational-regulation perspective. In M. Zanna (Ed.), *Advances in experimental social psychology* (Vol. 26, pp. 215–292). New York: Academic Press.

Fogel, A. (1993). *Developing through relationships.* New York: Harvester Wheatsheaf.

Fogel, A., Nwokah, E., Dedo, J. Y., Messinger, K., Dickson, K. L., Matusov, E, et al. (1992). Social process theory of emotion: A dynamic systems approach. *Social Development, 1,* 122–142.

Fontaine, J. R. J., Poortinga, Y. H., Setiadi, B., & Markam, S. (2002). Cognitive structure of emotion terms in Indonesia and The Netherlands. *Cognition and Emotion, 16,* 61–86.

Foucault, M. (1970). *The order of things: An Archaeology of the human sciences.* London: Tavistock Publications.

Foucault, M. (1976). *The history of sexuality (L'histoire de la sexualité).* New York: Vintage Books.

Fraley, R. C., & Shaver, P. R. (1999). Loss and bereavement: Attachment theory and recent controversies concerning "grief work" and the nature of detachment. In J. Cassidy & P. R. Shaver (Eds.), *Handbook of attachment: Theory, research, and clinical applications* (pp. 735–759). New York, NY: Guilford Press.

Franks, D. D., & Hefferman, S. M. (1998). The pursuit of happiness. In W. F. Flack & J. D. Laird (Eds.), *Emotions in psychopathology* (pp. 145–158). New York: Oxford University Press.

Fridlund, A. J. (1991). Sociality of solitary smiling: Potentiation by an implicit audience. *Journal of Personality and Social Psychology, 60,* 229–240.

Fridlund, A. J. (1992). The behavioral ecology and sociality of human faces. In M. S. Clark (Ed.), *Review of personality and social psychology 13: Emotion* (pp. 90–121). Newbury Park, CA: Sage.

Fridlund, A. J. (1994). *Human facial expression: An evolutionary view.* San Diego, CA: Academic Press.

Frijda, N. H. (1953). The understanding of facial expression of emotion. *Acta Psychologica, 9,* 294–362.

Frijda, N. H. (1986). *The emotions.* Cambridge, UK: Cambridge University Press.

Frijda, N. H. (1993). The place of appraisal in emotion. *Cognition and Emotion, 7,* 357–387.

Frijda, N. H., & Mesquita, B. (1994). The social roles and functions of emotions. In S. Kitayama & H. R. Markus (Eds.), *Emotion and culture: Empirical studies of mutual influence* (pp. 51–87). Washington, DC: American Psychological Association.

Fung, H. (1999). Becoming a moral child: The socialization of shame among young Chinese children. *Ethos, 27,* 180–209.

Gaffin, D. (1995). The production of emotion and social control: Taunting, anger, and the Rukka in the Faeroe Islands. *Ethos, 23,* 149–172.

Galati, D., & Sciaky, R. (1995). The representation of antecedents of emotions in Northern and Southern Italy. A textual analysis. *Journal of Cross-cultural Psychology, 26,* 123–140.

Geertz, C. (1973). *The interpretation of cultures.* New York: Basic Books.

Geertz, H. (1959). The vocabulary of emotion. A study of Javanese socialization processes. *Psychiatry, 22,* 225–237.

George, J. M. (1989). Mood and absence. *Journal of Applied Psychology, 74,* 317–324.

George, J. M. (1990). Personality, affect, and behavior in groups. *Journal of Applied Psychology, 75,* 107–116.

George, J. M. (1995). Leader positive mood and group-performance: The case of customer service. *Journal of Applied Social Psychology, 25,* 778–794.

George, J. M. (1996). Group affective tone. In M. A. West (Ed.), *Handbook of work group psychology* (pp. 77–93). Chichester, UK: Wiley.

George, J. M., & Brief, A. P. (1992). Feeling good—doing good: A conceptual analysis of the mood at work-organizational spontaneity relationship. *Psychological Bulletin, 112,* 310–329.

Gerber, E. R. (1985). Rage and obligation; Samoan emotion in conflict. In G. M. White & J. Kirkpatrick (Eds.), *Person, self and experience: Exploring Pacific ethnopsychologies* (pp. 121–167). Berkeley: University of California Press.

Gergen, K., & Davis, K. (1984). *The social construction of the person.* New York: Springer.

Gibson, J. J, & Walk R. D. (1960). The visual cliff. *Scientific American, 202,* 64–71

Goddard, C. (1996). The "social emotions" of Malay (Behasa Melayu). *Ethos, 24,* 426–264.

Goddard, C. (1997). Cultural values and "cultural scripts" of Malay (Bahasa Melayu). *Journal of Pragmatics, 27,* 183–201.

Goffman, E. (1956). Embarrassment and social organization. *American Journal of Sociology, 62,* 264–271.

Goffman, E. (1967). *Interaction ritual.* New York: Doubleday Anchor.

Goleman, D. (1995). *Emotional intelligence.* New York: Bantam Books.

Goodwin, C. (1980). Re-starts, pauses, and the achievement of a state of mutual gaze at turn-beginning. *Sociological Inquiry, 50,* 272–302.

Goodwin, C. (1981). *Conversational organization: Interaction between speakers and hearers.* New York: Academic Press.

Gordijn, E. H., Wigboldus, D., & Yzerbyt, V. (2001). Emotional consequences of categorizing victims of negative outgroup behavior as ingroup or outgroup. *Group Processes and Intergroup Relations, 4,* 317–326.

Gordon, R. M. (1974). The aboutness of emotions. *American Philosophical Quarterly, 11,* 17–36.

Gordon, S. L. (1989). The socialization of children's emotions: Emotional culture, competence, and exposure. In C. Saarni & P. Harris (Eds.), *Children's understanding of emotion.* (pp. 319–349). New York: Cambridge University Press.

Gordon, S. L. (1989). Insitutional and impulsive orientations in selectively appropriating emotions to self. In D. D. Franks & E. Doyle McCarthy (Eds.), *The sociology of emotions: Original essays and research papers* (pp. 115–137). Greenwich, CO: JAI Press.

Gotlib, I. H., & Colby, C. A. (1987). *Treatment of depression: An interpersonal systems approach.* New York: Pergamon Press.

Gottman, J. M. (1979). *Marital interaction: Experimental investigations.* New York: Academic Press.

Gottman, J. M. (1994). *What predicts divorce: The relations between marital processes and marital outcomes.* Hillsdale, NJ: Erlbaum.

Gottman, J. M., Guralnick, M. J., Wilson, B., Swanson, C. C., et al. (1997). What should be the focus of emotion regulation in children? A nonlinear dynamic mathematical model of children's peer interaction in groups. *Development and Psychopathology, 9,* 421–452.

Gould, S. J., & Lewontin, R. C. (1979). The spandrels of San Marco and the Panglossion paradigm: A critique of the adaptationist programme. *Proceedings of the Royal Society of London, 205,* 581–598.

Grammer, K., Kruck, K. B., & Magnusson, M. S. (1998). The courtship dance: Patterns of nonverbal synchronization in opposite-sex encounters. *Journal of Nonverbal Behavior, 22,* 3–29.

Greenwood, J. D. (1994). *Realism, identity and emotion: Reclaiming social psychology.* London: Sage.

Grice, H. P. (1975). Logic and conversation. In P. Cole & J. Morgan (Eds.), *Syntax and semantics 3: Speech acts* (pp. 41–58). San Diego, CA: Academic Press.

Gross, J. J. (1998). Sharpening the focus: Emotion regulation, arousal, and social competence. *Psychological Inquiry, 9,* 287–290.

Guerra, N., Huesmann, L. R., & Hanish, L. (1995). The role of normative beliefs in children's social behavior. In N. Eisenberg (Ed.), *Social development* (Review of Personality and Social Psychology, Vol. 15, pp. 140–158). Thousand Oaks, CA: Sage.

Halberstadt, A. (1983). Family expressiveness styles and nonverbal communication skills. *Journal of Nonverbal Behavior, 8,* 14–26.

Halberstadt, A. (1984). Family expression of emotion. In C. Z. Malatesta & C. E. Izard (Eds.), *Emotion in adult development* (pp. 235–252). Beverly Hills, CA: Sage.

Halberstadt, A. (1986). Family socialization of emotional expression and nonverbal communication styles and skills. *Journal of Personality and Social Psychology, 51,* 827–836.

Halberstadt, A., Crisp, V. W., & Eaton, L. (1999). Family expressiveness: A retrospective and new directions for research. In P. Philippot, R. S. Feldman, & E. J. Coats (Eds.). *The social context of nonverbal behavior* (pp. 109–155). New York: Cambridge University Press.

Hall, J. A., & Friedman, G. B. (1999). Status, gender, and nonverbal behavior: A study of structured interactions between employees of a company. *Personality and Social Psychology Bulletin, 25,* 1082–1091.

Hamilton, D. L. (1981). Illusory correlation as a basis for stereotyping. In D. L. Hamilton (Ed.), *Cognitive processes in stereotyping and intergroup behavior* (pp. 115–144). Hillsdale, NJ: Erlbaum.

Hansen, C. H., & Hansen, R. D. (1988). Finding the face in the crowd: An anger superiority effect. *Journal of Personality and Social Psychology, 54,* 917–924.

Harré, R. (1986). (Ed.). *The social construction of emotion.* New York: Basil Blackwell.

Harré, R., & Finlay-Jones, R. (1986). Emotion talk across times. In R. Harré (Ed.), *The social construction of emotion* (pp. 220–234). New York: Basil Blackwell.

Harris, P. L. (1983). Children's understanding of the link between situation and emotion. *Journal of Experimental Child Psychology, 36,* 490–509.

Harris, P. L. (1989). *Children and emotion: The development of psychological understanding.* Oxford, UK: Blackwell.

Harris, P. L. (1995). Developmental constraints on emotion categories. In J. A. Russell, J. M. Fernández-Dols, A. S. R. Manstead, & J. Wellenkamp (Eds.), *Everyday conceptions of emotion: An introduction to the psychology, anthropology and linguistics of emotion* (pp. 353–372). Dordrechl, NL: Kluwer Academic/Plenum Publishers.

Hart, S., Field, T., & Del Valle, C. (1998). Infants protest their mothers' attending to an infant-size doll. *Social Development, 7,* 54–61.

Harter, S., & Whitesell, N. R. (1989). Developmental changes in children's understanding of single, multiple, and blended emotion concepts. In C. Saarni & P. L. Harris (Eds.), *Children's understanding of emotion* (pp. 81–116). Cambridge, UK: Cambridge University Press.

Harvey, R. D., & Oswald, D. L. (2000). Collective guilt and shame as motivation for White support for Black programs. *Journal of Applied Social Psychology, 30,* 1790–1811.

Hatfield, E., Cacioppo, J. T., & Rapson, R. L. (1994). *Emotional contagion.* New York: Cambridge University Press.

Hatfield, E., & Rapson, R. L. (2000). Love and attachment processes. In M. Lewis & J. M. Haviland-Jones (Eds.), *Handbook of emotions* (2nd edition, pp. 654–662). New York: Guilford Press.

Hatfield, E., & Rapson, R. L. (2002). Passionate love and sexual desire: Cultural and historical perspectives. In A. L. Vangelisti, H. T. Reis, & M. A. Fitzpatrick (Eds.), *Stability and change in relationships: Advances in personal relationships* (pp. 306–324). New York: Cambridge University Press.

Haviland, J. M., & Lelwica, M. (1987). The induced affect response: 10-week-old infants responses to 3 emotion expressions. *Developmental Psychology, 23,* 97–104.

Hebb, D. O. (1946). Emotion in man and animal: An analysis of the intuitive processes of recognition. *Psychological Review, 53,* 88–106.

Hebb, D. O. (1949). *The organization of behavior.* New York: Wiley.

Hecht, M. A., & LaFrance, M. (1998). License or obligation to smile: The effect of power and sex on amount and type of smiling. *Personality and Social Psychology Bulletin, 24,* 1332–1342.

Heelas, P. (1986). Emotion talk across cultures. In R. Harré (Ed.), *The social construction of emotion* (pp. 234–267). New York: Basil Blackwell.

Heider, K. (1991). *Landscapes of emotion: Mapping three cultures in Indonesia.* Cambridge, UK: Cambridge University Press.

Henley, N. M. (1977). *Body politics: Power, sex, and nonverbal communication.* Englewood Cliffs, NJ: Prentice-Hall.

Herrmann, R. K. (1985). *Perceptions and behavior in Soviet foreign policy.* Pittsburgh, PA: University of Pittsburgh Press.

Hess, U., Banse, R., & Kappas, A. (1995). The intensity of facial expression is determined by underlying affective state and social situation. *Journal of Personality and Social Psychology, 69,* 280–288.

Hess, U., Philippot, P., & Blairy, S. (1999). Mimicry: Facts and fiction. In P. Philippot, R. S. Feldman, & E. Coats (Eds.), *The social context of nonverbal behavior* (pp. 213–241). Cambridge, UK: Cambridge University Press.

Hesse, E., & Main, M. (2000). Disorganized infant, child, and adult attachment: Collapse in behavioral and attentional strategies. *Journal of the American Psychoanalytic Association, 48,* 1097–1127.

Hewstone, M., & Brown, R. J. (1986). Contact is not enough: An intergroup perspective on the contact hypothesis. In M. Hewstone & R. J. Brown (Eds.), *Contact and conflict in intergroup encounters* (pp. 1–44). Oxford, UK: Blackwell.

Hewstone, M., & Greenland, K. (2000). Intergroup conflict. *International Journal of Psychology, 35,* 136–144.

Hirschman, A. O. (1970). *Exit, voice, and loyalty: Responses to decline in firms, organisations, and states.* Cambridge, MA: Harvard University Press.

Hobson, P. (2002). *The cradle of thought: Exploring the origins of thinking.* London: Macmillan.

Hochschild, A. R. (1979). Emotion work, feeling rules, and social structure. *American Journal of Sociology, 85,* 551–575.

Hochschild, A. R. (1983). *The managed heart: Commercialization of human feeling.* Berkeley, CA: University of California Press.

Hofstede, G. (1980). *Culture's consequences.* Newbury Park, CA: Sage.

Hogg, M. A. (1992). *The social psychology of group cohesiveness: From attraction to social identity.* Hemel Hempstead, UK: Harvester Wheatsheaf.

Hohmann, G. W. (1966). Some effects of spinal cord lesions on experienced emotional feelings. *Psychophysiology, 3,* 526–534.

Hornik, R., Risenhoover, N., & Gunnar, M. (1987). The effects of maternal positive, neutral, and negative affective communications on infant responses to new toys. *Child Development, 58*, 937–944.

Howell, S. (1981). Rules not words. In P. Heelas & A. Lock (Eds.), *Indigenous psychologies: The anthropology of the self* (pp. 133–144). London: Academic Press.

Huesmann, L. R., & Guerra, N. G. (1997). Children's normative beliefs about aggression and aggressive behavior. *Journal of Personality and Social Psychology, 72*, 408–419.

Hupka, R. B. (1981). Cultural determinants of jealousy. *Alternative Lifestyles, 4*, 310–356.

Hupka, R. B. (2003). The social construction of romantic jealousy. *Emotion Researchers, newsletter of the International Society for Research on Emotion*. New York: ISRE.

Hupka, R. B., Buunk, B., Falus, G., Fulgosi, A., Ortega, E., Swain, R., & Tarabrina, N. V. (1985). Romantic jealousy and romantic envy: A seven-nation study. *Journal of Cross-Cultural Psychology, 16*, 423–446.

Hupka, R. B., Lenton, A. P., & Hutchison, K. A. (1999). Universal development of emotion categories in natural language. *Journal of Personality and Social Psychology, 77*, 247–278.

Huynh-Nhu, L., Berenbaum, H., & Raghavan, C. (2002). Culture and alexthymia: Mean levels, correlates, and the role of parental socialization. *Emotion, 4*, 341–361.

Irvine, J. T. (1990). Registering affect: Heteroglossia in the linguistic expression of emotion. In C. Lutz & L. Abu-Lughod (Eds.), *Language and the politics of emotion* (pp. 126–162). New York: Cambridge University Press.

Islam, M. R., & Hewstone, M. (1993). Intergroup attributions and affective consequences in majority and minority groups. *Journal of Personality and Social Psychology, 64*, 936–950.

Iyer, A., Leach, C. W., & Crosby, F. J. (2003). White guilt and racial compensation: The benefits and limits of self-focus. *Personality and Social Psychology Bulletin, 29*, 117–129.

Izard, C. E. (1977). *Human emotions.* New York: Plenum Press.

Izard, C. E. (1978). Emotions as motivations: An evolutionary-developmental perspective. *Nebraska Symposium on Motivation, 26*, 163–200.

Izard, C. E. (1994). Innate and universal facial expressions: Evidence from developmental and cross-cultural research. *Psychological Bulletin, 115*, 288–99.

Jakobs, E., Manstead, A. S. R., & Fischer, A. H. (2001). Social context effects on acial activity in a negative emotional setting. *Emotion, 1*, 51–69.

James, W. (1884). What is an emotion? *Mind, 9*, 188–205.

Jansz, J., & Timmers, M. (2002). Emotional dissonance: When the experience of an emotion jeopardizes an individual's identity. *Theory and Psychology, 12*, 79–95.

Johnson-Laird, P. N., & Oatley, K. (2000). The cognitive and social construction in emotions. In M. Lewis & J. M. Haviland-Jones (Eds.), *Handbook of emotions* (2nd ed.)(pp. 458–475). New York: Guilford Press.

Jones, S. S., & Raag, T. (1989). Smile production in older infants: The importance of a social recipient for the facial signal. *Child Development, 60*, 811–818.

Jones, S. S., Collins, K., & Hong, H. (1991). An audience effect on smile production in 10-month-old infants. *Psychological Science, 2*, 45–49.

Kakar, S. (1978). *The inner world: A psycho-analytic study of child and society in India.* Oxford, UK: Oxford University Press.

Keating, C. F., & Doyle, J. (2002). The faces of desirable mates and dates contain mixed social status cues. *Journal of Experimental Social Psychology, 38*, 414 –424

Keltner, D., & Buswell, B. N. (1976). Evidence for the distinctness of embarrassment, shame, and guilt: A study of recalled antecedents and facial expressions of emotion. *Cognition and Emotion, 10*, 155–171.

Keltner, D., & Buswell, B.N. (1997). Embarrassment: Its distinct form and appeasement function. *Psychological Bulletin, 122*, 250–270.

Keltner, D., & Haidt, J. (1999). Social functions of emotions at four levels of analysis. *Cognition and Emotion, 13*, 505–521.

Kemper, D. (1978). *A social interactional theory of emotions.* New York: Wiley.

Kemper, D. (1991). An introduction to the sociology of emotions. In K. T. Strongman (Ed.), *International Review of Studies on Emotion* (Vol. 1, pp. 301–349). New York: Wiley.

Kemper, D. (2000). Social models in the explanation of emotions. In M. Lewis & J. M. Haviland-Jones (Eds.), *Handbook of emotions* (2nd ed.) (pp. 45–58). New York: Guilford Press.

Kendon, A. (1967). Some functions of gaze direction in social interaction. *Acta Psychologica, 26,* 100–125.

Kenny, A. (1963). *Action, emotion, and will.* London: Routledge and Kegan Paul.

Kim, U., Triandis, H., Kâgitçibasi, Ç., Choi, A., & Yoon, G. (Eds.) (1994). *Individualism and collectivism: Theory, methods, and applications.* Thousand Oaks, CA: Sage.

Kirouac, G., & Dore, F. Y. (1982). Identification of emotional facial expressions by French-speaking subjects in Quebec. *International Journal of Psychology, 17,* 1–7.

Kirouac, G., & Dore, F. Y. (1985). Accuracy of the judgment of facial expression of emotions as a function of sex and level of education. *Journal of Nonverbal Behavior, 9,* 3–7.

Kitayama, S., & Markus, H. R. (Eds.). (1994). *Emotion and culture: Empirical studies of mutual influence.* Washington, DC: American Psychological Association.

Kitayama, S., Markus, H. R., & Kurokawa, M. (2000). Culture emotions, and well-being: Good feelings in Japan and the United States. *Cognition and Emotion, 14,* 93–124.

Kitayama, S., Markus, H. R., & Matsumoto, H. (1995). Culture, self, and emotion: A cultural perspective on self-conscious emotions. In J. P. Tangney & K. W. Fischer (Eds.), *Self conscious emotions: The psychology of shame, guilt, embarrassment, and pride* (pp. 523–550). New York: Guilford Press.

Kitayama, S., Markus, H. R., Matsumoto, H., & Norasakkunkit, V. (1997). Individual and collective processes in the construction of the self: Self-enhancement in the United States and self-criticism in Japan. *Journal of Personality and Social Psychology, 72,* 1245–1267.

Klass, D., Silverman, R. P., & Nickman, S. L. (Eds.). (1996). *Continuing bonds: New understandings of grief.* Philadelphia, PA: Taylor and Francis.

Kleinginna, P. R., Jr., & Kleinginna, A. M. (1981). A categorized list of emotion definitions with suggestions for a consensual definition. *Motivation and Emotion, 5,* 345–379.

Klinnert, M. D., Campos, J. J., Sorce, J. F., Emde, R. N., & Svejda, M. (1983). Emotions as behavior regulators: Social referencing in infancy. In R. Plutchik & H. Kellerman (Eds.), *Emotions: Theory, research and experience* (Vol. 2, pp. 57–86). New York: Academic Press.

Kövecses, Z. (1990). *Emotion concepts.* Berlin: Springer-Verlag.

Kramer, R. M., & Jost, J. T. (2002). Close encounters of the suspicious kind: Outgroup paranoia in hierarchical trust dilemmas. In D. M. Mackie & E. R. Smith (Eds.), *From prejudice to intergroup emotions: Differentiated reactions to social groups* (pp. 173–189). New York: Psychology Press.

Kraut, R. E., & Johnston, R. E. (1979). Social and emotional messages of smiling: An ethological approach. *Journal of Personality and Social Psychology, 37,* 1539–1553.

Kroon, R. M. (1988). *Aanleidingen en structuur van schuld gevoel.* Masters thesis, Psychology Department, University of Amsterdam. No. psy.11.8.88.225.

Kundera, M. (1980). *The book of laughter and forgetting.* New York: Knopf.

Kupperbusch, C., Matsumoto, D., Kooken, K., Loewinger, S., Uchida, H., Wilson-Cohn, C., et al. (1999). Cultural influences on nonverbal expressions of emotion. In P. Philippot, R. Feldman, & E. Coats (Eds.), *The social context of nonverbal behavior* (pp. 17–44). New York: Cambridge University Press.

LaFrance, M., & Hecht, M. A. (1999). Option or obligation to smile: The effects of power and gender on facial expression. In P. Philippot, R. S. Feldman, & E. Coats (Eds.), *The social context of nonverbal behavior: Studies in emotion and social interaction* (pp. 45–70). Cambridge, UK: Cambridge University Press.

Langlois, J. H., Kalakanis, L., Rubenstein, A. J., Larson, A., Hallam, M., & Smoot, M. (2000). Maxims or myths of beauty? A meta-analytic and theoretical review. *Psychological Bulletin, 126,* 390–423.

Lanzetta, J. T., & Englis, B. G. (1989). Expectations of cooperation and competition and their effects on observers' vicarious emotional responses. *Journal of Personality and Social Psychology, 56,* 543–554.

Larsen, R. J., & Ketelaar, T. (1991). Personality and susceptibility to positive and negative affect. *Journal of Personality and Social Psychology, 61,* 132–140.

Latané, B., & Darley, J. M. (1968). Group inhibition of bystander intervention in emergencies. *Journal of Personality and Social Psychology, 10,* 215–221.

Lazarus, R. S. (1984). On the primacy of cognition. *American Psychologist, 39,* 124–129.

Lazarus, R. S. (1991a). *Emotion and adaptation*. New York: Oxford University Press.

Lazarus, R. S. (1991b). Cognition and motivation in emotion. *American Psychologist, 46,* 352–367.

Leach, C. W., Iyer, A., & Pedersen, A. (2002). *The politics of emotion: Inter-group guilt and anger predict political action regarding an apology to Aboriginal Australians.* Unpublished manuscript, University of California, Santa Cruz.

Leach, C. W., Snider, N., & Iyer, A. (2002). "Poisoning the consciences of the fortunate:" The experience of relative advantage and support for social equality. In I. Walker & H. J. Smith (Eds.), *Relative deprivation: Specification, development, and integration* (pp. 136–163). New York: Cambridge University Press.

Leach, C. W., & Spears, R. (2002). *"Without cruelty there is no festival:" Gloating over the suffering of a lower status group.* Unpublished manuscript, University of California, Santa Cruz.

Leach, C. W., Spears, R., Branscombe, N. R., & Doosje, B. (2003). Malicious pleasure: Schadenfreude at the suffering of an outgroup. *Journal of Personality and Social Psychology, 84,* 932–943.

Leary, M. R, Landel, J. L., & Patton, K. M. (1996). The motivated expression of embarrassment following a self-presentational predicament. *Journal of Personality, 64,* 619–636.

Lenneberg, E. H. (1967). *Biological foundations of language*. New York: Wiley.

Leonard, C. M., Rolls, E. T., Wilson, F. A. W., & Baylis, G. C. (1985). Neurons in the amygdala of the monkey with responses selective for faces. *Behavioural Brain Research, 15,* 159–176.

Levenson, R. W., & Gottman, J. M. (1983). Marital interaction: Physiological linkage and affective exchange. *Journal of Personality and Social Psychology, 45,* 587–597.

Levenson, R. W., Ekman, P., Heider, K., & Friesen, W. V (1992). Emotion and autonomic nervous system activity in the Minangkabau of West Sumatra. *Journal of Personality and Social Psychology, 62,* 972–988.

Leventhal, H., & Scherer, K. (1987).The relationship of emotion to cognition: A functional approach to a semantic controversy. *Cognition and Emotion, 1,* 3–28.

Levine, R., Sato, S., Hashimoto, T., & Verma, J. (1995). Love and marriage in 11 cultures. *Journal of Cross-Cultural Psychology, 26,* 554–571.

Levy, R. (1973). *Tahitians*. London: Chicago University Press.

Levy, R. (1984). Emotion, knowing, and culture. In R. Shweder & R. Levine (Eds.), *Culture theory: Essays on mind, self, and emotion* (pp. 214–237). Cambridge, UK: Cambridge University Press.

Lewin, K. (1948). *Resolving social conflicts*. New York: Harper.

Lewis, M. (2000). The emergence of human emotions. In M. Lewis & J. M. Haviland-Jones (Eds.), *Handbook of emotions* (2nd ed.) (pp. 265–280). New York: Guilford Press.

Lewis, M., Alessandri, S. M., & Sullivan, M. W. (1990). Violation of expectancy, loss of control, and anger expressions in young infants. *Developmental Psychology, 26,* 745–751.

Lewis, M., Feiring, C., & Rosenthal, S. (2000). Attachment over time. *Child Development, 71,* 707–720.

Lewis, M., Sullivan, M. W., Stanger, C., & Weiss, M. (1989). Self development and self-conscious emotions. *Child Development, 60,* 146–156.

Leyens, J. P., Demoulin, S., Desert, M., Vaes, J., & Philippot, P. (2002). Expressing emotions and decoding them: In-groups and out-groups do not share the same advantages. In D. M. Mackie & E. R. Smith (Eds.), *From prejudice to intergroup emotions: Differentiated reactions to social groups* (pp. 135–151). New York: Psychology Press.

Leyens, J. P., Paladino, P. M., Rodriguez, R. T., Vaes, J., Demoulin, S., Rodriguez, A. P., et al. (2000). The emotional side of prejudice: The role of secondary emotions. *Personality and Social Psychology Review, 4,* 186–197.

Leyens, J. P., Rodriguez-Perez, A., Rodriguez-Torres, R., Gaunt, R., Paladino, M. P., Vaes, J., et al. (2001). Psychological essentialism and the differential attribution of uniquely human emotions to ingroups and outgroups. *European Journal of Social Psychology, 31,* 395–411.

Lindholm, C. (1982). *Generosity and jealousy: The Swat Pukhtun of Northern Pakistan*. New York: Columbia University Press.

Lipps, T. (1907). Das Wissen von fremden Ichen. In T. Lipps (Ed.), *Psychologische Untersuchungen* (Band 1, pp. 694–722). Leipzig: Engelmann.

Lott, A. J., & Lott, B. E. (1965). Group cohesiveness as interpersonal attraction. *Psychological Bulletin, 64*, 259–309.

Lu, L., Gilmour, R., & Kao, S. (2001). Cultural values and happiness: An East-West dialogue. *Journal of Social Psychology, 141*, 477–493.

Lutz, C. (1983). Parental goals, ethnopsychology, and the development of emotional meaning. *Ethos, 11*, 246–262.

Lutz, C. (1985). Ethnopsychology compared to what? Explaining behavior and consciousness among the Ifaluk. In G. M. White & J. Kirkpatrick (Eds.), *Person, self, and experience: Exploring Pacific ethnopsychologies* (pp. 35–79). Berkeley: University of California Press.

Lutz, C. (1986). The domain of emotion words on Ifaluk. In R. Harré (Ed.), *The social construction of emotion* (pp. 267–289). New York: Basil Blackwell.

Lutz, C. (1987). Goals, events and understanding in Ifaluk emotion theory. In D. Holland & N. Quinn (Eds.), *Cultural models in language and thought* (pp. 290–312). Cambridge, UK: Cambridge University Press.

Lutz, C. (1988). *Unnatural emotions: Everyday sentiments on a Micronesian atoll and their challenge to Western theory*. Chicago: University of Chicago Press.

Lutz, C. (1990). Gender, power, and the rhetoric of emotional control in American discourse. In L. Abu-Lughod & C. Lutz (Eds.), *Language and the politics of emotion* (pp. 69–91). New York: Cambridge University Press.

Lutz, C., & White, G. M. (1986). The anthropology of emotions. *Annual Review of Anthropology, 15*, 405–435.

Lutz, T. (1999). Crying. *The natural and cultural history of tears*. New York: Norton.

Mackie, D., Devos, T., & Smith, E. R. (2000). Intergroup emotions: Explaining offensive action tendencies in an intergroup context. *Journal of Personality and Social Psychology, 79*, 602–616.

Mandal, M. K., Bryden, M. P., & Bulman-Fleming, M. B. (1996). Similarities and variations in facial expressions of emotions: Cross-cultural evidence. *International Journal of Psychology, 31*, 49–58.

Manstead, A. S. R., & Fischer, A. H. (2001). Social appraisal: The social world as object of and influence on appraisal processes. In K. R. Scherer, A. Schorr, & T. Johnstone, (Eds.), *Appraisal processes in emotion: Theory, methods, research* (pp. 221–232). New York: Oxford University Press.

Manstead, A. S. R., & Fischer, A. H. (2002). Culture and emotion: Beyond the universality-relativity dichotomy. Introduction to Culture and Emotion, Special Issue of *Cognition and Emotion, 16*, 1–9.

Markus, H. R., & Kitayama, S. (1991). Culture and the self: Implications for cognition, emotion and motivation. *Psychological Review, 98*, 224–253.

Markus, H. R., & Kitayama, S. (1994). The cultural construction of self and emotion: Implications for social behavior. In S. Kitayama & H. R. Markus (Eds.), *Emotion and culture: Empirical studies of mutual influence* (pp. 89–130). Washington, DC: American Psychological Association.

Markus, H. R., Kitayama, S., & Matsumoto, H. (1995). Culture, self, and emotion: A cultural perspective on 'self-conscious' emotions. In J. P. Tangney & K. W. Fischer (Eds.), *Self-conscious emotions* (pp. 439–464). New York: The Guilford Press.

Matsumoto, D. (1989). Face, culture, and judgments of anger and fear: Do the eyes have it? *Journal of Nonverbal Behavior, 13*, 171–188.

Matsumoto, D. (1990). Cultural similarities and differences in display rules. *Motivation and Emotion, 14*, 195–214.

Matsumoto, D. (1992). More evidence for the universality of a contempt expression. *Motivation and Emotion, 16*, 363–368.

Matsumoto, D. (1996). *Unmasking Japan: Myths and realities about the emotions of the Japanese*. Stanford, CT: Stanford University Press.

Matsumoto, D. (1999). Culture and self: An empirical assessment of Markus and Kitayama's theory of independent and interdependent self-construal. *Asian Journal of Social Psychology, 2,* 289–310.

Matsumoto, D. (2001). *The handbook of culture and psychology.* New York: Oxford University Press.

Matsumoto, D., Consolacion, T., Yamada, H., Suzuki, R., Franklin, B., Paul, S., et al. (2002). American-Japanese cultural differences in judgements of emotional expressions of different intensities. *Cognition and Emotion, 16,* 721–747.

Matsumoto, D., & Ekman, P. (1989). American-Japanese cultural differences in intensity ratings of facial expressions of emotion. *Motivation and Emotion, 13,* 143–157.

Matsumoto, D., Kasri, F., & Kooken, K. (1999). American-Japanese cultural differences in judgements of expression intensity and subjective experience. *Cognition and Emotion, 13,* 201–218.

Matsumoto, D., & Kupperbusch, C. (2001). Idiocentric and allocentric differences in emotional expression, experience, and the coherence between expression and experience. *Asian Journal of Social Psychology, 4,* 113–131.

Matsumoto, D., Takeuchi, S., Andayani, S., Kouznetsova, N., & Krupp, D. (1998). The contribution of individualism vs. collectivism to cross-national differences in display rules. *Asian Journal of Social Psychology, 1,* 147–165.

Mauro, R., Sato, K., & Tucker, J. (1992). The role of appraisal in human emotions: A cross-cultural study. *Journal of Personality and Social Psychology, 62,* 301–317.

Mayer, J. D., & Salovey, P. (1997). What is emotional intelligence? In P. Salovey & D. J. Sluyter (Eds.), *Emotional development and emotional intelligence: Educational implications.* (pp. 3–31). New York: Basic Books/Harper Collins.

McGraw, K. M. (1987). Guilt following transgression: An attribution of responsibility approach. *Journal of Personality and Social Psychology, 53,* 247–256.

McHugo, G. J., Lanzetta, J. T., Sullivan, D. G., Masters, R. D., & Englis, B. G. (1985). Emotional reactions to a political leader's expressive displays. *Journal of Personality and Social Psychology, 49,* 1513–1529.

Mead, G. H. (1934). *Mind, self, and society.* Chicago: Chicago University Press.

Medvec, V. H., Gilovich, T., & Madey, S. F. (1995). When less is more: Counterfactual thinking and satisfaction among Olympic medalists. *Journal of Personality and Social Psychology, 69,* 603–610.

Meltzoff, A. N., & Borton, R. W. (1979). Intermodal matching by human neonates. *Nature, 282,* 403–404.

Meltzoff, A. N., & Moore, M. K. (1977). Imitation of facial and manual gestures by human neonates, *Science, 198*(4312), 75–78.

Menon, U., & Shweder, R. A. (1994). Kali's tongue: Cultural psychology and the power of shame in Orissa, India. In S. Kitayama & H. R. Markus (Eds.), *Emotion and culture: Empirical studies of mutual influence* (pp. 241–284). Washington, DC: APA.

Mesquita, B. (2001). Emotions in collectivist and individualist contexts. *Journal of Personality and Social Psychology, 80,* 68–74.

Mesquita, B., & Frijda, N. H. (1992). Cultural variations in emotions: A review. *Psychological Bulletin, 112,* 179–204.

Mesquita, B., & Karasawa, M. (2002). Different emotional lives. *Cognition and Emotion, 16,* 127–142.

Mesquita, B., & Markus, H. R. (2004). Culture and emotion: Models of agency as sources of cultural variation in emotion. In A. S. R. Manstead, N. H. Frijda & A. H. Fischer (Eds.), *Feelings and emotions: The Amsterdam Symposium* (pp. 341–359). New York: Cambridge University Press.

Miceli, M. (1992). How to make someone feel guilty: Strategies of guilt inducement and their goals. *Journal for the Theory of Social Behaviour, 22,* 81–104.

Millar, K. U., & Tesser, A. (1988). Deceptive behavior in social relationships: A consequence of violated expectations. *Journal of Psychology, 122,* 263–273.

Miller, J. G. (1984). Culture and the development of everyday social explanation. *Journal of Personality and Social Psychology, 46,* 961–978.

Miller, R. S. (1995). On the nature of embarrassability: Shyness, social evaluation and social skill. *Journal of Personality, 65,* 315–339.

Miyake, K., & Yamazaki, K. (1995). Self-conscious emotions, child rearing, and child psychopathology in Japanese culture. In J. P. Tangney & K. W. Fischer (Eds.), *Self-conscious emotions: The psychology of shame, guilt, embarrassment, and pride* (pp. 488–504). New York: Guilford Press.

Montada, L., & Schneider, A. (1989). Justice and emotional reactions to the disadvantaged. *Social Justice Research, 3*, 313–344.

Moore, C. C., Romney, A. K., & Hsia, T. L. (2002). Cultural, gender, and individual differences in perceptual and semantic structures of basic colors in Chinese and English. *Journal of Cognition and Culture, 2*, 1–28.

Morris, J. A., & Feldman, D. C. (1996). The dimensions, antecedents, and consequences of emotional labor. *Academy of Management Review, 21*, 986–1010.

Morsbach, H., & Tyler, W. J. (1986). A Japanese emotion: Amae. In R. Harré (Ed.), *The social construction of emotion* (pp. 289–308). New York: Basil Blackwell.

Moscovici, S. (1976). *Social influence and social change*. London: Academic Press.

Mumby, D. K. & Putnam, L. L. (1992). The politics of emotion: A feminist reading of bounded rationality. *Academy of Management Review, 17*, 465–485.

Munroe, R. L., Munroe, R. H., & Winters, S. (1996). Cross-cultural correlates of the consonant-vowel syllable. *Cross-Cultural Research, 30*, 60–83.

Murray, L., & Trevarthen, C. (1985). Emotional regulation on interactions between two-month-olds and their mothers. In T. M. Field & N. A. Fox (Eds.), *Social perception in infants* (pp. 177–197). Norwood, NJ: Ablex.

Myers, F. (1979). Emotions and the self: A theory of personhood and political order among Pintupi Aborigines. *Ethos, 7*, 343–370.

Nagy, E., & Molnár, P. (2003). *Homo imitans or homo provocans? A human imprinting model of neonatal imitation*. Unpublished manuscript.

Neisser, U. (1979). The concept of intelligence. *Intelligence, 3*, 217–227.

Nelson, K. (1993). The psychological and social origins of autobiographical memory. *Psychological Science, 4*, 7–14.

Neumann, R., & Strack, F. (2000). Mood contagion: The automatic transfer of mood between persons. *Journal of Personality and Social Psychology, 79*, 211–223.

NICHD Early Child Care Research Network. (1997). The effects of infant child care on infant-mother attachment security: Results of the NICHD study of early child care. *Child Development, 68*, 860–879.

Nietzsche, F. (1967). On the genealogy of morals (W. Kaufmann & R. J. Hollingdale, Trans. originally published 1887). New York: Random House.

Nisbett, R. E., & Cohen, D. (1996). *Culture of honor: The psychology of violence in the South*. Boulder, CO: Westview.

Oatley, K. (1992). *Best laid schemes: The psychology of emotions*. Cambridge, UK: Cambridge University Press.

Oatley, K., & Johnson-Laird, P. N. (1987). Towards a cognitive theory of emotions. *Cognition and Emotion, 1*, 29–50.

O'Connor, T. G., & Croft, C. M. (2001). A twin study of attachment in preschool children, *Child Development, 72*, 1501–1511.

Öhman, A., Lundquist, D., & Esteves, F. (2001). The face in the crowd revisited: A threat advantage with schematic stimuli. *Journal of Personality and Social Psychology, 80*, 381–396.

O'Malley, M. N., & Greenberg, J. (1983). Sex differences in restoring justice: The down payment effect. *Journal of Research in Personality, 17*, 174–185.

Ortony, A., Clore, G. L., & Collins, A. (1988). *The cognitive structure of emotions*. New York: Cambridge University Press.

Ortony, A, & Turner, T. J. (1990). What's basic about basic emotions. *Psychological Review, 97*, 315–313.

O'Toole, A. J., Edelman, D., & Buelthoff, H. H. (1998). Stimulus-specific effects in face recognition over changes in viewpoint. *Vision Research, 38*, 2351–2363.

Oyserman, D., Coon, H. M., & Kemmelmeier, M. (2002). Rethinking individualism and collectivism: Evaluation of theoretical assumptions and meta-analyses. *Psychological Bulletin, 128*, 3–72.

Page, T., & Bretherton, I. (2001). Mother- and father-child attachment themes in the story completions of pre-schoolers from post-divorce families: Do they predict relationships with peers and teachers? *Attachment and Human Development, 3*, 1–29.

Parkin, D. (1985). Reason, emotion, and the embodiment of power. In J. Overring (Ed.), *Reason and morality* (pp. 135–141). London: Tavistock.

Parkinson, B. (1991). Emotional stylists: Strategies of expressive management among trainee hairdressers. *Cognition and Emotion, 5*, 419–434.

Parkinson, B. (1995). *Ideas and realities of emotion.* London: Routledge.

Parkinson, B. (1996). Emotions are social. *British Journal of Psychology, 87*, 663–683.

Parkinson, B. (1998). What we think about when we think about emotions. *Cognition and Emotion, 12*, 615–624.

Parkinson, B. (1999). Relations and dissociations between appraisal and emotion ratings of reasonable and unreasonable anger and guilt. *Cognition and Emotion, 13*, 347–385.

Parkinson, B. (2001a). Anger on and off the road. *British Journal of Psychology, 92*, 507–526.

Parkinson, B. (2001b). Putting appraisal in context. In K. R. Scherer, A. Schorr, & T. Johnstone (Eds.), *Appraisal processes in emotion: Theory, methods, research* (pp. 173–186). New York: Oxford University Press.

Parrott, W. G. (1991). The emotional experiences of envy and jealousy. In P. Salovey (Ed.), *The psychology of jealousy and envy* (pp. 3–30). New York: Guilford Press.

Parrott, W. G. (1993). Beyond hedonism: Motives for inhibiting good moods and for maintaining bad moods. In D. M. Wegner & J. W. Pennebaker (Eds.), *Handbook of mental control* (pp. 278–305). Englewood Cliffs, NJ: Prentice Hall.

Parrott, W. G. (1995). The heart and the head: Everday conceptions of being emotional. In J. A. Russell, J. Fernandez-Dols, A. S. R. Manstead, & J. C. Wellenkamp (Eds.), *Everyday conceptions of emotion. An introduction to the psychology, anthropology, and linguistics of emotion* (pp. 73–84). Dordrecht, NL: Kluwer.

Parrott, W. G., & Smith, R. H. (1993). Distinguishing the experiences of envy and jealousy. *Journal of Personality and Social Psychology, 64*, 906–920.

Parrott, W. G., & Smith, S. F. (1991). Embarrassment: Actual vs. typical cases, classical vs. prototypical representations. *Cognition and Emotion, 5*, 467–488.

Patterson, M. L. (1996). Social behavior and social cognition: A parallel process approach. In J. L. Nye & A.M. Brower (Eds.), *What's social about social cognition?* (pp. 87–105). Thousand Oaks, CA: Sage.

Paykel, E. S., Myers, J. K., Dienelt, M. N., Klerman, G. L., Lindenthal, J. J., & Pepper, M. P. (1969). Life events and depression: A controlled study. *Archives of General Psychiatry, 21*, 753–760.

Pennebaker, J. W. (1982). *The psychology of physical symptoms.* New York: Springer-Verlag.

Pennebaker, J. W., Zech, E., & Rimé, B. (2001). Disclosing and sharing emotion: Psychological, social, and health consequences. In M. S. Stroebe, R. O. Hansson, et al. (Eds.) *Handbook of bereavement research: Consequences, coping, and care.* (pp. 517–543). Washington, DC: American Psychological Association.

Peristiany, J. G. (Ed.). (1965). *Honour and shame: The values of Mediterranean society.* London: Weidenfeld and Nicolson.

Pettigrew, A. (1979). On studying organizational cultures. *Administrative Science Quarterly, 24*, 570–581.

Pettigrew, T. F. (1986). The contact hypothesis revisited. In M. Hewstone & R. J. Brown (Eds.), *Contact and conflict in intergroup encounters* (pp. 169–195). Oxford: Blackwell.

Pettigrew, T. F. (1998). Intergroup contact theory. *Annual Review of Psychology, 49*, 68–85.

Piliavin, J. A., & Piliavin, I. M. (1972). Effect of blood on reactions to a victim. *Journal of Personality and Social Psychology, 23*, 353–361.

Plutchik, R. (1980). *Emotion: A psychoevolutionary synthesis.* New York: Harper and Row.

Pugliesi, K. (1999). The consequences of emotional labor: Effects on work stress, job satisfaction, and well-being. *Motivation and Emotion, 23*, 125–154.

Rafaeli, A., & Sutton, R. I. (1989). The expression of emotion in organizational life. In L. L. Cummings & B. M. Staw (Eds.), *Research in organizational behavior* (Vol. 11, 1–42). Greenwich, CT: JAI Press.

Ramirez, J. M., Andreu, J. M., & Fujihara, T. (2001). Cultural and sex differences in aggression: A comparison between Japanese and Spanish students using two different inventories. *Aggressive Behavior, 27,* 313–322.

Ramirez, J. M., Santisteban, C., Fujihara, T., & van Goozen, S. (2002). Differences between experiences of anger and readiness to angry action: A study of Japanese and Spanish students. *Aggressive Behavior, 28,* 429–438.

Ratner, H. H., & Stettner, L. J. (1991). Thinking and feeling: Putting Humpty Dumpty together again. *Merrill-Palmer Quarterly, 37,* 1–26.

Reddy, V. (2000). Coyness in early infancy. *Developmental Science, 3,* 186–192.

Reisenzein, R. (1983). The Schachter theory of emotion: Two decades later. *Psychological Bulletin, 94,* 239–264.

Rimé, B. (1995). The social sharing of emotion as a source for the social knowledge of emotion. In J. A. Russell, J. M. Fernández-Dols, J. Wellenkamp, & A. S. R. Manstead (Eds.), *Everyday conceptions of emotion: An introduction to the psychology, anthropology and linguistics of emotion* (pp. 475–489). Dordrecht, NL: Kluwer.

Rimé, B., Philippot, P., Boca, S., & Mesquita, B. (1992). Long-lasting cognitive and social consequences of emotion: Social sharing and rumination. In W. Stroebe & M. Hewstone (Eds.), *European Review of Social Psychology* (Vol. 3, pp. 225–258). Oxford: John Wiley & Sons.

Rimé, B., Philippot, P., & Cisamolo, D. (1990). Social schemata of peripheral changes in emotion. *Journal of Personality and Social Psychology, 59,* 38–49.

Rodriquez Mosquera, P. M. (1999). Honor and emotion. *The cultural shaping of pride, shame and anger.* Unpublished doctoral dissertation, University of Amsterdam.

Rodriquez Mosquera, P. M., Fischer, A. H. & Manstead, A. S. R. (in press). Inside the heart of emotion: on culture and relational concerns. In L. Tiedens & C. W. Leach (Eds.), *The social life of emotions.* New York: Cambridge University Press.

Rodriguez Mosquera, P. M., Manstead, A. S. R., & Fischer, A. H. (2000). The role of honor-related values in the elicitation, experience and communication of pride, shame and anger: Spain and the Netherlands compared. *Personality and Social Psychology Bulletin, 26,* 833–844.

Rodriguez Mosquera, P. M., Manstead, A. S. R., & Fischer, A. H. (2002a). The role of honor concerns in emotional reactions to offenses. *Cognition and Emotion, 16,* 143–164.

Rodriguez Mosquera, P. M., Manstead, A. S. R., & Fischer, A. H. (2002b). Honor in the Mediterranean and Northern Europe. *Journal of Cross-Cultural Psychology, 33,* 16–36.

Rohner, R. (1984). Toward a conception of culture for cross-cultural psychology. *Journal of Cross-Cultural Psychology, 15,* 11–138.

Rolls, E. T. (1999). *The brain and emotion.* Oxford: Oxford University Press.

Rolls, E. T., & Baylis, G. C. (1986). Size and contrast have only small effects on the responses to faces of neurones in the cortex of the superior temporal sulcus of the monkey. *Experimental Brian Research, 65,* 38–48.

Rönnqvist, L., & van Hofsten, C. (1994). Neonatal finger and arm movements as determined by a social and an object context. *Early Development and Parenting, 3,* 81–94.

Rosaldo, M. Z. (1980). *Knowledge and passion: Ilongot notions of self and social life.* Cambridge: Cambridge University Press.

Rosch, E. (1973). Natural categories. *Cognitive Psychology, 4,* 328–350.

Roseman, I. J. (1984). Cognitive determinants of emotions: A structural theory. In P. Shaver (Ed.), *Review of personality and social psychology 5: Emotions, relationships, and health* (pp. 11–36). Beverley Hills, CA: Sage.

Roseman, I. J. (1991). Appraisal determinants of discrete emotions. *Cognition and Emotion, 5,* 161–200.

Roseman, I. J. (1996). Why these appraisals? Anchoring appraisal models to research on emotional behavior and related response systems. In N. H. Frijda (Ed.), *ISRE '96: Proceedings of the IXth Conference of the International Society for Research on Emotions* (pp. 106–110). Toronto: ISRE Publications.

Roseman, I. J. (2001). A model of appraisal in the emotion system: Integrating theory, research, and applications. In K. R. Scherer, A. Schorr, & T. Johnstone (Eds.), *Appraisal processes in emotion: Theory, methods, research* (pp. 68–91). New York: Oxford University Press.

Roseman, I. J., Dhawan, N., Rettek, S. I., Naidu, R. K., & Thapa, K. (1995). Cultural differences and cross-cultural similarities in appraisals and emotional responses. *Journal of Cross-Cultural Psychology, 26*, 23–48.

Roseman, I. J. & Smith, C. A. (2001). Appraisal theory: Overview, assumptions, varieties, controversies. In K. R. Scherer, A. Schorr, & T. Johnstone (Eds.), *Appraisal processes in emotion: Theory, methods, research* (pp. 3–19). New York: Oxford University Press.

Roseman, M. (1988). Head, heart, odor, and shadow: The structure of the self and the emotional word, and ritual performance among Senoi Temiar. *Ethos, 16*, 227–250.

Rosenhan, D. L. (1973). On being sane in insane places. *Science, 179*, 250–258.

Runciman, W. G. (1966). *Relative deprivation and social justice: A study of attitudes to social inequality in twentieth-century England*. Berkeley: University of California Press.

Russell, J. A. (1979). Affective space is bipolar. *Journal of Personality and Social Psychology, 37*, 345–356.

Russell, J. A. (1991a). Culture and the categorization of emotions. *Psychological Bulletin, 110*, 426–450.

Russell, J. A. (1991b). In defense of a prototype approach to emotion concepts. *Journal of Personality and Social Psychology, 60*, 37–47.

Russell, J. A. (1994). Is there universal recognition of emotion from facial expressions? A review of the cross-cultural studies. *Psychological Bulletin, 115*, 102–141.

Russell, J. A. (1997). Reading emotions from and into faces: Resurrecting a dimensional contextual perspective. In J. A. Russell & J. M. Fernandez Dols (Eds.), *The psychology of facial expression* (pp. 295–320). New York: Cambridge University Press.

Russell, J. A. (2003). Core affect and the psychological construction of emotion. *Psychological Review, 110*, 145–172.

Russell, J. A., & Feldman, Barrett L. (1999). Core affect, prototypical emotional episodes, and other things called emotion: Dissecting the elephant. *Journal of Personality and Social Psychology, 76*(5), 805–819.

Russell, J. A., & Fehr, B. (1994). Fuzzy concepts in a fuzzy hierarchy: Varieties of anger. *Journal of Personality and Social Psychology, 67*, 186–205.

Russell, J. A., Fernandez Dols, J.M., Manstead, A. S. R., & Wellenkamp, J. (Eds.) (1995). *Everyday conceptions of emotion: An introduction to the psychology, anthropology, and linguistics of emotion*. Dordrecht: Kluwer.

Russell, J. A., & Sato, K. (1995). Comparing emotion words between languages. *Journal of Cross Cultural Psychology, 26*, 384–391.

Russell, J. A., & Yik, M. S. M. (1996). Emotion among the Chinese. In M. H. Bond (Ed.), *The handbook of Chinese psychology* (pp. 166–188). New York: Oxford University Press.

Rutter, D. R. (1987). *Communicating by telephone*. Elmsford, NY: Pergamon.

Ryle, G. (1949). *The concept of mind*. Harmondsworth, UK: Penhuin Books.

Saarni, C. (1990). Emotional competence: How emotions and relationships become integrated. In R. A. Thompson (Ed.), *Nebraska Symposium on Motivation Vol. 36: Socioemotional development* (pp. 115–182). Lincoln, NE: University of Nebraska Press.

Saarni, C. (1999). *The development of emotional competence*. New York: Guilford Press.

Sabini, J., Siepmann, M., Stein, J., & Meyerowitz, M. (2000). Who is embarrassed by what? *Cognition and Emotion, 4*, 213–240.

Salovey, P., & Mayer, J. (1990). Emotional intelligence. *Imagination, Cognition, and Personality, 9*, 185–211.

Salovey, P., & Rodin, J. (1986). The differentiation of social comparison jealousy and romantic jealousy. *Journal of Personality and Social Psychology, 50*, 1100–1112

Saltzman, K. M., & Holahan, C. J. (2002). Social support, self-efficacy, and depressive symptoms: An integrative model. *Journal of Social and Clinical Psychology, 21*, 309–322.

Sarbin, T. R. (1986). Emotion and act: Roles and rhetoric. In R. Harré (Ed.), *The social construction of emotions* (pp. 83–97). Oxford: Blackwell.

Sastry, J., & Ross, C. E. (1998). Asian ethnicity and the sense of personal control. *Social Psychology Quarterly, 61*, 101–120.

Schachter, S. (1959). *The psychology of affiliation*. Stanford, CA: Stanford University Press.

Schachter, S. (1964). The interaction of cognitive and physiological determinants of emotional state. In L. Festinger (Ed.), *Advances in experimental social psychology* (Vol. 1, pp. 49–80). New York: Academic Press.

Schachter, S., & Singer, J. E. (1962). Cognitive, social, and physiological determinants of emotional state. *Psychological Review, 69*, 379–399.

Schaubroeck, J., & Jones, J. R. (2000). Antecedents of workplace emotional labor dimensions and moderators of their effects on physical symptoms. *Journal of Organizational Behavior, 21*, 163–183.

Scherer, K. R. (1984). Emotion as a multicomponent process: A model and some cross-cultural data. In P. Shaver (Ed.), *Review of personality and social psychology* (Vol. 5, pp. 37–63). Beverly Hills, CA: Sage.

Scherer, K. R. (1992). What does facial expression express? In K. T. Strongman (Ed.), *International review of studies in emotion* (Vol. 2, pp. 139–165). Chichester: Wiley.

Scherer, K. R. (2001). Appraisal considered as a process of multilevel sequential checking. In K. R. Scherer, A. Schorr, & T. Johnstone (Eds.), *Appraisal processes in emotion: Theory, methods, research* (pp. 91–120). New York: Oxford University Press.

Scherer, K. R., Schorr, A., & Johnstone, T. (Eds.) (2001). *Appraisal processes in emotion: Theory, methods, research.* Oxford: Oxford University Press.

Scherer, K. R., & Wallbott, H. G. (1994). Evidence for universality and cultural variation of differential emotion response patterning. *Journal of Personality and Social Psychology, 66*, 310–328.

Scherer, K. R., Wallbott, H., Matsumoto, D., & Kudoh, T. (1988). Emotional experience in cultural context: A comparison between Europe, Japan, and the United States. In K. R. Scherer (Ed.), *Facets of emotion: Recent research* (pp. 1–30). Berkeley: University of California Press.

Scherer, K. R., Walbott, H. G., & Summerfield, A. B. (1986). *Experiencing emotion: A cross-cultural study.* Cambridge: Cambridge University Press.

Schieffelin, E. L. (1985). Anger, grief, and shame: Toward a Kaluli ethnopsychology. In G. M. White & J. Kirkpatrick (Eds.), *Person, self, and experience: Exploring Pacific ethnopsychologies* (pp. 168–182). Berkeley: University of California Press.

Schimmack, U. (1996). Cultural influences on the recognition of emotion by facial expressions: Individualistic or Caucasian cultures? *Journal of Cross-Cultural Psychology, 27*, 37–50.

Schmidt Atzert, L., & Park, H. S. (1999). The Korean concepts of dapdaphada and uulhada: A cross-cultural study of the meaning of emotions. *Journal of Cross-Cultural Psychology, 30*, 646–654.

Selby, J. M., & Bradley, B. S. (2003). Infants in groups: A paradigm for the study of early social experience. *Human Development, 46*, 197–221.

Semin, G., & Fiedler, K. (1991). The linguistic category model: Its bases, applications, and range. In W. Stroebe & M. Hewstone (Eds.), *European Review of Social Psychology* (Vol. 2, pp. 1–30). Chichester, UK: Wiley.

Semin, G., & Fiedler, K. (1992). The inferential properties of interpersonal verbs. In G. R. Semin, & K. Fiedler (Eds.), *Language, interaction and social cognition* (pp. 58–78). Thousand Oaks, CA: Sage.

Semin, G. R., Goerts, C. A., Nandram, S., & Semin-Goossens, A. (2002). Cultural perspectives on the linguistic representation of emotion and emotion events. *Cognition and Emotion, 16*, 11–28.

Semin, G. R., & Manstead, A. S. R. (1982). The social implications of embarrassment displays and restitution behaviour. *European Journal of Social Psychology, 12*, 367–377.

Shaver, P. R., Morgan, H. J., & Wu, S. (1996). Is love a "basic" emotion? *Personal Relationships, 3*, 81–96.

Shaver, P. R., Schwartz, J. C., Kirson, D., & O'Connor, C. (1987). Emotion knowledge: Further exploration of a prototype approach. *Journal of Personality and Social Psychology, 52*, 1061–1086.

Shaver, P. R., Wu, S., & Schwartz, J. C. (1992). Cross-cultural similarities and differences in emotion and its representation. In M. S. Clark (Ed.), *Review of Personality and Social Psychology: Emotion* (pp. 175–212). Thousand Oaks, CA: Sage Publications.

Sherif, M. (1966). *Group conflict and cooperation.* London: Routledge and Kegan Paul.

Shields, S. A. (1987). Women, men, and the dilemma of emotion. In P. Shaver & C. Hendrick (Eds.), *Sex and Gender* (pp. 229–250). Newbury Park, CA: Sage.

Shields, S. A. (2002). *Speaking from the heart: Gender and the social meaning of emotion.* Cambridge, UK: Cambridge University Press.

Shweder, R. A., & Haidt, J. (2000). The cultural psychology of emotions: Ancient and new. In M. Lewis & J. M. Haviland Jones (Eds.), *Handbook of emotions* (pp. 397–414. New York: Guilford Press.

Shweder, R. A., Mahaptra, M., & Miller, J. G. (1987). Culture and moral development. In J. Kagan & S. Lamb (Eds.), *The emergence of morality in young children* (pp. 1–83). Chicago: University of Chicago Press.

Singelis, T. M., Bond, M. H., Sharkey, W. F., Lai, & C. S. Y. (1999). Unpackaging culture's influence on self-esteem and embarrassability: The role of self construals. *Journal of Cross-Cultural Psychology, 30,* 315–341.

Singelis, T. M., & Sharkey, W. F. (1995). Culture, self construal, and embarrassability. *Journal of Cross-Cultural Psychology, 26,* 622–644.

Smith, C. A. (1989). Dimensions of appraisal and physiological response in emotion. *Journal of Personality and Social Psychology, 56,* 339–353.

Smith, C. A., & Lazarus, R. S. (1993). Appraisal components, core relational themes, and the emotions. *Cognition and Emotion, 7,* 233–269.

Smith, E. R. (1993). Social identity and social emotions: Toward new conceptualizations of prejudice. In D. M. Mackie, D. Hamilton, & D. Lewis (Eds.), *Affect, cognition, and stereotyping: Interactive processes in group perception* (pp. 297–315). San Diego, CA: Academic Press.

Smith, H. J., Pettigrew, T. F., & Vega, L. (1994). *Measures of relative deprivation: A conceptual critique and meta analysis.* Paper presented at the Annual Meeting of the American Psychological Association, Los Angeles, CA.

Solomon, R. C. (1976). *The passions.* Notre Dame, IN: University of Notre Dame Press.

Solomon, R. C., (1981). *Love: Emotion, myth, and metaphor.* Garden City, NY: Anchor Press/ Doubleday.

Sorce, J. F., Emde, R. N., & Campos, J., & Klinnert, M.D. (1985). Maternal emotional signaling: Its effect on the visual cliff behavior of 1 year olds. *Developmental Psychology, 21,* 195–200.

Spackman, M. P. (2002). How to do things with emotions. *Journal of Mind and Behavior, 23,* 393–411.

Stearns, C. Z. & Stearns, P. N. (1986). *Anger: The struggle for emotional control in American's history.* Chicago: The University of Chicago Press.

Stearns, P. N. (1994). *American cool: Constructing a twentieth-century emotional style.* New York: New York University Press.

Stearns, P. N., & Stearns, C. Z. (1985). Emotionology: Clarifying the history of emotions and emotional standards. *American Historical Review, 96,* 63–94.

Steele, C. M., & Liu, T. J. (1983). Dissonance processes as self-affirmation. *Journal of Personality and Social Psychology, 45,* 5–19.

Steele, H. (2002). Attachment theory: The state of the art. *The Psychologist, 15,* 518–522.

Steele, H., & Steele, M. (2001). *Expectant fathers' (not mothers') Adult Attachment Interviews predict their children's mental health at age 11.* Presentation, Conference of the Society for Research in Child Development, Minneapolis.

Steele, H., Steele, M., & Fonagy, P. (1996). Associations among attachment classifications of mothers, fathers, and their infants. *Child Development, 67,* 541–555.

Steele, S. (1990). White guilt. In S. Steele (Ed.), *The content of our character. A new vision of race in America* (pp. 77–92). New York: Harper Collins.

Stemmler, G. (1989). The autonomic differentiation of emotions revisited: Convergent and discriminant validation. *Psychophysiology, 26,* 617–632.

Stephan, W. G., & Stephan, C. W. (1985). Intergroup anxiety. *Journal of Social Issues, 41,* 157–175.

Stern, D. N. (1985). *The interpersonal world of the infant: A view from psychoanalysis and developmental psychology.* New York: Basic Books.

Stern, D. N. (2000). Putting time back into our considerations of infant experience: A microdiachronic view. *Infant Mental Health Journal, 21,* 21–28.

Stern, D. N., Hofer, L., Haft, W., & Dore, J. (1985). Affect attunement: The sharing of feeling states between mother and infant by means of intermodal fluency. In T. N. Field & N. Fox (Eds.), *Social perception in infants* (pp. 249–268). Norwood, NJ: Ablex.

Strack, F., Martin, L. L., & Stepper, S. (1988). Inhibiting and facilitating conditions of the human smile: A non-obtrusive test of the facial feedback hypothesis. *Journal of Personality and Social Psychology, 54*, 768–777.

Stroebe, M. S. (2001). Bereavement research and theory: Retrospective and prospective. *The American Behavioral Scientist, 44*, 854–865.

Stroebe, M. S. (2001). Gender differences in adjustment to bereavement: An empirical and theoretical review. *Review of General Psychology, 5*, 62–83.

Stroebe, M., Gergen, M. M., Gergen, K. J., Stroebe, W. (1992). Broken hearts or broken bounds: Love and death in historical perspective. *American Psychologist, 47*, 1205–1212.

Stroebe, M. S., & Schut, H. (1999). The dual process model of coping with bereavement: Rationale and description. *Death Studies, 23*, 197–224.

Stroebe, W., & Stroebe, M. S. (1987). *Bereavement and health: The psychological and physical consequences of partner loss.* New York: Cambridge University Press.

Suh, E., Diener, E., Oishi, S., & Triandis, H. C. (1998). The shifting basis of life satisfaction judgments across cultures: Emotions versus norms. *Journal of Personality and Social Psychology, 74*, 482–493.

Szasz, T. S. (1961). *The myth of mental illness.* Garden City, NY: Doubleday.

Tajfel, H., Flament, C., Billig, M., & Bundy, R. F. (1971). Social categorization and intergroup behaviour. *European Journal of Social Psychology, 11*, 149–178.

Tajfel, H., & Turner, J. C. (1986). The social identity theory of intergroup conflict. In S. Worchel & W. G. Austin (Eds.), *Psychology of intergroup relations* (pp. 7–24). Chicago: Nelson Hall.

Takahashi, K. (1990). Are the key assumptions of the "strange situation" procedure universal? A view from Japanese research. *Human Development, 33*, 23 30.

Tangney, J. P., Wagner, P. E., Hill Barlow, D., Marschall, D. E., & Gramzow, R. (1996). Relation of shame and guilt to constructive versus destructive responses to anger across the lifespan. *Journal of Personality and Social Psychology, 70*, 797–809.

Tavris, C. T. (1982). *Anger, the misunderstood emotion.* New York: Simon & Schuster.

Tedeschi, J. T., & Bond, M. H. (2001). Aversive behavior and aggression in cultural perspective. In R. M. Kowalski (Ed.), *Behaving badly: Aversive behaviors in interpersonal relationships* (pp. 257–293). Washington, DC: American Psychological Association.

Tennant, L., & Bebbington, P. (1978). The social causation of depression: A critique of the work of Brown and his colleagues. *Psychological Medicine, 8*, 565–578.

Thoits, P. A. (2004). Emotion norms, emotion work, and social order. In A. S. R. Manstead, N. H. Frijda, & A. H. Fischer (Eds.), *Feelings and emotions: The Amsterdam symposium* (pp. 359–379). New York: Cambridge University Press.

Tiedens, L. Z. (2001). Anger and advancement versus sadness and subjugation: The effect of negative emotion expressions on social status conferral. *Journal of Personality and Social Psychology, 80*, 86–94.

Tiedens, L. Z., & Fragale, A. R. (2003). Power moves: Complementarity in dominant and submissive nonverbal behavior. *Journal of Personality and Social Psychology, 84*, 558–568

Timmers, M., Fischer, A. H., & Manstead, A. S. R. (2003). Ability versus vulnerability: Beliefs about men's and women's emotional behavior. *Cognition and Emotion, 17*, 41–63.

Tomkins, S. S. (1962). *Affect, imagery, consciousness: Vol. 1. Positive affects.* New York: Springer.

Tomkins, S. S. (1981). The role of facial response in the experience of emotion: A reply to Tourangeau and Ellsworth. *Journal of Personality and Social Psychology, 40*, 355–357.

Tomkins, S. S. (1995). *Exploring affect: The selected writings of Sylvan Tomkins* (edited by E. V. Demos). Cambridge, UK: Cambridge University Press.

Tooby, J., & Cosmides, L. (1990). The past explains the present: Emotional adaptations and the structure of ancestral environments. *Ethology and Sociobiology, 11*, 375–424.

Tooby, J., & Cosmides, L. (2001). Evolutionary psychology and the emotions. In M. Lewis & J. M. Haviland-Jones (Eds.), *Handbook of emotions* (2nd edition, pp. 91–115). New York: Guilford.

Totterdell, P. (2000). Catching moods and hitting runs: Mood linkage and subjective performance in professional sports teams. *Journal of Applied Psychology, 85*, 848–859.

Totterdell, P., Kellett, S., Teuchmann, K., & Briner, R. B. (1998). Mood linkage in work groups. *Journal of Personality and Social Psychology, 74,* 1504–1515.

Tourangeau, R., & Ellsworth, P. C. (1979). The role of facial response in the experience of emotion. *Journal of Personality and Social Psychology, 37,* 1519–1531.

Trevarthen, C. (1984). Emotions in infancy. In K. R. Scherer & P. Ekman (Eds.), *Approaches to emotions* (pp. 129–157). London: Erlbaum.

Trevarthen, C., & Hubley, P. (1978). Secondary intersubjectivity: Confidence, confiding and acts of meaning in the first year. In A. Lock (Ed.), *Action, gesture and symbol: The emergence of language* (pp. 183–229). New York: Academic Press.

Trevarthen, C., Kokkinaki, T., & Fiamenghi, G.A. (1999). What infants' imitations communicate: With mothers, with fathers, and with peers. In. J. Nadel & G. Butterworth (Eds.), *Imitation in infancy* (pp. 127–185). Cambridge, UK: Cambridge University Press.

Triandis, H. (1989). Self and social behavior in different cultural contexts. *Psychological Review, 96,* 269–289.

Triandis, H. (1990a). Cross-cultural studies of individualism and collectivism. In J. Berman (Ed.), *Nebraska symposium on motivation, 1989* (pp. 41–133). Lincoln: University of Nebraska Press.

Triandis, H. (1990b). Cultural syndromes and emotion. In S. Kitayama & H. R. Markus (Eds.), *Emotion and culture* (pp. 285–336). Washington, DC: APA.

Triandis, H. (1995). *Individualism and collectivism.* Boulder, CO: Westview press.

Triandis, H. C., Marin, G., Lysansky, J., & Betancourt, H. (1984). Simpatico as a culutral script of Hispanics. *Journal of Personality and Social Psychology, 47,* 1363–1374.

Tronick, E. Z. (1989). Emotions and emotional communication in infants. *American Psychologist, 44,* 112–119.

True, M. M., Pisani, L., & Oumar, F. (2001). Infant mother attachment among the Dogon of Mali. *Child Development, 72,* 1451–1466.

Tsai, J. L., Chentsova Dutton, Y., Freire Bebeau, L., & Przymus, D. E. (2002). Emotional expression and physiology in European Americans and Hmong Americans. *Emotion, 2,* 380–397.

Turner, J. C. (1982). Towards a cognitive redefinition of the social group. In H. Tajfel (Ed.), *Social identity and intergroup relations* (pp. 15–40). Cambridge, UK: Cambridge University Press.

Turner, J. C. (1991). *Social influence.* Milton Keynes: Open University Press.

Turner, J. C., Hogg, M. A., Oakes, P. J., Reicher, S. D., & Wetherell, M. S. (1987). *Rediscovering the social group: A self-categorization theory.* Oxford, UK: Blackwell.

Uzgiris, I. (1984). Imitation in infancy: Its interpersonal aspects. In M. Perlmutter (Ed.), *Parent child interaction and parent child relations in child development. The Minnesota Symposia on Child Development* (Vol. 17, pp. 1–32). Hillsdale, NJ: Erlbaum.

van Brakel, J. (1994). Emotions: A cross-cultural perspective on forms of life. In W. Wentsworth & J. Ryan (Eds.), *Social perspectives on emotion* (Vol. 2, pp. 179–237). Greenwich, CO: JAI Press.

Vandell, D. L., Wilson, K. S., & Buchanan, N. R. (1980). Peer interaction in the first year of life: An examination of its structure, content, and sensitivity to toys. *Child Development, 51,* 481–488.

Vangelisti, A. L., Daly, J. A., & Rudnick, J. R. (1991). Making people feel guilty in conversations: Techniques and correlates. *Human Communication Research, 18,* 3–39.

Van Goozen, S., & Frijda, N. H. (1993). Emotion words used in six European countries. *European Journal of Social Psychology, 23,* 89–95.

Van Maanen, J., & Kunda, G. (1989). "Real feelings:" Emotional expression and organizational culture. *Research in Organizational Behavior, 11,* 43–103.

Vaughn, B. E., Goldberg, S., Atkinson, L., Marcovitch, S., MacGregor, D., & Seifer, R. (1994). Quality of toddler mother attachment in children with Down Syndrome: Limits to interpretation of strange situation behavior. *Child Development, 65,* 95–108.

Viki, G.T., & Abrams, D. (2003). Infra humanization: Ambivalent sexism and the attribution of primary and secondary emotions to women. *Journal of Experimental Social Psychology, 39,* 492–499.

Vygotsky, L. S. (1978). *Mind in society.* Cambridge, MA: Harvard University Press.

Vygotsky, L. S. (1986). *Thought and language.* Cambridge, MA: MIT Press.

Wagner, H. L., & Lee, V. (1999). Facial behavior alone and in the presence of others. In P. Philippot, R. S. Feldman, & E. J. Coats (Eds.), *The social context of nonverbal behavior* (pp. 262–286). Cambridge, UK: Cambridge University Press.

Wagner, H. L., & Smith, J. (1991). Facial expression in the presence of friends and strangers. *Journal of Nonverbal Behavior, 15*, 201–214.

Wallbott, H. G., & Scherer, K. R. (1986). How universal and specific is emotional experience? Evidence from 27 countries on 5 continents. *Social Science Information, 23*, 763–795.

Walbott, H. G., & Scherer, K. R. (1995). Cultural determinants in experiencing shame and guilt. In J. P. Tangney & K. W. Fischer (Eds.), *Self-conscious emotions* (pp. 465–487). New York: The Guilford Press.

Watson, D., & Tellegen, A. (1985). Toward a consensual structure of mood. *Psychological Bulletin, 98*, 219–235.

Watson, D., Clark, L. A., & Tellegen, A. (1988). Development and validation of brief measures of positive and negative affect: The PANAS scales. *Journal of Personality and Social Psychology, 54*, 1063–1070.

Watson, J. B. (1929). *Psychology from the standpoint of a behaviorist* (3rd edition). Philadelphia: Lippincott.

Watson Gegeo, K. A., & White, G. M. (Eds.)(1990). *Disentangling: Conflict discourse in Pacific societies.* Stanford, CA: Stanford University Press.

Wegner, D. M. (1994). Ironic processes of mental control. *Psychological Review, 101*, 34–52.

Weinberg, K. M., & Tronick, E. Z. (1996). Infant affective reactions to the resumption of maternal interaction after the Still Face. *Child Development, 67*, 905–914.

Wellenkamp, J. C. (1988). Notions of grief and catharsis among the Toraja. *American Ethologist, 15*, 486–500.

Wellman, H. M., Harris, P. L., Banerjee, M., & Sinclair, A. (1995). Early understanding of emotion: Evidence from natural language. *Cognition and Emotion, 9*, 117–149.

Wharton, A. S. (1993). The affective cconsequences of service work: Managing emotions on the job. *Work and Occupations, 20*, 205–232.

White, G. M. (1990). Moral discourse and the rhetoric of emotion. In C. A. Lutz & L. Abu-Lughod (Eds.), *Language and the politics of emotion* (pp. 45–68). Cambridge, UK: Cambridge University Press.

White, G. M. (2000). Representing emotional meaning: Category, metaphor, schema, discourse. In M. Lewis & J. M. Haviland Jones (Eds.), *Handbook of emotions* (2nd ed.) (pp. 30–45). New York: The Guilford Press.

Wierzbicka, A. (1991a). Japanese key words and core cultural values. *Language in Society, 20*, 333–385.

Wierzbicka, A. (1991b). Talking about emotions: Semantics, culture, and cognition. *Cognition and Emotion, 6*, 285–319.

Wierzbicka, A. (1992). *Semantics, culture and cognition.* Oxford, UK: Oxford University Press.

Wierzbicka, A. (1994). Emotion, language, and cultural scripts. In S. Kitayama & H. R. Markus (Eds.), *Emotion and culture: Empirical studies of mutual influence* (pp. 133–196). Washington, DC: APA.

Wierzbicka, A. (1999). *Emotions across languages and cultures: Diversity and universals.* New York: Cambridge University Press.

Wittgenstein, L. (1953). *Philosophical investigations.* New York: McMacmillan.

Wouters, C. (1990). *Van minnen en sterven [About loving and dying].* Amsterdam: Bert Bakker.

Yik, M. S. M., & Russell, J. A. (1999). Interpretation of faces: A cross-cultural study of a prediction from Fridlund's theory. *Cognition and Emotion, 13*, 93–104.

Yzerbyt, V., Dumont, M., Gordijn, E., & Wigboldus, D. (2002). Intergroup emotions and self categorization: The impact of perspective taking on reactions to victims of harmful behaviors. In D. M. Mackie & E. R. Smith (Eds.), *From prejudice to intergroup emotions: Differentiated reactions to social groups* (pp. 67–88). New York: Psychology Press.

Zaalberg, R., Manstead, A. S. R., & Fischer, A. H. (2004). Relations between emotions, display rules, social motives and facial behavior. *Cognition and Emotion, 18*, 183–207.

Zahn Waxler, C., Friedman, R. J., Cole, P. M., Mizuta, I., & Hiruma, N. (1996). Japanese and United States preschool children's responses to conflict and distress. *Child Development, 67*, 2462–2477.

Zahn Waxler, C., Radke Yarrow, M., & King, R. A. (1979). Child rearing and children's prosocial initiations toward victims of distress. *Child Development, 50,* 319–330.

Zelli, A., Huesmann, L. R., & Cervone, D. (1995). Social inference and individual differences in aggression: Evidence for spontaneous judgments of hostility. *Aggressive Behavior, 21,* 405–417.

Zillmann, D., Weaver, J. B., Mundorf, N., & Aust, C. F. (1986). Effects of an opposite gender companion's affect to horror on distress, delight, and attraction. *Journal of Personality and Social Psychology, 51,* 586–594.

Zuckerman, M. (1991). *Psychobiology of personality.* Cambridge: Cambridge University Press.

Zuckerman, M., DePaulo, B. M., & Rosenthal, R. (1981). Verbal and non-verbal communication and deception. In L. Berkowitz (Ed.). *Advances in experimental social psychology* (Vol. 14, pp. 1–59). Orlando: Academic Press.

Author
Index

Subject
Index